Brian Day was born near Nottingham and brought up in a family whose elder members still had a considerable knowledge of folk lore, folk medicine and folk ways. He acquired an early interest in folk traditions, herbalism, music and linguistics, which led to a lifetime of study of the folk culture of the British Isles.

With awards of degrees in chemistry, biochemistry and computing, Brian has enjoyed a career as an international educational consultant, university lecturer and computer analyst. He has written and lectured extensively on folk culture and is a keen singer of folk, operatic and choral music, having discovered and transcribed several 'lost' English traditional carols. He is the author of *The Celtic Calendar*.

By the same author:

The Celtic Calendar
A Chronicle of Folk Customs
Chronicle of Celtic Folk Customs

The Modern Pagan

How to Live a Natural Lifestyle in the Twenty-first Century

Brian Day

RIDER

London . Sydney . Auckland . Johannesburg

Copyright © 2006 Brian Day

Brian Day has asserted his right to be identified as the author of this
Work in accordance with the Copyright, Designs and Patents Act 1988.

First published in 2006 by Rider,
an imprint of Ebury Press, Random House,
20 Vauxhall Bridge Road, London SW1V 2SA

Random House Australia (Pty) Limited
20 Alfred Street, Milsons Point, Sydney,
New South Wales 2061, Australia

Random House New Zealand Limited
18 Poland Road, Glenfield,
Auckland 10, New Zealand

Random House South Africa (Pty) Limited
Endulini, 5A Jubilee Road,
Parktown 2193, South Africa

The Random House Group Limited Reg. No. 954009

Papers used by Rider are natural, recyclable products made
from wood grown in sustainable forests.

Typeset by Palimpsest Book Production Limited,
Polmont, Stirlingshire
Printed and bound in Great Britain by Mackays of Chatham plc, Kent

A CIP catalogue record for this book
is available from the British Library

ISBN 1-8441-3294-3

Contents

Introduction

What is modern paganism?

It is my aim to describe in this book, and also put into modern context, a traditional pagan lifestyle, indigenous to the British Isles. This lifestyle represents the most fundamental level, and therefore the foundation, of British folk culture, and by extension the folk culture of those of British descent throughout the world. Such a lifestyle has survived in families throughout the English and Celtic areas of the United Kingdom, many of whom live on the margins of current, popular British society. The ways in which they interact with one another and with their fellow inhabitants of the natural world are, however, anything but marginal in relevance to the majority who have traditionally excluded them. That majority is currently experiencing serious discord, disruption and imbalance in its families, communities, and natural environments. Many people from all walks of life are now taking a keen practical interest in the ways of those who have preserved the harmonious lifestyle to which the beleaguered majority now desperately aspire. This book offers a window into the world of those whose lifestyle has become of great relevance today to the mainstream society that long ago tried to consign it to oblivion. It is this lifestyle that I describe in this book as traditional paganism at, and evolving from, its roots, and as modern paganism in its evolved current form.

The modern pagan lifestyle represents a synthesis of the ways in which traditional non-spiritual pagans have adapted the traditions they have preserved since ancient times, through the march of social change into the present modern world. The earliest recorded examples of elements of this pagan lifestyle come from descriptions of the ways of the ancient Celts in Western Europe and the British Isles, and in the latter these appear later amongst the Anglo-Saxon and Norse communities. Today, traditional – or true – British pagans may be of Celtic, Germanic or mixed descent, and because they are a disparate group their surviving lifestyles differ in aspect and application.

Drawing together these cultural threads, I have woven them into what I hope is a tapestry displaying a coherent, integrated picture of the collective ways in which traditional pagans have adapted their philosophies and practices to the demands of modern life. Thereby, this compelling, practical, caring, nature-based way of life is made available to all as a complete package. However, it is a package that lends itself to individual or collective variation and evolution as the occasion demands or the desire decides.

The evolution of traditional paganism into modern paganism has, perhaps remarkably, occurred with little change in fundamental characteristics. So, modern paganism can succinctly be described as a non-spiritual, non-supremacist, nature-based lifestyle, whose principal strengths are high regard for: the quality of personal character; family togetherness; equality of worth and opportunity in the community; environmental awareness and ecological responsibility; development of sensual, imaginal, creative, intellectual and communicative abilities; and for achievement of simplicity in life, especially through ethical and sustainable use of resources and the meeting of demonstrable, practical needs.

For those who wish to follow a practical life with no attendant spirituality, modern paganism offers a foundation upon which to shape your lifestyle, whatever your ethnic or cultural background. As a core lifestyle, modern paganism can serve as a template for people who wish to add a spiritual dimension to their life, or a fully fledged religious commitment. There is no conflict between the fundamental personal and natural aims of traditional paganism and the development of a spiritual dimension within that lifestyle. Put simply, we all have the same basic personal and survival needs.

What are the elements of the pagan lifestyle described here?

Pagans have always guarded their traditions closely, and have tended to be deeply suspicious of anyone seeking to write their history on their behalf. This is not just a consequence of oppression, persecution and marginalisation, and these are not the dominating issues they once were, not that they are yet a thing of the past. Still less than biography written by others do they like to define or categorise themselves and their way of life, for that can be the precursor of a creed, and thus the beginning of a process of codifying traditional paganism in the way of a religion. But in support of the recommendation that traditional pagan folk culture, or significant parts of it, offers a meaningful twenty-first century lifestyle for all, a summary of the principal characteristics of this culture is provided below. This initial summary is not intended to be an exhaustive list of characteristics, beliefs and practices, and it is drawn from across pagan communities. The latter are seldom discrete settlements like villages, but are most likely to be a scattered group of households consisting of extended families and their friends. Other features will emerge as the book unfolds, and by the end you will have the measure of what collectively constitutes the character of modern paganism today.

A non-spiritual way of life

Traditional paganism, even in its modern form, is non-spiritual, and as such can co-exist, as a basic folk culture, with any spiritual dimension.

- *Traditional pagans believe that by rejecting the alleged existence of, or the need for, a superior being at the rudder of the Universe, they can pursue an essentially biological lifestyle without the demands of religious obligation, nor its by-products, side effects, conflicts, historical baggage, or mental or physical constraints.*
- *The belief exists among some true pagans that their culture is historically pre-spiritual.*
- *True paganism is not an evangelising culture, but is welcoming and sharing, and disseminated by example.*

Human and personal characteristics shown by modern pagans

Modern paganism is a simple, harmonious lifestyle in which people demonstrate a strong sense of humility, personal responsibility and consideration for others.

- *There is a pronounced humanist element, and an absence of human supremacist views. For example, personal harmony, interpersonal harmony, and harmony in nature at large are equally valued.*
- *Pagans have human failings like everyone else, and recognise this without shame, so all are welcome amongst them.*
- *Values-based unity of purpose is more important than 'targets' as life objectives.*
- *Responsibility to others is held in higher esteem than upholding one's 'rights'. Total freedom of action is not endorsed, but rather tempered by consideration of the consequences. Such caution stems from a belief in the ancient Law of Returns, which says that all adverse actions rebound in some measure on the perpetrator.*
- *Dishonesty, violence and criminal tendencies are very rare, whereas straightforwardness, gentleness, and senses of obligation and honour are characteristic.*
- *There is a strong current of egalitarianism, with recognition and practical utilisation of the different aptitudes and characters of the sexes.*
- *Diet and health, and therefore intake of food and herbal or chemical preparations, are related as consistently to our place in the natural order as with our metabolic and physiological requirements, and with our responsibility to our dependants.*

Family togetherness

The immediate family is the most fundamental unit of modern pagan life, but the importance of the extended family means that its values are applied in dealings with all relatives, the community, and the natural world.

- *A strong bond of family togetherness generates mutual responsibility, respect and support.*
- *There is a tradition of protection of the structure and sequence of pagan celebratory life, such as living by the pagan calendar, pagan modes of celebration and life-cycle commemoration, but this does not itself imply exclusion of others willing to share and participate.*

- *Upbringing and education are highly valued and distinctive, and reflect the allegiance to the extended family as well as focussing on a child's intellectual, social, physical, artistic and other human developmental needs.*
- *There remains the desire to preserve family and community history and respect for tradition, ancestors and elders.*
- *Checks and balances and generational contributions and viewpoints are respected in family debate.*

Community spirit

The community is regarded in many ways as an extension of the family, in which all contribute, participate, and support each other.

- *Personal and practical worth in the community is more important than superficial differences. Who, or that which, harms no-one is tolerated.*
- *Standards of personal and social behaviour, especially in public, are expected to be high. Over-indulgence and excess are frowned upon.*
- *Equality of worth and opportunity are very important, as is the absence of all forms of discrimination.*
- *The natural instinct is to care for and rehabilitate rather than condemn and punish, if possible, and only the most irredeemable recidivist would ever be abandoned.*
- *Disrespect for, denigration of, or desecration of other cultures and their adherents and artefacts are unthinkable actions for pagans.*
- *There tends to be a distrust of institution, the media, centralisation and corporation, and anything else that usurps responsibility for the family and its values.*

Environmental awareness

In all aspects of lifestyle, modern pagans never forget that they are just one species in a mutually dependent natural world.

- *Modern pagans have a keen appreciation of humankind's position in local and global dynamic ecosystems as an equal partner with other forms of life, and they acknowledge their responsibility to preserve natural equilibrium by minimising or eliminating the environmental consequences of human actions.*

- *All plots created from nature, such as garden, farm, and park, are treated as extensions of the countryside, with local species and breeds and natural cycles encouraged. Ecological and ethical management are practised by the owner as far as possible.*
- *Fellow organisms and their inanimate associates are considered part of the pagan extended family, to all of which the pagan consciousness feels allegiance.*
- *There is a practical emphasis on equipping oneself for survival as an aspect of personal wellbeing.*
- *Ethical and environmental consumerism are championed.*

Intellectual development

The development of the mind is held to be just as important as a fit, healthy body.

- *There is a high regard for the sensual, imaginal and the creative, and unfettered thought is not found threatening.*
- *There is high appreciation for communicative ability, whether linguistic, artistic, musical, or through other modes of expression.*
- *The rational is not seen as superior to the intuitive.*

Technological

Simplicity, practical need, sustainability, and ethical and considerate use are key elements in modern attitudes to technology.

- *Adaptation by pagans to change, such as through pressure from the march of commerce and technology, varies with individual conscience. Some pagans are technologically progressive within the constraints mentioned in the next paragraph, while others may appear 'old-fashioned', but it is the personal choice of the latter to prefer tradition to conformity with what they regard as forces controlling their lives.*
- *In technological matters there is an emphasis on simplicity, sustainability by low energy and resources consumption, and demonstrable practical need. There is thus*

a tendency to minimal use of technology, maximum use of alternatives, or doing without and reverting to traditional manual and physical methods.

- *The ethical dimension of, and considerate use of, technology is more important than relentless technological change or progress.*
- *Regular personal audits of technological usage are undertaken, as is exercise of choice.*
- *Vocational education is considered no less valuable than academic education. There is considerable interest in the applications of science and technology, especially in practical skills and craftsmanship rather than in relentlessly usurping human skills by automation and mechanisation.*

This is how modern pagans respond to how they find things in the world today. With the exception of the first section of the list, there would seem to be nothing that compromises or denies personal spiritual belief and practice, but a great deal that is of relevance to every citizen of every culture. Pagans, like all people, put their personal gloss on many of the aspects of their lives, and have always done so because of a dislike of prescription. Non-pagans are no different, and there is within this framework the same scope for their individuality to be expressed as pagans have cherished for centuries.

The chapters that follow will expand upon these basic characteristics of modern pagan life, and once you close the last page I believe you will never think of your own life in quite the same way again. To what extent you choose to allow modern paganism to influence your future choices in life is of course a deeply personal decision. This book will also endeavour to show that modern paganism offers the only realistic hope for human survival and social harmony. This is another pressing reason why modern paganism is presented here as a new folk culture for all in the twenty-first century.

Why is this book structured as it is?

Part One

In the first part of this book, we will consider the events in history that led to the near destruction of the earliest pagan folk culture that traditional pagans claim descent from – that of the ancient Celts. This demise was due to the effects of the Roman invasion of the British Isles and then the subsequent spread of Christianity. The pagan sub-structure was a core folk culture that the invaders and evangelists, as fellow Europeans, shared in large measure. But the desire strongly existed to overlay this with a dominant spiritual dimension, and subsequently to seek to replace the pagan foundation by a remodelled, Christianised version of it, leaving few aspects uncorrupted. This led inexorably to the near extinction of the nature-based way of life that served so dynamically and reciprocatingly the needs of people and the natural world alike.

In addition to giving readers an insight into the origins of traditional British paganism, it is an aim of this historical section to provide an analysis that may persuade Christians to look humbly and self-critically at the dire consequences of their centuries-old association with paganism for humankind as a whole. This is done in the hope that they may recognise that what they originally sought to eliminate was their own folk culture too. It serves neither pagans nor Christians to pretend these events never happened, and it is as well to emphasise that the consideration here in the first part of the book is from a pagan perspective. Christians have already taken ample opportunity in literature to express their analysis of, and justification for, these events. But it serves neither group to perpetuate centuries of animosity, mistrust and misunderstanding by neglecting by absence of dialogue to inform one another of where the two traditions stand today with regard to each other. Christians will, therefore, find towards the end of part one a plea for reconciliation, which I hope they and all pagans will respond to.

Part Two

This plea takes the form of a sincere hope that once again, after so long, Christians will consider the elements of the pagan folk culture described in the second part of the book as their own. They are, expressed in modern form, what they themselves lost when they forced pagans to abandon them on such a large scale during the Christianisation of the British Isles. Please take this culture with the blessing of those who have clung on to it. You can call it what you please, and can overlay it with the spiritual dimension that is so precious to you, as you did in the evangelisation period long ago, but this time please leave it in place, practise it and cherish it, and you may come to believe that there really is no serious conflict with spiritual beliefs in a lifestyle that puts family, community and interaction with the natural world from within at its heart, for these represent the bedrock of human existence.

If you are of a religious persuasion, you do not have to refer to your reclaimed folk culture as 'pagan' if you feel uncomfortable with the term. The re-adoption of all or selected aspects of this lifestyle, or indeed the recognition that you are following some of it now and may wish to add later what you feel fill gaps in your life, is more important to your future wellbeing than the label you use to describe it. But to all readers I would say this. Whatever connotations the word 'pagan' has been given in the long history of its use and abuse, it is time for it to acquire again the respectability that it once had. That respectability is now a deserved one, as witnessed by the growing numbers proud to call themselves pagan. They are proud because of the personal, family, community and environmental focus, fulfilment and equilibrium that their philosophies and values have enabled them to create. For the simple expedient of adopting this word in a new light, and studying this thesis with an open mind, that fulfilment can be yours too, whatever your station in life, and whether you are of religious persuasion or not.

Traditional, or true, paganism, in the fundamental but modernised form described in the second part of the book, is essentially a practical, survival lifestyle. But it has during the last two hundred years increasingly attracted interest from individuals and groups wishing to overlay their own customised spirituality upon it. In one sense this simply represents the creation of other religions, and mirrors the processes that Christians applied to Celtic paganism centuries earlier. But certain groups, of which wiccans are perhaps the best known, have retained far more in common with traditional pagans than Christians after the Middle Ages were ever prepared to countenance, and as such these groups often refer to themselves today as pagan, or are so styled by others. Traditional pagans would take issue with this on the grounds that the overlaying of a spiritual element on the basic pagan folk culture takes such groups beyond the boundaries of true paganism. Moreover, the persistent use of the word 'pagan' to describe such groups has led to much confusion over who is pagan and who is not. I can but emphasise my own position that true paganism is non-spiritual as described herein, but I recognise the strong bond that the groups referred to feel with the same tradition that I propose as the pagan plinth. Spiritual pagans are, like Christians, cordially invited to embrace or reclaim what is offered in these pages.

How may you wish to use this book?

This book is for all those who want to change, or are considering changing, their lifestyle, to a modern pagan lifestyle, or some chosen aspects of it. This may be because you seek a new direction in life, or you are unhappy with your life as it is, or curious for new experiences. There are no disqualifying factors of any kind that would prevent you from selectively taking up some of the advice offered, or indeed reorienting your life completely. On this matter at least you currently have freedom of choice, but it may not be too long before some of the features of the lifestyle described on these pages will take on a more urgent, even obligatory, imperative. The thesis presented is aimed at all who have the interest or see the need to read it, from whatever cultural background or spiritual persuasion, and with whatever motive, for modern paganism, or new paganism as it is sometimes called, is of international appeal and relevance.

Some readers may find particular chapters or sections of greater initial attraction than others, for modern paganism is treated from many angles, historical, calendrical, environmental, social and ethological (behavioural). Part one explores its ancient beliefs and practices, and part two explores beliefs and practices that sit more comfortably in, and are more relevant to, the modern world. Other readers may wish to go straight to part two and read about how to refashion all or part of their lives in a modern pagan way. You may have already done so but wish to read about philosophies that support your choice or ideas for further enrichment and progress along your chosen path. You can then delay reading until later about the significant events in history that preceded the modern pagan revival. Each chapter in part two is devoted to a specific aspect, or aspects with a common theme, and the extensive use of subsections in the chapters allows the reader to dip in and read about specific matters at any time.

You may well find that some items have instant appeal, and then in the light of your experience you will be drawn to others of kindred affinity. This is how you put together your personal lifestyle. For the independently minded, the modern pagan lifestyle can be looked upon as a resource for your present and future consideration as your life evolves. You may find yourself jotting down some more aspects of your life that would lend themselves to a modern pagan approach, and in this way you will develop consistency of purpose instead of drawing fad ideas randomly from conflicting or miscellaneous sources, or from vested interests. A lifestyle whose elements are drawn from disparate sources is inevitably fragmented by exposure to, and influence from, conflicting cultures and social expectations.

Many aspects have gained widespread popularity as individual pursuits already, such as recycling waste, relaxation therapy, reverting to a natural diet, or the use of folk remedies, but the synthesis of a complete modern pagan approach allows the reader to see these aspects as part of an organic, coherent, evolving whole. By adopting the complete lifestyle, or substantial parts of it, you can truly transform your life in the direction that your previous individual choices suggested to you then that you wanted to move towards. To whatever extent you do this, partial or whole, it is my belief that you will be making an indelible contribution to the greater wellbeing of your good self and of all who are influenced and persuaded by your example.

A minority who feel they cannot, or who refuse to, adapt to modern society seek to escape the rat race by leaving its confines, but for most people their personal, employment and financial circumstances do not allow them to do that. And really they don't actually want to escape in the generally accepted sense of the term, only to understand, adjust to and cope better with or more profoundly to change to a genuinely fulfilling and sustainable lifestyle. These objectives may be achieved with the guidance contained within this book, by choosing what would fill a particular gap, or solve a particular problem, in your life, or by restructuring your life more radically. Good luck with whatever options you choose, whoever you are!

Part One
Traditional Paganism in its Historical Context

This section of the book is, as far as possible, in historical sequence, starting with the earliest period of settlement in the British Isles that there is evidence for. The greatest emphasis is placed on what is known about the ancient Celts, from whose culture significant aspects of traditional paganism are derived. From there the account moves on to consider the Roman occupation and its devastating consequences for the indigenous Celtic way of life, and then to the spread of Christianity to these shores. From the time of the arrival of the early Christian missionaries to the British Isles the histories of Celtic paganism and Christianity became entwined. This account tells the pagan story of that association.

The word 'pagan' and its many historical connotations

The rural origins of paganism are strongly indicated by the etymological probability that the word 'pagan' is derived from the Latin *paganus*, meaning 'a countryman' or 'rustic', or from the related *pagus*, 'a rural district', or *pagani*, 'followers of the old ways', 'old' often implying 'nature-based'.

In the early years of co-existence between Celts and Christians it would have been reasonable to define a pagan as someone who was 'non-Christian' in the sense of being an adherent of an indigenous, pre-Christian corpus of beliefs, especially one associated with the natural world, but later the Roman Catholic Church assumed the right to define a pagan as one who was 'anti-Christian', and this label proved to be nearly indelible, for there are many still today who think of a pagan as someone who is anti-religious. The Roman Catholic

Church used both meanings to suit its objectives of spiritual domination and social control, and spread the view that paganism is a lower level of human existence than, and an inferior philosophy to, Christianity, and in opposition to it. Whilst the course of history cannot be changed, there is no doubt that the labelling of pagans as anti-Christian has prevented dialogue and mutual understanding between pagans and Christians for centuries, which is extremely unfortunate in view of such a long period of co-existence and the similarities in philosophies and lifestyle that they share.

The word 'pagan' is used herein to mean 'not Christian' or 'pre-Christian' in the parts of this book that deal with the conflict between Christians and those who did and do not share their beliefs, and to mean 'non-spiritual', 'not religious', or having a lifestyle where religion has no place, where the context makes no reference to this conflict. The word will never be used to mean 'anti-Christian', for modern paganism is not about perpetuating conflicts between paganism and Christianity but about re-orienting personal lifestyle. The Part One discussion from a pagan perspective of the historical association between paganism and Christianity keeps faithfully to what is represented in recorded history, as part of the historical development in preparation for the presentation of modern pagan philosophies in Part Two.

1

The Roots of Traditional Paganism

The Celtic cultural origins of traditional paganism

Traditional pagans have long claimed cultural descent from the ancient Celts, and for centuries, historians and folklorists too have sought detailed knowledge of ancient Celtic paganism (if indeed there ever was a pan-Celtic culture as opposed to local cultures) and information on how it responded and evolved in the face of waves of settlers and missionaries to the British Isles. It would then be possible to reconstruct a modern form of it such as would represent an alternative lifestyle for people who are unhappy about what history has provided for them and its suitability for the twenty-first century. Unfortunately, the difficulty of interpreting the archaeological record and the possession of only a small number of literary and artistic survivals mean that it is not possible through these alone to reconstruct old Celtic lifestyle, customs and beliefs. To achieve any sort of template for a modern pagan lifestyle it is necessary therefore to rely on folk beliefs, customs and traditions of all kinds that can reasonably be held to be of Celtic provenance, or adoption, even if remoulded and repackaged by various immigrant and locally evolving influences throughout the course of history. Myths, legends and folk tales often incorporate details of folk beliefs and ceremonial practices, and although a folk culture may no longer be practised, evidence of its rituals can survive as drama, custom or superstition. In the absence of witness testimony and archaeological evidence these survivals are often all that is available. Moreover, because of the strong oral tradition in the past, they must be scrutinised for natural exaggeration for an audience and the changes that tend to come about as a consequence of being passed on orally before being written down. Then there is the problem of a writer who wants to be critical, such as a Christian writing about druidism (druidic philosophy) or druidry (druidic practice), or to revamp the facts for a particular audience or as propaganda.

Such a process of reconstruction is not intended to represent the product of a historical sequence of events, but, by assuming that folk tradition is not largely invention, and using what historical sources exist, it is possible to fill in the gaps with a reasonable degree of extrapolation to construct a modern pagan lifestyle which reflects the pagan Celtic heritage. What is being rekindled is not druidic. The fall from power of the druids, who may be thought of as the ancient Celtic priesthood, is often blamed on the Roman invasions of Gaul and Great Britain, but the same happened in Ireland where the Romans never set foot. It was Christianity that was the agent of the destruction or abandonment of both druidry and druidism. The long association of the people of the British Isles with Christianity may have started by their being attracted to what seemed like a complete prescribed lifestyle, whereas the return to Celtic roots by traditional pagans is a quest for elements of the culture that can be pressed back into service in modernised form.

Long ago Celtic beliefs were chased from their sacred sites, which in many cases they had adopted from the pre-Celtic cultures that built them, into remote countryside, where the intellectual and communal strength of the people allowed aspects of old Celtic culture to survive, mostly fragments, not always obviously recognisable, and seldom unchanged with time. It is these that allow reconnection to the past, but retaining modern intellect, practicality and purpose. Add to this the derived aspects of Celtic, and Celtic-influenced Anglo-Saxon and Norse, culture from folk traditions, and the considerable degree to which traditional pagans have evolved and preserved a lifestyle embodying these aspects, and a basis for the development of modern paganism, is thereby created. The reliance on folk tradition should make the construction acceptable to ordinary folk, in that it embraces only beliefs and customs that are already part of their heritage.

The traceable roots of traditional paganism in the British Isles, then, lie in Old Celtic society and whatever components of pre-Celtic society it had absorbed. The practice of magic was an important part of this society, and persisted, with inevitable borrowings and changes, through Anglo-Saxon and Norse settlement. The way in which basic folk beliefs remained reasonably consistent throughout the British Isles during the Germanic invasions shows how much they were a part of common European folk culture, and how much devolving folk customs remained true to their roots. An analysis of folk beliefs, customs and ceremonies enables us to discern certain attitudes which recur and which one can reasonably assume were manifest in everyday life. Indeed it is still possible to interview elderly people in certain rural areas who remember the old ways, the skills, knowledge, social interactions and communal living. Further insights into ancient paganism come from our knowledge of: surviving ritual magic; spells, charms, amulets and talismans; depictions in art of, or references in oral lore and literature to, pagan images and ways; and life-cycle practices associated with birth, puberty, partnership and death. All these aspects of popular culture are the legacy of paganism past which, when expressed in modern form, are the basis of new paganism.

Whenever a group of people, like traditional pagans, with common cultural aspirations hark back to a past age for any part of their inspiration for living, they are sure these days to be labelled 'old-fashioned', or said to have been left behind by the march of 'progress'. Cartoonists will picture them in animal skins and carrying clubs! But pagans living in the modern world know perfectly well that any return to traditional ways must be selective and appropriate for today's conditions. They believe that their descendant philosophies, attitudes, family values, social interactions, communal practices, and the harmonising of life with the natural environment, are still relevant and adaptable to the modern world. Modern paganism is not a 'back to nature' movement, which is wholly idealistic in a technological age, nor does it seek to 'put the clock back' in various ways that would retard its own progress as an evolving culture. The spartanism characteristic of some extreme sects is not typical of modern pagan life, for modern pagans believe life is to be enjoyed, just not at the expense of adverse personal, communal or environmental consequences elsewhere.

Paganism grew out of people's needs, primarily to understand their environment and survive in it, and we could do well to re-examine it now for our continued survival and wellbeing in the face of the collapsing of social and environmental equilibrium under human pressure. As the disrespectful and unprepared traveller will witness, nature always gets her revenge, but pagans believe also that all negative actions rebound, and harm the perpetrator. Many of the old pagan practices may not now be relevant or acceptable, but the philosophies and attitudes that governed them are largely applicable today, and these, when applied to today's problems rather than past rituals and practices, form the basis of modern paganism. There are times in all our lives when we need the courage to admit that we may benefit from wiser counsel, and in this thesis the counsel is that of traditional paganism.

Paganism and the natural world

Once our early human ancestors developed the self-critical faculties to appreciate the range of skills and accomplishments that they themselves possessed, it is understandable that they might regard the vast complexities of the natural world as the handiwork of a humanoid too, but of an enormously more powerful and talented one than any they knew. Religion, to peoples of the ancient world, was the belief that powers superior to their own created, controlled and directed the forces of nature and the behaviour of living things, and the apparent reality of this belief necessitated the practice of propitiating and conciliating these forces in order to survive. It was assumed that the origin of these powers was in superhuman form. This essentially practical and logical view is perfectly understandable, but, regardless of who or what initiated the formation of the natural world and controlled events within it, people still had a basic need to understand it, thrive in it and try to bend it to their advantage. In this sense, pagans and those who developed religious beliefs were alike.

Pagan personification of nature and natural forces

The notion of personification is different from that of a religious belief in a superhuman creator and controller. For the early pagans, humans were part of the ecosystem, and some of their fellow inhabitants appeared to have attributes like theirs, especially animals. It must have been a source of humility to realise that some animals were stronger, faster, more alert and possessed of more acute senses than they, and this humility must have made it easier to accept the idea of a superhuman creator. But inanimate phenomena appeared to have some of their powers too; the wind could blow like they could, so perhaps it too has some human characteristics. In such ways, those who are now called pagans personified these familiar components of their environment, but misleadingly, these personifications are sometimes known as 'deities'. However, they were not thought of in the same way as the gods of religions, for these 'deities' were looked upon as fellow inhabitants, for whom the population had respect and with whom they felt oneness. Pagans undoubtedly sought ways to influence these personifications and were in awe of the more powerful, but their attitude towards them was not like the worship of a single omniscient creator or of a pantheon of ethereal, versatile, powerful gods and goddesses living in a supraterrestrial realm, and it is not helpful, therefore, where pagans are concerned, to regard these personifications as gods and goddesses. Instead of using phrases like 'worship of the sun god' it is better to say 'veneration of the personification of the sun' or simply 'veneration of the sun'. Whether the personifications were male or female may have rested on whether their observed characteristics were more in keeping with pagan notions of masculinity and femininity at the time, but they were all specific, natural and local.

Veneration starts with sensory recognition of presence, which in turn leads to aesthetic appreciation, admiration and assessment of attributes. These attributes may be seen as having utilitarian value, or as appealing to survival sensibilities and thus worthy of emulation. Upon the realisation that appreciation and utility have become dependency, admiration turns to veneration. Veneration may then result in the assignation of personification, in recognition of exceptional qualities that an ordinary human is unable to match.

However sophisticated humans think they are they are limited. Therefore they are not above veneration of the superior attributes of other animals, of the beauty of landscapes, of the permanence, solidity, multi-texture and sheer grandeur of geological formations. The stable, reassuring presence of the tree is a storehouse of resources, as is the stream, whose abundance includes food, drink, silt, gravel, driftwood and other natural materials. The wind too is a cornucopia, bringing rain, coolness, warmth, identifying sounds and odours, birds for food, and above all change. Fertilise and water the earth, and growth and regeneration ensue, as also happens after fire. Illustrations of the power of transformation of the elemental forces are all around to be marvelled at.

Some basis for the belief that personifications were not like deities to be worshipped comes from traditional feelings of oneness with natural phenomena and inhabitants as fellow travellers with whom one shared the environment, boxing and coxing for survival. Relationships in folk tales between Celts and personifications do not have the obeisant character to be expected of people in awe of, and subservient to, deities, for Celtic heroes took on natural forces; they were not bowed by their irresistible power.

Natural law

The belief that the Universe is not arbitrary but governed in some way is known as the concept of natural law. Examples of natural cycles are seasonal, meteorological and astronomical cycles, the latter including the diurnal movement of the sun, the phases of the moon, the returning patterns of the constellations, and solstices and equinoxes. Also, pagans came to admire the symmetry of anatomical and morphological form, as exemplified by the hexagon of the honeycomb, the pentagon of the starfish, the logarithmic spiral of the chambered nautilus, and the bilateral symmetry of their own bodies. No one who has gazed in awe and wonder at the beauty of snowflakes and mineral crystals can doubt that nature is the supreme geometrician. But faith in the orderliness of natural events was tempered by the realisation that there were chaotic aspects to the natural world. The sun rose in the east and set in the west, but the wind blew where it would, as did the lightning strike and the clouds drift. The concept of fate becomes inextricably bound up with order and disorder when it is realised that the future of a world showing both order and disorder is inexorable. But what pattern will develop, or will there be no discernible pattern? Death must come to us all, but how, where and when? When symmetrical leaves fall in autumn, why do they make disorderly piles on the forest floor? It was against these apparently form-less and aimless aspects of nature that early humans strove for meaning, and signs of order and regularity.

Paganism and magic

Actions designed to manipulate the natural world are collectively referred to as magic. Magic assumes that nature works in specific, predetermined ways, and an understanding of these ways leads to methods of altering them to advantage, normally by imitation or contagion. Making a noise like thunder to induce rainfall is imitative, sympathetic or homœopathic magic, and inserting pins into clay images of an intended victim so that he or she feels pain is contagious magic. The latter also worked on the assumption that possession of something belonging to the intended victim enabled the magician to exert control over that individual. Magic is essentially an immediate form of action, whose success depends on human ritual skill and not on the extraordinary powers of a deity, but *Homo sapiens* the philo-sopher would eventually want more than just sufficient grasp of natural events to aid daily survival. His curiosity sought deeper understanding of and, ultimately, explanations for events. Gradually, for the more curious and experimentally minded, the quest for order and regularity turned magic into science.

The rise of science and mathematics

Science probably began in much the same way as magic, when people's natural curiosity led them to recognise, describe and seek explanations for patterns in nature. Gradually, a framework of ideas and beliefs grew up, within which people developed concepts of their world, their fellow inhabitants of it and themselves, and were able to manifest these ideas in practical demonstration. Certain dualisms must have come to attention early on, and linguistic evidence supports this, such as light and dark, life and death, male and female, left and right, order and disorder, and these may have been the catalyst for creation of the pairs of, and dual characters of, ancient pagan personifications, and indeed of the twentieth-century wiccan Lord and Lady, although it is known that some personifications also had triple aspects to their characters.

Science as a search for order in the natural world, leading to attempts to understand and ultimately control it, is superficially similar in its objectives to magic. The more recent application of mathematics to science to find mathematical expressions that appear to behave like, and predict, physical phenomena is rather like sympathetic magic, but the efforts and degree of success in this regard gave the impression that somehow it had been demonstrated that the world was like a giant, complex machine, whose workings could be reduced to mathematical equations and therefore manipulated at will. The common purpose of mechanists and magicians appeared to be attainable, but if indeed the complexities of the physical world could be totally encoded in, and described and predicted by, mathematics, then science as a branch of human wisdom would come to a close and be entirely under human control.

This debasement of the course of nature as some sort of mechanistic chain of events rather than as a divinely created and controlled sequence led to hostility towards magicians and scientists from the Church. Science, magic and religion all require faith, and they all accept nature as exhibiting order. Scientists generally have faith that sooner or later the solution to a problem will be found, or that an orderly explanation will eventually be forthcoming. This faith is probably partly a product of their cultural background, in some cases of religious upbringing and belief in the perfection of the created world, partly developed intuition, and partly because of a belief in reason and rationality. Reason is the ordering of our own thought processes, inspired by our instinctive curiosity to know the world we must survive in. But, despite the successful understanding emanating from the ordering of our own thought processes, philosophies clash when it comes to whether there is a purpose for the creation and evolution of the natural world. Science and magic say no, religion says yes, for purpose is a human attribute. What should be our reaction to the things science cannot explain? Scientists would say 'be patient', for understanding will come from further experimentation, but those believing in a religious view of the creation of the Universe point to their God as being behind those inexplicable phenomena. However, this belief condemns the supposedly all-powerful God to perpetual retreat as scientific advances continue apace.

Religion tends to condemn, and even to punish, free thought, as religious guardians feel threatened by intellectual freedom, whereas scientists cherish and protect such freedom. An adverse consequence of the latter can be unrestrained research with insufficient consideration of the likely consequences. This issue, and those stemming from the imposition of the results of scientific research and the technological development of them, is far more important for pagans today than the science versus religion debate about creation, particularly whether the human race is doomed to a scenario where moral and ethical consensus constantly fails to keep pace with scientific and technological advances. Some eighteenth-century philanthropists actually thought that progress in providing food, clothing and housing for all would see an end to human ills and conflict, but they failed to observe the increasing number of potentially undesirable uses of scientific and engineering knowledge, and the fact that ethics was not keeping pace with these practical developments. Scientific success is never a substitute for morality, for moral failure and misuse of this powerful knowledge can have terrible consequences, not least of which is entrapment in a cycle of development and implementation followed by drastic counter-measures against the undesirable outcomes of the original development. The United States of America, at the time when the Native Americans alone were part of the ecosystem, supported less than a twentieth of the present population. For the country to abandon science now would be mass suicide, so it must instead concentrate urgently on the ethical and environmental dimensions of science and technology, as to various degrees must all countries.

A biological origin for religion

Accepting that it is reasonable for some of our ancestors to have formed the view that there was a superhuman at the helm of the Universe is not explaining why the idea has been so enduring and captivating. Such widespread and lasting notions could well have a biological explanation. Of course, religion may just be an instinct, like sexuality or aggression, linked to our innate desire to seek causes, meaning and pattern in life and to fulfil our perceived role in it. It resembles science in this way, as science is a search for order triggered by instinctive curiosity. But, to an outside observer, religious practice would seem to be rather curious in the behavioural sense, consisting as it does of prolonged submissive displays to appease an unseen but dominant individual. These appeasement ceremonies must be regularly repeated to avoid offending this individual, usually referred to as a 'god'. Since none of these gods has ever been shown to exist in a tangible form, and they are therefore only the product of an act of faith, one might ask why they arose and why belief in them has been so tenacious. Looking back to our anthropoidal origins may provide a clue. Before humans evolved from a forest-dwelling ape into co-operative hunters they in all likelihood lived in social groups of the type seen today in other ape and monkey species. There, each group has a dominant male, an overlord, who must be respected and appeased or the offender will be punished. The lead male has a protective role in the colony as well as a peacekeeping role, and can be said to possess, indeed, god-like status.

But with the growth of a co-operative spirit that is vital for group hunting, the dominant individual's authority had to be severely limited if he was to expect an active, rather than a submissive, loyalty from his group members. Eventually, as individual skills evolved and diverged, the single male could no longer command unquestioning allegiance, as he was no longer master of all skills. However, such inbred allegiance is not erased by the mere mechanics of evolution and in order to fill the need, which may well have evolved from a practical to a spiritual need, for an all-powerful figure hovering permanently and reassuringly above the group, a god was imagined. The success of religion can be ascribed to the strength of the fundamental biological tendency to submit ourselves to a dominant being. The value of religion to believers as a device for social cohesion can readily be seen as a corollary. But priests are not like dominant male (silverback) gorillas, and have never managed to assume the silverbacks' degree of authority, though not through want of trying, and no silverback ever let his group down as badly as over-zealous, murdering priesthoods were subsequently to fail their flock in the darker periods of religious history. Religion in its evolutionary context, therefore, can be regarded as originating from, and revolving around, folk memories of a dominant male. For traditional pagans today, the respect for the pack leader borne out of our ape origins is best transferred back to the elderly, who carry society's heritage and wisdom, and provide moderation and balance to temper the modernising young.

Whereas early pagans thought that the agency of natural forces could only be explained by personification, the modern pagan has a scientific understanding of these forces, but the legacy of personification endures as oneness with, and respect for, the natural world. The fact that we do not know ultimately how the Universe began is no reason *per se* to credit a being with that act of creation, if indeed it was created rather than being in a state of permanent existence. Cosmology is interesting to ponder but is far too ethereal and remote to be the practical basis of a set of beliefs and actions, which are trusted to help us conduct the everyday business of living our lives. It is better to establish that practical basis to suit the immediate and likely future need, and that basis is the foundation of new paganism, a code to regain harmony with the natural world and our fellow inhabitants of it. Religions generally adopt a human supremacist stance, which works against the restabilisation of disturbed natural equilibria, whereas in traditional paganism, spirituality and harmony with the natural world is one and the same thing. All people are animals, with all the instincts and attributes of animals, and are as much a part of the environment as other animals are, so pressure on the environment is pressure on humans too. Sooner or later all living things suffer the consequences of loss of natural equilibrium, for we are mutually dependent. There are consequences for the perpetrator of every action in the interlinked complexity of nature, and it is the humility of pagans that empowers them to recognise and accept this fact, and act accordingly.

The divergence of religion beyond its natural origins

From their first meetings with the pagan Celts in the British Isles and elsewhere, the early Christians made the assumption that Celtic paganism was a religion like Christianity, and therefore a rival to it. But their tactics were not initially those of elimination and replacement of paganism, for many had themselves been brought up in the ways of paganism, and Christianity was then far from being the all-embracing new lifestyle that could take over, and substitute itself wholesale for, a way of life that was centuries old. To pagans, belief in religions like Christianity is founded on unverifiable revelations, visions and other subjective phenomena; the unprovable existence and divinity of beings; and the imperfect consequences of recording after the event with subsequent translation and re-translation; all of which gives rise to unprovable claims of what people said and did and demonstrates clearly the impossibility of separating fact, deception and myth from the impenetrable tangle of vested interests. Belief in any aspect of religion is an act of faith, and every claim to universal truth and ultimate morality based upon it is merely another expression of an act of faith. On this basis, one religion has no more standing than any other, and the early Christians appeared to recognise this fact in their attitude to paganism as a perceived religion. Little by little, the Christians borrowed pagan traditions, beliefs, rituals and day-to-day practices and remoulded and reinterpreted them, in order that the foundations of the current society should not be shaken too violently, nor cherished beliefs challenged too forcibly, so that Christianity looked a more attractive alternative to embrace. In the pagan estimation, it was upon this fraudulent, carefully constructed framework that the power and character of Christianity was built, with certain events that were alleged to have taken place in far-off Palestine grafted on, forming a Christian veneer on a pagan Celtic carcass, a religious graft on an ancient well-rooted scion.

The traditional pagans who preserved their culture on the margins of the Christianised British island societies did so alongside a divergent religious radiation into sects of various types. Practices within these sects that were demonised by the Church were often ascribed to pagans or pagan influences, which constantly stoked the flames of vilification and persecution, although quite unjustly so. Satanism, for example, is the dark side of Christianity and part of that tradition, never a part of the history of paganism. Black Magic and other occult practices consist of rituals invented in and after the nineteenth century and are therefore also not part of the pagan tradition. By the same token, traditional paganism is not in any way related to the activities of secret societies with invented rituals and pseudo-religious creeds such as the Freemasons, The Theosophical Society and The Rosicrucians, and they too are neither described nor recommended in this book. Although modern paganism owes much to ancient Celtic ways and beliefs, the book does not suggest that anyone should attempt to recreate an ancient Celtic lifestyle, nor does it encourage the joining of neo-druidic groups or the revival of druidic-style rites. What it does offer is a folk culture common to all.

2

The Legacy of Paganism Past

The archaeological, historical and literary records of the ancient Celts

British Neolithic Period	*4300–2500 BCE*
Building of Megalithic Monuments	
in the British Isles	*4000–2000 BCE*
British Bronze Age	*2000–500 BCE*
British Iron Age	*700 BCE–43 ACE*
Celtic Culture dominant in Great Britain	*500 BCE–600 ACE*
Celtic Culture dominant in Ireland	*500 BCE–1200 ACE*

A short excursion through the findings of the archaeologist and the historian in their search for facts about ancient pagan ways will establish where extrapolation from folk traditions is necessary. But, however imperfectly the modern pagan lifestyle is arrived at, it is its relevance to modern times that it will stand or fall by, not its hybrid genesis, for folk cultures are seldom isolated and do not therefore evolve in perfectly linear and uncorrupted fashion.

Written records

There is always the possibility that aspects of culture recorded in writing or by other permanent means, and having free public access, may become fossilised. The maintenance of a solely oral tradition, as existed among the druids, allowed secrecy if desired, but also flexibility and innovation in handing down what was public. The ancient Celts left no written records, other than short oghamic inscriptions for ritual purposes, so it is not possible to be certain of any aspect of pre-Celtic or Celtic culture or religion as the Celts would have described it. Ogham was used only in magical incantations, never for vernacular communications, so the druids used oral communication to pass down their learning, be it philosophy, tribal history, law, beliefs, poetry, music or medicine. Druidic schools existed, sited away from settlements, but their curricula have not come down to us. It is known that oghamic writing was used for invocations, execrations, invectives and curses, the latter usually written on yew or hazel, so was not used freely or carelessly. The Celts thought all writing had magical power, not just oghamic inscriptions, and the ban on writing as a form of ordinary communication allowed druids to be selective about who inherited their knowledge and followed in their footsteps. Accounts about druidic times by others were mostly written after the ancient Celtic way of life had disappeared, so are not witness accounts.

Roman writers were writing about a people the Roman Empire were at war with and Christian writers about a people they considered ungodly, so the question of bias is one that the reader must bear in mind. The earliest Celtic commentators on their own previous lifestyle were part of a largely Christianised Celtic world and so were writing about a pagan past that they had probably been taught to be ashamed of, or at least had moved well away from. Unfortunately, as memories and ancestral tradition faded they were replaced by imagination, gradually leading to the romantic view of druidry today. Recognisably Celtic society lasted over all but remote parts of Great Britain from about 500 BCE (before Common Era) until about 600 ACE (after Common Era), whereas in Ireland it lasted until about 1200 ACE. Oral tradition, for example through folk tales, is unreliable because of the tendency of storytellers to embellish or invent facts and to fit a tale to a belief rather than relate a genuine folk memory; if indeed the latter can exist for long in an uninfluenced state. Welsh literature dates from only the ninth century and the earliest Irish literature from the twelfth century, but referring to times about as old as the Welsh references, and was transcribed by Christian monks. In any case these sources contain few references to pagan beliefs and venerative practices. One serious problem that researchers have with early Celtic literature written after Christianisation is the difficulty of disentangling fact from myth and legend. Another is the obscurity posed by the usual cultural assumptions made by any writer as to what a contemporary readership is expected automatically to know. There is a pagan tradition that holds that the druids saw no clear distinction between myth and history, which, if true, would probably represent an insurmountable barrier to full comprehension. Heroic tales date from the Viking era, so similar problems of interpretation exist, and it is, moreover, not clear that they represent a written version of an older oral tradition.

From these revelations stems the traditional pagan acknowledgement of the art, power and significance of communication, with oral no less worthy than written, and itself sufficient guarantee of integrity. Also they indicate respect for the skill, intellect and wisdom of the teacher and for the engaging style of the storyteller.

Excavated records

The archaeological record is no less tantalising. The earliest finds that lend themselves to some sort of interpretation date from the Neolithic period. It is likely that Neolithic stone monuments acted both as graves for the recently departed and as shrines for the veneration of ancestors. Tradition says that at least some were built with an astronomical orientation, especially alignment with sunrise at the Summer Solstice or sunset at the Winter Solstice, but relatively few can be shown to have had such a characteristic. To prove this assertion beyond reasonable doubt astronomers would have to be able to compute an accurate map of the heavens on the date when they were completed, which they can, and to be able to date the monuments accurately, which archaeologists cannot. What does appear to be the case is that the tombs were respected, as there is evidence of repair, refurbishment and avoidance of overbuilding and interruption of sight lines.

When the Bronze Age came to, or developed in, the British Isles, in about 2000 BCE, cremation, with the ashes kept in urns, became more popular than burial, and incised figures and motifs began to appear on stones. Although it has become custom to assume that the ⊕ symbol, or 'Celtic cross', indicates the sun, and by implication the existence of sun veneration, the association cannot be proved. There is, similarly, uncertainty that the incised cup and ring marks represent the moon and sun respectively. Some Bronze Age sites appear to have astronomical alignments at one or other Solstice, but again, without accurate dating, this must remain no more than a possibility. One factor to consider is that Neolithic and Bronze Age surveyors and builders were only able to produce a straight alignment of stones, as required for the construction of the so-called processional avenues, over a limited distance. Long avenues between sites changed course several times as adjustments were made. By the late Bronze Age, about 1200 to 600 BCE, the familiar round barrow burial mounds were rarely being constructed and urn cremation cemeteries ceased to be laid out too. A change of burial practice may indicate a change to a different system of beliefs or profound social changes, perhaps because of invasion and imposition of new beliefs. Another possibility is demographic movement brought about by a change of climate, which is known to have become cooler and wetter, or soil impoverishment. Preoccupation with these changes of circumstance, whatever they actually were, may have led to simplification of lifestyle, including burial rituals and modes of interment.

The megaliths of Great Britain, Ireland and Brittany were built during 4000–2000 BCE, whereas Celts arrived at the end of the Bronze Age, during the period 900 to 700 BCE, leaving evidence of their existence from 500 BCE, although few examples of constructions. They seem to have adopted and utilised the megaliths, and although pre-Celtic rituals or beliefs can scarcely be identified with any certainty, it is likely that the Celts did absorb something of them. By the time of the Iron Age, about 700 BCE, there were signs that earlier monuments were being treated with contempt, or at least with no pride of ownership, for some were plundered, violated, dismantled for reuse of stones or to extend field use, or even bisected by new boundaries. But as the Iron Age settled down and progressed both burial and cremation began to happen again.

There were two Celtic linguistic groups to come to these islands from mainland Europe, the Goidels or Gaels first – the ancestors of the Irish, Manx and Scots – and then the Brythons, whose descendants are the Welsh, Cornish and Bretons. Trading links were retained with the Gallic Celts of Gaul, and possibly also with Galician Celts. From what is known, there do not seem to have been major differences in their beliefs, culture, social stratification and political organisation. They had a tribal structure, and one such tribe, the Picts, was formerly held to be a pre-Celtic race with an oft-quoted matrilineal rule of succession, but no evidence for this aspect of their society has ever been uncovered. Iron Age structures, identified by post holes, from which votive offerings have been unearthed, often have entrances facing where the sunrise would probably have been, so these may have had a ritual purpose with astronomical connections. One of the few references to possible sun veneration is the remark made by St Patrick about the fate that would befall sun worshippers, but as even solar motifs cannot positively be identified, there is no way of knowing as yet where such ceremonies occurred and what was done. What rituals occurred at outdoor sites like oak groves and sacred wells are also unknown; recorded practices at the latter date only from Christian medieval times, after the surrounding walls and other structures like baptisteries were built and practices thereat were Christianised.

There are many clues here to the origins of traditional pagan ways and beliefs. Dependency on solar and lunar cycles requires regular study of the way the environment changes with the cycles. Burial practices indicate veneration of ancestors and point to the belief that although in another world after death (the Otherworld), where earthly things are still of value, they are still part of the family. A fondness for remote places is indicated, where passages to the Otherworld exist and communication with the natural world is more intense and meaningful, as is the significance of water as an interface between this world and the Otherworld.

The origins of druidic culture

It is not known with certainty whether druidry came with the Celts or whether they borrowed it from their predecessors. In its character and beliefs druidism does seem to be Indo-European. If it was of Mediterranean origin then it might be expected that the Greek and Roman writers would have mentioned it, especially the latter as they described other systems of beliefs that they encountered in their expanding empire, but none of these writers described early Celtic culture. Attempts to demonstrate links with Germanic or Nordic beliefs are not convincing, and it remains a fact that druidism is only known from its Celtic connection, as supported by Caesar, who stated clearly that it evolved in Great Britain and from there was exported to Gaul. In both Gallic and Irish circles Great Britain was regarded as the home of druidism and the place to go for advanced training in it.

Roman commentaries on druidic beliefs, practices and venerated figures

It is interesting to read descriptions by later Roman writers, notably Caesar, of Celtic beliefs and heroic figures. They assumed that these figures were gods and goddesses, and appear to have initiated a process of replacing them with Roman deities whose characteristics appeared to them reasonably to match those of the Celtic figures. Multiple aspects, and alternative naming, of the Celtic figures appear to have caused confusion, as did the existence of local venerated figures. Many of Caesar's remarks refer to the situation he found in Gaul, but he referred also to British druidism, as did other Roman writers.

According to Caesar the chief Celtic venerated figure was Lugh, whose name means 'light' or 'whiteness', and who was designated 'Master of all the Arts'. His association with the sun and other characteristics compare well with the Norse god Odin. The festival dedicated to him was Lughnasadh, originally a great assembly on the plain of Meath in Ireland in honour of his adoptive mother Tailtiu. The Romans in Gaul replaced Lugh with Mercury, and the Christians in turn replaced him with St

Michael the Archangel. Next in order of importance was Lugh's grandfather Diancecht, to give him his Irish name, alternative names being Belenus, Maponos or Mabon (the young sun and prisoner of the night) and Grannus. All had a solar aspect, although the principal aspect of Diancecht appears to have been healing. He could heal any warrior who still had his head on, hence the practice of severing the heads of the slain so they could not be reanimated. Diancecht presided over the Fountain of Health and conducted the ritual of lighting the fire under the Cauldron of Resurrection and immersing dead and wounded warriors in it. Such rituals as the casting of votive offerings at thermal springs may have a related origin. The Romans replaced Diancecht with Apollo, whose name may have the same root as the sacred apple, and Christians replaced them both with St Michael. Apollo had a youthful aspect, and was associated with the Otherworld, seen as the land of eternal youth.

Third in Caesar's hierarchy was Teutas/Teutatis. This word may be titular, referring to any tribal totem figure, but it appears as one of the triad Teutas, Esus and Taranis. Cognomens appear to be Vellanus, Camulos/Cumal, Alborix, Smertrios, Segomo, Lucetius, Olloudius and Lovantucarus. It would appear that this figure was identical to Noden/Nuada and indeed to Ogma/Ogmios, said to have invented oghamic writing. The principal aspect was that of a warrior, but also the providence of the earth and its distribution. It is not surprising that the Romans replaced Teutas with Mars, portrayed both as a warrior-king and a warrior-druid, reminding one of the king-druid partnerships. Next in order of importance came Dagda, the all-powerful father, or Ollathir, the father of all, one of whose aspects was master of the land of the dead, and in this sense equivalent to the Roman Pluto or Dispater. He was depicted with a club, betraying a military aspect, but also had sacerdotal characteristics, and was a skilled harpist and magician. He was sometimes depicted as a ram-headed serpent. Yet another aspect was as Sucellos, who had a mallet, possibly the same as Dagda's club, and was often accompanied by a crow, one of whose associations was death. Dagda possessed the cauldron of abundance, from which issued an inexhaustible supply of food. Summing all this up, it would seem that a figure who was druid, warrior and provider was held in the highest esteem, and this may be why the Romans replaced him with Jupiter, and portrayed him in company with a wheel, symbolising his all-seeing gifts, and perhaps giving rise to the idea of the wheel of fortune, symbolic of past, present and future knowledge. Dagda had similar characteristics to the mythological Celtic character Gargantua/Gargan, meaning 'the lame one', but who was paradoxically very strong and had equally prodigious appetites for food and sex. The wheel was also identified with Taranis ('thunder'), the master of fire, to whom sacrifices were burned alive in wicker cages. Esus is an aspect that is good (Optimus), and symbolised by a woodcutter or tree, possibly the oak, or by a bull with three cranes. Sacrifices to Esus were hung upside down from a tree and bled. The third member of the triad, Teutas/Teutatis, received human sacrifices who were suffocated and then had their heads plunged into a cauldron of boiling water.

The last of Caesar's top five was Bride/Brigit, patroness of blacksmiths, bronze workers, artisans, physicians, poets and female fili (the lowest order of druids in Ireland), and whose aspects also include fecundity and abundance. She had a triple aspect, which may have been those of Bodbh ('crow' or 'victory'), Macha and Morrigan. She seems similar to Airmed, daughter of Diancecht, as she does to Epona, who had a strong association with horses, Belisama and Sirona of Gaul; Sul of Bath, England; Arianrhod and Rhiannon of Wales; and the Irish Tailtiu and Boinn/Etaine. Some references to Bride imply that she is a female fili, although no knowledge of the duties of this position has been preserved. Male venerated figures who appeared to be counterparts of Bride include Goibniu the master smith, and the Welsh equivalent Govannon, Credne the master artisan, and the master healer Diancecht. Bride was supplanted by the Roman Minerva, the latter portrayed as a teacher of arts and crafts and patroness of warriors, craftsmen, artisans and artists.

From Caesar's writings, we also know of other venerated figures of lesser importance. The horned Cernunnos, depicted with antlers, was symbolic of abundance, and sometimes appeared with three heads. Artio, depicted as a she-bear, represented royalty and sovereignty; other animal figures being the Gallic

Epona, associated with the horse, and Arduinna, from the Ardennes, shown as a boar. The shortage of agrarian figures may be a reflection of the fact that agriculture was a lowly activity to the Celts, generally done by servants, whereas animal husbandry had much higher status. The Welsh Amaethon had agrarian aspects. There did not seem to be an equivalent to the Roman god of the sea Neptune, only guardians of springs and rivers. This may have been a consequence of the development of Celtic beliefs in landlocked central Europe, before the migrations to the western European coast and the British Isles. Manannan mac Lir, the last word meaning waves or ocean, was not really an equivalent, as he was said to be in charge of the 'Otherworld', though described as if it was a parallel world rather than the destination of souls, and the mysterious islands, and places of the sidhe (spirits of the dead) such as megalithic monuments and mounds. He is best known from the Isle of Man, a land originally called Mider.

The aspects of venerated figures tell us of important traditional pagan associations and identities, and what skills someone had to possess to be revered and respected. Once again we find solar associations, but also the possession of many talents, the power of healing, and divinatory ability. Military prowess, artistic talent and technological skills are all respected, and the head is shown to be the powerhouse of life. Admiration for the greater attributes of animals, notably in strength, speed and courage, demonstrates a measure of humility.

Celtic personification and veneration

It is not obvious from archaeological sources whether what Roman commentators refer to as Celtic 'deities' were worshipped, as in religious practice, or venerated as personifications of natural forces. But as has been noted earlier in the text, literary sources and oral traditions, such as the heroic tales and character of folk customs, would support veneration of personifications. Certainly there is no clear reference in folk tales to a pantheon of Celtic gods and goddesses, the emphasis being on local venerated figures and individual or communal communication with them, examples being the guardians of sacred pools, rivers, glens and mountains, the sponsors of battle or patrons of clans. However, some figures were clearly more powerful and important than others, possibly as a result of local figures having been adopted so widely by neighbours that they acquired regional if not national significance. It may be that the Irish Danu was the origin of the image and perception of the Earth Mother or Mother Nature, and representations of Bride, in whose honour a sacred flame was kept alight at her shrine in Kildare, Ireland, with a triple aspect may have given rise to the triune maiden, mother and crone. Characterisation of Welsh venerated figures is more difficult as their appearances in literature are rarer, but even if such Celtic figures could be identified this would not of itself provide understanding of the rituals that were performed in their honour. Characters mentioned in Welsh literature and once thought to be deities, such as Ceridwen and her cauldron, Gwyn ap Nudd and Arianrhod, appear to be purely literary as they do not appear in the historical or archaeological records.

The Celts only venerated figures who possessed the protective functions that they needed. For example, early Irish farmers were principally herdsmen, not growers of crops, so no venerated figure with an agricultural aspect was needed. When cultivation of the ground became more common it was largely worked by slaves, and there was still no considered need for such a figure. Societies believing in a single all-powerful god or similar figure are termed monotheistic, and those believing in a pantheon of such personalities are known as polytheistic. But whether polytheism may be considered as monotheism with the god having all the aspects required by the people and varying its name and depiction accordingly, like the trinity but with many more than three aspects, needs to be determined separately for each culture. In old Celtic society, Lugh, the Master of all the Arts, would seem to be the best candidate for the principal venerated figure, but he was not regarded as the creator of the world, only as a polyfunctionary. How far the cognomens of Celtic venerated figures recorded by the Romans represent multiple aspects or different figures is not clear. The same polyfunctionality mentioned above is seen in the heroes of folk tales and the symbolism they project, there being no equivalent known of the cosmogonies and theogonies found in the mythology of other peoples.

But the folk tales do tell us about the scope and powers of the druids, for these powers are wielded by heroes in the tales. The belief that St Patrick had druidic-type powers may have assisted him to convert the Irish to Christianity without bloodshed. Just as the druids directed society so were the missionaries and later the clergy to do. It has been mooted that the relatively painless acceptance of Christianity by the Celts, especially by the Irish fili, who became the guardians of druidic thought and practice there, was because they did in fact have one multiple-aspect god, and Christian missionaries convinced them that their God was one and the same, but requiring just a different style of obeisance. The fact that old Celtic society seemed not to recognise a difference between the sacred and profane probably allowed Christianity to filter into every aspect of daily life, where it remained until recent times.

The existence of, and, from our perspective, absence of, specific aspects, points to the practical nature of Celtic personification, demonstrating a keen understanding of the workings and components of the natural world and how they can be utilised. This understanding has been maintained by traditional pagans.

Druidic responsibilities

Roman writers record that three positions existed in the druidic hierarchy, namely bard, druid and vates, of which the latter two had ritual functions. At least one popular image of druids stands up to historical scrutiny, that of them in white robes, and they also sported tonsures. Druids, according to Caesar, regulated all venerative observance; instructed the young; and judged in boundary and other disputes, inheritance claims, damages claims and trials for criminal behaviour. They were poets, soothsayers, skilled in the art of augury and other divination, performers of rituals and sacrifices, healers, magicians, astronomers, philosophers, priests, historians and annalists, legislators and musicians. Being experienced in liaison, druids would be sent as ambassadors to negotiate with kings. In legal matters druids were solely responsible for judgement, the sentence being carried out by the king. Such a sentence may have been a punishment, ostracism, public shame or a demonic visitation from the Otherworld. As soothsayers, druids interpreted omens for divination, and were held to be able to control the elements, such as is necessary for the calming of storms.

Some prophetesses are known, which indicates that women could at least assume some druidic roles. Morgan le Fay of the Arthurian tales may have been one such. All druidic rituals described were performed by men, which possibly is a disappointment to those who believe, despite lack of historical verification, that Celtic society had a considerable degree of sexual equality, but women were certainly involved with healing, magic, and divination, and were wardens of shrines.

Important druidic ceremonies and sacrifices were done in sacred forest clearings, but in other cases the druids would have advised on the conduct of them or just presided over them. The druids' healing role involved knowledge of plant medicine in particular, and also, if folk tales are to be believed, surgery. They believed that there was a psychic dimension to every illness and discomfort, so both the soul and body had to be treated appropriately. So broad was their scope that healers, bonesetters, cunning folk (herbalists) and hypnotists may all claim in some measure to be their occupational descendants. Druids performed a ceremony of anointing babies with water, which may have been part of a naming ritual. Two privileges druids had were that they were excused military duties and the payment of taxes.

In charge of the druids of a tribe was a chief druid, elected by the senior druids – that is to say, the most capable and intellectual – and together they shared both secular and sacerdotal authority, which did not appear to be distinct in old Celtic society. A druid assembly was called a gorsedd, and there are records of grand druidic gatherings, perhaps to elect a regional or national archdruid. Perhaps Christian priests modelled their assumption of secular as well as spiritual authority on the all-embracing role of the druids. The lowest order of druids was the vates, called fili (singular file) in Ireland, one of whose special duties was augury and divination. Below the druids in society were the warriors or equites, and below them the ordinary folk or plebeians. These were classes, not castes, so anyone, through the necessary study and probation, could attain higher office in society.

Druids did not have the pacifist leanings associated with many orders of priesthood today, and would take up the sword if necessary, to defend their tribe and their position in it, but remained in the service of the tribal king and saw no conflict between their sacerdotal and warrior roles. The King and chief druid were like a warrior–priest double act, perhaps the model for the legendary figures of Uther Pendragon and Merlin, and later King Arthur and Merlin. Kings were elected by their senior warriors, in like manner to the chief druid, and from records and the survival of identifiable inaugural mounds and stones some idea can be discerned about how Celtic kings were admitted to office. After a trial period where they demonstrated their physique and physical prowess, resistance to temptation to break tribal taboos, and underwent a ceremony of union with the tribe's patronal venerated figure, they were prepared for inauguration. They bathed, donned a white robe, and stepped into footprints carved into the inaugural stone. Kings would normally consult druids about their actions, but could act without such consultation, although strictly within the law. In most cases the chief druid and King depended on, and acted on the advice of, the other. The Christian missionary technique of initially converting and allying with a ruler possibly drew its inspiration from this partnership, and such an association also explains how Christians were able to fill the vacuum left by the collapse of druidism.

More is known about early Celtic ways from the British Isles than from Gaul, possibly indicating greater Roman suppression in the latter region. Caesar commented that druids from Gaul went to Great Britain for advanced studies, a fact which must have contributed to Caesar's decision to subjugate Great Britain in order that his hold on Gaul could be consolidated without fear of interference from the west. The druidic education centre may have been in Wales, at Bangor or on Anglesey, and its existence implies that there were at least common cultural bonds among the Celtic peoples, if not regular trading and social links.

Druidic polymathy provided many role models handed down by traditional pagans, who look up to the educated, the experienced and the wise. Those with a sense of history, who maintain the threads of culture and philosophy, are still, in pagan eyes, deserving of respect, and their judgement, and powers of negotiation and persuasion, sought after. From the druidic example we also note the ascent on merit rather than by birthright, and the election to office on the basis of intellect and variety of accomplishments. The druids' approach to healing has brought down to us the belief in holistic medicine – treating both mind and body – and the interest of women (who were often assistants to druids) in healing and divination comes from these times.

Initiations and plant rituals

There is no literary or archaeological evidence of temple building by the Celts in druidic times. During the period of early recorded history the Celts ritually walked sunwise round the tombs of great warriors and this may have been the inspiration for the building of ambulatories in Christian churches containing tombs of saints or martyrs, although no temples are known to have preceded these churches. Instead of temples the Celts used a nemeton, a sacred forest clearing, where sacrifices were made and effigies for veneration stood. A nemeton was, like the bed of a sacred well or lake, an interface between this world and the Otherworld. It may be that Christian hermits emulated the idea of communion with nature in forest sanctuaries when they chose isolated sites for communion with their god. As the druids left no liturgical pronouncements and no sacred writings it is not known exactly what happened in these groves, but Roman writers have recorded some initiations and rituals.

Pliny the Elder described the importance of mistletoe and the oak from which it was cut. He referred to a ritual carried out on the sixth day of the moon, at an unspecified time of year, although the mistletoe had berries so it must have been winter in Pliny's description. The mistletoe was cut with a golden sickle, by a druid in a white robe, and caught in a piece of white linen, presumably to prevent it touching the ground and losing its power. As gold is a soft metal and unsuitable for tool manufacture, the sickle was probably gold-plated iron or bronze. After the cutting young white bulls were sacrificed. Mistletoe was credited with magical properties; it was regarded as a panacea, and a beverage made from the berries was taken to cure sterility. Other botanical lore was mentioned in Roman commentaries. The apple was the fruit of wisdom, knowledge and immortality, and a number of trees were held in special regard. Rowan was used for magical purposes, especially if a suitable oghamic inscription was carved in it, and oak, yew and hazel also gave the ogham letters extra power over carvings in rock. For the cutting of lycopodium, or selago, a druid dressed in white and had bare feet, the latter newly washed. An offering of bread and wine was made first, then the druid turned to the rising sun, with his right side forward, and drew his blade by extending the right hand to his left side, which would be in shadow. The blade could not be of iron. A bog plant known as samolus was cut by a blade held in the left hand, taking care not to look behind and to store the cut stems where drinks were stored. Vervain was mentioned as an important plant in divination rituals, accompanied by appropriate incantations.

Here we see the roots of traditional pagan hero veneration, and the importance of ritual in preparing mind and body for communion with nature. The importance of trees in true paganism, and the familiarity with the properties of woods, both practical and magical, arises during this period.

The four elements

The Celts seemed to consider the four natural elements, earth, water, air and fire, as means by which energy was manifest or transmitted. The earth they regarded as belonging to no one person, and the burial or cremation of the deceased was the giving back of a body to the earth. Favourite possessions were interred with it, and in the case of those of high social status their slaves and even dependants. The grave was marked with a stone pillar, upon which an epitaph was carved, and the implanting in the ground was accompanied by the singing of a lament and the reading of a eulogy in verse.

As water flows from the earth, this ubiquitous and vital liquid was symbolic of fertility, and as the preserver of life and the prime cleansing agent it was symbolic of healing. The Celts anointed people in sacred watercourses to purify their souls by way of purifying their body, a practice that may have been copied by Christians as baptism. Rituals carried out for other purposes, such as to cure specific ailments, were the precursors of those recorded in Christian times at healing wells rededicated to saints. Druids claimed to be able to induce thirst, especially in enemy kings engaged in combat, and to cause new springs to appear in dry areas, and such powers were later to be attributed to saints, for example by making springs gush forth by thrusting their staffs into the ground. It may be a legacy of their terrestrial central European culture that the Celts of the British Isles had few rituals where sea water was concerned, save for the druids attempting to calm storms, something they presumably only applied themselves to on reaching the maritime coasts of Gaul, Galicia, Great Britain and Ireland. There arose a number of accounts of mysterious, magical islands, to which souls were transported and from which invaders came. Inundations from the sea were seen as punishment for an unwholesome lifestyle in coastal towns.

In addition to being the medium through which the winds and clouds moved, the air was the place of sacred beings and faeries, the former able to change into animal forms like birds. Druids claimed to have the ability to control the winds, and could even whip up a 'druid wind', which could influence people's actions or change the outcome of events like battles.

Fire was thought of as the manifestation of the outpouring of energy from the other three elements, and was a common component of many rituals. It may be that the uses of symbolic and memorial flames elsewhere, for example at the Olympic

Games and at the Yad Vashem memorial in Israel, also have their origin in such ceremonial employment of flame. The Celtic tradition of Beltane bonfires was borrowed by Christians for their created customs of Lenten fires and the Easter Fire, the latter having a claimed origin from St Patrick deliberately lighting a fire prior to the King's druids igniting the sacred fire on the Hill of Tara in Ireland. Such druidic fires were meticulously prepared, but details have not survived in the form of witness records.

Notions of the elements are central to a nature-based lifestyle like that of true pagans, from which they arise, and to which they return by transformation. The warmth and light of the sun, the life-giving, sustaining and pre-serving powers of water, and the fertility and regenerative functions of the earth, are all elemental aspects in the traditional pagan mind. The air is the common medium of all terrestrial and Otherworld life, and its highway, and the cleansing and regenerative powers of fire, used for saining (ritual purification, with fire and smoke), enable it to represent the sun in rituals.

Sacrificial rituals

Ancestors were revered, and their souls were believed to return on Quarter Days, the junctures of the seasons, especially Samhain, the dawn of Winter, when a room was made ready for them with fire and sustenance. Ancestors' bones or ashes were protected and burial sites cared for. Offering up the bones of an ancestor or recent family member as a sacrifice would have represented a very significant gesture. Animal bones were more commonly offered, or the animal itself, but this was still significant as families depended on their animals. Caesar recorded the sacrifice of men in willow wicker cages, and in Gaul both animals – from the wild and from farms – and men were so treated. The wicker cage became known as the Wicker Man, and may have been the precursor of the Carnival Giant. Roman writers commented that the victims included criminals after five years' incarceration. In Gaul, victims were also drowned by holding their heads under water in a cauldron, or by being hung from a tree and bled. It seems likely that the Romans, who regularly fed Christians to wild animals and forced captives to engage in gladiatorial combat, criticised Celtic sacrifice in order to discredit it. A ritual of regeneration is described in Irish and Welsh folk tales in which 'sacrificial victims' are given a feast in a hollow dug in the ground and a bonfire built above them. Hemp was put in the bonfire, whose fumes after combustion then had a narcotic effect on the 'victims'. When the fire died down the 'victims' emerged and were considered to be 'reborn' from the embers. There is the suggestion that in real life lepers were chosen for this ritual. Bonfire rituals, some with echoes of former sacrificial practices, survive as folk customs to this day, as does the rolling downhill of a flaming wheel, bound with hay and oakum, to imitate the sun's declination.

Sacrifice literally means to make something sacred by offering it, and is thereby felt to be a positive action. The negative aspect of sacrifice is when an individual or community seeks to transfer their sins or frustrations on to a scapegoat. Many animals were chosen as positive sacrifices, often male like bulls, stags and rams, but also female such as mares. Dogs and pigs featured too. Plant offerings included branches from sacred trees, flowers and newly harvested fruit and vegetables. Burying human or animal bodies under the foundations of walls of buildings or fortifications may have served to give them added strength or for consecration. General offerings at sacred sites, notably pools, bogs and rivers, perhaps considered to be links with the Otherworld, were commonly made, gold, weapons, cauldrons and other examples of the smithy's art, ornaments and jewellery being usual, and often damaged first so that they could not be reused in this world. As indicated above, some sacrificial rituals were symbolic, another example being the 'sacrifice and rejuvenation' of kings. The possibility exists that the collecting of tithes by Christian priests was an offshoot of the idea of sacrifice, with a subtle change of recipient.

The severing of heads from enemy corpses was a rite that immediately followed the conclusion of battle, the victorious warriors nailing the heads above their doorways. This act, it was believed, prevented the resurrection of the soul, as the head was considered to be the receptacle of whatever defined the individual. When kings or valiant warriors fell in battle their compatriots cut off their heads to prevent enemy warriors taking them. Prized heads became sacred skulls, and were sometimes employed as vessels for rituals at sacred wells and springs.

It remains important to traditional pagans to reaffirm kinship with deceased relatives, to welcome their return in spirit, and to remember their contribution and lasting influence. The belief in sacrifice shows itself in a willingness to go without for the common good, and to train oneself in self-control and resistance to indulgence and materialism, such as by deliberately offering precious things.

The Otherworld

To reach the Otherworld was everyone's objective in life. The soul, or essence of life, though not defined clearly in Celtic sources, was thought not to die but to pass after death into another body, a belief that supports the observation that the Celts did not fear death. The place of this transmigration was the Otherworld, so the Celts did not believe in reincarnation in this world. The idea of the Christian hell as a place of eternal punishment for sinners would not have applied to the Otherworld. Earthly toils were not needed there, earthly time no longer applied, and there was no death as the Otherworld was beyond this state. When mortals travelled to it, stayed a short while and then returned, they found they had been away for a very long time. It was described as a place of natural beauty, diversity and abundance, where teaching of all the arts was available to everyone. There were no earthly ills, conflicts and weaknesses of character; and fine food, especially sacred apples, mead and wine, music and sensual pleasures were all on tap. The weather was always fine, and there was no hierarchy of social classes, not even druids, so all were equal.

Some writers described the Otherworld as on an island away towards the setting sun, that is, behind the observer. Other locations mentioned for the Otherworld were often in mounds (sidh). On Quarter Days, especially Samhain, the two worlds could be accessed from each other, through entrances in certain lakebeds, hills, chasms, and mounds or from certain islands. One path to the Otherworld was through death, but it was possible to make the journey without dying, and to return, although it was a difficult path to discern and follow, along which the traveller was beset by all manner of obstacles, confusions, monsters and supernatural beings, intent on preventing progress. Overcoming these barriers needed wisdom, decisiveness, courage and resourcefulness, as it did to overcome one's own despair and self-doubt. Such personal quests are to be found in folk tales, in which the narrative focuses on the individual and his or her actions on route through life to the ultimate transmigration of the soul. Theirs was not a passive, fatalistic outlook waiting for inevitable death, but a determination to reach the Otherworld after striving to perfect such aspects of their own world as could be addressed to assist their passage, fairness and justice among them. It was portrayed as a duty to attempt the quest, and to experience all the struggles, setbacks and adversities. To fail to undertake the quest was to bring shame upon oneself, but his or her community would also feel it, just as they all shared in the glory of a successful quest. There is the suggestion in descriptions that one purpose of the quest was actually to try and convert this world into the character of the Otherworld so that it could be experienced without dying.

Whether the similarity of the Celtic notion of immortality of the soul and the Christian idea of resurrection is but another example of borrowing by Christians from the Celts or offers an explanation for the ready assimilation of Christian ideas of death by the Celts is not entirely clear.

White was the colour associated with the Otherworld and red signified death and destruction. In folk tales, supernatural creatures were often white with red ears. Belief in supernatural beings and animals persisted amongst the Celts into recent times, as folk customs and their attendant lore recorded as late as the early twentieth century testify. For example, the belief existed that whilst asleep one's spirit could be appropriated to ride in a ghostly cavalcade called the Wild Hunt, which was led by a female or male hunter and accompanied by spectral dogs.

Tales of Wildmen were persistent too, appearing to represent a belief that personified spirits haunted the sacrilegious and anti-social, possibly used by parents to frighten unruly children and possibly arising through demonisation of an ancient venerated figure or forest sprite.

The Otherworld is still regarded by true pagans as a quest on life's journey. The absence of a notion of death enables pagans to have a more positive and progressive outlook on life, constantly improving themselves for the next phase of the journey, and maintaining creativity and purpose into old age. This outlook benefits others too, so all share in one's accomplishments.

The druidic calendar

Although druids were keepers of the calendar only a few details of this calendar have been passed down. It was based on the lunar cycle, a month lasting from one full moon to the next, hence the importance of the moon in old Celtic folk customs. Thirteen festivals marked the full moons, one opening each lunar month, in a year. Each lunar month had a bright half when the moon was waxing, during which it was held to be propitious for positive magic and felt to be an optimistic time, and a dark half when the moon was waning, a time when people were apprehensive and cautious. Each full moon was symbolised by a tree, usually a sacred tree or one associated with herbal medicine. The cycle began at the darkest time of the year, with the full moon nearest the Winter Solstice, and this midwinter full moon was symbolised by the birch (November/December). Under this moon it was a time for beginnings or renewal. The sequence continued with the rowan moon (December), followed by ash (January), alder (February/March), willow (March), hawthorn (April), oak (May/June), holly (July), hazel (August/September), grape vine (September), ivy (October), reed (October/November), and finishing with elder (November), a time for endings and exorcism.

The druidic year was divided into two principal seasons, Winter (Geamhradh) and Summer (Samhradh). The beginnings of these seasons were marked by the fire festivals of Samhain, beginning at sunset on what is now 31 October, and Beltane, beginning at sunset on what is now 30 April, respectively. Samhain was at the most important new moon, when life started to decay, the harvest ended, and people prepared to venerate their dead relatives. Beltane was traditionally the time of the most important full moon, and the festival was a fertility rite, in celebration of the reawakening of life as Winter died. These two occasions were very important for divination and saining purposes.

Midway between were two less important festivals, Imbolc at the start of Spring (Earrach), the warming of Winter, beginning at sunset on what is now 31 January, and Lughnasadh at the start of Autumn (Foghara), the cooling of Summer, beginning at sunset on what is now 31 July. Imbolc was on the waxing moon, and was the celebration of lactating ewes and lambing. Lughnasadh was on the waning moon, and was the time to celebrate the first fruits of the harvest, especially corn, from which the first bread was ceremonially made. These four celebrations were known as the Quarter Days, each falling forty days after a solstice or equinox. It is natural for a lunar calendar to have reckoning by nights instead of days, and a calendar day was reckoned from sunset to sunset. Fire was very much in evidence on these occasions, for light, saining, and to augment the sun. There was a leap month every five years.

The old Celtic agrarian seasons were Summer, from Beltane to Samhain, when cattle were kept out in the pasture, and Winter, from Samhain to Beltane, when the cattle were confined to their byres.

The solar aspects of the pagan calendar, Solstices and Equinoxes, appeared much later than the druidic era. The Winter Solstice on 21 December saw the sun at its nadir, and bonfires were lit to ensure it had the energy to be reborn. At the Vernal Equinox on 21 March the lengths of day and night were equal, with the sun still in the ascendancy. The sun is at its zenith at the Summer Solstice on 21 June, and then starts to decline. By the Autumnal Equinox on 23 September day and night are again of equal length, and the sun begins to die. The solar festivals were probably added by the Anglo-Saxons and Vikings and adopted by the indigenous Celtic population, who transferred elements of the Quarter Day commemorations to the Solstices, but do not appear to have marked the Equinoxes. The latter appeared later in the witches' calendars of the Middle Ages.

These eight commemorations formed the basis of future British traditional pagan calendars.

It was expected that every member of the community attended Quarter Day celebrations. On these days there were family, community and tribal gatherings, the latter dealing with judicial and legal matters in Ireland, at Samhain; bonfires were lit, saining (ritual purification) done and cattle driven between two fires to ensure good health. The festival that marked the start of Winter, Samhain, was of particular importance. Pork was eaten at the feast, a meat believed on this occasion to bestow immortality. This world became connected to the Otherworld, and the sidh – the barrows where dwelt sacred and heroic figures – opened. To signify the death of the old year at Samhain all fires were extinguished, and then a new fire lit. At Imbolc three months later, which marked the middle of Winter, both fire and water were honoured, but it was a less important festival in terms of size and activity. Three months further on was Beltane, another fire ceremony and rites of Spring. Just as Samhain marked the slide into darkness and hibernation so Beltane heralded the brightening of the days and the reawakening of life. Branches were planted in fields and gardens, and fixed over house and stable doors. Animals and animal houses were sained, the former between two fires, the latter with flaming torches, spells being cast to protect them. Processions of flaming torches sained the fields. The final Quarter Day was Lughnasadh, the celebration of the harvesting of the first fruits. Games and sports, notably horse races, were held, as were poetry competitions.

Living on the basis of the pagan calendar allows a natural focus to life with the changing seasons. Calendrical celebrations take on special significance to regularly re-establish connection, input and dependency on nature, and feeling a part of natural cycles.

Orientational reckoning

To understand Celtic rituals it is important to know their orientational reckoning. The direction of the rising sun, that is to say, east, is assumed to be in front of the person conducting the ritual. Proceeding deisil, or sunwise, the south or luminous side is on the person's right, and west is behind the person. As west is therefore invisible, it is deemed to be where the Otherworld lies. Continuing sunwise, to the person's left is north, the obscure or sinister side. The right side, south, came to be more important than the left side, north, and Christianity adopted the north side as the Devil's direction, and no graves were dug on the north side of early churches, nor were doors or windows put in the north wall.

In terms of the life cycle, east was the direction of birth, proceeding sunwise to the right brought you to the south, taking you through a normal life. From there life continued until you were in the west, the place of death and the Otherworld, and after that you moved round to the north, the land of cold and shadow. To proceed left in the first instance was therefore to take a course that would lead to disaster.

It became customary to consider right as lucky and left as unlucky, and there arose a long-standing tradition of actions performed in a sunwise direction (east to south to west to north, or clockwise as we would now say), mimicking the direction of movement of the sun, being deemed favourable, and those done widdershins unfavourable.

Examples of actions still performed sunwise by traditional pagans, and indeed by most people in the British Isles today, are stirring a drink or cake mixture, coiling a rope, dealing a deck of cards, passing food round the table, processional perambulation and dancing, turning a boat in harbour, and many more.

The spoken word

The spoken word had force and respect in old Celtic society, and was chosen with care. For words of any kind to be effective they had to conform to a traditional order and style, with accompanying gestures and other body language. Ritual druidic formulae were kept secret, and only passed on to the chosen, but there were many other spoken formulae. A written formula would not do, as the intonation and actions would not be recorded with it. Sometimes musical accompaniment was used, for example on a harp, and sunwise circumambulation.

Casting spells, like writing, was also a very serious matter. The receiver of a spell, especially the notorious shouting spell, which we know of only by fearsome repute, had to decide whether to remain on their chosen course or risk the blame and wrath of the community, or worse suffer illness or deformity if considered guilty. If the receiver was shown to be innocent, the caster of the spell risked retribution, a fact that tempered the actions of the would-be spell-caster. Incantations also accompanied divinations, examples being the reading of entrails and the watching of the flight patterns of birds, and were similarly precise, and also accompanied sacrifices. A druidic ban was known as a *geis*. Most is known about the *geis* from Ireland, where it took the form of a druidic incantation designed to impose the prohibition, which may have been to determine or prevent an outcome, usually under pain of death. If two conflicting *geisa* were imposed then death was inevitable. Kings or warriors were mainly the recipients of *geisa*, never druids themselves. *Geisa* would determine the path of moral behaviour, and as such were acceptable to a population conditioned to expect a king to behave appropriately. Individuals could restrict themselves by a *geis*, normally by swearing an oath, which became a pledge to which all nature and any present witnessed. This then was the power of the spoken word, the force and conviction of which all modern pagans may consider to be worth remembering in their communication with others.

True pagans regard listening very highly and admire a speaker who chooses words, expressions and body language appropriately, and who speaks with a clear, straightforward style. Care with the spoken word was an art garnered in close-knit communities, where gossip, rumour, innuendo and unfounded accusations could have dire consequences for its integrity. Pagan self-discipline comes partly from the natural world being considered a witness.

Totemism

It seems a form of totemism existed among the Celts in that tribes, groups and individuals adopted an animal or plant whose characteristics or properties they admired and came to feel an association with. Animals known to have inspired feelings of kinship were the boar, bull, brown bear, horse, and dog, and of plants the yew. Animal symbolism particularly was used on warriors' shields and helmets. It was prohibited to kill one's own totem animal, although it could be consumed on one special feast day each year. Dressing in totem animals' skins was done to better imagine, identify with and act out their attributes and habits. Whether through incantations and trances the Celts actually believed, in a shamanistic way, that they could become animals is not known, but characters in folk tales certainly do transform themselves into animals by metamorphoses. The wheel is sometimes used to symbolise metamorphosis in these tales, just as bridges, fords and the ferryman are the ways in which spiritual journeys, such as those between this world and the Otherworld, are alluded to. It is likely, though not known for certain, that Celts took fungal preparations, perhaps from the Fly Agaric (*Amanita muscaria*), to induce hallucinatory states, or inhaled the fumes from burning hemp, or drank alcoholic beverages such as beer, mead and wine. The large consumption of alcohol in surviving folk customs may attest to this heritage.

Dreams may also have constituted a way to 'cross the bridge' – the ultimate journey, by whatever agency, being to cross over to the Otherworld and then return, overcoming all obstacles, supernatural beings and monstrous creatures. Those who study ancient Celtic folk lore are left with the impression that the Celts did not seem to recognise the difference between the real and the imaginary, and this made the dream more powerful as a means of regenerating and reorienting the mind and body. The dream seemed to inspire and prepare, and conditioned the belief that what is conceived in the subconscious could become conscious reality.

*There remains a true pagan tradition of adopting a
totem animal and plant, or of just having a favourite,
whose attributes and habits are studied, admired and even
emulated. Belief in the power of the imagination and
the meaningfulness of dreams remains strong amongst
traditional pagans.*

Druidic philosophy

As no druidic records have come down to us there is no
treatise on druidic doctrine that can be consulted. Roman and
Greek commentators made remarks about it, but they were
often commenting on the past, or relying on second-hand
information. Attempts to describe another people's culture carry
the risk of making judgements by one's own standards rather
than by those that held sway in that culture. Celtic reality,
lifestyle and philosophy were unique to the Celts and not
readily comprehensible to their Roman, Greek or Christian
observers, so the written accounts that they produced could not
have carried, and did not carry, a Celtic context that can now
be reconstructed and understood with clarity. And nothing that
has been passed down can possibly help us understand the
Celtic imagination and mentality. Where such an interesting
culture is concerned this is an enormous and irreplaceable loss.

Druidic philosophy does not seem to have considered dualities such as good and evil to be opposites, because it did not
establish absolute values against which to measure them. Evil
seen as an individual act of weakness or improperly selected
application was not regarded as the same as straying from
a norm. Achievement was seen in terms of the destiny of
the individual or community, and failure as the meeting of an
obstacle, albeit temporary. In this sense, actions were seen as
wholly positive. Negativity, in the sense of what shouldn't be
done, seems more likely to have come from Christianity than
old Celtic philosophy. Thus, anything that did not harm the
Celtic individual or community was acceptable, and although
geisa imposed limits, which if strayed beyond presented a risk
to the individual, they were not seen socially in a negative light.
Celtic dualities, then – other examples being life and death,

light and dark, day and night – were seen as parallel and inter-dependent rather than as conflicting opposites. Thus, the Celtic warrior's disregard for death and his enjoyment of all aspects of life can more readily be appreciated. There was also no concept of absolute truth; truth, and indeed falsehood, was believed to be multi-faceted like a diamond and immediate to the situation. Even though the Celts did not regard sin in the same light as the Christians, as a deviation from the norm, they accepted that freedom came with responsibility, and that actions had consequences that had to be faced. Compensation was an important part of the judicial process, and was not seen so much as a punishment as a re-establishment of equilibrium. This too was not, therefore, a moral issue.

Traditional pagan behavioural norms show an absence of absolutism and duality of qualities and attitudes as opposites. That which harms no-one is tolerated, as long as individual quest does not cut across the common path of progress and prosperity. Responsibilities are balanced between oneself, the family and the community. Consequences for one's actions are faced, with reparation or compensation as appropriate; a practical rather than moral-laced approach to justice.

The decline of druidism

Roman troops under Julius Caesar land in Kent	*27 August 55 BCE*
Second Roman invasion under Julius Caesar	*8 July 54 BCE*
Third Roman invasion under Aulus Plautius, south-east England occupied	*Summer 43 BCE*
Druid sanctuary on Anglesey sacked by Gaius Suetonius Paulinus	*60 ACE*
Wales under Roman control by	*77 ACE*
Agricola reaches the Solway/Tyne, late in	*79 ACE*

Agricola reaches the River Tay, limit of Roman conquest, end of	*81 ACE*
Evidence of Christian practice in Britain (Celtic and Roman) from	*205 ACE*
Roman forays into northern Scotland under Septimus Severus	*208 ACE*
Start of phased Roman withdrawal to defend empire from Germanic tribes	*211 ACE*
Spread of Christianity in Britain as pagan practices decline, from about	*350 ACE*
Roman withdrawals cause power vacuum, civil unrest	*360 ACE*
Significant Roman withdrawals to defend Italy, and ultimately Rome	*408 ACE*
Records of Christian missionaries arriving in Great Britain	*429–448 ACE*

After the Roman conquest of England and Wales had been consolidated and ordinary life became more settled there were no further references by Roman commentators to druids and their activities in Celtic society. Druids were killed in large numbers during the conquest, but doubtless some survived, carrying on their ministry in secret or concentrating on activities like magic or soothsaying that were less likely to attract the attention of the Roman authorities. Many druids were converted to Christianity early and so abandoned druidic practices that Christians disapproved of. After Christianity took hold, bards, who were poets and singers, were the druids' heirs in Wales and Brittany, whereas fili took over duties in Ireland. Possibly some converted willingly to Christianity, to regain some power, influence and status while this religion spread and had the support of the ruling classes. St Patrick may have converted the fili first to become the new Christian religious elite and the rivalry between fili and druids was thus exploited, the latter losing out. Certainly some druidic practices would have been unacceptable to Christians, who were growing in number and influence, and either through Christian pressure or reluctance to occupy only the margins of society practitioners of druidry gradually ceased their activities, leaving as its legacy local customs and traditions that were tolerated by the new spiritual guardians. It becomes difficult from records referring to the latter part of the Roman occupation of the British Isles to discern in some cases which of these customs were Celtic and which Roman, for a large part of the western Roman empire was Celtic or in contact with Celts, and cross-fertilisation would have been extensive.

It was during the missionary Christian period that the localisation of Celtic pagan culture was to become a weakness in its attempts to resist Christianisation and maintain its integrity. The adoption of Christianity by the rulers of the Roman Empire made it easier for missionaries to travel and work and led to many pagan chiefs adopting the new religion because it was seen as the spiritual arm of a powerful and influential empire and the means to acquire access to the new sources of trade and wealth. So, after much persecution, Christians saw a reversal in their fortunes and a reversal of the status of their religion, which they were not slow to exploit. The more successful Christian Roman emperors and generals were in battle the better Christianity stood in the eyes of victor and defeated alike. The darker sides of Roman life – slavery, brutality, excessive punishments and the like – seem not to have attracted the refining intentions of the missionaries, who were loath to upset their new masters and concentrated instead on spreading 'the word', capturing 'souls' for their faith, and correcting minor misdemeanours throughout the least powerful classes of society. Their calling was not so strong that they attempted to cleanse the sadism of their masters and their associates.

Although Romans were generally tolerant of different religions in the Roman Empire they put druidry down mercilessly, possibly because as teachers druids had a strong secular influence and were seen as a threat to Roman order and control. The spread of Christianity stopped any druidic revival, and then Celtic society itself began to change, first under Romanisation and then under the Anglo-Saxons and Vikings. In Ireland elements of druidism persisted as Christianity gradually replaced it with no serious disruption to Irish social structure. The institution of druidry gradually crumbled but the druidic threads of Celtic society were not broken overnight. Druids may have continued to practise in remote areas, possibly declining in status to mere diviners or healers, until eventually their legacy was to be found only in folk tales, folk songs, customs, superstitions, rituals, games and other everyday activities.

The meaning of the word 'druid'

The word 'druid' may be equivalent to an original Gaelic word meaning 'sorcerer', and in Ireland this is probably what they became after their spiritual duties were taken over by Christians and other duties given to the Christianised fili. Other possible meanings of 'druid' are 'all-seeing' or 'all-knowing' and 'men of the trees', referring to the sacred oaks.

Legislation against pagan practices

Roman Emperor Constantine converted to Christianity	*28 October 312 ACE*
Constantine orders Christian observance throughout Roman Empire	*3 July 321 ACE*
Constantine refuses to conduct customary pagan sacrifice at the Temple of Jupiter	*25 July 326 ACE*
Constantine orders confiscation of pagan treasures	*331 ACE*
Constantius II issues decree that offering a pagan sacrifice or obeisance to household gods carries the death penalty	*353 ACE*
Emperor Julian passes edict tolerating all religions, but bans Christian teaching. Pagan practices resurface in British Isles	*362 ACE*
Theodosius bans all faiths except Christianity in the Eastern Empire. Identical ban imposed by Gratian in Western Empire	*c380 ACE*

Theodosius outlaws all pagan
     practice, public and private   *391 ACE*
Theodosius outlaws magic,
     divination and necromancy   *428 ACE*

In the fourth century a series of legal rulings determined the intended fate of paganism and pagan lands, property and funds. With these rulings the Romans enshrined Christianity as the only officially acceptable religion, ordered the closure and confiscation of pagan sacred sites and funds and an end to sacrifice. Implementation was patchy, probably because some local officials were still pagan at heart whilst others were pre-occupied with Anglo-Saxon raids. After a brief restoration of pagan practices under Julian, Theodosius, towards the close of the century, brought in tough new laws outlawing paganism. The fact that Germanic tribes were becoming more and more troublesome to the Roman authorities did not halt the decline in support for paganism and by the middle of the sixth century there is no evidence of any public pagan ceremonial. The localisation of pagan veneration ensured that there was neither an organised campaign of revival nor any missionary or evangelical opposition to Christianity. Paganism was not a proselytising religion, and it had no central organisation like the Christian Church by which to co-ordinate resistance. There is evidence from votive offerings and inscriptions that some people practised both paganism and Christianity, perhaps the former for personal satisfaction and the latter for insurance and security, indicating, if true, a rather utilitarian attitude towards religion in troubled times.

The Christian missionary period in the British Isles

Christian missionaries arrive in
     numbers in the British Isles   *c429–448 ACE*
Extensive missionary activity in
     England and the Celtic regions   *c470–600 ACE*

By the middle of the fifth century the Church began to turn its attention to the elimination of heresy, no doubt regarding paganism as no longer a serious spiritual threat to the supremacy of the Church over most of what is now England, although increasingly there was both a serious physical and spiritual threat from invading pagan Germanic warriors. Missionaries moved into the remoter northern and western parts of Great Britain and Ireland, and their missions were largely successful, using the method of converting the chiefs and the noble families first to reduce the likelihood of popular reaction. By the end of the sixth century, missionaries were spreading Christianity to the Western Highlands of Scotland and the Western Isles, having already converted the whole of Wales, Cornwall and Ireland.

The period of Germanic invasion and settlement in the British Isles

First Saxon settlement on the East Anglia coast	c420 ACE
Jutes, led by Hengist and Horsa, take over east Kent	449 ACE
Saxon and Angle kingdoms established	c477–491 ACE
Pagan burial of King Radwald at Sutton Hoo, Suffolk	c625 ACE
First Christian Anglo-Saxon king, Eorconbert of Kent, bans pagan rites and orders destruction of pagan treasures	640 ACE
King Cadwalla of Wessex takes over the Isle of Wight, the last pagan Anglo-Saxon kingdom	686 ACE
The Anglo-Saxon poem 'Beowulf' written down	c725 ACE
Bede completes 'The Ecclesiastical History of the English People', Jarrow	731 ACE
Vikings attack Lindisfarne after four years of forays	8 June 793 ACE

Norse raids and settlement in the
    British Isles   *c795–1011 ACE*
'Anglo-Saxon Chronicle' commissioned
    by King Alfred of Wessex   *893 ACE*

Another significant event had occurred by the close of the sixth century. Pagan Anglo-Saxon invaders had established themselves in Eastern and Southern England, and were soon to control most of the area east and south-east of the Pennines and the River Severn. Of all the threats that they faced from day to day, early Christian missionaries seldom felt the threat of redundancy. Anglo-Saxon immigration had been under way since the mid fifth century, and within a century their lands were surrounded by Christian territory, Celtic Christians to the north and west, and Christian Gaul, having been conquered by the Franks, across the English Channel. Missionaries sent from Rome at the end of the sixth century converted and baptised the Kentish King Ethelbert and within another hundred years all Anglo-Saxon kingdoms were functionally Christian.

As with the conversion of the Celts the process had not been excessively violent, with few martyrs created, although sacred sites and artefacts were again destroyed. It is likely that the initial conversion of kings had again ensured relatively resigned compliance by the population at large, although some newly inaugurated kings did temporarily return to paganism in some regions. By now Celtic tribal structure was probably fragmented to some degree and the persistence of local cults ensured that no organised resistance against the relentless march of Christianity and its warrior power base was possible.

But, as if to warn missionaries that their job was no sinecure, Viking raids were to turn into invasion by the end of the eighth century, beginning a 300-year period of settlement and influence. Their arrival was characterised by attacks on coastal monasteries and villages, but on finding much in harmony with Anglo-Saxon beliefs and lifestyle they settled down quickly and adopted Christianity widely. However, as most commentators of the time were Christian it is not clear to what extent Celtic, Anglo-Saxon and Viking paganism survived. As all Scandinavian kingdoms were Christian by the early eleventh century, it would then have been most unlikely that Norse areas of the British

Isles, which kept up regular contact with the Scandinavian homelands, would have left the Christian fold.

Surviving pagan folk customs from the post-missionary period

There are no witness accounts known of actual pagan ritual practice from the eleventh century onwards, and it can be assumed that when the Church spoke of eradicating paganism after this time it was referring to folk traditions that may have had their origins in paganism, such as magic, superstitions, saining and divination. The degree to which such campaigns were successful probably depended on the degree of tolerance or zealousness of local clerics. Despite their efforts, many beliefs, customs, and artistic and literary images have survived beyond the passing of their original cultural origins, even though memories of their proper function have long since faded. Examples of surviving customs thought to be of ancient origin are the lighting of sacred fires and saining livestock by driving them between the fires; rolling blazing straw-covered wheels downhill to represent the sun's declination; decoration with greenery and flowers; the Mumming Play theme of the killing and resurrection of one member of the cast; dressing up as old women and animal guisers, such as Hobby Horses, Hooden Horses, Mari Lwyd and Horn Dancers; animal or human sacrificial elements such as burning effigies; libations and offerings; and bogeys and monsters, which may be demonised personifications, or folk memories of earlier creatures or inhabitants.

But there are traps for the unwary folklorist, for appearances may be deceptive. Many pagans adopted the Green Man, depicted by a male head surrounded by entwined foliage; which may be coming out of his mouth and nose, and often to be found on roof bosses in churches. It has been said to be a borrowing, from the pagan May Day character Jack-in-the-Green, the personification of the renewed plant growth in Spring, but the Green Man is a post-Christianisation figure. As leaves are symbolic of carnal sin it may represent an anguished soul gone astray, and as such a visual warning to parishioners. Another such warning dating from after the Christianisation of the British

Isles may be the Sheela-na-Gig, more usually carved on the outside of buildings, including churches. It is a naked, usually bald, ugly, squatting female, revealing her vulva between spread legs, and may represent a warning against lust, presumably for the clergy of the time as well as the congregation. Another symbol held to be of pagan origin is the maze. Despite tradition again, there is no evidence that mazes had an ancient ritual purpose, for the only certain association is with games played within them. A game of mounted riders negotiating a maze was played in the Roman Empire, and the practice goes back further to the ancient Mediterranean civilisations. Sport also may have been the motive for carving the turf mazes in England, some of which survive.

This completes the summary of the archaeological and historical records of old Celtic society.

Neodruidic orders

The absence of both druidic texts and an unbroken oral tradition has allowed all sorts of groups to claim that they are druids and that they are in some way maintaining, or have rediscovered, druidic tradition. Invented rituals have accompanied these claims in an attempt to pass them off as authentic. In 1659 the scholar John Aubrey proposed that Stonehenge might have been a druidic temple after conducting some fieldwork on the site. He discussed the idea with the Deist John Toland, who had been brought up in an Irish Catholic family in Co Donegal, and Toland expressed great interest in the idea. In 1717 the antiquary William Stukeley embraced the suggestion enthusiastically, and in the same year Toland founded the Universal Druid Bond on 22 September. It was really a secret society, and one of its members was author and poet William Blake. During the seventeenth and eighteenth centuries a number of mystical societies became popular, such as the Hermetes, the Freemasons, the Theosophists and the Rosicrucians, and they often had members in common. William Blake was also a member of the next neodruidic order to be founded, The Ancient Order of Druids, by Henry Hurle, a carpenter, in 1781.

The character of Hurle's order was much influenced by Scottish Freemasonry. In Corwen, Wales, in 1789, Thomas Jones organised a bardic gathering, and it was three years later that a freemason Edward Williams from Glamorgan, Wales, under his assumed name Lolo Morganwg, founded a neodruidic gorsedd (assembly) on top of Primrose Hill in London, some sources say on 21 June 1792, the Summer Solstice, and some say on the Autumnal Equinox of that year. Although interested in old Celtic folktales and medieval Welsh literature his knowledge did not unfortunately extend to the fact that the real druids did not mark solstices or equinoxes, nor to the fact that the megaliths of the British Isles and Brittany pre-dated druidic times by a considerable period. His gorsedd evolved into the Fraternity of Druids, Bards and Ovates of Britain, and from 1819 his invented ceremonial was incorporated into the Welsh Eisteddfodau, whose objectives nowadays are nationalistic, encouraging the development of Welsh language, literature, poetry, music and other aspects of Welsh culture. Other neo-druidic groups have since sprung up, and, like the ones above, all have created individual, syncretic philosophies and rituals, like those seen at Stonehenge at the Summer Solstice, none of which have any lineage with anything genuinely druidic, but the revival of interest in Celtic culture that they have inspired is to be welcomed.

Although those seeking to rediscover their cultural roots in north-west European culture have turned to druidry in the past, today they can turn to modern paganism, and instead look forward.

The pagan Celtic legacy

Pagan societies of old recognised talent in the community, and gave due status to those who had practical or artistic skills, and philosophical leanings. Anyone rising above the norm and benefiting the community was given credit and standing. In return for communal contributions the community offered support to members when they needed it, such as at harvest time, when planting, or when illness, natural disaster or poverty had struck. There was mutual respect and courtesy, but also a communal expectation of behavioural norms. Ostracism of criminals, gossips, adulterers, etc was a strong deterrent in a closely knit community, as was lifelong friendship a strong incentive to conform to certain attitudes and standards of conduct. Individualism and eccentricity were always tolerated as long as they did not become anti-social or threatening. People's self-containment today means that communal intra-dependence has lessened, and in consequence community spirit has waned. A worthy objective after the adoption of new paganism would be to seek to re-establish the pooling of skills and assistance within communities, and the mutual support that that invites.

The family unit was more than just a group of relatives thrown together by birthright. It was a mutual support group of great inner strength that defended its integrity yet recognised that its independence was limited within the community. Everyone worked to support the common enterprise, and scrounging, indolence and disloyalty were not tolerated. Solidarity came from a common set of values as well as a unity of purpose, and what was tried and tested was good enough for them. In the survival stakes, it was risky to be too experimental, and this resulted in great persistence of an ancient way of life, well into the twentieth century. Practices and attitudes ultimately changed, but they are still not totally alien to what are found in society today, so they can be selectively and appropriately reintroduced and reintegrated.

The strength of the family unit derived from a belief that to bring a child into the world committed the parents to its lifelong support and education. Handing down communal attitudes and wisdom was as important as handing down particular family skills such as a trade and the homemaking skills that would serve when children grew to adulthood to restart the cycle, but the naturalness of the cycle today is now barely recognisable in these times of fractured relationships and artificial aids. There were good practical reasons in the past why no opposition from children to parental guidance would be tolerated. A girl without homemaking skills would not attract a good suitor and be able to extend the family, and a boy without a trade would be unable to earn a living and attract a good partner to do likewise. Mutual support within the wider family circle continued when extra labour was needed, for example for the harvest, planting, calving and lambing. Taking in grandparents also provided domestic help and enabled their communal wisdom to be handed down to grandchildren. Each extended family member had a valued place, each contributed, and therefore each deserved care when needed. It is staggering today that the value of the family unit is so often unappreciated and its strengths underestimated and underused. Friendships outside the family seem to count for more than those within nowadays, although many are fair-weather friendships without the durability of family ties. Commitment to the family has in many instances been replaced by selfishness and self-aggrandisement. Once, each member of a family had respect for its elders, and this reduced rebellion and tantrums, and acted as a binding force, for rocking the boat affected every-one's survival in a hand-to-mouth existence, and no youngster could match an elder's experience. As career opportunities multiplied in their variety, this respect for, and reliance on, elders could and did wane, and go-getting families began to see their older relatives as a nuisance and a hindrance.

Much is made of the fact that old pagan societies were male-dominated. They were, as far as is known, but the co-operative and complementary strengths of the male and female partnership were recognised by both sexes, and it was an effective co-operation when it came to protecting and enhancing the individual, family and community. Present-day unisex is an unfortunate narrowing of social character and variety of personality and perspective. Although there is no clearly identifiable duality of male and female personifications in traditional paganism, the wiccan Lord and Lady acquired in the nineteenth century an image of sexual equality and of division of spiritual responsibility. This contrasts with images of a male supreme being, as in Christianity, which reinforce male domination. Masculine and feminine parallels were seen in the natural world – for example, the fact that the earth gave rise to new life each Spring led to the image of Mother Earth, or Mother Nature as she came to be called, and, as if to balance an unstated duality, her offspring, the animals and plants, were given masculine symbolism, as the Horned Man and Jack-in-the-Green respectively. It was believed that they were then reborn by union with her. The superior attributes of animals, in terms of strength, speed, sensory powers and the like, inspired admiration, as well as a sense of humility, as did the beauty, toughness and variety of adaptations of plants, in contrast to the arrogance and cruelty shown to our fellow creatures today, and the peremptory way in which meadows are ploughed up and whole forests are felled.

The oneness pagans felt with nature clearly seems to have been at the root of their relationship with their environment, which was fond, familiar and essential. They could take time out to admire it because they had studied it, understood it, learned to use it to advantage, and felt at home in it. Familiarity reduces the intensity of the struggle to survive, so there was a direct payoff from patient observation, keeping records, knowing the seasons and being prepared. The ancient Celts had a passion for colour and associated different colours with different properties. For example, the Celtic elemental colours were green for the Earth, nature, herbal imagery, the colour of faeries and the colour of enchantment, yellow for the air, red for fire and blue for water. The ancient imagination has now gone, and there are but few glimpses to enable us to understand it, so it is not possible to appreciate the full implications of such associations today, but we can at least re-establish connection with our environment, in order once again to save ourselves, but this time most seriously from the pressure caused by man-made environmental demise, and to a lesser extent from natural disaster or failed or incompetent management.

The Celts protected both the animate and inanimate environment, for rocks and living things were seen as equally important components of the natural scene. Indeed, rocks were imbued with properties like the living, and their cultural importance caused the early Christians to vandalise them by carving Christian symbols like crosses on them or to reuse them in the building of churches. From the Celts' study of nature came skill in horticulture, husbandry and agriculture, and an appreciation of ecology, especially the interdependence of the natural environment and its human inhabitants. Recognising their life-giving importance, the ancient Celts venerated and protected water sources and courses, and had a great attachment to the family plot of land, and a sense of duty towards its care and fertilisation. There is a pagan tradition of only taking from nature what is needed, for destructiveness was thought to herald a natural backlash. Conservation was essential then for survival, and still is, but so many people now have no closeness to their natural environment, are unaware of nature's fragility or limited resources, and are too arrogant to care. This is in part a legacy of the Christian view that humankind is God's special creation. True pagans believe that association with our fellow living things inspires humility and respect, and counters the arrogance that can arise amongst urban dwellers. In olden times people would ask permission before cutting a flower, fruit or branch, a practice which is continued by many today. A part of a plant was never put on the ground or its magic or properties would be lost, hence the widespread use of the trug when gathering natural produce. Properties were enhanced by tying the plant or parts thereof with red thread. The ancient Celts used herbal preparations, environmental awareness and ancient magic to achieve harmony with the self and the cycles of nature. They developed extensive knowledge of the medicinal uses of plant and animal extracts, and apothecaries and healers were people of high standing.

There is value too in astronomy and weather-gazing to achieve oneness with the sky and space, and acquire knowledge about it, always provided that light and other forms of atmospheric pollution allow you to see anything. The clear skies of the British Isles in old Celtic times encouraged astronomical and meteorological studies, and the relationship between the passage of the moon and the ebb and flow of the tides was known. By going with, and adjusting to, the seasons and the weather, rather than fighting them and attempting to change the environment, the Celts learned to appreciate their own vulnerability, which persuaded them to be prepared and organised, and to respect ecological equilibrium.

Passing on their cultural heritage was seen by the ancient Celts as essential in the cycle of life. Ancestors were revered and long remembered, and there was reverence too for the wisdom and contribution of the elderly, who were part of a structure of mutual generational care, support and respect.

Cycle-of-life celebrations, such as birth, puberty, partnership and death were family and community affairs, and the strong tradition of storytelling disseminated a common heritage and wisdom. Besides stories for children, Celtic oral lore embraced myths and legends; proverbs; riddles and conundrums; ballads, lullabies and work songs; and invocations. Travellers, gipsies, tramps and itinerant tradesmen also had a valued role as storytellers and news bringers, and as such were welcomed in, offered refreshment and even a bed for the night, and respected as part of the community for their characteristic skills and perceptions. Nowadays, to be different in lifestyle is to be ignored, rejected or harassed, as pagans know only too well. Much of what old Celtic society can teach us is as relevant today as it was in former times, and this is both its attractiveness and strength as the basis for modern paganism.

3

How Paganism as a Folk Culture was Nearly Lost

Early contacts between pagans and Christians in the British Isles

From their earliest meetings with Celtic pagans in Gaul and the British Isles, Roman commentators and missionaries and officials of the Roman Catholic Church sought to discredit and demonise the pagan way of life and beliefs, and it is not difficult to see why. To the Roman invaders the pagan Celts were formidable enemies in battle, having no fear of death, and fair game for dirty tricks and propaganda. Vilifying the powerful and influential druids helped break their hold over the population, although such was the standing of druidism in Celtic society that Roman generals put druids to death rather than prolong the battle for people's minds beyond that necessary for territorial control. It is likely that descriptions of druidry by Roman writers were influenced by the prevailing military attitudes towards a tough, courageous foe and the need for a united front against both druidism and druidry. Quite forgetting their own brutality and orgiastic indulgences the Romans portrayed the Celts as a barbarous, degenerate people who practised unspeakable acts. Much was made of human sacrifice, although it had but a specific ritual function, whereas little mention was made of the Celts' skills in metalworking and other craftsmanship, art, agriculture, and husbandry. As the Celts had no written records, appreciation of the times is mainly from the Roman view of history, and this has shaped popular understanding. It was to serve the Church's missionary purposes later as it served the Romans' imperial ambitions then.

Just as Celtic warriors were obstacles to the expansion of the Roman Empire, so druidism and the pagan way of life were seen as obstacles to the spread of Christianity, the religion that became pre-eminent in the late Roman Empire. Whether they truly were obstructive was not relevant, and whether co-existence was possible was never entertained. With its domination of the recording of events at the time the Church controlled the opinions that its readership formed and its parishioners heard. Celtic paganism thus became maligned and misunderstood from early in recorded history. The prevailing view of the immigrant Christians was that paganism was anti-Christian, anti-social, amoral and decadent, and the activities of its priesthood licentious, indulgent and depraved. Gradually, that lethal combination of ignorance and intolerance drove pagans to the margins of society and to remote places, thereby helping to generate further mystique and the self-perpetuation of their image.

The imposition of one set of beliefs upon another by a conquering army or dominating religious group often follows a now familiar path. Deities, or venerated animate beings, or sacred inanimate objects, are vilified, and become demons, devils and the like. The new rulers and their cronies take on the duties, even claiming the powers, of these deities, and they and the new priesthood that allies itself with them systematically re-educate the people and redirect devotions towards themselves or to the newly introduced deity or deities. Rituals and all their ceremonial trappings are replaced or remoulded, taking their place alongside military dominance as part of the mechanism of control. It may be, of course, that the Celts themselves adopted these tactics on their triumphant migration west across central Europe, but they would soon be on the receiving end. Being an ancient, proud and culturally fairly homogenous people, their ways were deeply ingrained and cherished, prompting extraordinary measures by the Roman Catholic Church to assume control of thoughts and lives.

The Christian missionaries' fear of the power of paganism was understandable. It was an integrated way of life, a strong communal adhesive, which did not need the enforcement that would have to accompany the imposition of an alien creed or political system. Much pagan lore was dispersed amongst the community, with only selected aspects concentrated in the hands of a few powerful figures, and regional and local aspects of pagan culture were common and tolerated. Sacred sites were scattered, were of many types and served many functions. Some were natural like springs, streams, oak groves, mountains, caves, and some were stone monuments erected by the pre-Celtic people of the British Isles. By contrast, the focussing of all spiritual activity on one village church must have seemed to the Celts restrictive, artificial and environmentally isolated.

The consolidation by the Roman Catholic Church of the missionaries' incursions into the pagan British Isles

The tactics to be adopted by the missionaries were as predictable as their fears. They converted first, and allied themselves with, the ruling and warrior classes, so that religion, together with politics and military might, became the agents of control of mind, heart and body. But, however skilled at oratory these men were, they must have found it difficult to make Christianity an enticing package, focussed as it was on events a long time ago in a distant land, whereas paganism was here and now and relevant to daily lives and the struggle for survival. The missionaries' response was to employ a tried and tested programme of adapting what was already familiar to the populace.

Before its arrival in the British Isles, Christianity had adopted pagan symbolism, vestments, rituals and philosophies, and reused pagan sites, in order to give it a familiar and more acceptable character on its passage from the Middle East, and this wholesale borrowing of both the tenets and trappings of paganism continued apace in the British Isles. Significant events, current and historical, were reinterpreted; ancestors and folk heroes had their lives remodelled, and were even renamed. Pagan myths and legends were reworked in Christian guise with Christian characters, and pagan lifestyle changed to suit, by enforcement if necessary. If this manipulation of history with its accompanying creed was not to anyone's taste then there was always the threat of excommunication, eternal damnation and burning in hell to fall back on. Fundamental pagan beliefs were challenged and replaced, and even something as natural and unchanging as the death and rebirth of deciduous vegetation had a new explanation, in what must have been a very bewildering and stressful period for the indigenous inhabitants of the British Isles. These tactics were awesomely reinforced by impressive ceremonies and rituals, much of which was purloined from the pageantry created by the Roman Emperor Diocletian. He ruled like a god and expected to be worshipped as one, and the popes continued this tradition.

Systematically, the missionaries set about destroying pagan artwork and craftsman-made items that depicted pagan subjects and inscriptions. Carvings, sculptures, metal and ceramic work, murals and mosaics of priceless historical value were disposed of. Historical and archaeological evidence indicates that among pagan artwork to be destroyed in the missionary period were inscribed stone memorials, figurines, jewellery and other adornments, ornamental weapons and insignia, carved staffs, and other personal and household decorated items. Folk art was originally just a natural extension of craftsmanship, but gradually motifs, geometric patterns, colour combinations, styles and decorative methods became the common property of a community, and eventually tradition. Functionality always came first in humble households, no decoration ever being allowed to interfere with efficient use. It was natural that after the first ecclesiastical buildings were erected, popular vernacular styles of decoration were used within, such as stencilling in the Middle Ages, popular in both house and church interiors.

But with the growing tendency of the Church to flaunt its wealth and seek to augment its religious message with impressive grandeur, popular motifs and styles were purloined and elaborated into an ostentatious show. This policy contrasted sharply with the parochial distaste made clear to individuals who adorned themselves. Ecclesiastical designers effectively claimed these styles and motifs as their own, so important pagan cultural symbols and designs were now being used to convey a religious message instead. The pagan cross, representing the four principal phases of the moon, became the Christian cross. Pagan art such as scrollwork, interwoven designs such as knotwork, decorative borders and corners, charted patterns and spirals found their way into manuscript illumination, engravings, and carvings in or as ecclesiastical architectural features.

Pagan sacred sites and monuments suffered rather less than artefacts, because some had already been abandoned so were no threat, and others, though certainly not all, were Christianised by incised crosses, inscriptions or other religious motifs, or dismantled and the stones reused for Christian or secular buildings. In no recorded case did a Christian historian refer to the artistic, architectural or technological merits of the pagan treasures destroyed. To be certain of being spared, an item had to be plain and utilitarian.

The lengths the missionaries went to are indicative of their fear of druidic power and influence and the persistence of a deeply ingrained pagan culture. To have the job of wrenching whole nations from their roots and substituting an alien religion from a far land was not to have an enviable task, unless one could call on the nobility for support. As only about thirty of several thousand pagan monuments were reconstructively Christianised, it seems there was still a deep-seated and lasting reverence for them in the population at large, causing all but the most zealous clergy to leave them alone. Constructive abandonment of the pagan sites, using appropriate threats and bribes, was probably regarded as the least risky option where alienation was a distinct possibility if the sites were desecrated.

Gradually, the clergy became so powerful that would-be politicians and warrior-rulers allied themselves with the Church in a symbiotic mission for power and control. Each used the techniques and public position of the other, until eventually there was really very little difference between the power and control objectives of political leaders, generals, monarchs, the pope, archbishops and the Christian god. As part of the entice-ment of people away from communion with nature and their social units, the influence of independent thinkers was forcefully curtailed and their reputations stained by whatever means suited. To maintain the momentum of mass conversion, the mainstream of paganism had, at all costs, to be diverted down the channel of Christianity by fair means or foul, by force of argument or just force.

The Christian clergy felt threatened by humanism because it gave ordinary people power over their own destiny, taking the reins from the Church. It was to the Church's advantage for people to think their lives were predestined by a god for whom the clergy are the agents and on whose behalf they can intervene and make decisions. The dominance of the clergy was constantly reinforced, lest it come under threat from liberty and independent thought. Christian predestination appeared to pagans to be essentially negative, because if their lives and ultimate destiny, whether it be heaven or hell, were already mapped out there was nothing the individual could do to change things. Therefore life had no purpose other than subservience to the god who made the decision. Pagan divination, on the other hand, was not negative. It warned of what *might* happen if the individual continued on his or her present course, but events could change if the individual made appropriate decisions. This degree of control was a valuable spur, for it encouraged engagement and a positive attitude in life's progress, not supine resignation in a world where fate was predetermined.

The Christianisation of pagan beliefs in the British Isles

The Christian attitude to sex

The pagan view that the purpose of sexual union was for the male to put the essence of life into the female body to create new life – in other words, that creation is under the control of people and not God – led to the early Christian condemnation of pagan sexual habits, and possibly even to disapproval of sexuality itself. Pagan attitudes to sex were bound up with the necessity to maintain their own, their animals' and their crops' fertility, and ritual sexual activity was for this end. Any licentiousness during calendrical celebrations was overspill of natural urges rather than orgiastic indulgence, but such a distinction was lost on the Church, which sought vigorously to ban all such ritual activities.

Christianity and magic

Having initially been schooled in paganism in many cases, the early Celtic Christian converts continued to practise pagan ways like magic within the confines of their orthodox religion, and this helped the principles survive during the period when zealots remoulded them to become 'Christian' principles. Some pagan philosophies, practices, and accoutrements transferred easily into a Christian setting because of the pagan influence that was already apparent in Christianity, lasting examples being the use of candles and meditation, but also crystals and herbs for quite a long time. Although their cultural background made them fairly tolerant to practices like magic, early Christian priests and monks decided that to compete effectively with witchcraft in people's affections they had to show they could match witches' magic, and they made appropriate claims for their own, and later for saints', powers to encourage people so awed to convert to Christianity. After their death, saints' relics carried on the good work, as did the head and bones of a Celtic hero after he was slain or a revered ancestor after passing away. The miracles of Christ and the Church's rituals such as baptism and the Eucharist were no different to magic rituals, indeed it is likely that they were simply modified pagan rituals in the first place. Baptism, for example, was probably adapted from pagan immersions performed at sacred springs and other water-courses. The population were used to their witches performing miracles, particularly of healing, so they readily accepted that Christ and his lieutenants could do likewise, but they did not willingly embrace the view put to them that it was now only acceptable for saints to perform miracles and that the same miracle performed by a pagan was fraudulent. This apparent hypocrisy led inevitably to tensions in a population still reliant on the witches' arts.

The boundaries between religion and magic were areas of constant conflict because of the consistent claim by Christians that magic was being performed by pagans for religious reasons, and was thus a survival of ancient religious practice. In religion, the adherent has no control over whether or not a deity acts according to his or her wishes, but in magic the practitioner expects to have control over the result. As magic was used for day-to-day purposes such as medicinal practice it sat comfortably with religion at a time when most Christians still had pagan backgrounds or were close to pagan culture. Religion was seen as being involved with weightier matters such as the salvation of souls. But as the pagan past receded in Christians' minds attitudes to magic changed. The claim was now made that magic could be done only with the active assistance of agents of the Devil, and divination was an attempted usurpation of the divine power of God, who alone could determine the future. The idea that something so mundane, ubiquitous and helpful as magic was sinful must have initially caused confusion to ordinary folk, for it was part of their lifestyle. What the Church deemed to be magical acts, and therefore old-style religion, came under attack from all sides, regardless of their function or provenance.

Sacrificing an animal because the herd is sick, or to put it in the foundation of a building to give its occupants luck in their use of it, is magic, but not a religious act because there is no offering to a deity. The same is true for termination rites, sacrificing an animal when the site is to be abandoned. Such practices in fact continued until the 1940s, showing how magic and religion can coexist when what may have once been a spiritual act continues as just a folk magical rite. The wishing well was used long after veneration of water sprites had ceased, by Christians and pagans alike, and Christian pilgrims continued to cast votive offerings into streams they crossed on their way to shrines. This fact illustrates how persistent culture can be, even in the face of religious onslaught.

The veneration of sacred trees, notably the oak, yew, beech, ash and rowan, was stamped upon, although some tree adornment customs survived as part of other village occasions. Preachers continued the practice of issuing sermons from under sacred oaks, the so-called gospel oaks, even though the practice arose in druidic times, although this may have also been an attempt to neutralise the power of the sacred oak trees over the people. The role of sacred animals similarly faded under ecclesiastic pressure to view them as just God's creatures with no special attributes. The latter were reserved solely for humankind, who may thus have acquired the arrogance towards wildlife that is so characteristically unpagan. The inscribing of ogham and runic characters on objects before critically important usage such as casting spells continued into Christian times. Despite the Church's condemnation of magic practice as a survival of 'the old pagan religion' it had no reasonable basis for this supposition, and far less to fear than it had supposed. Even if the rituals once had a venerative purpose that purpose was way in the past for most people because magic had simply become utilitarian folk tradition.

The pagan spirits who were intermediate between the Otherworld and this world were demonised by the Roman Catholic Church as evil spirits, the messengers and agents of Satan. The Otherworld became Hell, possibly named after the Norse goddess of the Underworld Hel, who presided over the place where souls went to await rebirth, and life became a battleground between good and evil, even creation itself was so reinterpreted. The Evil Eye was portrayed as one of Satan's weapons, and witches regarded as his apostles. Finally, in the early fifth century, magical practices of all kinds were outlawed by the Church, the legislation specifically banning consultations with magicians or diviners, the practices of necromancy (the foretelling of the future by the raising of or communicating with the dead) and magic. Magicians could, under this law, be condemned to death, with no rights of appeal or inheritance for their families. The Church, however, generally stopped short of attaching the death penalty in its edicts, preferring to try to 'cure' and 're-educate' offenders. Until the period of the witch-hunts, therefore, witches and clergy coexisted uneasily, more acceptably in rural communities, and much more so with beneficent than with maleficent magic. The more practical sides of witchcraft such as healing were tolerated more than practices seen as endangering the soul.

Christianity and witchcraft

The recording of the Canon Episcopi
  documenting incidences of witchcraft   900
The bull of Pope Eugenius IV initiates trials
  for witchcraft under Canon Law   1437

Pope Innocent VIII orders the Inquisition against heresy and witchcraft	*1484*
Publication of **Malleus Maleficarum**, *giving detailed instructions for the prosecution of witches*	*1486*
Henry VIII's parliament passes laws against witchcraft	*1542*
The death penalty introduced for witchcraft in Elizabeth I's reign	*1563*
Last alleged witch, Alice Holland, to be hanged in England	*1684*
Last alleged witch, Janet Horne, to be hanged in Scotland, at Dornoch	*1722*
Revised, and last, Witchcraft Act	*1735*
Last person, Helen Duncan, to be charged with (and found guilty of) witchcraft in the UK	*1944*
Last recorded ritual murder, of Charles Walton on Meon Hill, Warwickshire, of someone suspected of witchcraft	*1945*
All UK witchcraft laws repealed	*1951*

The term 'witchcraft' was not current until the Middle Ages, and then, as the skills of witchcraft – for example, herbalism, divination and control of elemental forces – were widely known and practised, a member of the clergy could call almost anyone a witch. The Church outlawed certain practices, but not necessarily the practitioners, who were just ordinary citizens in other ways. Other practices it sought to monopolise by Christianising those magical beliefs and rituals which did not harm the soul or could not be viewed as heresy, and insisted on being in control and approving every practice. If a priest prayed for relief from bad weather, that was acceptable, but a pagan ritual to do the same was not. Thus, as anything the Church did not sanction could be classified as heresy, so magic became heresy and the whole practice of paganism with it. Significant aspects of the lifestyle of a pagan thus became officially condemned, not overnight, but over a period of time, as the tolerance of the early Christian period was replaced by insistence on orthodoxy and relentless persecution of dissenters.

Witch persecutions began in the thirteenth century, and it was not long before what was termed witchcraft was regarded as a surviving pagan tradition that had become an organised, anti-Christian movement, whereas in reality it was neither, and once the Church had control of the secular authorities, the inquisitions were not far in the future. The King James Bible says 'Suffer not a Witch to live'. Trials for witchcraft under Canon Law, following the bull of Pope Eugenius IV in 1437, were supported by more and more secular authorities in Europe and the British Isles. Magic was seen as the agency of demons, who were angels that had fallen from heaven, and therefore from grace, and degenerated under Satan's control. These evil spirits were said to make pacts with witches and thus control their magic. Therefore, witches were accused of making pacts effectively with the Devil, and so they were the enemies of God. Church propaganda against witches and their gatherings led to wildly exaggerated claims of vile, licentious and murderous behaviour at Sabbats and Esbats, including flying through the air on beasts and broomsticks. The latter was an example of the Church manipulating folklore for its own ends, for although witches may have claimed the power of flight, possibly under the effects of hallucinatory fungal extracts, they never actually had it, of course. Many of the so-called witches put to death in the witch hunts were solitary women, condemned by their neighbours to settle old scores or because they were despised for their healing techniques or magic practices. They became easy victims for those wanting to revive Christian fundamentalism and to 'cleanse' the population of likely dissenters by using scapegoats.

The actual persecution, as opposed to verbal denuciation, of witches was largely by males, not only for religious fundamentalist reasons or revenge, but also for political and religious dominance over rich, property-owning, as well as poor, women. There was a strong misogynist undercurrent, with opposition to the education of women thrown in to keep them subservient to men. Even female midwifery was cut back so male doctors could take over, and since those times the male-dominated medical profession has had a history of opposition to natural medical practice, like herbalism, that has traditionally been the province of women.

The twin forces of adaptation and reinterpretation

It has long been held by pagans that the enduring similarity between Christian beliefs and practices, and those of the pagans whom they supplanted, is no coincidence, but part of a deliberate process of promoting acceptability through adaptation and reinterpretation. Striking similarity is often evident, and there is ecclesiastical historical evidence in some cases – for example, in the biographies of many saints, and in other archived material. In other cases it is generations of pagan tradition that provide the associations. In what follows, only these cases are quoted. As in all historical sections of the book, these associations and interpretations are from a pagan perspective.

Beneath the public face of Christianity, reinterpretations of paganism continued to be absorbed into Christian doctrine, even at a fundamental level. Making Eve from Adam may well be a Christianised corruption of the pagan dualism of the Horned Man and Earth Mother represented as an androgyne, half man, half woman. The rituals formerly used to communicate with the Earth Mother seem to have been taken over by early Christians and adapted for their cult of the Virgin Mary. She was impregnated, gave birth and was undying, just as the Earth Mother was. The son of God, Jesus Christ, had a composite character reminiscent of the European Oak King of the Winter Solstice and Spring and of the Holly King of Autumn and Winter. The miraculous birth, crucifixion, and resurrection are all reminiscent of pagan themes, relating to the agrarian/seasonal cycles. Even the name Jesus is remarkably similar to the Greek version of the Aramaic Isha, which is the name Lord in the Hindu religion reserved for Shiva, possibly taking the roots of paganism back to the earliest known Dravidian culture, in the Indus Valley. This culture was assimilated by the Aryan Vedic tribes from Central Asia, who conquered the Dravidians, and through Aryan migrations it was brought to Europe and the British Isles. To aid the rapid conversion of the masses the Christian missionaries adapted the cakes and ale ceremony as their communion ritual with bread and wine. To pagans the cake symbolised Mother Earth and the ale the moon or life-giving water, and their consumption was an expression of unity with nature. An even older ritual was the consumption of the bodies of relatives or slain warriors so that they or their characteristics would be reborn or absorbed respectively.

The adapted pagan views that when someone 'dies' they are reborn in the Otherworld, and that energy (or the 'life force') is immortal, seem to be those used by Christianity to threaten non-believers with eternal torment in Hell. As part of the process of replacing Celtic venerated personifications with saints the early Church demonised the former and actively tried to eliminate dedications to them and fertility rites. But in some ways the acceptance of Christianity was made easier because of some similarities in belief, for example, in the immortality of the soul. 'If you can't beat them, join them' was an adage the early Christians took to heart during their missionary work. So powerful was pagan solar imagery that the symbol of the sun seems to have been that which was incorporated into the Celtic cross, the cross itself being a pagan symbol also. Another inspirational borrowing by the Church appears to have been the triple aspect of certain pagan personifications, which became the Holy Trinity.

The Christian cult of saints

The cults of saints arose as the Roman Catholic Church persuaded people to revere those who allegedly imitated Christ by demonstrating outstanding holiness – that is to say, what the Church deemed to be worthy of note to suit its evangelising purpose – and/or dying for their faith. In reality, the super-human qualities of the early saints were just an attempted re-personification of pagan myths and legends in Christian guise, as the remarkable biographical similarities indicate. Stephen was the first Christian martyr to be made a saint, in about the year 35 ACE, and the memory of him and those who followed was kept alive in cults, whose superficial elements, such as shrines and iconography, seem ultimately to have been derived from those of Greek and Roman polytheism. Dates of saints' deaths were commemorated on saint days, or feast days, to celebrate their arrival in heaven. Believers prayed for intercession between God and themselves or others through saints, often focussing their requests through relics, the Christian versions of talismans. Saints became guardians, protectors and workers of miraculous cures, in fact anything the Church wanted of them to maintain people's attachment to them and to keep the pilgrims visiting their shrines. Each saint had an appropriate life history provided for him or her, and their powers and exploits became increasingly fantastic, especially when one of their tasks was to usurp a revered pagan hero. This appeared to pagans to be Church-approved idolatry, and Protestants were later to reject it, giving this as one of their reasons for breaking away from Roman Catholicism.

Saint days were deliberately created to coincide with pagan festivities, to redirect people's attentions and thoughts, although the saints Peter, Paul, Andrew and James were given feast days that were not pagan festivals. There may have been no suitable vacancies on significant pagan days for these saints. To have one's saint day chosen to replace a pagan festival day a saint had to have appealing credentials to pagans, according to the nature of the festival, not just status within Christianity. Eventually the number of saints grew to an extent that several, as many as ten in some Celtic regions, had to share the same saint day. The life histories of the saints, real or invented, were further re-moulded around the pagan traditions associated with the rituals, but appropriately Christianised.

It does not need a professional historian to recognise that many of the details of the lives of saints bear an uncanny resemblance to the myths and legends of the venerated figures and heroes of the pagan folk whom Christians were trying to convert, and the people's acquiescence to this reinterpretation of their own folk lore was but part of their acceptance that Christianity was one arm of the irresistible ruling trinity of monarch, nobility and Church. In 1969 it was announced by the Roman Catholic Church that many saints were to be removed from the official calendar of saints because there was no historical basis for their existence.

The Christianisation of pagan rituals in the British Isles

As part of its policy of avoiding civil unrest caused by blatant antagonism of the pagan populace, the early Christian Church preferred remodelling and reinterpretation of pagan beliefs to outright condemnation and ban, but sometimes the latter course of action was seen as the only acceptable way forward. The populace joined in festivities with joy and abandon, as they were a welcome relief from the struggle for survival. But the sight of people getting more pleasure, in indulgent, boisterous and lusty ways, than they got from religion was regarded as impious by the Church authorities, who sought to curtail and dampen down the jollifications. Moreover, a ban may have been in response to public demand, when festivities long tolerated had finally become unacceptable through the changing Christian expectation of what constituted tolerable social order during celebration.

Some of the first festivities to be 'cleaned up' or banned, during the Reformation, were the Feast of Fools in the first week of January, May Day celebrations and Hallowe'en fires. The Calvinists banned Christmas in Lowland Scotland from 1574 to 1642, which may explain the transfer of jollifications to Hogmanay, and in England Christmas was banned in 1644. The Church never found a satisfactory replacement for May Day and could not dampen enthusiasm for it, so a ban, with Oliver Cromwell's help, was its only option. May Day festivities and Christmas were allowed again by Charles II after the Restoration of the Monarchy and sustained public pressure. The Church also hijacked and revamped Mummers' Plays, in which pre-Christian stories of life, death by sacrifice and resurrection are enacted, for example, the death of Winter and the resurgence of Spring. These were reshaped as the triumph of good over evil or as Miracle Plays acting out biblical equivalents such as the death and resurrection of Christ. Folk carols had their words adapted for Christian purposes, a well-known example being the Coventry Carol, originally part of a Mumming Play.

The list of Christianised pagan rituals is a very long one. By the Middle Ages, the Roman Catholic Church had already borrowed heavily from paganism in terms of its adoption of the symbol of the cross, church design, the use of altars, chants and sermons, the lighting of candles and incense, priests' vestments, the display of wreaths and garlands, and its style of inconography. When pagan sacred buildings became Christian churches little changed within except the message. The medieval Christians, however, tended to build churches on new land rather than convert any more pagan structures, although they continued to destroy pagan images. The Christianisation of ritual was a logical step in bringing every celebratory aspect of ordinary life under the ecclesiastical wing.

Spring rituals

The first significant Spring rite was the fertility custom of Wassail, and the Church made strenuous efforts to replace the Wassail customs, on what became Twelfth Night, with its own rituals of Epiphany. This commemorated the story of the three Wise Men finding Christ and recognising him, a suitable substitute for the pagan naming day that was one of the functions of Twelfth Night. Superficially respectable elements of Twelfth Night celebrations, such as those surrounding the making and consumption of the Twelfth Cake, were moved to Christmas Eve, and from there to Christmas Day. Blessing the plough on Plough Monday was intended to replace the rituals accompanying the return of the Corn Dolly to the earth in Spring, as was the Harvest Festival intended to supplant the making of the Corn Dolly at the end of the harvest.

The partnership divination customs normally observed on a Celtic Quarter Day like Imbolc (31 January/1 February) were probably regarded as relatively innocuous, so were just transferred by the Church to St Agnes' Eve (20 January) because St Agnes was patron saint of maidens. Candlemas was a Christian ritual because it represented the presentation of Christ at the Temple, which had to be done so many days after a birth. If the latter was 25 December, the presentation had to be on 2 February, leading to the suspicion by pagans that transferring the birth of Christ from the Winter Solstice, where it had been placed to try and eliminate the shortest day fire rituals, to 25 December allowed Imbolc to be replaced. Imbolc was the Celtic veneration of Bride, a Celtic Spring personification, done at the start of the lambing season, and rededicated by the Church to St Bridget of Kildare. This dedication was done on Candlemas Eve as the Celtic day started at sunset, a concession opportunely made by the Church. Just as Bride visited the poor and hungry to provide for them, so St Bridget was said to visit and bless them, although this can hardly have been regarded by ordinary folk suffering from Winter shortages as a useful substitute. Gradually, St Bridget's life history was rewritten to provide a convincing and important replacement; she even became the Virgin Mary's midwife. The candle was made the focus of Candlemas blessings in church because at Februa, the Roman festival dedicated to the mother of Mars, candles were carried by women as part of their purification rites, and, in post-Roman Britain, women were reluctant to abandon the tradition.

By having rents and other land tenure administration due on Quarter Days the Church hoped that people would have little time for the festivals on these significant days in the Celtic calendar. Lady Day was such a rent day, which originally had the Virgin Mary standing guard over the Vernal Equinox, and may have led to the virtual disappearance of Spring equinoctial commemoration.

The replacement of the sacrifice of goats and puppies at what was originally the Roman festival of Lupercalia was possibly the start of church clipping, the linking of hands and dancing around the church. The tradition of rush bearing to cover house floors was also redirected to the local church. The Lupercalian pairing of boys and girls by drawing names was made more respectable by association with the chaste St Valentine and the replacement of the sexual element with the pairing of innocent sweethearts. Shrove Tuesday feasting and carnival, on the last day before Lent, conveniently replaced the feasting, with its conspicuous consumption, that had originally been in honour of the Roman Bacchus. Lent, a period of fasting and abstinence, appeared to be so placed in the ecclesiastical calendar because going without food after Winter shortages was part of life before the first crops of Spring became available. In addition the Church imposed severe social restrictions on the Sabbath, food restrictions on Fridays and Advent fast days, and behavioural restrictions on many other days, further drawing the population into common adherence. The Church also tried to redirect April foolery towards the commemoration of the mocking of Christ before his death, but this was not popular and the tradition of japery was retained.

The pagan rituals honouring the death of Winter and the re-emergence of plant growth were absorbed into the Christianised

Easter celebrations with the focus on Christ's death and resurrection instead. Easter was originally timed to follow the Hebrew Spring festival of the Passover as Christ's arrest was just after this festival, but the date as reckoned and prescribed in 664 ACE by the Synod of Whitby made Easter variable from year to year, and the date of the Christian Easter is so calculated to this day. After Winter dormancy, pagan fertility rituals were designed to bring forward new growth, symbolised by the egg and young chicks, leverets, etc, and this enduring symbolism was retained as harmless. Hot Cross Buns, originally made as pagan offerings, were adopted as symbolic food for Good Friday, but the pagan cross, symbolising the four quarters of the lunar cycle, remained on top as Christianity had already adopted it. The old tradition of burning a scapegoat to banish Winter ills was replaced on Good Friday by the burning of Judas effigies, and some aspects of Spring rites were turned into the Pace Egg plays, which in character resembled Mummers' Plays.

Summer rituals

The important saints Peter and Paul were assigned to Beltane, but the association of the honouring of the Virgin Mary and of the Holy Cross with Beltane on the eve of 30 April were both unsuccessful. The Celtic ritual of rolling eggs downhill at Beltane to imitate the movement of the sun appeared to be that which was recast by the Church as the rolling away of the stone in front of Christ's tomb. Also, the tradition of watching the Beltane sunrise at the start of the Celtic Summer, from which pagans could not be dissuaded, became the early morning Easter Sunday observation to see the sun dancing for joy at the resurrection of Christ. From pagan celebrations at this time Christians appeared to have taken the idea of resurrection of the life of Christ from death, and the Church adopted the egg as the symbol of resurrection, probably to deflect association with fertility rites. Beltane divination later came to be done on St Mark's Eve. The Passion Sunday ecclesiastical tradition of eating grey peas on the day when Christ's death was announced is also not a Christian custom as it comes from the ancient practice of eating beans at feasts to honour the dead.

The veneration of water sources and the sprites who guarded the wells and springs is considered by pagans to be the source of well-dressing in honour of God as the supposed supplier of life-giving water. Chapels were built on the sites of wells and springs and traditional rites Christianised and dedicated to the assigned saints. Visits and well-dressing were encouraged on Sundays and saint days, rather than the traditional Quarter Days like Beltane, the offerings formerly left to the water sprites then being left in honour of the saints. Fertility rites on farms and fisheries, originally to ensure good yields and catches respectively, seem to be those at the root of the Christian blessings of plough, fields and boats and thanksgivings for what was regarded as God's bounty. The pagan beating of the earth to awaken the spirits of growth almost certainly became the Beating of the Bounds and their perambulation during Ascension Week, the time when well-dressing was also performed. The marking of parish boundaries aided their recollection as there were no detailed local maps and many villagers were illiterate. These Rogationtide customs resemble, and appeared also to incorporate elements of, the Roman blessing of the crops (Ambervailia) and beating of the bounds (Terminalia, in honour of the god of boundaries, Terminus). Church commemorations at Whit appear to have been an attempt to keep the lid on early summer frolics, and Whitsun Ale festivities had some of the character of May Day celebrations. Whit Walks may have had a similar origin to Rogationtide perambulations.

Midsummer excesses and their long-entrenched association with sun veneration were replaced by devotions to St John the Baptist. St Anne, who is now known not to have existed, was probably invented to replace Anu, the Earth Mother, the similarity of name being no coincidence. To further add to St Anne's status she was held to be the mother of the Virgin Mary, thus proving that the Immaculate Conception was at least not hereditary.

Autumn rituals

The similarity of the Anglo-Saxon Lammas to the Celtic Lughnasadh is striking, and it seems highly likely that Christians substituted a Christianised Lammas (loaf-mass) for the Celtic corn harvest festival of Lughnasadh, the sacrifice of the first fruits of the soil, retaining its association with bread and lamb and making the first grain into a loaf and presenting it in church. As with some other formerly pagan festivals Lammas was transferred to the nearest Sunday, in this case the first Sunday in August. The Church imposed the celebration of the imprisonment and miraculous escape from his chains of Saint Peter at Lughnasadh, but this was never regarded by the populace as a significant alternative. The burning of Bartle the strawman, originally a human harvest sacrifice, on the Saturday nearest 24 August was almost certainly that which was replaced by the saint day of the similarly named St Bartholomew. Towards the end of the harvest period was the Autumnal Equinox, presided over by another important saint, St Matthew. After the hop harvest, altars were draped with hops and a church ceremony devised, but the persistent pagan Hooden Horses were never admitted to the churches. Harvest Thanksgiving was initiated by the Church to Christianise the rowdy Harvest Home celebrations and the Corn Dolly making, which had formerly involved human sacrifice.

The traditional end of harvest, considered a Quarter Day, was 29 September, which was put in the charge of St Michael the Archangel, from which comes the designation Michaelmas. He at least was a saint of Christian origin, not a remodelled pagan hero, and churches dedicated to him were built on high places, presumably to be near his angels. The sea god cults of the Hebrides were redirected towards St Michael, who was made patron of fishermen and horsemen, for the horse featured prominently in the pagan ceremonial. The special cakes baked, Struan Micheil, had a cross on top, in the fashion of that on hot cross buns. The Christianised festivities were transferred to the eve of 28 September.

Winter rituals

The end of the Celtic year was marked by Samhain, whose rituals survive in elements of our Hallowe'en celebrations. The wake (vigil for the deceased) on this highly important day, the Feast of the Dead, was Christianised as a revamped All Saints' Day or Hallowmas, when people were encouraged to remember all dead saints instead of their dead relatives. Wakes generally were changed to dedications to parish saints. Originally, Hallowmas was on the 21 February, put there to replace the Roman Feralia, but Pope Gregory moved it to 1 November to replace Samhain, illustrating once again the elasticity of the ecclesiastical calendar in the face of expediency. The resited Hallowmas was followed by All Souls' Day, when it was hoped the departed would ascend from purgatory to heaven, instead of return to the Otherworld. Other aspects of Samhain, such as the bonfire, were transferred to Guy Fawkes' Night on 5 November. The traditional day of slaughter of surplus beasts for Winter meat, which may originally have been pagan rites in honour of the ox god Hu, was rededicated to St Martin, and hence 11 November became known as Martinmas. The Church seems most likely to have remoulded the ritual of the rolling of a blazing straw wheel downhill to represent the declination of the sun as a story about St Catherine, invented for the purpose, being tortured on a wheel, her saint day being 25 November. For all her suffering, St Catherine did not survive the 1969 purge of invented saints, but at least on Bonfire Night her wheels give us an annual reminder of the power of spin.

The Norse fire festivals on or about 13 December were part of their Yule celebrations, and this day was rededicated to St Lucy, whose life story appears to have been changed so that she was conveniently burned to death. Pagans believe that Christians borrowed the pagan belief in the rebirth of the sun at Yule (the Winter Solstice) to create the story of the birth of Christ, the son of God replacing the sun. At this time of rebirth fires and candles were lit to welcome the returning sun and enhance its power. The departing Holly King gave gifts as he rode his solar sleigh, pulled by eight reindeer, on Yule Eve. He was called Old Nick, and would seem to be the origin of the Christian St Nicholas, and hence Santa Claus. The term 'Old Nick' was then applied by Christians to the Devil, who may simply have been the Christian version of the Horned God. But the pagan evergreen Christmas Tree with the five-pointed star remained. On the Holly King's departure the Oak King arrives, and he seems to have been replaced by Christians with Jesus. The pagan figure who became Father Christmas was doubtless also reborn as St Nicholas, or Santa Claus, as part of the Christianisation of both the Roman Saturnalia and the pagan Yule.

The care of the Winter Solstice, on a day when there was a festival in honour of the Celtic Fingan, was entrusted to St Thomas, and people were encouraged to make charitable gifts (thomassing) to the needy rather than wait for the returning sun. The trappings of the day – evergreens, Yule log and candles – were transferred to Christmas Day. Such was the people's attachment to the hanging up of evergreens that the Church even allowed it in churches to try and take ownership of the practice. The Christianisation of the Roman Saturnalia (at the Winter Solstice) and the Norse Yule began in the fourth century when the Roman Emperor Constantine was converted to Christianity, and the date of the birth of Christ was originally deliberately fixed on the Winter Solstice. The Church discouraged the Christmas Day (and New Year's Day) gatherings at stone circles and market crosses, formerly held at the end of the old Celtic year at Samhain, by instituting church services.

Hunting the wren on 26 December was a highly persistent activity unsuccessfully replaced by dedication of the day to St Stephen, so the wren was woven into a story about St Stephen. The diminutive bird allegedly woke up Stephen's jailer and prevented his escape, hence providing a Christian justification for the annual slaughter they could not cause to cease. There was probably little Christian sympathy anyway for a bird that was in pagan lore the messenger of the druids.

Dedicating 31 December to St Sylvester, a saint whose name would not have been on everybody's lips, was not a success. The saint did not have sufficient clout to make inroads into the established New Year's Eve celebrations in Scotland and elsewhere, the Hogmanay celebrations in Scotland probably deriving from a transfer of Christmas Day festivities after the banning of Christmas by the Calvinists. First-footing (the desire to be the first of the year to step over a relative's or neighbour's threshold), saining with flame and sprinkled water, divination, guising in animal costumes and holming (flagellation with holly leaves) were all transferred. In Wales the Mari Lwyd horse continued on its rounds, sometimes appearing on Christmas

Night, sometimes on Twelfth Night, the custom having elements of wassail, Mumming and pagan horse cult practice.

The Christianisation of the folk customs of the British Isles

For a long time after the original pagan purpose of many rituals had ceased to be common knowledge, the activities having taken on the character of communal folk customs, pressure for their discontinuation lessened, and was often only at the hands of zealous individuals or local disapproving authorities. Nevertheless, the Churches, both Catholic and Anglican, remained too influential to defy, and more and more folk practices were caused to cease or were abandoned. Particular damage to folk culture was done by the Protestants in Ireland, the Calvinists in Scotland, the Methodists in the Isle of Man and Cornwall and by most non-conformist churches in Wales.

Every form of communication and entertainment came under scrutiny. The universal adoption of the ecclesiastical calendar caused the demise of local folk calendars. The use of the Celtic languages was forbidden in many areas, ensuring that pagan traditions retained by the elders were less likely to be passed on to the younger generations. Folk singing and carolling, folk dancing, and street theatre were either discouraged or the content Christianised or bowdlerised. Links with the pagan past gradually dissolved over large areas of the British Isles, although it was noted by pagans that any activity cherished by the ruling and influential classes, with whom the clergy shared social power symbiotically, such as blood sports, remained uncondemned.

The ecclesiastical calendar in the British Isles

In times past when pagan society was still significantly nature-based, the loss of the pagans' ability to regulate their lives by their own calendar was disorientating and distressing. A folk calendar is more than just a handy chronicle of periodic events in people's lives. It embodies their unbreakable links with the natural world and its own cycles of events, a vital cog connecting pagans to their natural origins in Mother Nature's engine. The early Christian Church opposed lunar and solar veneration, and therefore the basis of the pagan calendar, but adopted it because it didn't have one of its own. It then modified it to establish its own commemorative days and conformity of behaviour and practice thereon.

What was to become the ecclesiastical calendar evolved over several hundred years, and was conveniently changed many times, as the campaign to eradicate paganism grew and with it the need to substitute Christian for pagan commemoration. In the first century only Easter and Pentecost (Whit) were marked, and in the second century Lent and the Birth of Christ were added. By the fourth century there were saint days, Candlemas, Holy Cross, St John's Day, Lammas and Hallowmas, dates being manoeuvred as appropriate. The ecclesiastical calendar, far from being just a holy chronology, must have appeared to pagans to be an elastic, evangelising tool.

One legacy of the dovetailing of the pagan and ecclesiastical calendars is the current mixture of fixed and movable dates, and for a long time there was confusion over two sets of Quarter Days. The establishment of a date for Easter commemoration caused particular disagreement with the Church. Eventually, the Synod of Whitby, in Northumbria, in 664 ACE, fixed the method of determining the date as the first Sunday after the Paschal full moon after the Vernal Equinox. The lunar component of this calculation made the Christian Easter a date that varied from year to year, and this calculation is still applied annually. The entire movable Easter Cycle, of Septuagesima, Sexagesima, Shrovetide, Lent, Easter, Hocktide, Rogationtide, Whitsuntide, Trinity and Corpus Christi, became an additional complexity in a calendar bursting with saint days and days of observance. But, as the society within which pagans were now a minority became more secular, the ecclesiastical calendar gradually ceased to have the relevance, or indeed the religious function, it once had. What were once religious occasions with a defined purpose, themselves Christianised variations of former pagan rites with strongly retained pagan elements (such as the lights, evergreens, mistletoe, decorations and giving of presents at Christmas and eggs, young animal symbolism and Spring flowers at Easter), had become simply secular occasions for enjoyment, indulgence and a break from routine. The pagan folk calendar did not disappear, and forms the basis of the modern pagan calendar, introduced in chapter four.

The Christianisation of pagan society in the British Isles

The borrowing and remodelling of pagan culture enabled the Roman Catholic Church, through the agency of its missionaries, to gain power and authority over ordinary folk, and land and wealth for the clergy and their noble and warrior associates. The role of the missionary, as witnessed through pagan eyes, was one of intentional destruction and replacement of a rival culture, a process that must have bewildering, if not frightening, and which at worst led to death by introduced disease or, in the case of dissenters, death by the hand of zealotry. The pagans had their native cultural stability taken from them, and in its place, through promises of 'salvation' and 'paradise', they found themselves grappling with an alien philosophy and way of life. If the effects of missionary work in more recent times can serve as an example, the pagans would soon have descended into a state of low self-esteem, helplessness and despair. Their state of mind would have been characterised by emotional and moral confusion, and some would have shown a tendency to resort to crime, alcohol abuse, and anti-social behaviour of other kinds. Family problems would have emerged as parents failed to cope with alien ways and modes of thought. The 'converted' would have acquired an insatiable, unrealistic desire to be 'civilised' like the missionaries, and enjoy what they regarded as the perks of 'civilisation', when in fact they were perfectly civilised in the first place. All of these factors to some degree would have paved the way down for pagan societies visited by missionaries, for the latter had to be prepared to sacrifice the stability of family, community and oneness with the environment so that new souls could be 'saved'. For traditional pagans, this sacrifice was the terrible price of being 'converted' to religion.

Stable pagan communities were wrenched from Mother Nature, who provided for their fundamental needs, to the Christian God, who added only an alien spiritual dimension to their lives. The conventions, constraints and observances of religion worked against the pagan oneness with the natural world, and destroyed the social cohesion upon which their tradition of mutual support relied. Indeed, they were compelled to put the Church before family and community, and even to make a financial contribution to the institution that had irrevocably changed their culture. An organisation in which an all-male hierarchy fashioned privileges and position for itself, while women remained subservient, dutiful handmaidens, was not one that traditional pagans would have warmed to or felt prompted to emulate.

Towering over pagan hovels, magnificent ecclesiastical structures were built from the spoils of power. To pagans they were but showcases of looted, melted-down and remanufactured pagan treasures and artefacts, but with characteristic lack of originality, and perhaps a sense of history, the artefacts were often reshaped into images that betrayed the pagan provenance of the originals, even if superficially Christian.

It is perhaps no coincidence that the Protestant Reformation, a movement to revert to a simpler expression of religion, found fertile ground amongst the stronger pagan and rural traditions of the Celtic and Germanic peoples of northern Europe. And it is amongst their descendants that the repaganisation of residual British Christian society is most likely to proceed, and succeed.

The effects of urbanisation and industrialisation on surviving pagan ways

After the dramatic military consequences of the Roman occupation, the waves of conquest and settlement in the British Isles by Jutes, Anglo-Saxons and Scandinavians, and the profound spiritual and social reorientation and zealous excesses of the Christianisation period, one would have thought that surviving pockets of paganism deserved a period of abatement, but there was more to come, though not an onslaught of a kind that had gone before. In the agrarian Celtic and English heartlands, and indeed elsewhere, miscellaneous elements of pagan belief, ritual, custom, habit, and of artistic, technological and linguistic heritage, had endured, often much changed but recognisable nonetheless. Paganism as a complete way of life no longer existed, the original folk calendar was but a memory, and daily life was tightly regulated by the Churches, local nobility, and increasingly by legislative and commercial changes brought about in response to the growing complexity of urban society and its overspill effects on rural communities. But what these heartlands were to find the most difficult to fend off, and ultimately to recover from, was the drift away of villagers to the expanding urban centres with their industry and promise of a more materialistic lifestyle, and to fight in wars whose devastating cost in human lives ensured most would never return.

The growth of materialism and self-aggrandisement, combined with the growing demands of an increasingly complex social order, drew people further and further away from self-sufficiency and a life oriented around family and community. Once-distinct communities disappeared in urban expansion, and the anonymity of, and feeling of dispensability in, city life replaced the communal value and importance of the individual. Science, technology, and commerce seemed to be the new controllers, and just as those caught up in the turmoil of industrial and commercial life had little time for pagan ways, so Christianity was also to be a casualty for much the same reason.

The fact that ancient folk customs had survived thus far indicates their value as a cohesive force in self-sufficient, mutually dependent communities, and they continued long after their original function had largely been forgotten and their character altered by the march of time and expedient. Those high-minded observers now living a much more sophisticated lifestyle in towns and cities increasingly looked upon rural villages as outposts of rustic, primitive ways, where the evolving, superior urban attitudes, social conventions, language and materialistic objectives had not yet penetrated and begun to exert their 'civilising' effects. An urban life so thoroughly dependent on servants, tradesmen, patronage, birthright and the lure and power of wealth was alien to rural communities dependent largely upon individual effort and each other. In these communities, conformity, co-operation and versatility were more important that one-upmanship, hierarchical control and delegation.

The bonds of folk culture were to prove fragile in several respects. Customs either had to change radically to suit new social values or be abandoned. The Christian Churches and various Christian-influenced authorities began a further period of intolerance towards, and again sought to discredit, folk culture for what they deemed to be unacceptable excesses, which were out of character with new urban norms. The licentiousness, high spirits, drunkenness and damage to property that accompanied some ceremonies made them obvious targets, and when they were quietened and whittled down then less robust occasions found themselves under threat. Youngsters were experiencing a tug of loyalties. On the one hand, authoritarian efforts sought to belittle their parents' lifestyle and expose it as backward, which must have caused loss of pride and feelings of shame and embarrassment. On the other hand, they felt the lure of more attractive prospects in the towns. But the hectic pace of life of an industrial town where folk worked long hours for little pay and struggled to feed and clothe a large family was no basis to have time or inclination to pursue folk customs with rural roots and significance. So, when villagers left their homes, they left their folk culture behind too.

Back in the country, now slowly being denuded of human resources, public transport, such as trains and motor vehicles, was ending rural isolation. Commercialisation of various kinds started to weaken local bonds, and new values, habits and attitudes were adopted, along with the lifestyle changes of which they were an integral part. So, eventually, even the youngsters' parents started to look upon their lives as backward and uncultured and sought something 'better'. Their edification and a response to the iniquities of the new, 'progressive', urban lifestyle saw the growth of campaigns by philanthropists and the nonconformist Churches in both rural and urban areas to further 'protect' ordinary people. In reality their objective was to regulate their lives still further by focussing them on chapel and institutions instead of their communities, to save them from the temptations of urban life. This further assault on paganism seriously eroded surviving pagan ways in the predominantly Celtic areas of the British Isles. By now, many local folk customs were barely recognisable as traditional and were in some cases to be supplanted by popular pressure to adopt hybrid, commercialised customs such as those at Christmas, New Year and Easter.

The demise of the Celtic languages and English regional dialects

The near death-knell of paganism was sounded when the vernacular use of the Celtic languages and English regional dialects declined, as standard English spread ever northwards and westwards, replacing all before it, pushing the Celtic languages to the Atlantic coastal regions. The process of contraction of the Celtic languages is well documented.

Once spoken throughout Ireland, Irish Gaelic survived as the vernacular in the twentieth century only in Counties Donegal, Mayo, Galway and Kerry, and in small areas in the south near Cork, and in Counties Waterford and Meath. After absorbing large numbers of English settlers, particularly from Lancashire, the Isle of Man became virtually all English-speaking by the 1920s. The last speaker taught Manx Gaelic as a child was Ned Madrell, who died in 1962. By the seventeenth century Scots Gaelic was rapidly in retreat as English spread first into the eastern lowlands, up to and around Edinburgh, and then into the western lowlands. By the early years of the twentieth century it was heard only in north west Scotland and the Western Isles.

In the sixteenth century, Welsh could still be heard in the English border counties of Gloucestershire, Herefordshire, Shropshire and Cheshire, surviving in Shropshire into the nineteenth century and in Oswestry into the twentieth century. Before long, only in areas of north Wales was there a substantial unbroken Welsh linguistic tradition. Cornish succumbed to the spread and dominance of English by the end of the eighteenth century, being confined to the far west of Cornwall. It did not survive as a vernacular into the nineteenth century. Breton, which is still spoken in Brittany, is descended from the Cornish of those who fled from the Anglo-Saxon occupation of south west England in the fifth century. The ancient Gaulish and Galician languages did not survive into recent times. Gaulish came even more recently to public notice in the Asterix cartoons, but no druidic potion proved strong enough to revive it.

As the average age of speakers of these minority languages and dialects rose, fewer and fewer young people had access to their oral lore, with its distinctive cultural references, vocabulary, modes of expression and vocal style. Communal linguistic threads were broken as the elderly, the repositories of tradition, became isolated; their lore valued only by the likes of traditional pagans. In some cases the disappearance of language or dialect happened through concerted efforts to eliminate them, in others through their becoming moribund because there was little future and influence through any discourse but standard English. This loss caused much local distinctiveness to vanish, and helped media communications to take hold. When children can no longer converse with their grandparents the oral tradition fades, and also the cultural relevance and uniqueness that surviving literary heritage embodies and preserves. There are many recorded instances of children being made to feel ashamed of their dialect or language by their teachers and social superiors, even punished for using it. By this means, another significant, perhaps critical, bond with the pagan past was broken. Paganism was a lifestyle no more, but a collection of spiritual, ritual, habitual, linguistic and behavioural fragments, but those fragments have sufficient substance to be reassembled with the adhesive of folk history, memories and tradition, as this book attempts to show.

Modern paganism and Christianity

The end of the pagan victim culture

The foregoing summary of the historical relationship between paganism and Christianity, from the pagan view of that history, is as it is, and neither Christians nor pagans can change the past. We are all descendants of some people that we would rather not have to identify ourselves with, and we all carry balls and chains forged by their unfortunate actions. A pagan interpretation of ecclesiastical history inevitably highlights some episodes that most ordinary Christians are probably now ashamed of, but it is important to present these episodes from a pagan perspective, to inform Christians today of the reasons why pagans take issue with the Christian version of historical events, and over the way its current aftermath affects modern pagan lives. Probably, most pagans today accept that Christians would rather Christian excesses of the past had not happened, and especially had not happened at the expense of ordinary folk, pagan or not. For all pagans it is time to move on and forge new relationships with all groups in society, spiritual or non-spiritual, from whatever cultural background.

When engaging personally with Christians and others of spiritual persuasion, one hopes that pagans will find as much interest in talking to those with thoughtful beliefs and sound conviction as with those less committed and more ambivalent in their views. The former are just as likely to be receptive to understanding the pagan position, but the latter probably more likely to take it up. In such conversations, pagans should not feel reticent about expressing pride in those aspects of their culture that were used to lay the foundations of Christianity, and indeed other religions in other parts of the world. Those aspects include their humanity, family ties, mutual communal support, artistic and technological creativity, the importance placed on music and other aesthetic pursuits, and the value of sensual, intuitive, imaginative and psychic exploration in the development of the whole person.

The dialogue could remind Christians of the power of paganism as a basic cultural adhesive, which the missionaries recognised by choosing to retain it in reinterpreted form. Do go into religious buildings and admire the recycled and revamped examples of pagan artistic brilliance and technical skills, and make a contribution to their preservation if you feel able. If you get an opportunity to talk to members of the clergy, do so in a positive way about the common heritage and values you both share, and make it clear that modern pagans are not anti-religious; that they want a society where everyone can follow freely their chosen path in life, spiritual or not.

DeChristianisation of British society

There remain issues and consequences for pagans of life in a society with substantial residues of its once extensively Christian character and influence at all levels of the social hierarchy, administration and government. Some may seek active deChristianisation by lobby for legislative action in those areas of life where Christian privilege, procedure and influence remain enshrined in law, procedure and custom. Privilege through royal birthright, inheritance or historical precedent does not sit comfortably with modern pagan philosophy, neither does the continued insistence by the Churches that they have a monopoly on morality, and therefore a right to perpetuate their unelected representation on governmental and public bodies and committees, and legal intrusion into life-cycle ceremonies, court proceedings and the right of free speech, such as in laws on blasphemy. The removal of anachronistic ecclesiastical baggage from these offices and from public education systems, and the consideration of Church personnel as ordinary citizens and the business of religious institutions as falling under common law like all others, would open the way for modern pagans and good Christians to share on an equal footing the great deal that they have in common. Religious activity, or association with life-cycle ceremonies, then simply becomes a personal freedom like any other, a matter of personal conscience and preference, just as modern pagans ought to have, for the first time in recorded history, complete freedom to conduct their own affairs in their chosen way, to their own calendar.

For the most part the process of deChristianisation is happening anyway and making its own momentum, for most ordinary folk now either rate various aspects of their lifestyle above any religious affiliation, or have gone in another spiritual direction, as dwindling church congregations testify. As on a piece of ageing furniture consigned to the attic, the Christian veneer is rapidly peeling off the pagan carcass, as the adhesive loses its power and people who so wish can rediscover their pagan consciousness and roots.

Self-entrapment by the trappings of religion

It is certainly not advocated that modern pagans lose their lack of spiritual encumbrance by attempting to create the trappings of religion, such as 'churches', icons, vestments, chants, creed and ceremonial rituals. That would put them on a par with the neo-druids of England, Cornwall and Wales, who have invented such embellishments and accoutrements in the belief that they have somehow revived druidism proper. Modern paganism is not a modern version of druidism, and has no idolatry, as it is a lifestyle whose roots lie in the ancient Celtic past but whose philosophy has evolved beyond it and whose behavioural norms belong inextricably to the present. Modern pagans will obviously want to meet one another, and the ancient Celtic preference for meeting outdoors is just as worthwhile today, even though the oak groves are long gone. Ancient sacred sites, even though laid bare by the exigencies of history, are perfectly acceptable for those wanting to establish in their minds a sense of connection with the past, although the conversation and discussion will be relevant to the present and future. But meeting anywhere will do, for it is the company and their mutual quest, not the surroundings, which matter.

Reclaiming pagan culture

There are more opportunities than ever for modern pagans to reclaim their culture. Interest groups and classes abound to promote the study and performance of folk music, instruments, songs and carols; the learning of ancient arts, crafts and constructional techniques; and the application of old woodland and other environmental methods of management. The quest for spirituality and what is seen as sophistication in culture has somewhat left a void at more basic levels of cultural experience. Modern paganism is a foundation culture for all, from which your individual leanings can sprout.

Many pagans today have adopted Celtic art and crafts and developed new directions in design from them, but new pagans are not in any way constrained to feel they must give a Celtic look to anything they design or make, for the danger is that this could lead to iconography and the visual trappings of religion. In all material matters they have the same choices as anybody else. Modern pagans of Celtic descent will naturally lean towards their own artistic traditions, but modern paganism transcends all boundaries between nations and between existing communities and social groups within a nation. Important aspects of cultural identity that are not in conflict with the common attitudes of modern pagan lifestyle need not be obscured by them, and certainly should not be abandoned. Paganism always had a local flavour, and can continue to do so. Breadth of thought, character and opinion is welcome in modern pagan circles, for there are no stakes at which to burn dissenters, only force of argument and strength of common purpose.

Repaganisation of British society

It will be a natural corollary for some, that after reclaiming their pagan heritage they will seek repaganisation of British society. Modern paganism is not a movement designed specifically to achieve this, as it is a foundation lifestyle for everybody, but modern pagans recognise that some may wish to use it to take steps in the direction of repaganisation.

Modern pagan family and community values, founded on sexual and human equality, and on co-operative endeavour, are in sharp contrast to male-dominated, hierarchical Christian society, but it is questionable if repaganisation of society is best done by evangelising, that is to say, using the methods of the Churches. Christianisation had tragic consequences for pagans, but it is not part of the modern pagan mentality to retaliate in a vengeful way. Permeation by example and lawful lobby is really the only way to bring about a quiet pagan revolution, and example can only be transmitted by contact and engagement, not by isolation. The latter would lead to new pagan society becoming like the Amish sect, trapped in a time warp, they and their ways being seen as no more than animated museum exhibits. Modern pagans should have great respect for other religions and spiritualities, for their buildings and properties, and for the beliefs and ways of other groups generally. The paganism/Christianity interface need not be a source of conflict in society or indeed in a relationship, for they are not rival religions. Modern paganism is a lifestyle, not a religion, and its tenets should not be strange or uncomfortable to a good Christian, just as ancient pagan ways were not alien to the early Christian missionaries. Modern pagans are encouraged to turn away from all religious-based conflict, and seek harmony and mutual understanding.

The silent journey

After centuries of persecution and suppression, traditional pagans learned to guard their tongues and quietly protect their traditions, beliefs, philosophies and ways of living. The custom of secrecy and exclusiveness among traditional pagans throughout their history is known by some as 'the silent journey'. The traditional pagan journey continues, but now that they recognise they have something to offer the world, their journey can be silent no longer. The traditional pagan voice speaks for the first time from this book, and the message is now one of reconciliation, inclusive and modern. That message is Part Two.

Part Two
The Establishment
of a Modern Pagan
Lifestyle

In this section the principles of modern paganism will be explained, and in consideration of their application you will be asked to examine and audit certain aspects of your current lifestyle. Some key aspects are discussed at length, as these are of great significance in successfully reorienting your lifestyle, wholly or in part, in the modern pagan way. But on many matters no comment is made, for individuality in those aspects is part of the variety and vibrancy of society, and it is not the place of modern paganism to express advice or pass judgement upon them. The key aspects that you will be invited to reflect upon are the calendar you follow, how you see your place in the natural environment, the quality of the food you eat and your state of health, your attitudes towards other people and living things in general and your relationships with them, your senses of family togetherness and of community purpose, how your children are to be brought up and educated, and how you respond to life in a commercial and technological age.

Rise and fall, ebb and flow
Stars are born and sooner or later, however mighty they are, they die, and the same is true of their attendant planets and the geological structures of which they are made, and which are in constant flux. Upon our planet, and possibly on many others, are living organisms, and these too are born and later die, a certainty applying to individuals, populations, species, families and higher taxonomic groups. Within human society, organisations as vast, complex and highly ordered as empires,

rise, expand, contract and fall, and within any tribe or nation social structures develop, change and decay; dominant individuals come to power, enjoy the fruits and then fade from grace. Every dog has its day, for nothing lasts for ever.

Homo sapiens alone as a species has the wherewithal to modify and enhance its lifestyle and environment in ways no other species has managed to do, and such unique ability could be said, therefore, to be most unlikely to have survival value, otherwise many other species in the Earth's long biological history would probably have evolved such an ability. It is one thing to have a neutral ability that has no bearing on survival, but quite another if that ability has destructive potential. It is a thread in the tapestry of the present that human ingenuity and the capacity and desire to change our natural environment to suit an increasingly abiological lifestyle has created a fearful realisation in many people's minds. Either human lifestyle, for increasing globalisation means that the term can be used with some justification, or even the human species itself, is now on the downward slope to eventual destruction. Human society is no more immortal than each human within it.

But this is by no means the first time in history that such feelings have been felt and expressed, and always a further human-induced change has engendered optimism for the future and a revival of human fortunes, until the next period of decline sets in. Celtic paganism rose to prominence as a lifestyle a long time ago and then declined over much of the interval between the rise of the Roman Empire and the present day. Then the Roman Catholic Church rose to prominence, followed by the growth of Protestantism, but their imperial grip is now weakening and their congregations shrinking. Developments in science and technology and their applications in various fields of engineering inspired and catalysed the Industrial Revolution, with its attendant urbanisation and the evolving complexity of life within it, but that phase too appears to be past its zenith. The human ills and wants that the leaders of this revolution thought they could cure are still with us, and growing in extent and variety.

Increasingly, urban life, which the majority in the British Isles and many other countries now share, is condemned as stressful, impersonal, crime-ridden, and out of individual – and even collective – control. Like all of the aforementioned periods in British history this phase is everywhere now in serious decline after a series of conflicts and periods of excess, leaving ordinary folk of all nationalities and cultures to wonder what is best suited to succeed and replace it. Uniquely, according to the thesis herein, a rebirth of pagan lifestyle in modern form represents human society's best chance of embarking upon a journey through life that offers hope, optimism and a constructive way forward. It can do this by reversing the normal mode by which power has operated in British and other societies towards pagans. Pagans and their culture have been on the receiving end of a series of top-down wieldings of power, by no means all with the intention of eliminating either pagans or their culture, but nearly having those effects nevertheless. But now that modern popular culture appears to be in decline it is time for modern pagans to start wielding their power, from the bottom up, and that power is a combination of their personal conviction, freedom of choice, unshakeable determination to exercise both, and the willingness to offer their lifestyle to all who share this ailing planet with them.

Towards a personal strategy by audited change

Adopting modern paganism means embracing a new calendar, new attitudes, and a new lifestyle, in order that old family, community and environmental harmony can be regained. It will not happen overnight, and you may receive adverse comments from the uninformed. Despite what some may say, modern paganism is not about attempting to re-create the past, but is about applying forgotten principles, attitudes and practices to life today. Some alternative lifestyles have acquired a bad press because those who advocate them are seen as anarchists, anti-establishment activists, drop-outs or wasters, but the more responsible and better organised activist groups, such as those concerned with energy and wildlife conservation issues, can gain a wide public following and an even wider public sympathy. Something similar is the way forward for modern paganism, as it is a lifestyle that can be adopted by anybody, whatever their cultural origins, regardless of what the media and others who seek to stereotype may regard as their position in society. Its emphasis on harmony makes it an infectious philosophy and a contented way of life, and thus a serious rival to any other. New paganism can be passed on to children without fear that they will be socially isolated, for the elements of modern paganism are already widely respected, just not yet widely followed as a complete lifestyle, so modern pagan children will be the survivors, and pathfinders for others, the ones with a healthy, optimistic future.

Modern paganism is for modern people. It may be portrayed as nostalgia for the old days, but there is no golden age of the past for pagans, as it was full of hardship, tyranny and disease. What the past did have, however, was compensatory courtesy; helpfulness; respect; community spirit; self-discipline; parental and social responsibility and communal pressure, checks and balances to reinforce them; and an understanding of dependence on the environment and its conservation. It is unrealistic to think of going back to nature or dispensing with technology; the emphasis should now be on harmony with nature, conservation and eco-friendly technology. Early humans had space and time, but lack of these now imprison us. The success of new paganism requires the belief that it really can get off the ground, because it stems initially from individual action and wanting attainable objectives from sensible audited choices. This means examining your current lifestyle choices closely and changing them in the ways you feel are right for you, your family, community, and environment. This book will help you consider the options modern pagans recommend.

A great deal can be done without party politics or the support of the media or high finance, although it is likely that the mood of the public in regard to many new pagan issues, if properly represented, will eventually carry many influential people and organisations with it.

A relevant calendar to live by

A new calendar is an important framework for new attitudes

in that they receive a new daily focus. Only by adopting a solar/lunar calendar can people properly re-align their thoughts and actions with the needs of the environment, to bring back the astronomical, meteorological and natural cycles into their lives. The ecclesiastical calendar, with its largely irrelevant celebrations, has been secularised to the point of pointlessness, in a way that is now irreversible. It no longer has any meaning in most people's lives, and what is required more than ever today is meaningful focus in life, such as the modern pagan folk calendar offers. A key modern pagan objective should be to see the current calendar replaced by the folk calendar throughout the nation and not just in private celebration. It is your human right to be a modern pagan, to be able to follow the new indigenous lifestyle of the British Isles, and to demand pagan festival days, but you must be willing to work on ecclesiastical and on bank holidays. Whilst there is no imposed standard way to celebrate pagan festival days, guidance has been given herein because it is important to keep them in appropriate fashion, especially if you have children to set an example to. But, be tolerant of other people's lifestyles and their particular ways of celebration, for new paganism seeks to add positively to the experiences of those who so desire to embrace it. Many modern pagan celebrations can sit comfortably alongside celebrations of spirituality without conflict.

Lobby and consumer pressure

Despite all the predictions of planetary doom and social breakdown through rising crime, self-abuse and intolerance towards various groups within society, there has yet to be a concerted, collective effort to change environmentally and socially damaging habits. People and organisations are still wasting resources, still purchasing items from endangered species, still engaging in environmentally destructive practices and conducting themselves in selfish, anti-social ways that are damaging family and communal stability. They get away with it partly because so many governments have weak, ineffectively applied legislation on all these matters. Unless there are more effective ways of tackling these problems, and stiffer, deterrent penalties for such behaviour, there will not be full confidence that quality of life will improve. Modern pagans can bring about a review of such legislation by leading the campaign for improved personal and social behaviour through example, influence, lobby and consumer pressure. The more who take up the campaign the more exposed governments' weak positions will be. Just speaking out is not enough; ordinary folk can empower themselves by living the lives that personify and reflect their needs.

There are many social and environmental pressure groups whose objectives are close to pagan hearts and you may consider joining these, for they can provide carefully researched information, lists of contacts and valuable shared experience. Organised campaigns can be very effective in bringing an issue to public attention, but the power of example, where an individual act or position attracts the like-minded to follow suit, is often longer-lasting, beyond the immediate impact of the protest. This part of the book, therefore, has three objectives – to help you re-examine your current lifestyle, to invite you to adopt as many modern pagan principles as you feel comfortable with, and to encourage you to encourage others by your example. There are many who are modern pagans in spirit, and it is to be hoped that through these pages they will be prompted, and thereby persuade others, to be modern pagans in deed. Instead of drifting along in the same old, follow-my-leader fashion new paganism will only succeed if it enters the mainstream of everyday thoughts and actions. A difference in society will only come about if modern paganism is put into practice by those with the courage and conviction that can overcome the inertia bred by the states of helplessness and despair which pervade our fragmented, violent, stressful, polluted world.

Self-examination
We can all identify our weaknesses as individuals, but another important step is the realisation and acceptance of our dependence upon one another, and the damage to this mutual dependence that independent, selfish behaviour can cause. Peer pressure ought to function by helping to maintain everyone's

equilibrium for the common good, but too many people, organisations and governments today seem to think they know better or have priority or some sort of divine right to trample on the community and the individual in order to promote their agendas. Only the responsible and unselfish deserve rights, but these are so often taken from them by vested interests, whose public profile is largely hypocritical. If while eating pâté de foie gras you pause between mouthfuls to bemoan the extent of cruelty to animals you have missed the point of modern paganism, which is to think and live like a modern pagan the whole time, not be a Jekyll and Hyde with double standards that expediently serve your needs according to which hat you are wearing or what company you are keeping. Instead of sitting in a car discussing atmospheric pollution while you drive along you should be asking yourselves why you are in there at all, and shouldn't you all be walking, cycling or using public transport instead, if these options are available.

Individual responsibility

An individual is a link in a chain of responsibility, and one weak link breaks that chain, leading to failure of the initiative. Please consider the merits of being a strong link, and of boycotting what your principles and conscience tell you to avoid, and of resisting giving way to fashion, vested interest or ill-informed lobby. Were it not for public pressure and refusal to follow the crowd we would still live in a society that unashamedly kept slaves, used pit ponies, watched and enjoyed bear-baiting, and hung children for stealing a crust.

4
The Modern Pagan Calendar

The New Folk Year

The Folk Year has in times past been expressed in many different calendrical forms, but new paganism takes the following traditional form as its basis. In the New Folk Year, all commemorative days fall on the same day each year.

The New Folk Year

(• indicates the nine national holidays)

Winter
1 November to 31 January
21 December • The Winter Solstice or The Mid-Winter Festival (Yule)
31 December/1 January • Twelfth Night

Spring
1 February to 30 April
31 January/1 February • The Spring Festival or The First Day of Spring (Imbolc)
21 March • The Vernal (Spring) Equinox or The Mid-Spring Festival (Ostara)

Summer
1 May to 31 July
30 April/1 May • The Summer Festival or The First Day of Summer or May Day (Beltane)
21 June • The Summer Solstice or The Mid-Summer Festival (Litha)

Autumn

1 August to 31 October

31 July/1 August • The Autumn Festival or The First Day of
Autumn or The Harvest Festival (Lughnasadh)

21 September • The Autumnal Equinox or The Mid-
Autumn Festival (Mabon)

31 October/1 November • The Winter Festival or The First
Day of Winter (Samhain)

The New Folk Year is based on a combination of the traditional Celtic folk calendar and solar festivals of Anglo-Saxon
and Norse introduction. Variants of it have been used by pagans
since ancient times, but the basic format of the new calendar
is functional for all today. The Celtic folk calendar was based
on the four Quarter Days of Samhain, Imbolc, Beltane, and
Lughnasadh. Later, the annual cycle was expanded to include
solar festivals, and was often represented by a wheel, to
symbolise the cycle of life, death and resurrection/rebirth. The
ancient rituals were designed to ensure that the wheel kept
turning, but now its operation is in our hands, and it behoves
us all to protect and facilitate seasonal changes.

Modern pagans may wish to mark the phases of the moon
on their calendar; an almanac will give you the precise dates
for each year. By watching the new, crescent, half, gibbous and
full phases of the moon each lunar month, and by watching
the changing zenith and course of the sun, you will begin to
connect with both natural astronomical cycles and the growth
and regenerative cycles of nature. If weather permits, try to be
outside at the times of the full moons, in the garden, out walking in the countryside, or silently sit near the edge of a wood
or other vantage point, where you can experience the beauty
and tranquillity of moonlight and observe the activity of nocturnal wildlife. Those who do this regularly will not find it hard
to understand the reverence in which the moon was once held.

Your Modern Pagan Calendar

In parallel with the reintroduction of the folk calendar, which
has no variable dates like the Christian Easter, must come a

reinterpretation of its cusps, the points where one season changes into another, known as Quarter Days, so that what people do on these and other significant days is meaningful and relevant. Locally, where old folk traditions have been maintained on specific dates, those dates may be added to the new folk calendar. One of the values of performing and reviving folk customs is that they belong to local people, whereas the creeping internationalism of societies around the world belongs to nobody. Folk traditions, both national and local, and current and revived, the latter sometimes with a modern interpretation, form the basis of the new pagan calendar. Wiccans will, of course, continue with their traditions, but for the majority of users of the new folk calendar, the new pagans, guidance is offered below. It is to be hoped that existing folk customs and their current dates of celebration will continue unaffected for these are part of folk tradition and need not be subsumed artificially into the new folk year by holding them on Quarter Days or Solar Days. The combination of the new folk year and dates of folk customs forms your Modern Pagan Calendar, for it will have the local character that your folk customs give it.

The old pagan lunar and solar calendars were genuinely communal, and were variable because of the seasons and the weather, but tasks can be, and often were, done when conditions are right, regardless of what the calendar says. Therefore, a fixed calendar makes no difference to those tasks dependent on meteorological and ground conditions, and fits in better with modern life with its emphasis on planning, preparation and regularity of schedule. The modern pagan calendar also allows for the actual festival days to be kept, rather than the nearest weekend or bank holiday. Bank Holidays, named after the nation's most intractably grasping financial institutions, are incompatible with new paganism, and have neither function nor place in the new pagan calendar. The old Celtic start and end of the day at sunset would be nice to uphold privately but is no longer practical with life as ruled by the clock. It would similarly be nice to start the year at Samhain as did the old Celtic year but January seems firmly fixed now as the first month of the year, although privately many may choose to think of sunset at Samhain as the end of one year and dawn the next morning as the start of the next.

The Modern Pagan Calendar in its basic form has the dual practicality of being adaptable to modern lifestyle, by new pagan reinterpretation of the cusps and celebratory days, and can also be retained by those preferring to keep to the traditional pagan ways. It accommodates private and public celebration with equal ease, spreads festival days evenly throughout the year, and allows an improved term structure for the school year, organised around the fixed cusps and festivals. What is done at each of the revived commemorative days must be relevant to our times, but based if possible in an evolutionary sense on the ancient purposes and meanings of the festivals. These days are more meaningful with a family, community and Green emphasis to focus people's attention on such matters as a society, rather than on the more usual consumption, entertainment and other forms of self-indulgence as at present. Another important reason for maintaining pagan festival dates with updated ways of commemoration is to emphasise to children their place in the rhythms and cycles of nature and the Universe. This gives meaning to life and emphasises both its continuity and security. Commercialism has ruined many current festivals, such as Christmas, which now begins in September in some shops and Easter, for which chocolate eggs may be purchased in January. Perhaps it is also true to say that people have allowed commercialism to ruin these occasions. It is to be hoped that children will be encouraged to give eco-friendly gifts, preferably homemade, and to join in traditional pastimes. Excitement and enjoyment should ideally come from the relevance of the festival, not from expensive, manufactured presents and marketed entertainment.

Although there have been many revivals of pagan folk customs in the last fifty years, these are sadly just a small proportion of those lost. There is scope for more that have a meaning that modern pagans can readily identify with if they conduct the custom in traditional style and for its original purpose, albeit with a modern flavour. Well-dressing emphasises dependence on the purity and supply of fresh water and the need to conserve it, as should former fertility rites in fields and on the sea have the conservation of yields and catches and the need for good practice and stewardship as their theme. Beating the Bounds, originally to awaken the sleeping spirits of the earth after Winter, is a way to encourage village identity and togetherness, and respect for local wildlife and good soil management. Much the same applies to boundary walks and rides, as they too stimulate interest in local environmental issues. Wakes could readily be reinstated with their original function of honouring the dead of the district and rekindling respect for the elderly and their place in the family and locality. Doles and charities ought properly to be put into the hands of locally elected committees so that the most needy are selected as beneficiaries. The re-introduction of traditional sports and games, in place of the tribal warfare and crass commercial enterprises that sports like football have become, would strengthen family and village togetherness and perhaps steer children away from sedentary pastimes.

Examples of modern pagan practice, derived from traditional customs, on universally significant days follow, although it is to be hoped that local long-standing pagan customs will continue normally on their traditional days. All of the customs and activities below are authentically pagan, and will enable new pagans to revive ancient traditions but with a modern interpretation. Details of the full traditional celebrations may be found in books on folk customs.

21 December – The Winter Solstice or The Mid-Winter Festival (Yule)

At Yule the sun was said to be reborn after the shortest day had passed. Much of the style of current Christmas celebrations that has evolved over recent years may be retained as the pagan elements are substantial in number, but with the emphasis that lights and Yule candles, and traditionally bonfires, are lit just before sunset to encourage the sun to return, and kept alight until after dawn to welcome the returning sun. The bringing in of the Yule Log, the symbol of warmth in Winter, is important, and it too should remain alight until after dawn, a little piece being kept as symbolic of the continuance of life and used to rekindle the next one. The Yule Log has a human figure carved or chalked on it, a reminder of human sacrifice long ago to ensure the sun's return, and is doused with cider and sprinkled with corn before lighting.

Evergreen trees and hangings, including holly and ivy, similarly represent the continuance of life, and the entwining into a wreath of holly, with its masculine symbolism, and ivy, with its feminine symbolism, represents harmony between the sexes. The origin of this symbolism is not clear, unless the prickly male and the clinging female are stereotypes of long standing. The decorated evergreen conifer tree is a perfectly good pagan element of Yule, as are presents placed in stockings and under the tree. The displaying of tree lights stems from the belief that the woodland spirits, sheltering in evergreens after deciduous trees have lost their leaves, would welcome illumination. Rowan is hung over the door lintel, a practice originally to keep out Otherworld visitors. Mistletoe should be hung and should not touch the ground or floor during cutting and hanging, lest its powers be lost, and a berry should be plucked for every kiss granted under it. A Kissing Bush or Bough is also traditional, and is a small decorated bush of holly or yew hung upside down from the ceiling. Another traditional Yule decoration is a globe of blackthorn or hawthorn, doused in cider, which is suspended in the kitchen near the door, originally to keep disease out. Once Yule is over it is stuffed with straw and set alight to symbolically burn all old ills away.

Father Christmas is a renamed old folk character, probably originally an image of the Norse god Odin, who has a place in pagan Yule celebrations, but he should be given back his green jacket and green fur-trimmed cloak to go with the white beard, for the red attire is a recent commercial innovation. It is to be hoped that original versions of folk carols, such as wassail carols, may make a return to the domestic scene, and that wandering singers will once again carry a decorated holly or blackthorn bush, lantern, and wassail bowls for listeners to partake from, and give a contribution to charity. One bowl, for adults, traditionally contains Lamb's Wool, a wassail drink, and one for children might contain a non-alcoholic fruit punch. There are many pagan carols to choose from, such as the original versions of Deck the Hall, The Holly and the Ivy, Joy to the World, Tannenbaum, Here We Go A-Wassailing, Green Groweth the Holly, and Lord of the Dance. Wassailing emphasises our dependence on the fertility of the land, and well documented customs may be adopted by modern pagans everywhere. It is also traditional for children to stick evergreen twigs of box or rosemary into an apple, and go from door to door wishing a happy new year and getting contributions for charity. After wassailing the bush is burned or carried through fields for saining. Those with apple or other fruit trees can wish for a good crop by wassailing in the orchard, singing wassail songs, pouring cider over the roots of the trees and hanging cider-soaked toast for the robins in the branches. Noise was traditionally made with guns, horns, dustbin lids and pots and pans to scare away evil spirits.

Most traditional Yule food has now become a regular feature, although the boar's head and the traditions that surround it could make a comeback, as could Yule cakes and perry or cider. Oatcakes with a cross on, originally the symbol of the sun, may be baked and eaten. The custom of hanging up a wheatsheaf, and other suitable food, for birds would make a welcome revival.

Other folk customs at Yule are Burning the Bush, Mummers' Plays, guisers with blackened faces – so malevolent spirits don't recognise them – animal guising and Hooden Horse processions, calling the Waits (musicians hired to play music and sing carols in the streets), pantomime, torchlight processions and tar-barrel rolling, and traditional dancing such as sword dancing. A Lord of Misrule may be elected to preside over communal festivities. The bringing in of a burning ashen faggot was to cleanse the domestic scene as an act of renewal. Pagans customarily remember the needy at Yule and help provide for them, and collections made by Waits and carollers are freely given to the less fortunate. This day was an important time for divinations, and these were good family fun as well as tinged with a touch of serious soul-searching, reflection and consideration of the future as a family. The prospects of finding compatible partners, future careers and personal circumstances such as health and finances were traditionally the subjects of the divination rituals, after which resolutions for the coming twelve months were made. A focus on family fun and entertainment is the customary objective all evening.

It is no longer acceptable to hunt and kill the wren at Yule, the wren being the old pagan avian messenger between this world and the Otherworld, but parading a garland with a model of a wren in the centre, atop a beribboned pole, when guisers go carolling, would emulate the ancient parades. The carrier of the evergreen-decorated wren pole has a straw mask or horned animal mask, so as not to be recognised. There are also traditional wrenning songs to be sung as the wren effigy is paraded. It is probable that there will be only a few who want to revive holming – thrashing oneself, and formerly other people and animals too – with holly or nettles in the rejuvenated sun to improve health and stamina.

31 December eve – Twelfth Night

As midnight on 31 December approaches, or alternatively on Yule Eve, first-footing may begin, the visitors carrying traditional gifts (called handsel) to wish those visited good luck (something green), warmth (a piece of coal), prosperity (salt) and plenty of sustenance (food and drink) in the coming year. Traditionally, first-footers are led by a tall, dark man; not a fair-haired man to remind Celts of Anglo-Saxon and Norse infiltrators. Before admitting them the back door is opened to let the old year out, making a din by beating pots and pans, originally to drive any lingering malevolent spirits of the old year away. Those wishing to keep to the old Celtic yearly cycle should go first-footing at Samhain. After the first-footers have left, and the family has retired to bed, all should rise early in recognition of the principle of starting as you mean to go on throughout the coming twelve months. All leftovers are used up for breakfast, the house cleaned, all your possessions brought inside, and a gift given to each child. Don't lend money or otherwise display a personal weakness, as it may become a habit for the year.

This is the Naming Day for each new child, and until this ceremony a child is just a son or daughter, a state that could last until puberty. Traditionally, and for wiccans, this day was to commemorate important junctures in our life cycle, such as the coming-of-age ceremony or rite of puberty, involving initiation and dedication rites, wiccaning (or presenting) the newborn, handfasting or jumping the broom (establishing a partnership), handparting (dissolving the partnership) and crossing the bridge, a memorial ceremony for the deceased. Handfasting, which used to be done by a couple clasping hands through a holed stone, is a ceremony in which the couple commit themselves to create and uphold the principles of a modern pagan relationship and family. The choice of words and style of ceremony is entirely their own. Handparting is the mutual severing of the relationship, with agreed arrangements being made for children, parents and other members of the extended family. For modern pagans Twelfth Night is an ideal day on which to reunite family ties, celebrate these life-cycle occasions, renew vows, allegiances and friendships, and 'mend fences' where relationships have become strained.

The Twelfth Night Cake, the precursor of the Christmas Cake, is baked with a pea and bean inside. Whoever finds the pea in their piece is elected King, and the finder of the bean is elected Queen, of the Festivities, then leading the jollifications. Wassailing, singing of wassail carols, and passing round the wassail bowl of Lamb's Wool are also customs appropriate for this day, as are Mummers' Plays and sword dancing. Guisers take the wassail bowl from door to door, singing carols and receiving gifts. If you are celebrating a rite of passage then each guest takes a spoonful of toasted apple and Lamb's Wool from the wassail bowl and drinks the health of those present, especially any new baby. The Strawman, who may have once been a sacrificial scapegoat, may put in an appearance, after disappearing for so long from most village folk customs. He, or indeed she, dressed in straw from head to foot, may do antics and collect for charity before being burned in effigy at the end of the day. There are traditional fertility rites in fields, for the plough, on boats and in fishing grounds on this day, to remind us that when Spring arrives we shall once more be in nature's hands for our food. All Yule decorations are traditionally taken down before midnight, and all Yule cake and other Yule food eaten except the edible Yule log.

31 January eve – The Spring Festival or The First Day of Spring (Imbolc)

This day was traditionally associated with the start of lambing and planting and preparation in farm and garden for Spring, and in addition it is an ideal time to begin Spring-cleaning, in recognition of the saining (ritual purification) that was done on all Quarter Days, and to renew or mend clothes, furniture, and other essential belongings. Part of this ritual was even to smash crockery, but that is perhaps taking the notion of a fresh start too far these days. Rush-bearing and hay-strewing ceremonies are also appropriate on this day, to give a fresh floor surface for everyday life to proceed. Everyone rises early to bathe their faces in the morning dew, and then there are two things to consider – the needs of the poor and hungry, traditionally provided for this evening by going from door to door, and the welfare of pregnant women, who are honoured with gifts and candles.

The day has an association with youth, which can be brought out in private commemoration, although young people were noted for the creation of public mischief as a relief from Winter austerity, and roaming the streets singing songs in exchange for money or food. The environment generally receives a clean-up, with every new pagan making a contribution, and in parallel with these activities it is appropriate to re-examine our own lives and attitudes and re-appraise ourselves and our direction as a family and in our careers. As a Quarter Day this was a traditional time for divination about future prospects. The piece of the Yule log saved should be kept burning until sunset and the remaining edible Yule log finished up.

People of all ages, not just potential young sweethearts, could incorporate the pre-Christian tradition appropriated for Valentine's Day of drawing lots and pairing off in order to get to know someone you would not otherwise have an opportunity to do. A later tradition involves making and sending gifts and cards to actual or desired sweethearts – not buying those items, as this helps to perpetuate the commercial takeover of this custom. On this the first day of Spring, it is appropriate to eat pancakes, symbolising the period when Winter meat stocks had been exhausted and only a few staples were left. The day before, families could eat collops, originally strips of the last stock of preserved meat. This practice reminds us all of the need for good housekeeping, to eliminate waste and to curb extravagance.

21 March – The Vernal Equinox or The Mid-Spring Festival (Easter, Ostara)

As the days begin to lengthen, the letting off of steam after the restrictions of Winter, namely activities associated with All Fools' Day, is traditionally carried out at this time, until noon. There is evidence that post-Winter pranks and japery began at festivals to mark the end of the Spring Equinox, and the 'fool' may have been a scapegoat or sacrificial victim. As this is near the time when the first cuckoo is expected the fool was often called a 'cuckoo'. Less traditionally minded new pagans may prefer to keep All Fools' Day on 1 April.

The adoption of the new pagan calendar would be a good time to bring back the traditional Ostara Tree, hung with painted eggs and decorations representing young animals and Spring flowers. In moderation our chocolate Ostara eggs also have a place, alongside the more ancient hot cross buns. When Winter meat stocks had run out eggs were a staple food until Spring produce was available, so the giving of eggs was a much-appreciated generosity, later superseded by gifts of chocolate eggs. The hanging of decorated eggs on May trees gave rise to the Ostara Tree, which represents renewed growth after Winter dormancy, as the egg represents the force and sanctity of life. Rabbits and hares are symbols of good luck and fertility, the hare also having a more ancient connection with the dawn and the moon. Hence the new pagan family should rise early to see the dawn and stay up to see the moon.

Children have always played an active part in Ostara preparations, which can also include what has been transferred to Mother's Day, namely the making of a simnel cake by children for their mother and expressing gratitude for their mother's devotion and their parental upbringing. Maternity, the young and provision for their future are important issues at Ostara, as is an emphasis on creativity on account of the association of this festival with the dawn. There are traditional games to be played today, and Ostara carols sung outside houses, the traditional sign of appreciation being an egg. The attention of householders was formerly drawn by a noisy chorus of rattles or clappers. Ostara games include lifting or heaving, men lifting women in decorated chairs and then women repaying the compliment by lifting the men. Other activities are egg rolling, egg painting, egg shackling – where marked eggs are rattled in a sieve until one remains whole – and Pace-egg Plays. Rolling eggs downhill imitates the movement of the sun, and it is good luck if a shell remains intact or if your egg reaches the bottom of the slope first. Some local veneration of wells and watercourses takes place at this time. As at Imbolc this is a traditional time to buy or make new clothes.

30 April eve – The Summer Festival or The First Day of Summer (Beltane)

At the start of Summer the ancient theme was sexual union and fertility, and enjoying communion with nature. Rowan and elder adorn the outside of the house, originally to protect the occupants from malevolent visitors from the Otherworld, and also yellow (sun-coloured) flowers like St John's Wort are used. Flowers are strewn on paths, and sweet woodruff is steeped in white wine to make May Wine to drink. A horseshoe or other iron object is hung up in memory of the desire to keep malevolent faeries at bay tonight, for they were afraid of iron.

At sunset house fires are put out and the Beltane bonfire, made of nine types of wood, is lit, and kept alight until dawn. A brand from the fire is kept to rekindle the house fires. It was traditional not to use iron to create the spark, but friction of oak on oak. Walking or dancing round the bonfire sunwise emphasises the importance of the sun's light and heat for the forthcoming crops. Marked stones are put into the fire, to be searched for at dawn, it being lucky to find your own. Torchlight processions are in memory of the carrying of burning brands to sain (purify) the buildings, grounds and animals. Oatcakes are traditionally made, and offered so that each chooses one unseen – the one that has been blackened indicates who must play the role of the sacrificial victim and leap over the fire three times. The height of the crops will parallel the height of his or her highest jump. It is also traditional to roll oatcakes downhill, having marked one side with a cross to represent the sun, and good luck is accorded to anyone whose oatcake ends up with the cross uppermost. Divination is also done this evening.

A charming custom is to rise before the dawn, if you are not already up, and bathe the face in dew and draw the first water from the well if you have one. It may not actually improve the complexion but it is a lovely time of the year to be up early, and while you are up it is customary to 'bring in the May' – greenery to decorate the house. Leafy branches are brought in and decorated as May Boughs with yellow flowers and ribbons, and silver and gold balls, originally representing the moon and sun. When the day is over the Bough is burned. The May dawn is greeted by the blowing of horns, formerly done to scare away any lingering Otherworld spirits. Making May garlands, erecting Maypoles, crowning the May Queen and King, May dances, and singing May carols are all long-standing traditions, as are local ceremonies such as Beating of the Bounds, thanksgivings for crops, catches at sea, and watercourses and wells. The May King is dressed in greenery as he represents Jack-in-the-Green, the symbol of the regeneration of plant growth after Winter. Dancing round the beribboned Maypole (traditionally of birch) should be in a sunwise direction.

Sweeps' and milkmaids' parades were once common, in the case of the former to mark the end of the busy, dirty, Spring-cleaning season, the processions also including Jack-in-the-Green; the Hooden Horse or Hobby Horse and other animal guisers; gaudily dressed human guisers, sometimes dressed as the opposite sex; strawmen and strawwomen; and Morris, clog, step, Mollie, garland and long-sword dancers. These could be revived in areas with such traditions, and be instituted elsewhere too. Beltane is also an appropriate occasion for working in the garden as a family and for the study of herbs and the practice of healing. Well-dressing can be done today, or indeed on any Quarter Day, when there is not a tradition on any other day.

21 June – The Summer Solstice or The Mid-Summer Festival (Litha)

Midsummer, when the sun is at its zenith, is a wonderful time for outdoor pursuits, enjoyment of nature, picnics and outings, pageants, fairs, fêtes, horse parades, treasure hunts, and walks, either on a village scale or with the extended family, friends and neighbours as appropriate. This custom possibly arose because midsummer falls between sowing and haymaking so was a relatively slack period on farms. The sunrise may be viewed from ancient monuments known to have had an astronomical function, such as the Callanish Stones in Lewis in the Western Isles of Scotland, and it is a time when handfasting was done, as at the Stone of Odin at Stenness in Orkney, Scotland. Rise early and bathe the face in morning dew.

It is a suitable time to venerate mature trees and to vow to protect them. Midsummer bonfires are traditionally lit, suggestive of encouragement of the sun to continue to shine on the crops after its zenith. Walk three times round the bonfire sunwise, with linked hands, and jump through the flames, individually or in couples, or wait until there are just embers, for luck or in the hope that the height of the crops will be similar to that of the leap. Brands from the fire are carried round as was done in saining rituals, and effigies of disliked figures may be thrown onto the fire. Other traditional midsummer activities are Morris dancing, well-dressing, and rush bearing or hay strewing. Cartwheels bound with straw are lit and rolled downhill to emulate the start of the sun's declination. The house may be decorated with flowers and greenery, a St John's Wort garland being hung on the front door. Real ale is a favourite drink on this day. Although not a Quarter Day, a tradition has grown up of divination this evening, usually to see who will find a partner in the next twelve months or who will die during that period.

31 July eve – The Autumn Festival or The Harvest Festival or The First Day of Autumn (Lughnasadh)

On this day of the 'first fruts' of nature, traditionally the start of the harvest and the sacrifice of its first produce, fresh food is eaten, as we reflect on the bounty of our shared harvests and the need to protect the natural environment to ensure continuance of fertility, and to promote genuine organic agriculture and horticulture. If nearby, hilltops, lakeside or riverside sites are good choices for family picnics, especially where you can pick wild fruit such as bilberries and blackberries to make into pies to eat later at the Lughnasadh feast. Horse races and swimming races have a history of popularity on this day. The fruits of our labour are customarily shared with friends and strangers alike, especially the needy and elderly. Freshly baked bread or oatcakes and lamb are eaten. Bonfires are lit, brands carried round for saining and with linked hands people walk or dance round them. The Strawman is carried through the village, and an effigy ceremonially burned as a reminder of the sacrifices once made to ensure a good harvest. It is a time to reinforce ownership of common land and take steps to ensure it and its boundaries are protected. Corn garlands are made to decorate family graves. Handfasting, as at the Stone of Odin, is also traditionally done today.

21 September – The Autumnal Equinox or The Mid-Autumn Festival (Mabon or Madron)

As the days shorten, the sun wanes in strength, and inclement weather becomes more common, so attention ought now to be directed towards elderly relatives to ensure that they are comfortable, warm and provided for in every way before the Winter. As the traditional end of the harvest it is the time when a reaper cuts the last sheaf of corn with a sickle – the oldest or youngest worker being chosen – and binds it with flowers or ribbon to be used to make corn dollies. A corn dolly is a personification of a corn spirit, in which it has taken refuge. Some corn is saved to add to the first Spring sowing, or to plough in, or to feed to the horse pulling the first plough next season. A libation is poured onto the plough, to 'streak' it for the first furrow. At no time must the corn dolly touch the ground, or the corn spirit will be released prematurely and lose its fertilising power for the next crop. The corn dolly is hung up in the room where the harvest supper is to be held. After the harvest is safely in, a supper is held to celebrate the bringing in of the harvest from land and sea, when the guest of honour is the one who was chosen to cut the last sheaf. It is customary for those who prepare the harvest feast to bar out the reapers, and for the latter to use subterfuge to try and get in without being sprinkled with saining water. The last sheaf and guests are all sprinkled with water, and the guests wear a harvest knot at the feast. A fiddler plays for dancing when the food has all been consumed. Despite the mechanisation of harvesting today there is no reason whatever why these fine and enjoyable traditions should not be revived.

This is also the time when rush plaiting is done. Nuts are traditionally gathered (nutting), but only by boys as girls thought that this symbol of fertility would make them pregnant if they picked them. Nuts and blackberries – for it is traditionally the end of the blackberrying season – are eaten. Apple and pear picking begins for making cider and perry, traditional drinks which new pagans may like to encourage the making and consumption of. Goose is a traditional meal, or newly slaughtered meat, originally for salting down for Winter. Bonfires are lit and saining done. Parades with the Hooden Horse are held, and horse riding and races, the horses getting a treat of carrots for their exertions.

31 October eve – The Winter Festival or The First Day of Winter (Samhain)

At this the end of the old Celtic year, when the sun is dying, all household tasks should be completed, and preparations made for Winter. The dead, especially our ancestors, are remembered and their graves cleaned and tended. Pumpkins, candles, and traditional Samhain witchcraft and supernatural symbolism and games are pagan and wholly appropriate, and the extended family usually meets today. Pumpkin and turnip lanterns and candles originally lit the way for the returning souls of the departed, who were made welcome by food, drink and a fire left to warm them. This custom can be remembered by baking and eating soul cakes – also traditionally given to mourners – by extinguishing and re-lighting fires, and by holding lantern-lit or torch-lit processions to remember the dead, or firework displays in their honour.

The customs of lighting bonfires and rolling blazing tar barrels are part of the Samhain tradition, to ensure the sun rises next morning. Chestnuts, potatoes and lucky stones are put into the bonfire; the first two to eat when cooked and the latter searched for in the ashes after dawn and pronounced lucky if retrieved. People go sunwise round the fire, blacken their faces and jump over it, accompanied by the blowing of horns, originally to scare away evil spirits. Rowan is hung on the outside of the house, formerly to protect it from Otherworld malevolent spirits. House fires are extinguished prior to lighting the bonfire, and rekindled from a firebrand, as are the candles to light a room for returning ancestral spirits. Firebrands or torches with blazing faggots on poles are used for saining. Traditionally oatcakes and strips of roast, freshly slaughtered meat were eaten, and the rest of the beasts preserved for the Winter. Don't eat blackberries as our ancestors believed that the faeries had by now spat on them, although the 'spit' (mildew) at this time of the year makes them inedible anyway.

In the evening it is traditional to play Samhain games such as Apple-Ducking, combining the sacred apple with the custom of looking into sacred lakes to see the Otherworld and those passing to it, and Snap-Apple, apparently derived from an ordeal by fire. In Snap-Apple two pieces of wood are fixed together at their centres, making a cross, and this is suspended from the ceiling. On the end of one arm a lighted candle is fixed, and on the other end of this piece of wood an apple is fixed. The whole assembly is spun and people take it in turns to take a bite out of the apple, trying to avoid being burned. The older generation tell stories to the family, and all divine their futures. Snap-Apple is not advisable for children as they may get burned, but Apple-Ducking is great fun, trying to remove an apple, floating in a bucket of water, with the teeth. The tradition of guising and making mischief stems from the belief that at Samhain and other Quarter Days windows opened between this world and the Otherworld and spirits from there came into our world and created mayhem. The children wear masks or blacken their faces to prevent them being recognised by these spirits, who may take revenge for perceived past wrongs, as well as by their victims. Bribes of food or money to trick-or-treat guisers should always be respected, and the modern habit of always playing a trick whether a treat is given or not should not be countenanced by new pagans. Mummers' plays to mark the beginning of the dark, austere days of Winter are performed, and Mari-Lwyd-type horses go round with the Mummers.

Changing to your Modern Pagan Calendar

This, then, is the new pagan folk calendar, but how easy might it be to give up the ecclesiastical calendar? It would seem to be a remarkably easy task as the original purpose of the ecclesiastical calendar, to list the days of obligation, saint days, days of Church commemoration, etc, has largely disappeared in a secular society. Holidays are not holy days any more, they are what people want to make of them, and the last thing on most people's minds at Christmas, Easter, Whitsun, etc, is religious devotion. The latter has been replaced by commercialised celebration, fun and indulgence. In any case, most of the surviving trappings of Christmas and Easter – the only substantial survivors from the festivals of the old ecclesiastical calendar – are pagan, having been borrowed and adapted in the early days of spreading Christianity to make it more acceptable. Reconstituting these as the Winter Solstice and Spring Equinox festivals would mean no significant difference to most people. Beltane/May Day (Summer Festival) and Samhain (Winter Festival) are reviving anyway, and when the Summer Solstice and the Autumnal Equinox, Spring Festival and Autumn Festival are revived too, we would be back to a yearly cycle of reasonably spaced-out festivals with both meaning and function. Just their regular spacing alone would be a benefit for the working person and for schools, and the sooner the folk calendar is re-established on a national basis the sooner these benefits will accrue.

You could start your personal folk calendar by purchasing, or creating with word processing software, a blank universal monthly calendar. Write on the Quarter Days, Solstices, Equinoxes, and Twelfth Night, and then any local folk customs you intend to participate in. This can serve as a template for future use. There are so many celebratory activities for each festival you can ring the changes from year to year. Having decided for the coming year, noting them down will enable you to plan ahead with regard to invitations, meals, and making any items required.

The New Folk School Year

The issue of the school year and its inconveniently different term lengths can be dealt with by basing it on the folk calendar, so that the folk school year has spaced-out holidays and roughly equal terms. During the days immediately preceding holidays, schools can readily devise special activities on Green, family and social issues, the heart of new pagan culture as well as the foci of its calendar. The relationship between the New Folk Year and a proposed Folk School Year is shown below, and will be considered further in Chapter 9.

The New Folk Year

(• indicates the nine national holidays)

Winter

1 November to 31 January
21 December • The Winter
  Solstice
31 December/1 January •
  Twelfth Night

Spring

1 February to 30 April
31 January/1 February •
  The Spring Festival
21 March • The Vernal
  Equinox

Summer

1 May to 31 July
30 April/1 May • The
  Summer Festival
21 June • The Summer
  Solstice

The Folk School Year

(• indicates national holidays)

Winter Holiday

12 December to 2 January
Winter Term
3 January to 11 March
31 January •, 1 February •,
  2 February •

Spring Holiday

12 March to 1 April
Spring Term
2 April to 8 June
31 April •, 1 May •, 2 May •

Summer Holiday

9 June to 2 July
Summer Term
3 July to 10 September
31 July •, 1 August •,
  2 August •

Autumn

1 August to 31 October

31 July/1 August • The Autumn Festival

21 September • The Autumnal Equinox

31 October/1 November • The Winter Festival

Autumn Holiday

11 September to 1 October

Autumn Term

2 October to 11 December

31 October •, 1 November •, 2 November •

5
Garden, Farm and Countryside

The Home–Garden Continuum

The unnatural garden

Gardens and land under private ownership have traditionally reflected the social status of the human owner or creator, from the landscaped pleasure grounds of the rich to the fruit and vegetable plots of the rural and urban poor, and have seldom been created with the needs of the natural environment in mind. Much the same may be said of land in public ownership, such as parks. As urban dwellers prospered they attempted to create landscapes in miniature, but used designs that were more geometric than inspired by nature, with plants in regimented order instead of in natural juxtaposition. Such personally designed creations were unnatural in both conception and execution, and if any native species dared infiltrate or pop their heads up through the soil they were ruthlessly eliminated. Each area had its purpose, like the rooms in the adjoining house, and plants were there to display their beauty, their natural functions as food for butterflies or nesting places for birds being incidental. To modern pagans, however, the function of the garden is quite different.

Stewardship or ownership?

To modern pagans, all land is countryside, and the only thing separating garden from countryside, and farm from countryside, in essence, is the boundary walls and fences, or other marks of stewardship. The concept of ownership of land, whilst it may have legal force, is not, in the pagan mind, looked upon as a licence to treat that land and its natural occupants in an unnatural way. Within land enclosures everywhere, activities have diverged more and more from sustainability and ecological balance, and it is one of the missions of modern paganism to reverse this trend. A garden, a common, and a farm can still have functionality, for food, pharmaceutical extracts, dyes, aesthetic pleasure, shade, windbreak, etc, yet still be managed on ecological principles. We who have made ourselves the guardians of our environment have become habitually inclined to adapt the natural world to our demands, rather than adapt our own lifestyle to the demands of the natural world, which we should do before we change it irreversibly. Selfish human activity has denuded land of forests; polluted it with fertilisers and pesticides; overgrazed and eliminated local flora; and allowed top soil to be blown away by removing windbreaks, hedges and natural cover. We have concentrated for commercial reasons on monocultures with consequent vulnerability to disease and environmental change; and allowed locally bred varieties of crop plants and farm animals to die out, so losing genetic stock adapted to local conditions. Tree felling and wetland draining have caused serious loss of wildlife breeding areas and changes to weather patterns. However, in gardens and on farms, where tree planting with native species and re-establishment of wetlands such as ponds and marshes could be an effective ecological enhancement, these strategies are rarely carried out. The problems outlined above are global problems, as is well known, and many caring people are actively engaged in seeking restitution on a suitable scale. But for most people the principal area of interest is their own immediate environment. This is where individuals and small communities can make a lasting impact, especially if they can recreate the sense of local belonging that was so important to our self-sufficient ancestors.

A garden as an extension of the countryside

Ideally, the modern pagan garden is designed to be an extension of the local countryside, with native plants in natural settings, and the more wild visitors it attracts the better the balance will become. As an ecosystem in its own right, a mature natural garden is cyclical, evolving and self-adjusting when natural external forces impact upon it. Not only can you see, hear, touch, smell and taste more in such a garden, but there is a great deal going on that you won't immediately be aware of, some on the microbiological level and some you can see only if you search. Exploring a wild garden is an endless fascination compared with the relatively sterile conventional garden. Without natural cycles of reproduction, growth, consumption, death and decay, no ecosystem can form, so the managed, well-maintained conventional garden, with its 'design' and imported plants, is a poor approximation and needs constant, manual intervention to enable its occupants to thrive. It is not surprising that busy, working residents neglect their gardens, but they are wasting a huge amount of potentially valuable ecological space.

The natural, local garden

The four ancient elements are essential for a new pagan garden as for any garden, earth, water, air and fire, the last being really the heat and light from the sun. Without them the biosphere's natural cycles cannot exist or maintain momentum. Instead of being a product of the control of the availability of these elements and the natural cycles they fuel, the new pagan garden is allowed to reach a state of natural equilibrium as far as possible so that these cycles are self-perpetuating and the four elements naturally interacting. It takes time for a balanced community to form from successive colonisation by visitors joining the planted inmates, and there will be jostling for position and sustenance, and combat resulting in winners and losers, until a balance is struck. A natural, or wild, garden is therefore a long-term project. But of course it is still a personal plot, and you will want to intervene sensitively and productively to ensure that it does not become overgrown or choked by vigorous plants that cannot naturally be checked in such a small space, and to ensure that you derive whatever food you wish to grow or special features or habitats you wish to maintain and whose small size necessitates a degree of management. Thus, there will have to be compromises, but the objective can still be to achieve as naturally balanced and as intervention-free an environment as possible.

Later in the chapter, some ideas will be provided for achieving a balance between access to the garden by the family for its education and enjoyment, the garden's functional use to provide food and herbs, and its purpose as the natural link between house and countryside. These are all important considerations for a small plot, but always with one primary aim in mind, to create as natural a scene as these different functions allow.

Whilst some algae can be troublesome in ponds, and mosses can make paths dangerously slippery, there are few reasons why the non-flowering plants should not have a place alongside flowering plants throughout the modern pagan garden, notably algae, lichens (symbiotic associations between algae and fungi), fungi, mosses, liverworts and ferns. Even the tiniest micro-organisms have a vital place in the garden, especially in the soil, where balanced communities of microfauna and microflora are as essential as the proportions of nutrients, organic content, minerals, water and air space.

Fruit and vegetables that are indigenous, or that have been bred from indigenous species, allow the most numerous opportunities to establish stable ecological conditions; just as farming animals is most successful when stock is descended from native species, or indeed is the native species itself. Farming of ostrich in Africa is an example. But if you import alien species or varieties, or if you grow vegetables and fruit bred just for size and taste, and therefore likely to have had protective features such as hard skin, prickles, unpleasant taste or odour bred out, then other local herbivores are going to enjoy them too, so preventative measures will be needed. If you want to keep a natural garden, these will have to be natural, that is to say, organic, methods, such as encouraging natural predators, using naturally occurring pesticides, planting plants which repel unwanted insects, and so on. Non-organic farmers and gardeners have much in common. They use chemicals to enhance growth and to kill so-called weeds and pests. Just as modern pagan attitudes to health involve a holistic approach, with as much self-healing as possible, so does the modern pagan approach to gardening and farming. A naturally balanced plot can adjust and heal itself when threatened or invaded, especially if populated by local species and local breeds, using appropriate local techniques, thereby standing up to local conditions and, in the case of farms, catering for the needs of local people.

The planning and occupation of a modern pagan garden

The process of balancing the management and natural occupation of your garden, so that it is as inviting an extension of the local countryside as possible, will require planning, on account of the small scale of the project. Just leaving the garden to run, or remain, wild will not enable you to have a small, varied, multi-purpose plot, because a few rampant species may swamp it. In any case, the process of ecological management is valuable in that it encourages the feeling of stewardship rather than the potential problems of ownership.

You will need to know what soil types, flora and fauna are typical of your area and what microclimates – for example, dry, damp, sunny, shady, windy, sheltered, etc – you have or can create to accommodate wildlife that will thrive. Make a detailed plan of the existing plot, with compass bearings, contours, prevailing winds, movement of the sun, soil types and pH, and microclimates. Your plans will be all the better if you study the local wildlife, with the aid of the local knowledge of elders, and of local libraries and naturalists, to understand what habitats would be colonised and be a useful part of a garden in your locality. If you are creating a rocky area to match the local countryside, try to get hold of local stone and use this throughout, for it will have the properties like porosity that local rock plants require to thrive.

Knowing your garden's microclimates, and those you plan to create, you can then plan a viable layout for extending the countryside into them. If any rare plants and animals are characteristic of your area, try to find a place for the plants, if you can obtain them, and a habitat suitable for the animals. On no account transplant from the wild as this may be illegal for protected species and is undesirable for the others because of the likelihood they will die. Natural colonisation ensures that those species suited to the prevailing conditions will establish on your plot. As more and more land is used for building it behoves us to let our gardens provide a refuge for what has been displaced, and at the same time to create a place of education and interest, teaching us how to produce food, save energy and recycle. Perhaps the most important benefit is that of bringing us and our senses closer to nature.

Wild gardens and farms can form valuable links and migratory passages between patches of countryside isolated by urban and industrial development and its infrastructure of roads and railways, so plant as many trees as your plot can support, consistent with your microclimate plans. Creating isolated nature reserves is not sufficient action to save our biodiversity and the habitats it needs, whereas gardens and farms constitute a huge rural resource of links that could serve this purpose. It will take some time for modern pagan farming philosophy to be implemented widely, but the modern pagan garden can be functional in a year or two with proper planning and dedication. If you can get together with neighbours, or better, work on a community scale, then the result may become very significant in giving a boost to wildlife populations and bringing the countryside to everyone's doorstep.

Wild flowers are not as spectacular as modern cultivars and introduced varieties, as their design is for the attraction of pollinators, not us, but in gardens they can play a vital part in augmenting diminished or polluted wild habitats by providing what these threatened areas have lost, namely breeding and feeding areas. Typical of native species, they usually need minimum maintenance, and certainly no chemical treatments, require little or no acclimatisation, and will spread by natural propagation and attract creatures dependent upon them. The way one habitat merges into another in the wild garden has to be carefully thought out and landscaped, but there will be no problem areas in the long term as there are native species for all conditions. In such a wild garden Mother Nature is the manager, the gardener initiating checks and balances necessary because of the scale and scope of the plot size available. If you wish to grow food, then more, but still sensitive, intervention will be required because of the unnatural population size food plots are expected to serve.

Maintenance of a wild garden, when necessary, is straightforward. After seeds have set, scythe and remove hay when dry. In woodland areas leave fallen leaves, twigs and branches to rot naturally and provide homes for fungi and other colonisers of dead wood. If you adopt careful seasonal patterns of maintenance and are not fastidiously tidy about removing the likes of tangled undergrowth and windfalls, you will get a greater range of small mammals, reptiles, amphibians, birds and invertebrates. Hedges may need thinning and trimming periodically. Alternatively, if you wish to have a purely natural plot, you can dispense with maintenance and let colonisation, succession and competition determine the final appearance and range of inhabitants. If small it won't be greatly biodiverse, but it can be immensely satisfying to see, be in, and feel responsible for.

Your modern pagan garden can be a life-long project, with self-maintenance and minimal intervention. Forget what commercial concerns or television gardening programmes say gardens should be like, as their aim is largely to perpetuate and expand upon existing unnatural design and practice, in which they have vested interests. Of course, if you choose to have herb-, vegetable- and fruit-growing areas these will need regular attention, but wild areas of the garden can be ruined by digging, which never happens in the wild, and by liberal use of manure or compost, or by other methods of 'improvement'.

Access to the garden

Consider how people are going to walk through the garden as well as what areas you want and where they are best created. Modern pagan garden design should emphasise naturalness and informality, with secluded areas for quiet contemplation, somewhere for the family to sit together and eat, and areas for wildlife to adopt. Secluded areas also allow ecological themes to be used in their planting, and can arise naturally in garden design if meandering paths and screening shrubbery or arbours are used. A Celtic knotwork design gives scope for both seclusion and interconnectedness, using walkways with pergolas, archways, and climbing plants. Sensitive colour grouping can help you connect with the beauty and sublimity of colour. There is much to be said, therefore, for arranging your microclimates, subject to specifically required conditions being present, around traditional Celtic designs, or a traditional Celtic knotwork pattern or series of patterns, as they can be adapted flexibly to your plot. Also, the use of such a design for the vegetable plot will allow for the inclusion of plenty of paths so that the plants can be tended and observed more easily by children. Designs should be used only where these would enhance the character of the garden – for example, in formal or tended areas – as there would be good reasons for not employing any design features where the intention was to establish as natural a look as possible.

Knot pattern garden designs are known to have been used as long ago as the fifteenth century, the design being in the form of low hedging of box or yew, sometimes cotton lavender or rosemary. The pattern of plots was used for herbs and for bedding plants. Knotwork designs can provide scope for almost any shape garden, or for areas within a garden, with shapes which are linear, circular, elliptical, polygonal, corner, torus, or more complex in perimeter. Within or without one can incorporate other designs. The lemniscate, like Charles Darwin's sandwalk at Downe House, in the village of Downe in Kent, England, is a symbol representing infinity as well as the cyclical continuity of natural events. This could be used as an envelope within which other shapes could be employed. The spiral symbolises the inexorable march of time, and the triskele embodies the ancient belief in the magical properties of the number three, and the evolving radiation of life. Both can emanate from a central, quiet refuge or around a specimen tree or important plot, perhaps delineated by fruit or hedging. The triquetra has been widely adopted as a representation of the ancient triple aspect of natural personifications; of life, death and rebirth; and, through its resemblance to an interlocking triple mandorla, of the three stages of womanhood – virgin, mother and crone. The mandorla is an almond-shaped symbol denoting female fertility, and if a triple interlocking mandorla is overlaid by a circle then a triquetra is produced. A triquetra-shaped bed would make for easy access to plots via the paths, and would therefore be suitable for a rockery, vegetables – if you don't want to disperse them – or herbs. A monthly rotation of herbs could be established in a twelve-spoked wheel design, whose thirty degree sectors could also be used for establishing colour groups. Rather than have a garden entirely within the boundaries of traditional designs, a mixture of design and informal merging of natural microclimate areas can be very attractive.

When choosing materials for your access paths, consider natural ones like earth, stone chips or pieces, gravel, flint, pebbles or cobblestones. If you have a particular reason to use brick, to maintain historical precedent, for example, then you may like to research traditional patterns like Spanish bond, running bond and diagonal herringbone. Edging, steps and terracing could be of timber or stone, and fill all gaps in paths with plants such as creeping thyme and chamomile. Where boundaries or screening are to be sited, consider the merits of hedging rather than walls or fences, for a mixed species hedge is a habitat in its own right. Laying a quickthorn hedge can be learned quite quickly, and it will soon teem with life.

Nutrient/energy cycles in the garden

This is an aspect that cannot safely be left to chance in a small plot, and will have to be considered and planned in connection with your garden's microclimates, their elemental requirements, and your gardening activity. Avoid buying unnecessary items for the garden, as it is a natural place, not a junkyard for garden centre purchases you don't really need, and which don't enhance the natural scene. Not only kitchen and garden organic waste can be composted and reused, but newspaper and cardboard too as mulch. Reduce energy consumption in the garden by using hand tools instead of power tools. You can eliminate mowing and the use of petrol by eliminating grass and planting a wild-flower meadow instead. Both for house and garden look to employ eco-friendly materials, cleaning agents, and preservatives such as wood treatments.

Try to map the water flow on to and within your garden and plan to store what water you can catch from roofs into water butts, and divert from potentially waterlogged areas to dry areas, unless you are creating a bog garden. Attending initially to matters that can lead to erosion, leaching and poor drainage will reduce difficulties later. Water from household usage such as washing, cooking and cleaning can be utilised in the garden through filtering and irrigation. Mulching and planted under-growth help to conserve water by reducing evaporation.

The managed areas of the modern pagan garden

The fruit, vegetable and herb areas of the garden will inevitably be managed to some degree, and this management, if it is to conform to the notion of establishing as far as possible an ecologically balanced zone, should be strictly using what has come to be generally known as organic gardening. The modern pagan gardener uses wholly organic methods in all intervention gardening, that is to say, in all processes that depart from the sustaining of a natural extension of the countryside.

Growing your own food in as natural a way as possible saves you money, but to modern pagans this is the least significant reason for doing it. Fresh food is tastier, healthier and more convenient, and reduces the demand on agricultural land and the environmental impact of intensive food production. It is also great fun, and a satisfying and educational experience for children. You don't have to have a dedicated orchard or vegetable plot, for dispersal of fruit and vegetables in the garden helps to keep unwanted insects down and allows for interesting ways of integration. Yields may be lower, but this is a relatively small price to pay for quality in produce and experience. Mixed planting encourages the family to regard nature's bounty as just one part of the whole and to regard vegetables and fruit as plants in their own right and not just dispensable and utilitarian.

The most important organic task is to feed the soil, not the plants. A loamy soil rich in humus (organic material), minerals, micro-organisms and other natural soil life retains moisture and texture well, and is all a plant needs as a growing medium. The modern pagan gardener's job is to maintain this state or assist the soil to return to it after each growth cycle or other period of stress. By using natural methods of regeneration, ecological stress on the adjoining wild garden is minimised, and by ensuring biodiversity, a garden will have plenty of food chains and not be susceptible to pestilence. Good husbandry can keep disease in proportion and under control, and crop rotation helps recharge soil fertility and reduces concentrations of, and resistance in, unwanted herbivorous insects.

There is both an ecological and a moral dimension to modern pagan gardening, as will be illustrated by a few examples. Please avoid accepting plants that have been extracted from the wild or otherwise started in unnatural conditions, although success is likely to be limited anyway. Also consider not purchasing peat and other materials from non-renewable sources. Aim to make your modern pagan garden chemical-free as far as possible. The quick way to fertilisation is to use chemicals from a bag that dissolve and provide aqueous nutrients directly to roots, but this is not to be recommended for natural gardening. Using organic fertilisers such as bone meal, fishmeal, dried blood, and animal manure from farms or stables, is a better approach, but it is even better to recycle from your own garden's productivity. In general please avoid all synthetic fertilisers, herbicides, fungicides, and insecticides, and learn how to use cunning, traditional practices and natural methods. Good organic husbandry also involves choosing what plants or varieties are suited to your prevailing soil and external conditions. If you also practise good garden hygiene and promote air circulation on your managed plot, you will forestall potential imbalances that can help disease or unwanted attention from insect competitors.

By composting garden and household waste and recycling around the garden where beneficial, you will get plenty of humus into the soil. Any extra suitable animal or plant source can be used, including leaf mould, seaweed, farmyard manure, and even your own excrement. You don't normally dig it in, that's what worms are for. Put on top as a mulch, the material helps with moisture retention and actually encourages worm activity. As the texture of the soil improves, natural drainage is promoted. Mulching also controls wild annuals that might take over a bed.

Techniques commonly employed in the organic garden to use soil efficiently include staggering planting to get cropping over a longer period; catch-cropping by planting quick-growing crops, such as lettuce, radishes and baby turnips, to fill space temporarily while slow-growing ones develop; underplanting of large with small crops; and companion planting when one plant is known to assist another mutually by providing nutrients, reduced susceptibility to attack, or other important conditions. For example, peas and beans do worse next to onions than on their own, but do better next to sweetcorn.

Change your attitude to 'pests' and 'weeds'
A relaxed approach is needed for the wildlife garden. Coping well with 'pests', if indeed they really are, depends principally

on a change of attitude on the part of the gardener. After observing basic principles of garden hygiene, and siting and planting so as to make the best use of natural air circulation (stagnant air being a favoured condition for mildews and botrytis), you may on your managed plots still get problems with invertebrate competitors, especially insects. Of course, if you site a plant that is susceptible to mildew against a warm west-facing wall you have only yourself to blame, so it ought to be moved. Keep fungal complaints down by keeping soil and plants healthy, rotate crops and clear litter and lower leaves to encourage air circulation. A pest is what non-pagans call a natural competitor, but it is just a herbivore that you don't happen to want. Pesticides break vital food chains by killing pollinators and predators as well as prey, so avoid them if at all possible. There are both plants and animals which you can draft in, as well as a range of other tried and tested strategies. Encourage natural predators, and there will be indigenous plants that are favoured by predatory or parasitic insects, so grow them near vulnerable plants and allow them to flower. Changing seasons is a sly dodge, as Winter-sown broad beans, for example, are unlikely to get blackfly.

Crawling ground predators like slugs and snails dislike gravel or other sharp surfaces. Cosy traps of straw in flower pots on stakes, or barriers such as sacking or corrugated cardboard round fruit trees to trap codling moth grubs and weevils work well, as do grease bands to trap climbing insects. Some plants contain natural repellents, and some have insecticidal sap. Odour or other natural chemical barriers are very effective in companion planting. Interplanted carrots and onions mask the odour of each other's predators, or you can use mothballs to stop carrot fly homing in on the odour of bruised seedlings after thinning out. Peas coated in paraffin won't be located and dug up by mice, and paraffin on onion sets stops onion fly detecting them. A piece of rhubarb at the bottom of each planting hole for brassica seedlings, or watering with rhubarb water, controls club root. The odour of mint keeps white fly away from beans, and nasturtiums are known to repel several insects. The scent of several other perennial herbs deters pests – notably chives, hyssop, lavender, rosemary, sage, southernwood and thyme.

French marigolds discourage white fly and nematodes, possibly by a root exudate being taken up by neighbouring plants, such as tomatoes. Other plants with similar effects are golden feverfew and members of the daisy family, the latter also being sacrificial in that they attract black fly. Alliums like garlic and chives, and also nettles, keep fungal and bacterial diseases down.

You can actually lure many insects away by providing alternative, more tempting, plants ('scapegoat' or 'sacrificial' plants) in the vicinity for them to feast upon. Sweet tobacco, *Nicotiana sylvestris*, attracts white fly and thrips, which are trapped in its sticky leaves and stems. Aphids will prefer fox-gloves, lupins, honeysuckles and nettles to vegetables, and black fly love marguerites.

Take steps to encourage a number of hard-working voracious predators to your garden. If you have a wild part to your garden then they will probably already be there, but if not then your managed area can be made more inviting to them. Plants with seedy heads, like sunflowers, and redcurrants and cherries as sacrificial plants will attract birds. Any snails present will automatically attract song thrushes, and good cover will ensure the presence of hedgehogs in rural locations. Amphibians are also valuable predators if you have a pond. Interplant species known to attract ladybirds, hoverflies, centipedes (soil carnivores that also love slug's eggs), predatory wasps, and lacewings. Many of these plants are also favoured by good pollinators such as bees, butterflies and beetles. Butterflies seem to favour red, orange or yellow flowers, whereas bees prefer blue or white flowers. Yarrow, *Achillea millefolium*, is the top predator attractor, but also good are alliums, *Anthemis* species, *Convolvulus tricolour*, cosmos, fennel, *Foeniculum vulgare*, goldenrod, *Solidago* species, *Limnanthus douglasii* (beloved by hoverflies), and marigolds. Good butterfly and bee plants are Buddleia davidii, goldenrod, honeysuckles, lavenders, lilac, marjoram, *Sedum spectabile*, valerian, and violas.

As a desperate measure against caterpillars, black or green fly, you can safely use the natural insecticides Derris and Pyrethrum, which don't leave harmful residues and don't harm non-insects. If all fails with slugs, remember that they love beer even more than your vegetables.

'Weeds' too are just natural inhabitants you don't want in a certain place. You can't blame vigorous plants for colonising soil that you have made ideal for them by clearing and fertilising a patch of land, so if you don't want them, don't cultivate or artificially fertilise. Plant competitors are tough and well adapted, whereas cultivars are artificially selected for taste and productivity rather than hardiness and natural immunity. Soil texture and drainage can be improved by natural means if desired, allowing a natural equilibrium to establish afterwards. Using organic means, you can provide encouragement for sensitive, choice species and discouragement for the invasive go-getters. Ground cover plants and mulching inhibit competitor growth.

Remember the old adage, 'One year's seeding, seven years' weeding'. Cultivating ground allows competitive annuals to dominate at the expense of other plants, so the annuals should be hoed or pulled within two weeks or they will seriously compete with seedlings. You may have to remove successful perennials, especially rampant, invasive ones such as those with creeping roots, as these can swamp a small area, but do it selectively. Perennials often have deep roots, and some will grow from just a piece of root left in the soil. They are best dug up completely before planting other plants. Make use of vigorous plants by composting, digging in as green manure, or leaving them to enjoy and as food plants for butterflies and moths, some species of which are becoming very rare as intensive agriculture kills or shuts out their hosts.

Far from being the nuisance they are labelled as, some so-called weeds are positively beneficial in some circumstances, especially on otherwise vacant plots. Those that fix or accumulate essential elements include clovers and vetches that fix nitrogen; comfrey, nettles and thistles that accumulate potassium; and fat hen, sorrel, thornapple and yarrow that accumulate phosphorus. When their work is done they can be turned in as green manures, and they also make good mulches. Other green manure plants for the organic garden are lucerne (alfalfa), peas and beans, buckwheat, trefoil, chicory, fenugreek, grazing rye, lupins, mustard and Winter tares.

Some plants are simply amazing. The marigold *Tagetes minuta* not only kills eelworm, but controls ground elder and bindweed, suppresses couch grass and spear grass, and can then be composted or turned in as green manure! And not a chemical in sight.

The tool shed

This structure is more than a store to a modern pagan: it is a personal space in which to plan and reflect, and the choice of tools and other accoutrements within is very revealing. The construction of a traditional shed has a witchguard, a diamond-shaped piece of rowan nailed at the roof apex. Using iron nails to secure it also keeps malicious faeries at bay, as does a horseshoe nailed with iron above the entrance, points upwards. Once on your land a horseshoe will lose its powers to bring luck and give protection if it touches the ground. Complete the construction with a weather vane, and inspect it every day to improve your understanding of local weather.

Many garden and farm tools are essentially unchanged in design for centuries, only their quality falling with manufacturing standards, because they work and do the same jobs. Being traditionally minded, modern pagans will want to use the oldest hand-me-downs they can get their hands on, with good forged metalwork and natural, replaceable hardwood handles. Once you have got used to the feel of those handles, the balance of the whole tool, and learned how easy they are to use as soon as you learn to balance the body and use its weight upon or behind the tool, you will not be satisfied with currently manufactured tools. Clean and maintain your tools after use, oiling metal joints and sharpening blades and points as necessary with a grindstone.

Seek out as many items as possible made from natural materials in the traditional way, like besom brooms, wooden rakes and terracotta flower pots. The latter drain more efficiently than plastic ones, and being porous are less prone to water-logging and lack of air circulation. Plants in them will need watering more often, but they look as though they belong in them and show it as they grow.

When you are sitting in the tool shed planning your organic strategies, resolve to grow as much as possible from seed, nature's way, so that you can get the most healthy, vigorous plants. Save your own seeds whenever circumstances allow, and don't buy another plant if you can propagate existing stock, sexually or asexually as appropriate.

Before you lock up for the night, strew mint, cotton lavender and hyssop on the floor, for a delightful herbal ambience, or southernwood to keep unwanted insects at bay if you have stored any seed, fruit or vegetables in there.

Wild plants and wild animals in the garden

Once the wild character of your garden is firmly established it will begin to attract both diurnal and nocturnal visitors. It is then that your planning of habitats will pay dividends. Wild gardens offer all the opportunities the gardener would want for colour, height, habit and shape variation, once you know the soil and weather conditions. The types of habitat to be incorporated will depend upon prevailing local conditions, but opportunities to exploit light and shade, damp and dry conditions, exposure or cover, grading by height, and a range of ambient temperatures and nutrient sources, are very widespread. If the opportunities are there for you, they are there for wild creatures as well. Take care when maintenance is necessary to leave unmolested plants and animals that are in the process of reproduction, so that nests, dens and the setting and dispersal of seeds, are not disturbed.

Banks, rocky beds and dry stone walls offer numerous opportunities for habitat distinctions involving light and shade, different soil depths and pHs, and plant height and habit variation. Hedges and shrubberies will soon be alive with occupants if you resist the temptation to clip and clear. By including flowering, evergreen, nutting and berrying shrubs, and allowing fallen leaves and fruit to remain and rot, food chains will establish that include a range of invertebrates. These in turn will attract visiting birds, rodents, insectivores, reptiles and amphibians. Berried native plants that attract birds include crab apple, dogwood (*Cornus sanguinea*), elder, evening primrose (*Oenothera biennis*), the gean or wild cherry, the guelder rose (*Viburnum opulus*), holly, honeysuckle, rowan, the spindle tree (*Euonymus europaeus*), and yew. Deliberately placed compost heaps and piles of wood, and leaving windfalls, dead and fallen trees, encourages fungi and provides places for hibernation or shelter.

Your pagan credentials will be tested when the visitors to your plot decide to investigate the potential of your house as a source of food, cover or nesting places. By being as accommodating as you can, without compromising internal standards of hygiene, you will be giving your family a unique opportunity to observe wildlife at close quarters, and to learn that very few represent any sort of threat. You will also be helping beleaguered species to breed successfully and rear their young safely.

Woodland areas, if you have sufficient space, give dry shade for plants and bulbs liking these conditions and light in Spring. Woodland conditions are favoured by terrestrial orchids, if the patch is undisturbed. Leaving mature trees provides homes for a variety of wildlife, and not being too fastidious about clearing away dead or fallen trees provides in the former case perches for raptors, allows opportunities for woodpeckers to visit the garden and for a greater variety of invertebrates and fungi to establish. Don't collect all the windfall fruit from orchards but leave them for a while as a meal for birds, small mammals and insects. The more native trees and wildflowers are planted the greater the range of invertebrates and vertebrates that will find your garden a haven.

Set aside damp or shady places – don't drain or clear them – as they are ideal for planting ferns, mosses and liverworts, and letting them, and lichens, grow naturally. Many non-flowering plants are particularly attractive, with both subtle and spectacular differences of colour and form, especially if used with natural wood and rock in sculptural arrangements. Such diversity is often overlooked in managed gardens, especially when lopping and pruning allows unwanted light and heat and vigorous sun-loving invaders. It is important for the whole family to appreciate that their garden's non-flowering plants, and indeed the microfauna generally, have an ecological place and function no less significant than their showy, spectacular flowering cousins, and are certainly no less beautiful in form when the observer takes the trouble to look closely.

Think about nesting sites and roosting areas for birds when selecting the hedging and mature trees, provide nesting boxes, bird tables, feeders, baths so they can clean their feathers, and berries, and leave seed heads and windfalls. Feeding birds and small mammals in the garden is a delicate issue for modern pagans. A bird table is indeed a good way to attract birds, and often rodents as well, to the garden, but the food given should be their natural food as far as possible, not kitchen or table scraps. Dependence on bird table food, except in the most severe winter, is not advisable for the health of the bird population. It is better to plant so that the birds and other visitors can feed themselves, particularly trees and shrubs with berries, and those that have abundant seeds. If you do not fastidiously remove the parts of plants that naturally fall or die back when their purpose is fulfilled, birds and small mammals can use them as nesting materials.

Bat boxes or other artificial refuges are desperately needed for endangered bats in many countries, but if you have hollow trees or outbuildings they may attract bats for Winter hibernation and roosting during the day. Bats get a bad press in world folk lore, but in truth they are interesting, inoffensive creatures, many of which have a voracious appetite for flying insects. It is a joy to watch their aerial antics on a warm summer evening, but when they are roosting please do not touch or otherwise disturb them. The people who learn to love bats, or any of the other animals much vilified by handed-down ignorance, and who persuade their children to do likewise, have crossed a vital bridge of understanding by rejecting the supersition and irrational fear that the likes of vampire myths perpetuate.

A pond, a small stream and a natural marshy area help to ensure balance of local wetland habitats, and this provision is especially welcome where local ponds and water courses have disappeared. Wetland seed mixtures can be bought for poorly drained areas. Garden ponds are popular breeding places for amphibians, dragonflies, damselflies and many more species, and provide biodiversity in the garden. Birds and small mammals may be seen drinking from it and bathing in it, and you could also provide a birdbath for this purpose. A pool with a proper pump and filtration system is a better habitat than a still pool liable to stagnate, and building a cascade gives the soothing sound of running water, provided neighbours do not regard the sound as intrusive. Newts are friends of the gardener when out of the pond, feeding on insects, although they do take worms. In sharply seasonal climes, they spend the Winter in damp terrestrial hideaways. Frogs eat insects, slugs and worms, and they too over-winter in damp holes or hideaways. Toads are even more voracious nocturnal feeders, on flies, snails, worms, woodlice, caterpillars and various insects. They spend the day in dark nooks, some scooping out hollows under roots or stones. Without such niches in the modern pagan garden the value of the pond will be lessened. Children can become very fond of amphibians, because they present what is perceived to be a purposeful and adept, yet non-aggressive, character, but for these qualities to rub off the modern pagan parents must provide and be tolerant of the damp, dark conditions amphibians need.

Butterflies, moths, bees and other interesting insects may easily be attracted to the garden. Butterfly and moth populations throughout the world have fallen in recent years, but this is not always to do with a decline in the distribution of their food plants, which are often very specific, for the latter in many cases are still abundant. Nevertheless, if you can provide a good patch of a specific food plant, whose details appear below for British butterflies and some of the larger moths, you may be rewarded with breeding success. In addition, plants whose flowers produce abundant scent and nectar will serve to attract butterflies and moths to your patches of food plants, and once all are established you should have the annual pleasure of their graceful, colourful presence. Night-flying moths and other nocturnal insects can be attracted by night-scented plants. Bees are also drawn to many of the plants that are favoured by butterflies and their value as pollinators scarcely needs emphasising.

Because of the parlous breeding state of many British butterflies, and some of our larger moths, the introduction of their natural food plants into gardens has taken on an imperative not foreseen fifty years ago. To this end, the following comprehensive list is provided. You should enquire first at your local wildlife conservation organisation which species are likely to be found in your area.

Food plant (most important in italics)	Butterflies
Milkweed	Milkweed butterfly
Couch grass and cock's foot grass	Speckled Wood, Wall, Gatekeeper, Ringlet
Mat grass (bog plant)	Small Mountain Ringlet
Blue moor grass	Scotch Argus
Sheep's fescue, cock's foot grass, cat's tail grass	Marbled White
Various grasses	Grayling, Meadow Brown, Small Heath
Beak sedge and various grasses	Large Heath
Dog violet	Small Pearl-bordered Fritillary, Dark Green Fritillary, Silver-washed Fritillary
Dog violet and sweet violet	High Brown Fritillary
Devil's bit scabious, other scabious, honeysuckle	Marsh Fritillary
Narrow-leaved plantain	Glanville Fritillary
Cow-wheat, also foxglove, plantain, woodsage	Heath Fritillary
Stinging nettle	Red Admiral, Small Tortoiseshell, Peacock
Thistle, mallow, burdock, stinging nettle	Painted Lady
Elm, willow, sallow, aspen, poplar, cherry	Large Tortoiseshell
Sallow, willow, birch, elm	Camberwell Beauty
Hop, stinging nettle, currant, gooseberry, elm	Comma
Sallow	Purple Emperor
Honeysuckle	White Admiral
Cowslip	Duke of Burgundy Fritillary
Pea family, especially peas and lupins	Long-tailed Blue
Kidney vetch	Small Blue
Bird's foot trefoil	Short-tailed Blue
Gorse, bird's foot trefoil	Silver-studded Blue

Rock rose	Brown Argus
Bird's foot trefoil, rest harrow	Common Blue
Horseshoe vetch	Chalkhill Blue, Adonis Blue
Thrift, kidney vetch, clover, melilot	Mazarine Blue
Wild thyme	Large Blue
Holly, dogwood, buckthorn	Holly Blue
Dock, sorrel	Small Copper
Great water dock	Large Copper
Dyer's greenwood, needle furze, broom, Whortleberry, and berries of buckthorn, and buds of bramble and dogwood	Green Hairstreak
Blackthorn, plum, oak	Brown Hairstreak
Oak, aspen, bramble	Purple Hairstreak
Wych elm, common elm, bramble	White-letter Hairstreak
Blackthorn, damson	Black-veined White
Brassicas	Large White
Brassicas, mignonette, nasturtiums	Small White
Hedge garlic, mignonette, watercress	Green-veined White
Wild mignonette	Bath White
Hedge mustard, cuckoo-flower	Orange Tip
Buckthorn, alder	Brimstone
Milk parsley, angelica, fennel, wild carrot	Swallow-Tail
Clover, lucerne, bird's foot trefoil, melilot	Clouded Yellow, Pale Clouded Yellow
Hippocrepis	New Clouded Yellow
Bird's foot trefoil	Dingy Skipper
Wild strawberry	Grizzled Skipper
Brome grass	Chequered Skipper
Soft grasses	Small Skipper
Couch grass and other coarse grasses	Essex Skipper
False brome grass, couch grass	Lulworth Skipper
Hair grass	Silver-spotted Skipper
Cock's foot grass	Large Skipper

Food plant (most important in italics)	Large Moths
Lime, elm	Lime Hawk Moth
Poplars, sallow, willow	Poplar Hawk Moth
Sallow, willow, poplar, apple	Eyed Hawk Moth
Potato, Duke of Argyl's Tea Rose	Death's Head Hawk Moth
Large convolvulus	Convolvulus Hawk Moth
Privet, lilac, ash	Privet Hawk Moth
Pines	Pine Hawk Moth
Euphorbia paralias	Spurge Hawk Moth
Bedstraw	Bedstraw Hawk Moth
Grape vine, fuchsias, dock, bedstraw, antirrhinum	Striped Hawk Moth
Grape vine, common yellow bedstraw	Silver-striped Hawk Moth
Oleander, lesser periwinkle	Oleander Hawk Moth
Greater willow herb, other willow herbs, fuchsia, evening primrose, Virginia creeper, bedstraw	Large Elephant Hawk
Bedstraw	Small Elephant Hawk
Honeysuckle	Bee Hawk Moths

A sensual place for all generations

Gardening in all its aspects is an ideal activity for the whole family, who may thereby come to regard the garden as an extension of their living space. Use the garden freely, sit in it regularly, eat there and carry on as much daily discourse there as possible, but please don't make unnecessary noise if you have neighbours. Avoid especially playing music or other artificial sounds, or hanging up wind chimes, as this not only disturbs the neighbours but also conversation, meditation and the natural orchestra of sounds that makes the outdoor aspects of life so appealing.

It is glorious to experience dawn and dusk throughout the year and to relate to the light changes and seasonal variations in the sky and garden. Recording the first appearances of birds, butterflies, buds, flowers and berries can form part of a garden chronicle from year to year. If your sky is free from light pollution, the garden is also an ideal astronomical observatory, and you may like to site a sundial and an astrolabe. A deckchair at its lowest position will provide a comfortable viewing seat.

The more the whole family uses the garden and senses nature's cyclical ways the more you will all feel a part of it, and that is an essential step to take in healing yourselves of the deprivation caused by life in our concrete jungles and denuded rural wastelands. Here in the garden a child can experience influential aspects of upbringing, and the whole family can learn to appreciate the complexity, diversity and beauty of nature and the interdependence of humankind and environment.

When you walk through the garden try and get used to keeping all your senses alert, not just your eyes and ears, for no two days will be alike in terms of temperature, humidity, air currents, surface textures, odours and tastes. This is a sensual world, which young and old alike can soon feel a part of, whatever their individual sensory capacity or mobility. A child needs little encouragement, but the whole family might take the trouble, to look in every nook and cranny; to feel the textures and surfaces; to smell the scents, both fragrant and pungent; to taste, but with care and guidance; and to hear the sounds from every quarter. Plants with textured surfaces to their leaves are worth growing just so that they can be touched, as are trees with interesting barks. The range of odours in the garden is enormous, and all of us can occupy hours seeking them out. You may like to extend the odoriferous experience to the evenings and early night by planting Night-scented Stocks (*Matthiola* species), which also attract moths. But please avoid referring to the odour of, say, a compost heap as unpleasant or offensive, for it is just one of many characteristic natural odours. In countries where there are distinct seasonal changes, any garden is a seasonal feast for the eyes through the courtesy of snowflakes, frosted stems, dewy spiders' webs, Autumn colours and Spring blossom.

Many features of gardens specially planted for blind people are worthwhile in everyone's garden. You can ensure that at every time of the year there are fragrant blooms open, and a selection of plants with aromatic leaves and stems, some only emitting scent when rubbed. Low-growing species, some of which are fragrant, can serve as a grass-free lawn. Some species give off an aromatic odour after rain, while others scent the air in the evening only.

If you have one or more family members with mobility impairment, your garden design can, in a straightforward way, be adapted for them to enjoy and work in, and even provide a special area for them to tend. You may need wide, firm paths for wheelchair access and raised beds so that tasks can be done from the wheelchair. You may choose to avoid steps altogether, but certainly you can provide ramps and handrails for negotiation of any slopes between the reserved area and the house. Such an area can provide like the rest of the garden for the use of all senses, including particularly touch, smell and hearing. Smaller, lighter tools may be needed. It is most important that the disabled are no more excluded from the garden than from household routines and pleasures, for they are family, and the modern pagan garden is a family space, not the preserve of the able-bodied.

Nature's child in the garden

The garden is one of the first places that a baby meets his or her fellow living inhabitants of the planet, their variety of forms, habits and behaviour, and it is important for its upbringing that the experience should be an interesting and pleasurable one on the one hand, and the start of a lifelong, mutually educational relationship on the other. Encourage them to enjoy the natural pleasures of the garden by getting them used to sitting quietly and patiently to watch and record, at different times of the day and night, throughout the year. If encouraged, a child will observe at the minutest level, for there is wildlife of all shapes and sizes, and respond eagerly to opportunities to photograph and video what is found. Respect for the smaller inhabitants is very important as it steers children away from the vision of wildlife conservation as simply emergency action to save large, spectacular animals and plants, essential though these are, to a recognition that all parts of an ecosystem or food chain have a valued place, to be understood and protected.

It is, therefore, most important to show children the small as well as the large and spectacular, the plain as well as the colourful, predator as well as prey, in order to emphasise objectively the importance of each in nature's community. Seek out the quiet, plain and well-camouflaged as well as the colourful and noisy, for there are equally important niches for them all. Search together for signs of animal activity like tracks, remains of meals, broken twigs or scratch marks, snagged hair, droppings, shed skin, cracked nutshells, etc. A good pair of binoculars is a worthwhile purchase for wildlife spotting and astronomy, but above all urge children to use their noses, ears, tongues and fingertips as well as their eyes. The parents who modify and manipulate nature excessively in their garden are demonstrating to the impressionable infant what is being done to nature at large, and unwittingly giving approval to that destructive process. But by welcoming Mother Nature to the garden and allowing her to claim it back, the modern pagan parents are sending a powerful, lasting message to the child that its natural environment begins at the doorstep, not in some remote wilderness halfway round the world that has miraculously survived intact.

Children are observant of, interested in, and careful and caring towards all the living things in a garden unless they have learned otherwise from adults. When talking to children, please avoid using words like weed, pest, creepy-crawly, bug (unless it really is of that family of insects), as this reinforces negative attitudes, and invites the mental construction of stereotypes and the development of irrational fears and prejudice. Calling a hippopotamus ugly or a snake slimy is the equivalent of grimacing when you feel mud, or gagging when you smell compost, and a child will thereby fail to appreciate that nature's designs are functional, not to please or displease our senses. Bees sting and their wings buzz, but unless you over-react to this fact, children will see them as the industrious, inoffensive insects they really are. By keeping still and watching them in action, children will readily accept both their presence and ecological value. Please also try to avoid making egocentric remarks like, 'Bees are put on this earth to make us honey', as our standing in the natural world is no 'higher' or 'lower' than theirs. A garden is a place for the whole family to feel comfortable in as ordinary citizens of the natural world, not to acquire feelings of arrogance as though you are rulers over it. We may use terms like 'animal kingdom' and 'plant kingdom' for taxonomic reasons, but as the Martian invaders in H. G. Wells's novel *The War of the Worlds* found, when they succumbed to microbial infection, he who would be king can get his come-uppance from very lowly, but very powerful, sources.

A garden full of animal haunts is a pleasure day and night, and gives scope for exploration at any time. Parents often unwittingly pass on fear of the denizens of the night to their children by their reactions to them and the words they use to refer to them. A garden with twenty-four hour activity allows children in particular to identify with, and feel part of, events at all times of the day and night, at all seasons of the year, and to respect animals with a nocturnal lifestyle. It is very exciting for them to experience the mysteries of the night, its odours, sounds, fleeting movements and eerie atmosphere. A night spent badger watching, nightjar and owl spotting, or admiring fungal and algal bioluminescence, whether by moonlight or in total darkness, brings a new dimension to a child's appreciation of the natural world. The inhabitants of the global garden are friends and companions, who battle against the elements like we do, are a comfort when a stressful period is being experienced, and a reassurance that in a technically progressive world the natural framework is still in place to cling to and cherish.

It is a worthwhile and endlessly absorbing routine, every morning and evening, for children to look at the moon, the rising and setting sun, clouds and other weather phenomena, as part of a life-long engagement with the environment and the development of environmental awareness. They can experience great calmness by gazing upwards and making shapes from the clouds or patterns from the stars, or by hearing stories composed with natural characters and features, cast in their ecological roles rather than in those which perpetuate old misunderstandings, fears and superstitions. Encourage children to plot the move-ments of sun and moon throughout the year, the phases of the moon, the positions of the planets, the zodiacal constellations on the ecliptic, and the other constellations and stellar structures. It may well be a voyage of discovery for you too, to learn with your children. Expressing humility means you will never be a fallen idol, and an interest in astronomy engenders a sense of humility like no other as you begin to appreciate the vastness and complexity of the Universe, and the relative insignificance of humankind within it.

Children love to take part in the whole cycle of planting to maturity, as it is a project with a beginning, an end, a purpose and environmental relevance, as well as being fun. They like to keep records of what they see and do in the garden and when, and recording the arrival of wildlife visitors reinforces their appreciation of the cycle of nature and their place in it. Comparisons year to year show how climatic cycles affect the pattern and how bird and other populations fluctuate. Growing plants common in folk tales, and encouraging animals so featured, adds further interest. There is also great enjoyment and value to be had from propagating and caring for growing plants, and looking after pets, all of which teaches children about the responsibility of the carer.

A wheel design with twelve monthly sectors makes a good patch for children to maintain, with plants coming into flower/fruit/leaf colour/etc successively in each sector, to emphasise the seasonal cycle. Such a design may also be used for children to tend their own herb and kitchen gardens, where they can begin to learn and appreciate the culinary and pharmaceutical properties of plants. But there is more in the garden that is edible or otherwise useful than just familiar fruit and vegetables, and it would be a fascinating quest for a child to undertake to rediscover local botanical knowledge, from the elderly, about the culinary and pharmaceutical properties of familiar plants. Introduced food plants may give better yields, but they are often alien to local conditions, suffer from disease and infestation, and do not pay for their keep by being a valuable component of the natural scene. Nevertheless, it is to be hoped that the use of the garden for growing vegetables, fruit and herbs, the latter emphasising the value of nature's storehouse of useful plants for cooking and herbal medicine, will be regarded by the children as a vital element of modern pagan family life. Involve your children in growing and saving rare varieties of fruit and vegetables, just as some livestock farmers are returning to rare local breeds, to preserve the gene pool of varieties bred in and suited to local conditions. It is ideally part of every modern pagan's upbringing to regard the natural world as the first port of call when a medicinal, restorative or dietary preparation is sought, assuming it is really necessary, as the more widely such practice is adopted the more progress will be made to arrest the physiological deterioration of the human species caused by the use of synthetic substitutes. You won't always find what you want, but you will often surprise yourself how extensive is nature's multi-purpose storehouse.

Gardens are very educational places for children, but also reserve an area for them to relax and play in, bordered of course by robust plants and screened off from water features. Ideally the play area should be visible from the house, quickly accessible and free from hazards or access to them.

Modifying a conventional garden

You don't really need to call in the bulldozers to turn a conventional garden into a wild garden as it can be done in stages once your initial planning has been completed and the overall design finalised. Wildlife is quite accommodating to non-native plants and you need only to use native species for all new planting as you move around the garden developing one microclimate at a time. Even on a limited budget and with limited time a big difference can be made by just adopting modern pagan gardening attitudes and techniques. A small suburban garden can be very productive as mainly a fruit, vegetable and herb garden with careful choice of varieties and selective interplanting, or as a wild garden with just a small number of microclimates. With imagination and resourcefulness any plot can be an extension of the countryside, but far more effective is the communal approach where neighbours pool their ground and thereby increase the scope and possible biodiversity. This does not have to progress to common ownership, as that would create legal problems when properties are bought and sold, but can engender the same degree of common pride that once characterised ownership of common land. Such a project can also counter the socially corrosive effect of people zealously protecting their patches and imagining they can do what they like on them with no regard for the consequences suffered by their neighbours.

If you have little interest in gardening and currently have an untended plot then with a modest expenditure of time, effort and money you can create a wildlife garden. A wildflower area can be set aside where plants can grow without tending, for example from collections of wildflower seeds, and this will attract seed-eating birds and butterflies, and provide cover for small animals – more effectively if you include a few native trees and bushes. A wildflower meadow only needs to be cut to a few centimetres from the ground after blooming and the shedding of the seeds. If you have a grass area then turn it into such a wildflower meadow, and naturalise native bulbs in it to give it colour and interest. A country hedge is a much more interesting place than one planted with only one species, and can be created by grubbing out and replacing with native species. Plant ferns and other non-flowering plants in damp areas, and disperse refuges and nest boxes around as recommended above. Stop digging and 'weeding', and very soon you will have a low-maintenance garden teeming with wildlife.

Communal parks, orchards and gardens

In many countries of the world it has become usual for town planning to include the reservation of plots of land for relaxation and recreation. Such parks and gardens are valued as green oases in deserts of concrete, asphalt and habitation, and rightly so. Often they are beautifully and expensively planted with ornamental trees, shrubs and bedding plants, and public money is spent manicuring them, apparently to ensure they are as little colonised by nature as possible. But the setting aside of large urban areas of land, especially if on the edges of towns, purely as leisure grounds is to miss a significant opportunity to create an ecologically more useful multi-purpose plot.

Instead of ornamental planting, the community would benefit more from the functional planting of useful species and varieties, so that people can sustainably pick and use the fruit, leaves, or whatever part serves their culinary, pharmaceutical, or other practical needs. And such species should be native, so that beleaguered local wildlife can share the plot, thereby bringing nature back into the community. The sight and usage of natural produce in garden and community, especially urban communities, are important steps in weaning people away from processed foods and the physiological damage they do. Once the decision to reinstitute communal planting is made, the choice of species and varieties makes itself, for the most suitable are always the locally bred indigenous varieties, many of which are now extremely rare, as are local breeds of farm animals. When the site is established, the community then has the opportunity to start eating a greater variety of fresh produce and making traditional foods like preserves, cordials, wines, and many more.

Worthwhile communal projects would include a physic garden for medicinal and culinary plants, an orchard, or a village pond. In small communities a communal orchard or physic garden would work well simply from the residents being involved in the upkeep and then reaping the rewards of harvesting on a shared basis when the produce is ready. In larger communities, to avoid a free-for-all, projects with output would probably have to be more tightly managed, perhaps on a commercial but minimal-profit basis. Whichever scheme is chosen, it is the attitudes engendered that are as environmentally and personally valuable as the attractions provided by the plots themselves. Such schemes are the embodiment of the modern pagan view that where there is green it should ideally be as biodiverse, and its care as mindful of the health and welfare of all inhabitants, as the scale allows.

Journeying in the countryside

Planning an expedition

Non-pagan children learn about the natural world; modern pagan children are brought up in it, so they know its moods and ways, its bounties and dangers, its pleasures and perplexities. To know the countryside and to feel a part of it, modern pagans and their children must spend time in it, starting with short, planned expeditions, properly equipped and with objectives, although the unexpected will always provide diversions. Just the planning stage is a very good activity for all to be involved in, for it might bring in skills like map-reading and route planning;

using a compass; reading and summarising other travellers' accounts; learning how to use keys to identify wildlife and tracks, and sketching what is found; drawing up an essential kit list and packing a rucksack; arranging stops, refreshment and transport if necessary; and making provision for any other contingencies. There is no shortage of good literature on preparing for and conducting an expedition, but there is relatively little published information on what may be seen and experienced, because most walkers in the countryside use only their eyes, and even then see only a fraction of what is there.

Try to allow time on the proposed itinerary to explore and take short diversions, for it is what is encountered on the way, not the destination, that is most important. Walking more than twelve miles, or cycling more than fifty miles, in a day will not allow much exploration. Progress will be impeded if the equipment list is too long, so travel light, but do include pencil and paper to record what you see. Above all, engage all of your senses and interpret and react to what they tell you. Respect the countryside and those who live and work in it, and be especially careful not to damage wild plants or crops, not to disturb wild animals, and to leave field gates as you find them.

Artistic skills can always be put to use when on a trip or engaging in an activity out of doors, especially drawing and photography. A record illustrated with sketches is a much more vivid aid to the memory. Making scrapbooks is an engaging hobby for all ages, or making a record throughout the year of your local environment, or of just one feature such as a pond, park or landscape through the seasons. Artistic skills learned in youth will give pleasure throughout adult life and be useful in all manner of ways, and sketching develops powers of observation like no other skill.

Ponds

Ponds are good places to learn basic principles of ecology, as they are small but largely self-contained ecosystems. Starting with a sketched plan of the pond, the depths and plants growing in each depth or zone can be plotted, from the marginals to those with floating leaves, and the totally submerged. By observation and use of a net at different depths you can then plot vertically the animal life and its feeding zones, from the surface skaters to the bottom and mud dwellers. Anything caught should be returned when it is identified. The basic idea of food chains can readily be appreciated from even a small pond. The populations of the pond will be seasonal, for example as larvae and spawn mature into adults and leave, so several visits in the year will be needed. By having their first lessons in ecology round a pond, children will learn to value a local ecosystem that is in danger of disappearing through land development, drainage for agriculture, and climate change in many countries.

Rivers

To get to know a river you need to do more than walk its banks, interesting though this is. You need to swim in it, row or sail on it, learn about its currents and eddies, its shallows and depths, and observe throughout the year from summer trickle to winter flood. Rivers cascading down from mountains have a different character to those meandering through flat, fertile soil, and the colour of the water says much about the landscape and soil over which they have passed and picked up material, whether it be peat, clay, sandstone, or, over chalk, virtually nothing. If you are lost, and the weather is fine and you come across a river, you would normally go downstream, as you would be more likely to come to a bigger river and eventually a settlement. By talking to boat builders and those who sail or paddle traditional craft on rivers you will learn a great deal about rivers and their associated environment, but if you use a net to catch and observe their aquatic wildlife remember to keep the bottom of the net in the water and to return quickly what you have caught. Fishing, hunting or shooting for sport, taking aquatic life home in jars, and the collecting of wildlife are not acceptable hobbies for modern pagans; neither is the use of motor vessels on waterways. Rivers need protection just like ponds, but only those who know and cherish them ever lobby on their behalf, and you may care to ensure that you and your family are amongst them.

The seashore

Similar ecological awareness can be gleaned from exploration of a sloping, rocky shore. The cycle of exposure after the ebb tide and submerging on the flow dictates the tidal zones and the adaptation of their populations. Tides advance higher and recede further at new and full moons, and are called spring tides, being greatest in March and September in the northern hemisphere. Between the spring tides are the neap tides, when ebb and flow are least, so shore life must adapt to this changing pattern of cover and exposure, being exposed to drying out or freezing twice a day. Shore creatures must tolerate fresh water – that is the rain – and seawater; relatively few aquatic creatures can survive in both, salmon and some eels being examples. Starting above the highest tide line and working towards the sea, the family will soon, with guidance, understand the different zones and identify the differences in populations of plants and animals such as crustaceans and molluscs, all adapted to different degrees of exposure and food supply. There are also depth zones in the sand, best explored by digging near the low-water level after careful exploration for signs on the surface of what might be below.

As with all wildlife explorations, collecting specimens should not be done, either of living or dead, for observation of organisms in captivity teaches very little about the natural world and can generate the sort of collection mania that caused the Victorians to devastate the world's wild places for specimens. Every seashell taken is one less home for a hermit crab or other vulnerable creature.

At the seaside the least interesting activities for modern pagans are the commercialised amusements. No-one with the ability to swim, and the inclination to explore, use the senses and learn, or a child with a bucket and spade, will be bored on a beach or rocky coast. When exploring the beach remember to replace any stones and rocks you turn over, as they may be essential protection for marine life. It is important for landlubbers to understand the tides, waves and currents and to appreciate the need for judgement, caution and respect for the power of the sea. Snorkelling is a good observational activity for a confident swimmer, and can graduate to further exploration by diving.

A good beach activity is kite flying, as it is an absorbing exercise in co-ordination and learning about atmospheric movements. This could lead later to an interest in gliding. For making kites – other than box kites – one or more spars will be needed, and these are traditionally made from birch. If making a bow kite the bow is normally made from spruce or bamboo. Use proper kite string for the bridle and tail, or cotton or thread, but not nylon as this is elastic and makes the kite difficult to control in blustery conditions. The fabric parts, and the knots on the tail, are traditionally cut from heavyweight model aeroplane tissue stuck down with balsa cement.

Seabird and cetacean spotting can be done all over the world and provide further experience in developing powers of observation and identification from a key. Simply beachcombing by walking along the high tide line is an interesting way to exercise and enjoy the variety of things found. The calm after a storm, when the tide is beginning to ebb, is good beachcombing time, especially in spots that have a strong back eddy, as objects will naturally accumulate there, sometimes in abundance if the wind is blowing on-shore.

Farms

Provided the practices thereon conform at least to organic and free-range principles, then farms are worthwhile places for modern pagans to visit with their children, being particularly worthwhile for those brought up in urban areas. Many city children do not actually know where meat, fruit and vegetables come from, apart from out of tins or plastic wrappers. Simply learning about farms from books achieves little in the way of communion with nature; they must see and experience farm life first-hand. The so-called 'dirty' jobs upon which farm management depends are good conditioning for a youngster used only to the relative sterility of an over-clean urban house, as is the opportunity to exert themselves and discover muscles they didn't know they had. Farmers often have to hire workers from developing countries abroad because local people do not want, or are physically unable, to manage the hard work required on farms.

Making the most of a journey

Never mind about listening to music through headphones; look and note. It is commonplace today for travellers to regard a journey as dull and something to be endured. They seek mindless pastimes rather than observation of what is around them and engagement with fellow travellers. Admittedly there is often little scope for observation for many air passengers, but from the deck of a ship or through the windows of a car, bus or train there is much to see and learn, more so if the journey is followed with a map. The design of groups of buildings, towns, road and rail systems, farms and landscapes is fascinating, but it can only be appreciated properly by travelling at a leisurely pace. Few young walkers observe their surroundings these days, preferring to drown their senses with loud music through earphones or to replay their urban social relationships. Bird spotting is an excellent travelling hobby, as is spotting breeds of dog, cat, and farm animals, and species of trees, shrubs and garden plants. Admiring architectural styles helps imbue a sense of history, as does inspecting ancient monuments and other old structures. The building materials of houses are related to the local geology and availability of timber, thatch, tiles, and so on, and the type of farming activity is similarly dependent on local conditions such as climate, soil type, and vegetation. Names of public houses, civic buildings, streets and indeed place names generally are full of local historical association. So much is there for those who choose to seek.

Spotting and tracking wildlife

Whether you live in an urban or rural area, spotting and tracking wildlife is one of the great pleasures of life, especially in childhood. Whatever type of habitat you are exploring try to ascertain what wildlife surrounds you by looking for evidence of its movements and activities. Look for tracks, for example in damp earth, holes where observation or discards might reveal the occupant, bitten leaves or twigs, flattened grass where an animal has rested, a change of odour in bark revealing a spot with a grub underneath, sounds of water creatures diving or surfacing, the twittering of birds in hedges and trees, and so on.

Identification of what is seen is the precursor to the absorbing study of ethology, the behaviour of living things in their natural environment. A child may develop a particular interest in one category of wildlife later in life, but initially you should introduce all types of animals and plants, and learn with the child as you identify them, for identification is an engaging scientific study, a supremely challenging, sensory and deductive exercise for all.

All sorts of evidence can be gathered – date and time of day; weather; appearance; behaviour and sociability; call; habitat and locality are some. Children are often more patient than adults. They are also acute observers and very honest with their claims and record-keeping. They quickly learn and apply photographic and video camera skills. Having their senses closer to the ground also helps, as they perceive what adults often miss.

Watching mammals is on the whole more difficult than watching birds, as the former have to be more cautious because they can't just fly out of danger. It is very good training to keep still and quiet, and wait patiently. Both diurnal and nocturnal expeditions should be undertaken in order to appreciate fully the ecological and environmental diversity of nature. Tracking mammals is a skill that comes easily to no-one, for you are in their domain, where they are supreme, but a start can be made by trying to ascertain if a suspected burrow is occupied. Are there footprints in the earth around, or claw marks in bark or earth? Has hair been snagged nearby, especially on prickly stems or trees used as rubbing posts? Are there droppings, and what do they contain? If you find tracks, decide on the direction they are going. Was the animal running or walking? How many were there, and how many adults and young? Soft earth, damp sandy soil and snow show up tracks best. Follow them cautiously to see what the animal was doing on its trip. Does it stop at all? Does it dig, scratch on trees or posts, or sharpen its claws? Is there evidence of feeding? The debris of a meal, like the feathers and remains of a bird, carcass of a mammal, nutshells, snail shells, nibbled pinecones, or bird pellets regurgitated by owls or raptors, is very helpful in identification. Bird pellets are useful in telling you what the bird of prey has fed on recently, as they can be prised apart to reveal indigestible parts like insect wings, feathers, fur, bones, claws and beaks.

Getting near to wild animals by stalking is a complementary skill to tracking. Make sure the wind is blowing towards you so that your scent won't be detected, and learn to walk quietly and to use cover effectively. To stalk an animal expertly you need to know something of its habits and food preferences, but even without this knowledge basic tactics can work well. Most mammals have a good sense of smell compared with humans, although even we can smell the presence of a large mammal. Second to the use of the nose comes acute hearing, and then detection of vibrations through the ground. Birds' primary sense is their sight, their sense of smell being generally poor. Reptiles scent well with their tongues and detect ground vibrations. Amphibians do the latter and also hear very well, but their sight is short-range. These facts show you what you are up against and what your tactics should be. Tread on a dry stick, or even a dry leaf, rustle vegetation, brush a tree trunk, or cough, and your quarry will be gone. Wild animals are acutely sensitive to sharp movement, so move steadily, and crawl if in open country. If the wind changes so it is blowing against your back then change position, but at a distance if you can. Clothing for stalking could be dark green, dark grey, brown, white, sandy or other colour to suit the terrain. Although most mammals have poor colour discrimination they distinguish well between light and dark, so a white collar or cuff will give you away easily amongst temperate vegetation. Generally you will have more success stalking or tracking alone, or in a small like-minded group to minimise disturbance, but not with a dog unless it is very well trained, or it will simply pick up scents and chase.

Look around, look out, but also look up

Let us assume that we are in the northern hemisphere after dark and away from urban lights. If the night sky is clear the stars will provide a guide to your position and direction, and to the time. If you hold an arm out straight and spread the fingers of the hand, the distance between thumb and small finger is called the hand's span. This is useful for comparing apparent distances between stars. The angle subtended is commonly fifteen to eighteen degrees. Find the constellation Ursa Major (Great Bear, also known as the Plough) and observe the two stars on the opposite side to the tail. These are called the Pointers, and if you extend the line between them by just over a hand's span you will reach the Pole Star, which is due north. The stars appear, over a period of time, to 'revolve' around this star in a counter-clockwise direction (east to west). However many degrees above the north point of the horizon the Pole Star is, the stars within that angle, called circumpolar stars, never set at that latitude. The angle between the celestial pole and the horizon is the latitude of the observer.

The imaginary line at right angles to the north–south axis is the celestial equator, and the stars on it move fifteen degrees per hour. This is essential to know when steering by a fixed star. The sun and stars appear to move round the earth once every twenty-four hours because the earth rotates once on its axis in this time, and the stars appear to move round the whole sky once a year because the earth travels once round the sun in a year. If a star travels 360 degrees in 365 days, this is approximately one degree per day, or four minutes of time (sixty minutes divided by fifteen). So, wherever a star is on one night, on the next night it will be in the same position four minutes earlier.

All these basic astronomical facts allow you to find time and bearing from the stars. Using a star map, and starting with the Pole Star and Ursa Major, you should be able to identify the neighbouring stars and constellations. Over a year you will be familiar with the northern hemisphere night sky, or, by similar observation, the southern hemisphere.

By day, you can get a rough north–south bearing by looking at trees, for mosses generally grow only on the north side, away from the full heat of the southern sun. At the Autumnal and Spring equinoxes, when day and night are of equal length, in the northern hemisphere the sun rises due east, and sets due west. As the Winter solstice approaches the sun rises and sets nearer and nearer to due south, and the days get shorter and shorter. Once midwinter is passed the sun rises and sets nearer to the north and the days get longer until the Summer solstice. If you know the time, therefore, you can estimate the compass bearing. The sun will be due south at midday GMT and moves through an arc of fifteen degrees per hour (360 degrees divided by twenty-four hours). Wherever you are, hold your watch horizontally, point the hour hand at the sun, and due south is along the line bisecting the angle between the hour hand and twelve o'clock.

The inanimate is part of nature too

For geological exploration it would be advisable to have the best maps available, but as with the animate do not collect rocks or other specimens but get used to studying things where they are. Evidence for both the erosion and building of geological features is all around, as is the evidence of extinct life in the form of fossils and impressions. A geological map is useful for archaeology too, as this involves deciding why settlements were made where they were. Quarries, gravel pits, road and railway cuttings, river banks and sea cliffs are useful places to see exposed strata and search for fossils, which in turn are valuable to date the strata. Geology teaches observation, reasoning and deduction, and appreciation of the beauty and variety of the inanimate. The colourful, geometrical beauty of crystals is very appealing, but the urge to chip out and collect should be resisted.

Archaeological digs are very good activities for the whole family, as is exploring local history. Just as people wear their ethnic history and past experiences on their faces, so the face of the earth and what lies immediately underneath contains remnants and clues from our social, pastoral and industrial past. Just as you can read the lines and expressions on a face, so can you gather archaeological evidence to reconstruct past events in a locality, starting with aerial photography and land-based examination, continuing with excavation, and concluding with interpretation of the finds. Museums full of exhibits are all very interesting, but nothing compares with being on an archaeological dig and being in contact with ancient earth and its deposits.

Excavation teaches patience, concentration, organisation, self-control, and cautious reasoning and deduction. Nothing may be regarded as obvious or conclusive. If looking for sites yourself, low ground is often not productive as it may have been marshy in former times and drained for agriculture, despite the heavy soil, or overgrown with mature trees and shrubs rather than cleared for settlement. High ground often has lighter, better-drained soil and as natural vantage points hilltops were often the first places settled by immigrants to an unpopulated land.

Whether it be tracing the course of an ancient road, causeway, or field; delicately unearthing burial sites; excavating the lower remains of walls, buildings or an abandoned village; plotting the layout of hillforts or stone monuments; sorting through a midden; or just identifying fragments of pottery or lost or discarded personal items, archaeology enables the individual to feel a sense of belonging to the march of humankind through time and place, above all the place where they are digging. No-one on seeing the craftsmanship in a piece of ancient jewellery or wood carving can fail to admire the technological achievement of our ancestors, so often stupidly referred to as primitive.

Survival in wilderness

It is part of modern pagan destiny to try to achieve communion and oneness with nature, and the only way to do this is to experience it, learn to respect it and feel at home in it. The more remote your travel the more you can re-orientate your thoughts and actions to those which have a place, relevance and purpose in the natural world, but life in the wilderness will only be fulfilling if you prepare yourself fully and sensibly. The list of essential skills for survival is not very long, and includes common sense, humility, foresight and prevention, as well as the use of a compass, map reading, understanding the weather, first aid, tying knots and living off the land. These are practical skills for which adequate literature exists, but there is a shortage of information on the survival process itself and the mental preparation for it. Survival courses exist in many countries, covering local conditions, and, for your own safety, you should definitely attend one of these before venturing into wilderness.

Carelessness plays a big part in a situation becoming critical, common examples being not leaving the itinerary and estimated time of arrival (ETA) back with a responsible person; walking alone in remote terrain; inability to use a map or compass; not being dressed or carrying enough clothes for the worst possible weather; no first aid knowledge or kit; no headgear for wearing in the mountains; taking nothing to attract attention, such as a whistle or flares; insufficient food to maintain body warmth if delayed; insufficient water to maintain body fluids; no source of light; and no training for the activity undertaken. Another failing is not having the moral courage to make sensible decisions, like turning back when the odds are stacked against you, or changing course when the warning signs urge you to do so. Even if others accuse you of cowardice or of being a wimp you must follow your good sense.

When preparing for an expedition, planning must be meticulous, taking into account every reasonable possibility of mishap in the terrain or on the watercourse chosen, erring on the sides of caution and safety. Involve everyone in the expedition in this side of the planning, as well as listing basic equipment, so they appreciate its seriousness. The forces of nature are regularly underestimated, particularly wind, which can cause you to lose body heat very quickly, especially through the head, so wear headgear and, if conditions warrant it, several layers of thin woollen garments. Wear woollen socks and trousers or breeches, and thermal underwear if necessary. Keep waist, neck and wrists covered and wear gloves, all to stop heat loss from the body. Waterproofs should cover the whole body, and in severe conditions wear gaiters. It is easy to slip and injure yourself or to be gradually crippled by blisters and bruising, so wear stout, appropriate footwear, carefully waxed to make it waterproof. If you are likely to come across snow, take an ice axe and crampons.

If stalking or tracking you will want to blend in with the landscape and will be dressed in greens and browns or whatever colour combination allows your form to be broken up, but this makes you invisible to rescue services too, so always take a brightly coloured thin waterproof top to put on in an emergency.

A typical survival kit would include a detailed map (scale 1:50000, or 1:25000 for hilly terrain); compass; wind- and water-proof clothing, and a spare set; high-calorie foods such as chocolate and glucose; first aid kit; plastic survival bag; whistle; torch; knife; rope; matches in a waterproof container; and a candle. If appropriate take a packet of red flares. The standard distress call is six of however you announce yourself, for example six blasts on your whistle, then a one-minute pause, then six more. The standard answer is three blasts, a minute's pause, and then another three blasts. Every member of the party should have a copy of the route and schedule and their own survival kit. If travelling into remote wilderness leave a copy of your plans with at least two responsible people, otherwise one should suffice. The itinerary must show map references of all key points, distances, approximate travel times, ETA, and emergency telephone numbers.

The three most common causes of mishap are getting lost, having an accident, and unexpected bad weather. If someone is injured, one or more of the party is advised to stay with the injured person, and one or more to go for help if that is called for. The map reference of the injured party member must be taken by whoever goes for assistance. For wilderness journeying four in a party is the minimum safe number.

Navigation by map and compass

The ability to read a map and use a compass competently are essential survival skills. The style of reference of map grids varies from country to country, but most are based on a grid of vertical and horizontal lines, each of which has a cardinal reference. Any point on a map can be represented by an intersection of two grid lines, and the combined references of the lines gives the map reference of the point. Contour lines are a standard distance apart according to the scale of the map, so the closer they are together the steeper the gradient. To tell if land is rising or falling, the contour values on the lines normally read so they face uphill. Orienting a map is turning it so it matches the terrain; it can then be set with a compass. Set the magnetic variation on the compass first, then, with the arrow pointing north, place the compass on the map. Turn the map until the orienting lines on the compass are parallel to the grid lines on the map. This procedure will give you north.

The navigating skills you need to learn with map and compass should include the following: finding your position by re-section; translating the grid bearing into a compass bearing; calculating a back bearing (just 360 degrees minus the bearing) to retrace your route if lost; calculating distances and time of travel, including estimating with Naismith's Rule (three miles lightly laden takes an hour, as does climbing two thousand feet). Use the map and compass regularly, starting in your local area, and learn to trust them. Stop regularly to check your position until it is a quick routine task. Remember that metallic objects, telegraph wires and power lines can affect the compass needle. When you are experienced by day, try navigating at night and in fog, starting in your local area again. A good compass will have luminous paint to highlight key parts and positional markings. You can find north in the daytime by holding your watch horizontally and pointing the hour hand at the sun. The line bisecting the strap and the axis of the hour hand points due south. At night the Pole Star will give you north.

First aid

The next essential step after learning map and compass craft is to learn how to apply first aid, how to put together a first aid kit, and how to assess a situation and determine an appropriate course of action. You can't learn first aid from a book like this, so enrol on a reputable course that will give you realistic practical guidance. You should try to find a place for tried and tested herbal remedies in your first aid kit, such as homoeo-pathic arnica for shock, arnica ointment for bruises and sprains, lavender oil for pain relief, and distilled witch-hazel for sunburn or minor burns.

Understanding the weather

Another essential skill is understanding the weather and how to read meteorological maps. Generally, rising air pressure indicates improving weather and falling air pressure worsening weather, but the air pressure also falls as you ascend, so adjust-ment must be made for your altitude. Just as contour lines join points of equal height above sea level so isobars join points of equal air pressure. Close isobars mean strong wind. Learn both the Celsius and Fahrenheit scales of temperature and how to convert between the two. Temperature falls with altitude to the extent of about three degrees every one thousand feet. Relative humidity is often quoted in weather forecasts and measures the moisture content of the air as a percentage. Wind direction refers to the direction the wind is blowing from, not to.

Weather forecasts, which are generally reasonably accurate these days, should be consulted before travelling and the forecast for the duration of the trip noted if available. However, you will also benefit from local knowledge, particularly from seafarers, farmers, foresters and others who work outdoors. Knowing the usual prevailing wind and its moisture content and temperature at various seasons, as they will, is most useful. Rain at sea level may turn to sleet then snow as you climb if the tem-perature profile is right, whatever the time of year, so don't make the assumption that just because it's Summer it won't snow. Remember that wind chill is a significant hazard for lightly dressed walkers, giving an effective temperature lower than the true air temperature. If there are dark cumulonimbus clouds high up there may be a risk of lightning. Metal objects should be stowed, and you should keep away from isolated trees. Head for lower ground, but don't go into hollows. Woods are generally safe. Sit on a rubber ground sheet if you have one. You will need specialist advice if you plan to go over terrain that is subject to avalanches.

Survival decisions

If you are well equipped and have followed the guidelines on leaving a copy of your route and ETA, but are prevented from keeping to schedule by sudden mishap or bad weather, you may choose to wait for rescue. This is not normally a survival issue immediately. But if you, or members of your party, are lost, seriously delayed, injured or exhausted, improperly equipped or dressed, and have not lodged your route then your predicament may suddenly require your survival knowledge. This is where training on a course run by experienced personnel proves its worth, as you must critically assess the situation and decide which of several options to choose. It all depends on the nature and severity of the problem. Do you know your location? Are you way behind schedule? Did you lodge your route and ETA? Are you exhausted, freezing or injured? What is the weather like, and does it appear to be changing? Have you adequate food and drink? Do you have, or can you make, shelter? Is your clothing adequate? Weigh up the answers and decide on a course of action, which may be to wait for help, wait for the weather to improve, rest and wait for morning to reassess the position, retrace your steps, or carry on. Only training and experience can ensure you make the right decision, so do not venture into wilderness without them. Generally your priorities are, in order, health, safety and first aid first, then shelter, then warmth, then water, then food.

In a survival situation make for low ground if possible, to a spot in the lee of the wind. If falling temperature is a likelihood then put on extra layers of clothing under your waterproofs. If a survival bag is not adequate then build a windbreak, lean-to or bivouac from what is available. Your survival course should provide instructions; rocks, saplings, branches, reeds, and turf can all be made use of. In deep snow dig a snow hole, as this is warmer than a tent. Sit on a ground sheet to protect from ground chill, and huddle together to share body heat, especially when children are present as they have a higher surface area to bodily volume ratio than adults, so will lose heat more quickly. Light a fire if necessary. The floor and walls of a snow hole should be covered with pine branches so you are not resting directly against snow. If you decide to keep going, don't cross swollen rivers, or follow them downhill in poor visibility as they may lead you over a cliff. Don't walk on an ice-covered lake or watercourse, even to try to reach much-needed water, but break the ice at the edge.

If it is decided to send someone, preferably two, for help, make sure they have the precise map reference of the party. At least one ought to stay with the injured, which is why a minimum of four is sensible for wilderness trips. When deciding to press on with an injured party member the decision would only normally be taken if carrying the injured would not exacerbate the injuries. Other decisions your survival course will help you with will be when to call the rescue services, when to use the whistle to attract attention, when to light a smoky fire as a signal, and when to use flares. Life-or-death decisions come more easily when you have received training and gained experience by starting locally, or in easily accessible areas, and gradually going further afield. There is no place for heroics in the wilderness. If you run out of food and consider living off the land you must know what you are doing, for sampling fruit, leaves or fungi in a country where you are not familiar with the plant life can lead to poisoning. Most young grasses are quite nutritious, whereas older grass is more fibrous, but even in this case identification needs to be certain, not just probable.

The more at home in nature you and your family are the more you can safely enjoy what the wilderness areas have to offer, especially the tranquillity, abundance of wildlife and unpolluted air, land and waterways. If you live in an urban area, such trips will help you to recharge your lifestyle batteries and help to counterbalance the pressures of life in a concrete jungle, but only if you know how to prepare and how to look after yourselves. Mother Nature has little patience, tenderness or sympathy for those who abuse her or take her for granted.

Countryside and land use

Issues appertaining to the use of countryside are similar to those of relevance to plots of urban land, but more critical in scope because the pressures created by an ever-expanding urban population bear down more heavily upon that countryside. It falls to all who share the modern pagan philosophy of stewardship to remind landowners, land users, and authorities responsible for country planning and rural industrial development that the countryside belongs morally and ecologically to every living and non-living thing. The last reference is neither trivial nor abstractly romantic. To regard the fate of a potential quarry as important from the point of view of the fracture and dispersal of displaced rock is to understand and value the integrity and functionality of landscape, and this aspect is as significant as its biospherical dimension.

Like pollution, problems associated with land use are international in their scope, for such attendant consequences as economic instability and adverse meteorological reactions are global in their effects. As an individual you can make a difference on your own doorstep and examine what is happening locally, but you may be sure that the picture in your own back yard will be repeated all over the country. Pressure on land is not just from the urban sprawl that accompanies population growth and the necessity of feeding more people, it is also from the fuelling of technological development and expansion with raw materials and the extension of transport infrastructures. Those in charge of land development strategies seem to find it extraordinarily difficult, unless it is vested interest and corruption that are to blame, to return unused or surplus agricultural land to countryside, to develop only brown-field sites not green ones, to insist that industrial companies have an environmental audit of their activities to ensure they do not impact unacceptably on the environment, to deal with the plague of unnecessary road journeys and make more use of rail for both freight and passengers. But in democratic countries such people will be elected, and therefore accountable to the electorate. As far as private companies are concerned, modern pagans can offer another incentive, for it is extraordinarily easy for investors to select only companies that behave ethically for the communal good in such matters, and demonstrate sustainable, environmentally secure development. As a consumer, a voter, and an investor you have the power to be part of collective neighbourhood and national pressure to have all land use monitored, audited and properly accredited.

As an expression of your feeling of responsibility for your local landscape, you could join forces with others in your community to study the planning process and local structural plans so that development proposals can be scrutinised and challenged early if undesirable. Assessing the impact on watercourses, wildlife and tree cover is especially important, and sustained lobby is called for so that these aspects have a higher profile in applications for mining, quarrying, gravel extraction, and waste tipping. Planning controls on agriculture tend to be weaker than on urban or industrial development, and where this is the case, farmers can with impunity destroy or damage environmentally sensitive sites. In these cases there is an urgent call for modern pagans to be vigilant and active in calling for tighter controls and more accountability. The public have a responsibility too, in looking after farming infrastructure, carrying litter home, avoiding the degradation of paths, leaving all wild plants where they are, not breaking branches or rocks, and educating children to so protect and respect the countryside. There is a strong case for offering incentives to return farmland that is unnecessary or unproductive to countryside. Patches of countryside within urban boundaries are especially valuable, but also vulnerable to unscrupulous development. Sensible planting of trees and other plants will encourage wildlife, who may need routes in and out to connect patches of habitat, thereby enabling amphibians to reach breeding ponds, birds to have cover and nesting sites, and mammals and reptiles to have a sufficient feeding range. As advised already, more gardens could usefully be planted to attract and provide refuges for wildlife, and this sort of initiative would increase respect and care for islands of countryside and provide the incentive to link them. The rural traveller's code could have been written by a new pagan: 'Take nothing but photographs, leave nothing but footprints.'

There will undoubtedly be scope in your area for environmental initiatives. Just a small group of volunteers starting to clean up a neighbourhood can persuade many others to join in. Once it is clean, momentum to begin planting schemes, especially with trees, can be built up. Local authorities, grant-awarding bodies or charities may be willing to contribute financially, and just the regeneration of one unsightly corner can have a dramatic effect on people's morale and willingness to participate. Bringing in outside helpers or contractors does not have the same effect, for they have no ownership of the neighbourhood. It is your determination and that of your neighbours that alone will make a difference.

In general, controls on use of land, management of natural resources, extent of recycling, pollution control and transport planning are wholly inadequate globally at the moment for effective long-term confidence in the health of our environment. Environmental care is for the next generation as well as the present one, so you who are parents have a responsibility to incorporate it actively into your children's upbringing, not just talk about how desirable it is. Despite the amount of research done, and the publicity given, to the dwindling of the earth's natural resources it has not yet dawned on consumer societies as a whole that they cannot continue to produce and consume more. Continued pressure for economic growth, with its 'more is better' and 'the faster the better' syndromes gets us further from the simplicity and natural pleasures of life. We all know how valuable water, soil and forests are, yet we continue to pollute and waste them or their derivatives. Similarly, we know that fossil fuels and minerals are non-renewable, yet we fail to recycle most of what is recyclable and use up the rest. Such a situation is not sustainable, as we also know perfectly well, and neither is the lifestyle and lack of environmental management that has brought it about. Many countries, multinational and national companies are party to non-sustainable and unethical practices affecting population and environmental welfare, and consumer intention not to support, patronise or invest in them will come to be of great future significance.

It has been said with some truth that foreign aid is poor people in rich countries giving money to rich people in poor countries. There is a growing body of opinion amongst those concerned about the international dimension of conservation and sustainability that aid should only by given in the form of practical assistance, not money to be siphoned off into the bank accounts of corrupt leaders and their cronies, the assistance conforming to strict ethical and environmental standards. Monetary aid invites corruption and encourages debt repayment defaulting. The most important objectives for assistance are not to help create high-growth export-oriented economies, which are simply modelled unsuitably on our type of consumer society, but to tackle basic issues of land use, proper clean water supplies and irrigation schemes, agricultural improvements, protection and sustainable harvesting of natural resources, health, education and rural infrastructure. Much money for developing countries in the past has been swallowed up by capital-intensive projects like dams, airports and power stations, while most of the population of the country concerned still lacked clean drinking water, sanitation, fuel for cooking and heating, and food to eat. To repay loans, land and labour is then used for cash crops for export, or intensive mineral extraction, or hardwood tree felling, instead of meeting the basic needs of the people. When intensively farmed soil that was once forest, or open-cast mines, is exhausted the land turns to desert, and the means to sustain the debt repayments are lost. Modern pagans may, therefore, care to lobby for foreign aid to be given only in the form of practical help that enhances the lives of families and communities and protects their environment for sustainable harvesting. A stable, biodiverse ecosystem gives the international members of the extended family who live in it the best chance of not just survival but a contented, healthy future.

Modern pagan farming

The modern pagan farm

The garden, farm and countryside are viewed by modern pagans as a continuum. Like the natural garden, the modern pagan farm is an ideal whose achievement depends on the area available and the intended degree of diversification. Modern pagan farming is based on the sound ecological principles of sustainable populations, energy and nutrient recycling and crop rotation – in other words, what is generally known as organic farming or eco-friendly farming, but with the additional features of a mixed plant and animal community, and strict ethical standards. These five features characterise the modern pagan farm.

The modern pagan farm is like a garden in the sense that what grows there is as close to the farmer as the garden and its inhabitants are to the household, and both are just enclosed areas of the countryside. The degree of care shown to all the incumbent living things is as one would show in the garden, and arguments of scale that are used to justify less humane attitudes and treatment, or carelessness towards the rural periphery or internal ecosystems, have no moral or environmental validity in the new pagan mind. Indeed, the greater scale of a farm is an argument for more care and respect for the environment, not less, as a greater area could potentially be damaged. The fact that farm animals are generally docile and are classed as 'domesticated' does not justify rough treatment nor consideration of them as mere disposable, temporary assets. The well-managed organic farm has much in common with the wildlife-friendly garden, in the sense that what happens in both mirrors the temperature of society's earnestness in bringing up and providing for an environmentally conscious nation.

Of course, providing as natural an environment as possible for farm animals has to be balanced against the fact that a farm is a business. But no business ethic is acceptable to new pagans that means severe confinement, force-feeding or feeding unnatural foods, and lack of normal interaction with fellow animals, nor the growing of vast areas of chemically laced plant monocultures. With both incentives to reform and pressure from consumers interested only in genuinely organic products, business-conscious farmers will certainly respond, but under some present agricultural regimes, some farmers are paid to produce, store, and then destroy food. Monoculture farmers practise a style of farming that is wholly unbalanced in the natural, ecological sense, and it can only be continued by perpetually using artificial ways of boosting growth and fending nature off while it happens. Important though it is for new pagans to achieve natural balance and biodiversity in their gardens, the ultimate prize is to extend the techniques to farms. A farm is still just a piece of Mother Nature's jigsaw puzzle, but it is a large, significant piece. Small pieces like gardens are valuable for the environmental awareness they give to families, especially children, but farms have the potential for acting as nuclei of much larger spheres of ecological harmony, so inviting farmers into the modern pagan fold is vital for the world's environmental stabilisation.

A short history of alternative agriculture

The phrases 'developed world' and 'developing world' are interesting choices for, respectively, nations whose agricultural practices are environmentally damaging, and nations whose methods are sustainable, and it is satisfying to pagan objectives to note that the former is returning to the retained practices of the latter. Modern pagan consciousness, if not modern pagan practice, is much more in tune with what has curiously become known as 'alternative' agriculture in the so-called developed world, than it is with 'conventional' agriculture, because the former represents the first tentative steps back to organic farming. The greater challenge is to help the so-called developing world to either retain its local, traditional agriculture, or to wean itself off practices imported from developed countries, whose sterile farms are no example to recreate, especially where land is naturally of marginal fertility.

Wherever you live, the elements of successful agriculture are to be found in your local, natural surroundings. Many farmers in developed countries no longer appreciate this because they are living in an environment that their kind has created, and their methods have recently been chemical and interventionist. They think they understand country ways and the natural living cycles, but they don't, because the practices of their recent antecedents have disturbed natural mechanisms to a degree that makes the use of the word 'natural' to describe them highly questionable. The export of such practices to alien environments in the developing world has equally serious consequences, not least the failure to develop local knowledge and solutions.

Starting in the 1980s, a period of agricultural diversification began in developed nations as a reaction against the growing numbers of food mountains and lakes resulting from intensive monoculture production, and there were calls for a return to organic methods. At the same time came the realisation that the urgent planting of more forests was necessary, as the erosive effects of deforestation became ever more apparent, and that technology was becoming dominant and perhaps should play a less prominent role. However, rather than any sort of grand plan, a series of piecemeal strategies and initiatives resulted, revealing that more response was coming from environmental pressure groups and enlightened farmers and landowners than from governments. Early initiatives included replanting flax for linen, trials of possible high-protein crops, planting peas and beans for livestock feed, cultivation of herbs for culinary and medicinal use, trials of different varieties of sunflower, serious attempts to save indigenous rare breeds and food plant varieties, and the establishment of seed banks.

Organic farming started to spread in the 1990s, with little governmental assistance or encouragement, many of the most innovative projects being started by women, notably the supply of choice or unusual varieties of herbs, vegetables and fruit to restaurants and specialist food manufacturers. Some of these have been smallholding ventures, as the desire to make fields and farms ever larger was seen to be denuding the peripheral environment, and this reduction in scale is a development to be encouraged in the future. In many countries, therefore, there has been virtually no expansion in recent years in sizes of farms, and even a return to traditional co-operation between neighbouring small farms. With the loss of interest in large farms producing mainstream food to national quotas and for retail demands there has come a reversion to regional specialisation and a call for more local sales rather than farmers remaining in hock to supermarket purchasing power.

Smallholdings and small farms are not only easy to manage organically but can respond quickly to local demands by supplying directly to consumers and businesses the quality and type of produce required, harvested seasonally by local labour. Parochial initiatives have also seen the revival of rural crafts and their associated skills of traditional woodland management, catch cropping and crop rotation. By allowing intensively farmed land to regenerate into its former type of local habitat, whether it be forest, scrub, meadow, moor, heath, breckland, marsh or other wetland, and returning to the traditional ways in which it was harvested and managed, dependence on manufactured products or materials imported from exploited environments overseas can be considerably reduced. So, before you buy synthetic goods, enquire about a natural, biodegradable alternative. Examples are locally made fibreboard and strandboard instead of rainforest hardwood; flax and hemp instead of synthetic fibres; plant oils as lubricants, hydraulic fluid and preservatives; coppiced willow for basketry, wickerwork furniture, hurdles, and as a green fuel; plant dyes instead of synthetic ones; revival of proven herbal medicine; and essential oils for the food, perfumery and pharmaceutical industries, and for aromatherapy. People were once surrounded by the answers to their needs, and they can be again.

In summary, recent experience shows that in times of agricultural downturn it is individual and local initiative, not governmental leadership or support, that fuels expansion into alternative products. This development promotes more local projects and reduces dependency on imports. Modern pagans should support these initiatives wholeheartedly if methods are sustainable and environmentally friendly, and encourage the transfer of support from large, monoculture farms to small, organic farms and those diversifying into alternative crops and products such as those referred to above. Perhaps this trend will also see a move back to the land from urban areas plagued with unemployment and materialism, as one enormous field currently used to grow grain that is immediately put into storage can be converted into numerous, eco-friendly smallholdings.

Self-sufficiency

As the techniques of self-sufficient farming can already be found abundantly in print, this section will focus on its principles. The principles of self-sufficiency as practised on a smallholding could, if translated on a large scale, transform modern intensive farming into a modern pagan style of agriculture that would be sustainable. This would also have the effect of removing over-production, environmental impoverishment and damage, and subsidy. Monocultures, both animal and plant, are unnatural and therefore unsustainable without environmental degradation and artificial methods of production. Crop monoculture is a practice that leads to soil exhaustion and entrenched disease, and animal monoculture has similar pathogenic consequences. Mixed stocking and rotational grazing means that the life cycles of parasites in the animals' droppings are broken, which keeps all stock healthier. Modern pagan animal farmers not only keep animals but also grow their own animal food and recycle the animal waste.

Modern pagan self-sufficient farming, unlike conventional chemical agriculture, embodies strict environmental discipline, mutual dependency, organic principles of tending, humane husbandry, and creation of a natural, safe, unadulterated product. It also embodies the conviction that our land can always support us without artificial, chemical assistance, and intensive high-production farming can still occur, but on a long-term, sustainable basis. Monocultures are not part of modern pagan agriculture as they are created by attempting to wipe out the local ecosystem instead of using the biodiversity to advantage. Modern pagan farming doesn't exploit the land like conventional agriculture; it nurtures it by locally evolved techniques and a sense of oneness with the land. Reverting to dependency upon the land will ensure it is looked after, whereas no-one feels a sense of ownership for a food-processing factory.

An animal-free self-sufficient farm is unnatural in the sense that it is not a mixed animal/plant community, and its energy/nutrient cycles will therefore not easily equilibrate. It is of course accepted that as a matter of conscience a farmer employing modern pagan principles may, if vegetarian or vegan, decide to have a farm with no animals and be prepared to tackle the more difficult management of nutrient and energy recycling. As vegetarians tend to live in urban areas in developed countries there has been relatively little research done on vegetarian self-sufficient farming and no practical tradition anywhere as yet. The way animals are treated on farms, and indeed in zoos and in the home, is increasingly being seen as a measure of the natural environmental consciousness of the nation concerned. Many farm animals are doomed to have their lives curtailed, but new pagan principles demand that they have a dignified, unmutilated life, natural food, space and fresh air in which to relate normally to their kind, and shelter when the extent of their adaptation is insufficient for climatic conditions. Please consider making purchases of meat, fat, eggs, milk, cream, cheese, and other animal products only if these conditions have prevailed.

'Self-sufficient' farms are rarely wholly independent, for there is scope, and indeed community value, in co-operating with other modern pagan farmers to share labour, sell or barter supplies, share experiences, and generally help on a co-operative basis. Even a modest suburban garden can be self-sufficient in some produce, but a smallholding of a few acres offers considerable opportunity for a large measure of self-sufficiency, and larger farms can achieve it alone or in co-operation for a few items. However small a plot, some wild space will ensure the maximum biodiversity and opportunities to use wildlife as part of the farming process, such as natural 'pest' and 'weed' control.

Rotation and recycling

Where, as on true modern pagan farms, both animals and plants are tended, animals eat the plants and in turn manure the ground. Crop and animal rotation around the farm is used to avoid soil exhaustion and allow for natural regeneration. Animals are moved to their feeding field to save on the labour of gathering and clearing, and also to wherever needs manuring. In numerous countries, Mother Nature's own farm labourer is the pig. Pigs are so vigorous in their habits that they are a resident workforce, even turning over the land as they clear it. What is not trodden in by the pigs can be composted, and waste from any process, including bonfire ash, is returned to the land. Rotation of animals and plants prevents concentration of disease and parasites, the latter usually species-specific. Above all the soil is cared for, as without healthy soil there will be no produce of any kind worth harvesting. Maintaining elemental balance, as in the body, is very important, the four major elements to balance being nitrogen, phosphorus, potassium, and calcium, with a number of trace elements, such as boron, to consider too. This balance can be achieved by natural means, without the purchase and application of artificial fertilisers.

The practice of crop and plot rotation is fundamental to modern pagan farming. The English four-course rotation known as Norfolk Rotation can serve as an example. In a typical scheme, in the four fields are grown grass and clover; root crops and kales; corn and beans; and spring-sown grain such as wheat or barley. Briefly, the plan is as follows. In field one, the bacteria in the root nodules of the clover fix nitrogen so it will be available to plants. Grazing animals deposit manure and finally all remaining plant material is ploughed back in. In field two, potatoes are grown for human consumption, root vegetables like turnips, swedes and mangolds for winter animal feed, and kales. Manure from the farmyard is spread and the growing crops are 'weeded', thereby turning and aerating the soil. In field three, the now very fertile plot produces a cash crop of corn as well as the source of flour, and beans for animal feed. In field four, the barley is sown with an undercrop of grass and clover. The barley is harvested for malting for beer-making, and the grass and clover mixture could be used for grazing or haymaking. Some barley is fed to cattle as straw, and some spread, to be trodden into farmyard manure.

Such a system needs no artificial fertilisers, and can be adapted to a greater variety of animals and crops than was the case in the past. The following principles appertain to all rotational and recyclical farming:

1. All waste and residues from animal and plant produce are returned to the soil. Fields are manured by putting animals on them whenever possible as manure is more fertile than compost.
2. Mixed stocking and rotational grazing are used to prevent parasitic cycles establishing.
3. Crops are rotated so that disease micro-organisms do not establish.
4. Bare soil is prone to erosion and nutrient-leaching by rain, so a crop is grown and ploughed in as 'green manure'. Wild annuals such as chickweed and fat hen can just be ploughed in, or comfrey, grazing rye, lucerne (alfalfa), mustard, red clover, or tares can be planted.

5. Soil prone to waterlogging is drained and its texture regularly monitored. It is not ploughed too often or too deeply as this spoils and buries topsoil.

Natural energy

In addition to the sun, all regions of the planet have energy potential, from the wind, waves, running water and geothermal sources, for example, but most of these are only viable economically on a small scale. Few of us have scope for a small dam and water wheel, but solar energy could be more widely used. Large-scale electricity generation by solar, stream, wind or wave power is not possible with current technology, so individual effort is better spent in the short term making buildings better insulated against heat loss and making engines and other devices energy-efficient. Worthwhile tasks to this end include insulating roofs and lofts, filling cavity walls with foam or using exterior insulated cladding, and using heat-exchanger ventilation. House design does not always help, and could be improved, with more compact, rounded design and heat sources in the centre rather than on outside walls like the traditional chimney. The pumping windmill is quite an effective device, but like the water wheel and solar panels is small-scale and dependent on weather and seasonal conditions. Energy produced in favourable conditions can be stored and used later, but again on a small scale. Methane digesters allow dung to ferment anaerobically for a few weeks and the methane produced can be used as natural gas. The remains of the dung can be returned to the land. This process could be developed on a medium to large scale on modern pagan farms.

For larger farms, the extrapolation of these modern pagan farming principles to something like a five-acre self-sufficient smallholding is well documented and it is a matter of expansion of scale to employ these principles on large farms. Only then might farms once again be viewed as productive areas of countryside and not just as intensively exploited plots of land. Agricultural trade would become the selling of surplus stock and produce from otherwise self-contained farms. An example of a modern pagan farm would have about a third of its fields as grassland for mixed grazing animals, the others for crops of corn, pulses, and roots; a woodland area for timber; orchards for hard and soft fruit; beehives for honey and pollination; and wild corners as sources of biodiversity and refuges for wildlife, and perhaps, from time to time, the farmer's family.

Commercial farming and food

The visions of a modern pagan approach to farming described and of a healthy eating revolution recommended in chapter six, by no means unrealistic in view of encouraging progress in alternative and organic agriculture, will be a reality only when consumers determine they have had enough of artificially, intensively, forcibly reared crops and livestock and the chemically tainted foods derived from them. We eat food for sustenance, and it is a bonus if it is enjoyable, but nobody these days who buys their food from retail outlets, whether it be deemed fresh, packaged or processed, can be quite sure of what they are eating. Food labelling is often unhelpful, incomplete and ambiguous, and additives, which are not normally nourishment, are seldom properly identified.

If you audit and examine your food intake you can specify strict conditions when it comes to source and production methods, and some research in your local area will establish these to your satisfaction. Buying locally enables you and your community members to apply ecological criteria to the methods of land stewardship of your local farmers. Is the farming sensitive to the desirability of preserving hedges, copses, meadows and other wildlife refuges? Is the fertilisation cycle natural, using manure and humus, or chemicals? Are crops rotated? Are pests controlled by natural means and good management, or by chemicals? Are chemical sprays used to produce blemish-free surfaces or other enhancement, or is the produce allowed to mature naturally? Is meat produced by processes in which chemicals are injected, or water added to increase bulk? Are the animals kept in humane, free-range conditions, and fed on their natural food? By insisting on these conditions, pressure will be applied to farmers to break out of their cycles of chemical dependency.

A chemical farm is like a self-abused body in that it is in a downward spiral of action and reaction to successive waves of over-exploitation and attempted chemical restoration. The soil needs natural intake to promote natural restorative mechanisms, so that the chemically driven cycle, as with the treatment of bodily over-indulgence with pharmaceuticals, is broken. Depletion of trace elements, and even major nutrients, is a significant reason why the soil is treated with chemicals, as this is better for the farmer's immediate finances than the long-term strategy of employing organic fertilisers, instituting crop rotation and controlling undesired insects with natural products and good practice. The desire for maximum crop yields prompts the application of massive doses of artificial fertilisers, with consequent lush growth and more large concentrations of insects able to thrive. But what is not given is protection to soil structure, as provided by manure and humus, and resistance to erosion. Repeated intensive cropping leads to further nutrient exhaustion and disease epidemics associated with the growing of the same few varieties. Regular spraying with pesticides leaves residues in the depleted soil, along with chemical-resistant bacteria. Aerial spraying causes health problems in people living nearby, and cosmetic spraying to produce blemish-free surfaces is a further example of the unnecessary saturation of farms with chemicals and the accumulation of residues from them in food.

Meat and egg production on farms is often an inhumane and chemical-laced process. Intensive animal rearing, with unnatural feed and growth-accelerating chemicals, in close confinement, encourages stress and disease, which is then treated with antibiotics. Thus, resistant strains of bacteria accumulate in tainted meat to pile up alongside the vast amounts of animal waste that find their way into watercourses rather than on to fields. Additional unnatural practices are the dosing of animal feed with antibiotics to combat epidemics, the injection of cows' udders with antibiotics, injection of stimulants and growth hormones, and the feeding of livestock on recycled, reprocessed animal remains. It is a grim list, but now you have it you can take it into account when deciding on your purchasing strategy.

Once you have found suppliers of the food that meets your requirements, advertise them and use them regularly, and tell the provider why you are giving your custom. Modern pagans probably don't actually pay more for the pleasure of eating because the modest proportions of their natural diet are filling and nutritious, and they do not indulge in unnecessary extra intake unless it is a celebratory occasion. Moreover, the absence of chemical residues in your diet will pay dividends in terms of better health and fewer calls on medical services. There is a great deal of published research on the residues of chemical farming and their effects, but the long-term consequences of consumption of such a large variety of residues as is now present in food are still not fully understood. Pesticide residues in food have been linked to cancers, allergies, skin irritation, mutagenic effects and birth defects. Animal fat concentrates pesticide residues and other foreign chemicals so for this reason it is sensible to remove it from meat. There is also the danger from antibiotic-resistant bacteria in meat and residues from hormonal injections given to cows to increase milk yields. Chemical residues tend to concentrate in offal like liver and kidneys, and heavy metal residues, from coastal industrial discharges, in fish, so these nutritious foods should only be purchased from organic sources.

Food irradiation, far from preserving food safely, produces chemical changes, which have been linked to damage to internal organs, immune response, cells and growth rate, and to lowered birth rate. Chemical contaminants are not removed and some bacteria are known to survive irradiation. Good food doesn't need to be irradiated, only food likely to deteriorate. In the absence of any conclusive evidence that genetically modified foods are safe to eat and have no long-term adverse effects, modern pagans are advised not to consume them.

Modern pagan farmers, as with the pioneers in organic and alternative farming, have shown that their methods are not only environmentally sound but make good business sense. The more they are supported by the public buying their produce, even if it is a little more expensive, the more their example will be copied by other farmers. Your food audit is not just for your health, it is for the health of the countryside. Farmers will respond to a discerning, demanding public like any business people, and only then will the world's sick agricultural holdings begin the process of natural recovery from the disastrous, poisonous agrochemical revolution of the twentieth century.

Food, Diet and Health

Food and the modern pagan mentality

Modern pagans eat to survive like everyone else, but eating to them is also an expression of their association with nature and its seasonal produce. The latter is not produced for our benefit, but as part of the natural cycle of reproduction, so it behoves us not to interfere with this cycle by over-managing and over-harvesting, for we are but one species that depends upon it. The sole criterion is to take from nature only what is needed for immediate use or preservation, and can be sustained. Harvest humanely and with respect, so that the remainder of a plant, for example, is not damaged, nor is the surrounding habitat. Failure to take care over harvesting will cause the crop to diminish over the years in both quantity and quality. Look after Mother Nature and she will look after you. In ancient times druids had specific rituals for harvesting important plants for rituals, the most notable being mistletoe, and this fact serves as an example for us to emulate in the company of our living companions. A derivative of this tradition, which survived into the twentieth century, was the asking of permission of a tree before pruning its branches.

In planning the day and its mealtimes, some may wish to keep to the traditional Celtic day of sunset to sunset, but that would mean variable times for eating breakfast at dawn and supper at sunset, which would not sit comfortably with the demands of modern working life. However, the early riser still has most to look forward to, and as with all tasks the morning is the most productive time for food preparation and preserving. Modern pagan cookery is more than just resurrecting and cooking old recipes – although this is an interesting thing to do – for many were suited only to their time and used ingredients no longer available. The more labour-intensive lifestyles of the past necessitated high-energy foods, such as the traditional cooked English breakfast, but working habits have changed and eating habits and dietary consciousness must change too if we are to stay healthy. It has become commonplace to lead a sedentary life and yet eat beyond one's needs, the result being an epidemic of obesity. There is much to be gained by modern pagans, as part of an ongoing acclimatisation to natural cycles, returning to seasonal eating, and it is also exciting, especially for children, to look forward to annual treats. The fact that foods are available all year round from somewhere or other, and that climates have changed to blur the traditional meteorological distinctiveness of the seasons, is no reason to dissociate oneself from natural cycles that still exist, continue to need protection, and of which we are indissolubly a part.

Returning to growing your own food, or just some of it, is another expression of seasonal association with nature. Involving children in the growing and preparation of food is an important activity for them and the product a reward for their care and labour. Most people will still buy some of their foods, for self-sufficiency is an option for only a few, but it is important that the practice of food production in natural conditions be part of family life and the upbringing of children. It gives meaning to festival days and the reasons why special foods are eaten, which may be natural, ancestral, historical, or a tradition of forgotten origin. There are obviously issues surrounding the management of meals by working parents, but many people eat convenience foods when they do have time to cook a proper meal; they simply do not value the process of food preparation. Family cooking is an important activity in its own right, especially when it is a special folk calendar meal. Children and adults alike have so much to gain from participating: enjoyment, being involved in a co-operative venture, the chance to be creative and productive, the potential to be artistic with presentation, stimulus of the senses, learning to make their own decisions instead of being led by advertisers, developing dexterity and the ability to use utensils, and a sense of achievement. And try always to eat as a family, with no music, radio or television on, so that it is quality family time for conversation, discussion and togetherness.

There are many edible plants in the garden and countryside and some of them have valuable components that aid our general health. The identification of fungi, berries, nuts and other parts of plants that are natural foods should be a task that every modern pagan undertakes in order to make use of these resources and to do so safely. Making your own wines and cordials from natural produce, particularly from abundant or invasive plants, as these can sustain regular harvesting, is an engaging hobby. Preservation of fruit by bottling or storage, and of meat and fish by smoking, is straightforward and an enjoyable family activity, as is the making of your own condiments, preserves and sauces. If you want to provide sweets for the family it is advisable to make your own so that you can control what is put in them, and you will have no trouble persuading children to help and sample.

With the exception of shops selling organic produce, food outlets, with their processed, additive-rich merchandise, are best regarded as sources of what cannot be grown, gathered or made in the home, not as a convenient way to purchase what can be so much more rewardingly acquired from Mother Nature's infinitely more tasty and nutritious emporium. With desire and a little effort it can be part of every new pagan family's routine to harvest natural foods whenever available, even from common garden plants, many of which are edible, although local knowledge of that fact is no longer widespread in many parts of the world. Recipes are relatively easy to come by nowadays, elderly people from the locality being much the best resource as they may well have been brought up in more self-sufficient times and will know thoroughly how the resources of the local area may be utilised. This applies particularly to culinary knowledge of woodland products and the bounty of the seashore, fungi and seaweed being particularly neglected, yet abundant, foods.

A walk through Mother Nature's larder

Let us take a walk from high downland down to the lowland woods and fields of a coastal plain and thence on to the beach, to see what we can find to eat. Discoveries made at different times of the year will be incorporated into the one travelogue, so that we can get a complete picture of what is on offer.

In the right locations with the right soil types, bilberries (or whortleberries) and, if an acidic bog, cranberries, can be picked for making into superb pies or yoghurts, or in the case of cranberries, sauce. Juniper berries give a fine tart flavour to savoury dishes. Lower down you will be able to harvest wild blackberries and raspberries, if you can possible manage to take some away with you. The leaves of ramsons, which grows in alkaline soil, betray their onion kinship when broken, and they and the white spindle-shaped bulbs can be chopped and added to a stew. Wild garlics can do the job of an onion, with more benefit to the heart. The crow garlic, found on alkaline soil, has a crown of little bulbils that can be chopped and also put in a stew. Another lime lover found nearer the coast is Alexander, also known as the black pot herb because its fat seeds turn black as they ripen. If powdered they can be used to flavour soups.

Were we to come across a damp place we might find wild celery. Fennel is found in drier places but is a plant of similar usage, although sweeter in taste. Other wild flavourings to seek are valerian roots, which can be dried and stored, and the wild forms of mint, thyme and marjoram. The roots of the wild parsnip and wild carrot are perfectly edible, if rather small compared to their cultivated descendants. Other edible roots are evening primrose, which must be boiled first, horseradish, vetch, dandelion, and burdock, although the last two have a bitter taste. Burdock stems can be eaten when young and have a taste like chicory. Remove the fibrous outer layer and boil in slightly salted water for ten minutes. And, of course, Dandelion and Burdock is a drink that sustained country folk for generations, in both alcoholic and non-alcoholic forms.

The young shoots of bladder campion may be boiled in slightly salty water and eaten. Stinging nettles are tasty, and can be treated like spinach, or made into a refreshing, detoxifying tea. Pick the young leafy shoots, no more than six inches long. Chickweed, fat hen, Good King Henry, ground elder, lungwort, shepherd's purse, and yarrow can be cooked similarly. If you peel off the skin of the stems of wild rose or bramble they may be boiled and eaten.

The fruit of the wild cherry, or gean, is perfectly edible but sometimes a little tart, as is that of the wild plum. Crab apples make a fine jelly, and assist the fermentation of mead. Rosehips can be made into a syrup rich in vitamin C. Rosehip and haw conserves are delicious, and set better if crab apples are added. Elderberry jelly may be made likewise. Bullace is a relative of the plum, and the fruit of the yellow variety is good for bottling as well as jam, the blue-fruited variety only for jam. Sloes, medlar and whitebeam fruits are high in tannin and need to be overripe to be edible, but do make very good wine and gin. Elderberries make excellent wine too, and also improve the flavour of fruit, or can be boiled in spiced vinegar to make a relish. Elderflower cordial and Sparkling Elderflower are country favourites, as is blackberry wine, and adding elderflowers to gooseberries or gooseberry jam improves the flavour in a delicious way. Rowan and guelder rose berries can be made into preserves, but their natural bitterness means you will have to control the taste carefully, one way being to use Sweet Cicely. If you come across a sugar maple, then try tapping it for maple syrup. The woods you walk through may once have been places where charcoal was made, and this was used as a filter in the making of beverages.

To judge if hazelnuts are ready, check that the shells are brown at the base and slip easily out of the husk. Leave the shells to dry completely before storing. Beech mast is tasty, if a little fiddly to extract, and sweet chestnuts may be eaten raw if ready, roasted in the fire, puréed, or made into stuffing. 'Pignuts' are the rootstock of a relative of the carrot, which may be dug up and peeled before eating. Ash keys may be boiled and pickled in vinegar. We are sure to see goat's beard climbing over shrubbery, but looking down reminds us that the roots are edible and taste like salsify, and should be dug before the plant starts to flower.

Salad vegetables abound. The young leaves of Jack-by-the-hedge were a popular seasoning for meat sandwiches, and have a flavour like a mixture of cress and onion. Other salad leaves are chickweed, dandelion, the sow thistles, and wild chicory, all with quite a tang. Milder is the aptly named salad burnet, whose taste is not unlike cucumber, and of similar taste are comfrey and borage leaves. The growing tips of wild hop are tasty in salads or when boiled for five to ten minutes in slightly salty water. For a sharper flavour use the leaves of wood sorrel, or of the sorrel dock that is found in meadows. The unfolded leaves of the hawthorn may be picked and chewed, and a wad was referred to as 'bread and cheese', as you may discover.

At the appropriate time of year, fungi may be identified and picked, but you will need to be certain of the species as some are poisonous. Those that are relatively easy to identify, and also delicious to eat, are the field mushroom, horse mushroom, cep, boletus species, morel, chanterelle, giant puffball, shaggy parasol, and shaggy ink-cap. The last is normally boiled lightly in milk, the others prepared like mushrooms or to individual taste.

Water lily roots are edible, and so is the root stock of the reed mace, although many other parts of the latter are edible too. The young male spike, which is found above the slender female spike, when its pale green sheath is removed, may be boiled in slightly salted water for five to ten minutes. The male flowers are edible and have a taste not unlike that of shrimps! Reed mace pollen is very nutritious and can be added to cake mixtures and used to dust the finished cakes. The inner parts of the young leafy shoots may be boiled and eaten as a vegetable, and the same is true of other reeds. Watercress is a well known wild vegetable, but eat only the non-flowering shoots, and similarly the related wintercress, or yellow rocket. Rushes, and indeed nettles, flax, hemp, coarse grasses and the marigold *Tagetes minuta* were once used to make paper.

When we arrive on the foreshore we may find a leafy vegetable in the form of the young leaves of the sea beet, which is prepared like spinach. The broad fleshy leaves of the coastal scurvy grass taste like cress. You can also try the young shoots of sea campion, which when boiled in slightly salted water have a flavour like peas. Sea kale can be picked, washed and cooked like greens, or blanched and eaten like asparagus. If you cultivate it, treat like rhubarb. Any driftwood you find may be used as fuel, or to decorate the garden and table as natural sculptures. You could also try extracting your own sea salt from sea water using an iron boiler. Something similar was used to make soap in the house, by boiling animal fat with lye (sodium hydroxide). Lye was made from straw and wood ash steeped in water, and improved with olive oil and peanut oil.

The common garden snail, like its maritime relatives winkles and whelks, is edible, and only has to be dropped into boiling salty water for a few minutes to be ready to eat. Extract the body with a pin. Winkles are boiled for about fifteen minutes, picked out with a pin and sprinkled with vinegar. Some like to eat them with bread and butter. Whelks will need to be boiled or steamed for thirty minutes, and mussels are cooked similarly. Pick mussels low off the rocks at low tide; the live ones are those that are tightly closed. Look for areas of sand greyer than normal, and there you can rake or dig out cockles. Allow them to stand in sea water for an hour or two so that the sand is easily removed, and boil or steam for about twenty minutes. Limpets can be cooked similarly, and made into soup. Oysters are normally eaten raw, but can be cooked. If you find clams, the traditional way to cook them is to heat stones in a pit, cover with seaweed and bake the clams on top. Shrimps and prawns can be netted from under near-shore rocks as the tide recedes, although their freshwater cousins, the crayfish, are best caught with a baited line. Any fish caught and not to be prepared immediately can be smoked, salted, pickled or potted in brine.

Seaweed makes good eating, especially laver weed, *Porphyra umbilicalis*, and samphire, *Salicornia europaea*. Laver weed is soaked for several hours in clean water, dried in the oven and powdered in a mortar. It is boiled for four hours, changing the water several times, then drained and dried. This is 'laver bread', and it is traditionally eaten with bacon for breakfast, notably in Wales. Sea lettuce, *Ulva lactuca*, and dulse, *Rhodymenia palmate*, are cooked like laver weed. Samphire is boiled until tender and served like asparagus, with butter. The flesh is drawn off between the teeth, leaving the rough fibres behind.

It is time now to return after the walk, with much to reflect upon and to admire in the availability of natural products, if only we know where to look.

The kitchen garden

In the kitchen garden of yesteryear, without the panoply of chemicals and technical aids available today, and despite the capriciousness of the weather, food had to be grown for the table, or the family suffered or starved. In the absence of anything to compete nowadays with the freshness and quality of home-grown food, there is much to be said for some determination to put ourselves into a similar position of dependency.

The monastic kitchen gardens of medieval times had plenty of paths and small, square or rectangular beds for compact growing and easy tending. Walled kitchen gardens became popular later in large country houses, the wall traditionally being a 5 x 3 parallelogram arrangement (with the long side having the most exposure to the sun) to allow places for fruit to ripen on trained trees, and shelter if needed. The idea of a kitchen garden was soon taken up on a smaller scale in properties throughout the country.

Typical structures in a kitchen garden include a fruit cage, greenhouse, cold frames for hardening off greenhouse-grown seedlings, and portable cloches to warm the soil before sowing, protect seedlings, and extend the sowing season. In addition to the compost heap, a dung hotbed could make a comeback as a source of energy for growing seedlings without using a heater burning fuel, and the forcing house with its ridge of manure on which to grow mushrooms, again without artificial heat. Rhubarb and sea kale are traditionally forced under special ceramic pots, but your own ingenuity will do. Blanching growing plants helps to sweeten and tenderise them if they have slight bitterness, as you may wish to do with celery, chicory and endives. Wrap them and earth up around them, or use large inverted flower pots.

You could also design the kitchen garden to the same principles as a managed garden, by using colour and habit attractively. Some cabbages have attractive glaucous foliage, in contrast to the silvery green of globe artichokes. Red Swiss chard is striking with its bright green foliage and red stems, as are the blue-green leaves of sea kale and its honey-scented white flowers. Modern cultivars may score on appearance, size, yield and shelf-life, but seldom on taste, so go for old varieties. They are often disease-resistant, relatively unfussy about conditions, and consistent croppers.

In kitchen garden beds, it is better not to plant in rows, but in a block with plants equidistant, as this gives each plant equal light and keeps unwanted plant competitors to a minimum. With larger crops, interplant with salad vegetables like lettuce, radishes and spring onions. This is a good activity for children to be involved in, as it is the start of the process of food production, and it is to be hoped that they will play their part in the tending, harvesting, preparation in the kitchen and cooking of the crops, so that they appreciate where food comes from and how it is naturally produced and prepared. Another favourite activity with children is to prepare sprouting seeds for the kitchen in shallow trays on layers of damp paper towelling. This works well for adzuki beans, alfalfa, barley, buckwheat, chickpea, fenugreek, lentil, mung bean, radish, rye, soya bean, sunflower, triticale and wheat.

Encompassing nutritional types, ease of cultivation, seasonal range and culinary versatility, the following are suggested as good fruits and vegetables for your kitchen garden.

Fruit
Soft fruit: blackberry, blueberry, cranberry (if on acid soil), currants (black, red and white), gooseberry, loganberry, raspberry, strawberry.
Tree fruit: apple, apricot, bullace, cherry, cherry plum, crab apple, damson, grape, greengage, medlar, mulberry, nectarine, peach, pear, plum, quince.

Nuts
Nuts: filbert, hazel (cob nut), walnut. Sweet almond will only fruit in mild, frost-free areas with warm summers.

Vegetables
Brassicas: broccoli, Brussels sprout, cabbage, cauliflower, kale.
Fungi: mushroom
Leaves: spinach, spinach beet, Swiss chard.
Onions: leek, onion, shallot, spring onion.
Pods and seeds: broad bean, French bean, haricot bean, pea, runner bean, sweetcorn.
Roots: beetroot, carrot, celeriac, kohlrabi, parsnip, radish, salsify, scorzonera, swede, turnip.
Salad: chicory, endive, lettuce, mustard and cress, and watercress, which grows quite happily in soil.

Stalks and shoots: asparagus, celery, Florence fennel, globe artichoke, rhubarb, sea kale.

Tubers: Jerusalem artichoke, potato.

Vegetable fruits: aubergine, courgette, cucumber, marrow, melon, pumpkin, squash, sweet pepper, tomato.

Herbs

Culinary herbs: angelica, anise, balm, basil, borage, caraway, chamomile, chervil, chives, coriander, dill, fennel, garlic, horseradish, hyssop, lavender, lovage, marjoram, mint, parsley, rosemary, sage, salad burnet, sorrel, summer savory, sweet bay, Sweet Cicely, tarragon, thyme, winter savory.

Angelica, comfrey, meadowsweet and mint prefer damp soil. Chives, fennel, lemon balm, lovage and parsley are tolerant of semi-shade, and comfrey, lungwort and mint of full shade. Comfrey, sorrel and Sweet Cicely will not thrive in alkaline soil, but catmint, chicory, hyssop, lavender, lungwort, marjoram and rosemary will.

Let us examine just one example of the value of adopting a grow-your-own mentality towards natural ingredients. If you are cutting out refined sugar from your diet and you want a natural sweetener there are plants and natural products that can oblige, but so seldom are they used. When a sweetener is desired as an ingredient, almost the entire population reaches for a jar of sugar (sucrose), even though such a vessel should carry a government health warning for reasons we are all familiar with. For sweetening beverages, some will add a synthetic chemical like saccharin. It is not as though nature's pantry is unstocked with sweeteners, and one wonders why beekeepers go to all that trouble to bottle honey, or purveyors of maple syrup the sap of the sugar maple. Then there is crystallised ginger, and numerous fruit preserves.

But, most versatile of all, and the least known about by the current younger generation, is Sweet Cicely, *Myrrhis odorata*. All parts of the plant can be used, and it has a long history of being the diabetic's friend in the kitchen. Two to four teaspoons of dried leaves will sweeten the tartest fruit, or fresh leaves with lemon balm can be added to the boiling water in which fruit is to be stewed. The unripe seeds, with their sweet, nutty flavour, can be tossed with fruit salads, or the ripe seeds added whole or crushed to fruit pies, especially apple. The root can be chopped to add to a salad, made into a good wine, or it can be eaten raw when peeled or grated. Sweet Cicely can even just be served as a steamed vegetable. Is it really worth reaching for the sugar bowl, to risk coming away with dental, weight and nutritional problems?

Storing your home-grown food

Wasting natural or garden harvest is thoroughly unpagan in its disrespect for the effort and resources consumed, and is a breaking of the bond with the soil. Stored food develops its own flavour, and allows a natural extension of a season with retention of quality and absence of synthetic preservatives. It also means less reliance on shops in the Winter.

Potatoes and root crops are traditionally stored by clamping, a technique whereby you make a pyramidal pile, covering it with straw or bracken, and then with a layer of dry earth. Provision is made for air circulation and drainage. Carrots, beetroot and sweet potatoes may be laid down in dry sand. Carrots, parsnips and potatoes can also be stored in moist peat in a cellar, but do make sure any peat you buy is from a sustainable source.

Celery, leeks and Jerusalem artichokes are either left in the ground or heeled into dry ground by the house for late season protection. Marrows, pumpkins and squashes may be hung in nets, or you can leave pumpkins in the sun to dry then store in a cool, dry place indoors. Onions and sweetcorn are strung with twine and hung against a cool, airy wall under the eaves. Cabbages and cauliflowers can be hung up in a dry, airy place. Peas and beans are dried, threshed and winnowed, and stored dry in crocks, barrels or bins. For centuries this enabled plant protein to be preserved for the winter.

Spread keeper apples and pears, to dry. Pick out the perfect fruit and wrap in paper. You will need to research good keepers amongst local varieties by asking the elderly of the area. Pears may also be kept in dry silver sand, or in dried fern or kiln-dried straw. Mushrooms can just be spread to dry.

Setting up a modern pagan kitchen

The kitchen is a family place, and ideally should have plenty of space and preparation area for all to be involved in preparing and cooking food. For the room in the house that is to receive the garden's produce, wooden furniture and fittings are most suitable, otherwise good-quality metal. The same holds for utensils and implements. Memories are still fresh of the best china on the dresser; plates vertically in racks; jugs and cups on rows of hooks; copper pots and pans hanging up, their lids on pin rails; cool slate slabs and iron hooks in the pantries; shelves and more shelves with bottles of preserved produce; knives and other implements on racks or hooks ready for immediate selection; and plenty of air circulating and space to work. The cooking range dominated the scene, and bains-marie kept everything hot. There is not much wrong with such ideas today.

It is part of modern pagan mentality to use utensils, bowls, etc, of natural materials sustainably harvested, and always try to keep old utensils as they are often well-made, with lovely, comfortable hardwood handles and no weak joints or other built-in obsolescence. If you want quality construction and blades that can take plenty of sharpening then hand-me-downs can't be beaten. Learning how to clean, maintain and sharpen kitchen tools is time well spent. There is no reason not to use labour-saving ideas and devices in the modern pagan kitchen, provided you have completed the technological audit outlined in chapter 10, as a natural approach to cookery does not mean drudgery. You may like to have a barometer at the exit furthest from the cooking area, although learning about the weather from the clues your garden gives is just as good in many ways.

When involving children in kitchen activities, please remember to ensure that all operations done by them are supervised and safely carried out through your initial instruction and demonstration, especially where handling hot liquids and sharp implements are required. Ideally children should be involved as early as possible, in the harvesting of food from nature and garden, and in its preparation in the kitchen, so that they can see where it comes from and what is done with it. Even when too young to actually undertake a task, a baby can, from a sling, watch what goes on and enjoy the aromas. Children love to wash foods, tear and prepare salads, stir and mix, shape pastry and dough, and arrange the food on plates. As they get older they can be taught to use implements as you feel they are ready and gradually take responsibility for a part of the meal. Being so involved will help to educate their senses, as they smell and taste at every stage, and you can teach them valuable tool-using and other dextrous skills. Witnessing the sequence from nature or field to pot and table, as with preparing a pheasant or rabbit, or baking bread, will also teach them about the seasonal food cycles, to which one hopes they will look forward with eager anticipation.

If you are going to follow the natural human omnivorous diet you will need to make provision in terms of storage and preparation for more fruit and vegetables than meat and seafood. It will be necessary to learn about cross-contamination and food spoilage, and how to both prevent and deal with them, for modern pagan eating habits are centred around fresh produce, and you will need to be familiar with storage times and rates of deterioration. Use separate preparation surfaces and implements for meat and seafood, and maintain strict cleanliness and hygiene of them. Meat should be stored separately from other foods, and cooked and raw meat separately from each other, cooked higher than raw. Indeed, cooked foods of any kind should be stored and prepared separately from raw foods, and utensils washed before re-using on the other. If using canned foods, don't keep food standing in an opened can, and never use a rusty, dented or leaking can. Only put food into a refrigerator when it has cooled to room temperature. Thaw frozen food slowly and thoroughly, covered and in a cool place. Cook as soon as possible. Reheated food should be hot throughout, not just on the surface, and never reheat again.

Natural eating means all the ingredients of a meal ought to be natural. Adding proprietary sauces and condiments full of synthetic additives to fresh foods is missing the point of modern pagan philosophy and practice. Some ideas will be given shortly on how to make your own accessories to a meal from the kitchen garden, so that the whole meal is as natural as you can make it. As with the kitchen garden, fill your kitchen and body with food, not chemicals. How much of a meal you make from your own produce and how much is purchased will inevitably depend upon the time you have available and the amount of assistance you have, but at least try not to compromise on natural quality. Regardless of how affluent you are, it is characteristic of modern pagan living not to waste nature's bounty. Peelings and other vegetable leftovers go onto the compost heap, the remains of a carcass, pea shells and vegetable trimmings to make stock, and crusts and stale bread may be browned to make breadcrumbs. 'Waste not, want not' is still a good axiom.

As a contribution towards the family saga, write down all the recipes and other ideas that turn out successfully, both in the kitchen garden and in the kitchen, so that your descendants can carry on the traditions that you have established.

Stocking a healthy store cupboard

Beans, pulses and pasta: adzuki beans, blackeye beans, chickpeas, flageolet beans, haricot beans, lentils (brown, green, red), mung beans, pasta (buckwheat, millet, rice, wholemeal), red kidney beans, yellow split peas.

Dried fruits: apricots, currants, dates, figs, mangoes, peaches, prunes, raisins, sultanas.

Dried herbs: basil, mint, oregano, rosemary, sage, tarragon, thyme.

Flour: arrowroot, brown rice flour, cake flour, polenta, soya flour (gluten-free), wholemeal flour (plain and self-raising – stoneground best), wholemeal pastry.

Grains: basmati rice, brown rice, buckwheat, bulgar wheat, cornmeal, couscous, cracked wheat, jasmine rice, millet, oat bran, oatflakes, oatmeal, pearl barely, pot barley, quinoa, wild rice. Store grains in sealed jars.

Nuts and seeds: alfalfa, almonds, brazil nuts, cashew nuts, desiccated coconut, hazelnuts, pecan nuts, pine nuts, pumpkin seeds, safflower seeds, sesame seeds, sunflower seeds, walnuts.

Oils (unrefined or cold-pressed): toasted sesame oil and olive oil for sautéing, and grapeseed and walnut oil for salad dressings and sautéing, sunflower oil. Oils should be in a cool, dark place, and kept for no more than a month.

Setting and gelling agents: gelatine, or seaweed products like agar-agar.

Spices: allspice, black pepper, cardamon pods, cayenne pepper, chilli, cinnamon, cloves, coriander, cumin, fennel, garam masala, garlic, ginger, mustard seed (yellow or black), nutmeg, onion, paprika, saffron, salt, star anise, turmeric.

Sweeteners: carob powder (instead of chocolate or cocoa), crystallised ginger, date syrup, honey, maple syrup, natural fruit preserves.

Vinegars: cider vinegar, rice vinegar, wine vinegar (red, white).

Coconut milk, which is low-fat and keeps ten days, soya milk.

Tamari soy sauce (naturally fermented).

Malt extract, yeast extract, dried yeast.

Tinned fruit and tomatoes in natural juices only.

Tinned beans only if additive-free (wash salt off before using).

Tinned fish in water, brine or oil.

Choosing and preparing food

If using food other than from your kitchen garden, endeavour to obtain or purchase organic produce. Organic, in this context, means, in the case of plants, grown without artificial fertilisers or pesticides, grown in soil whose fertility has been conserved by crop rotation, and grown in conditions that do not pollute the peripheral environment. In the case of meat, organic means produced in humane, free-range conditions, using natural feed, and without use of growth stimulants or antibiotics, save for essential veterinary care.

Purchasing organic food

Suppliers are now easier to find, but costs are generally higher because organic production is less intensive, relies on natural insect control rather than instant pesticide application, thereby giving lower yields, and grows at a natural pace instead of at a chemically induced accelerated pace, thereby taking longer to reach the market. If in doubt or mistrustful about organic provenance, grow your own if you can. Unfortunately the word 'organic' is sometimes used as an advertising ploy, and really it would not be necessary to specify the word at all if there had not been such a departure from traditional growing methods. If you have no garden, or insufficient space, it is now possible to buy all your food and drink requirements organically produced – notably baby foods, beers, cereals, cider, coffee, condiments, dairy products, eggs, fish, flour, fruit, fruit juices, herbs, honey, mead, meat, pasta, perry, pulses, rice, teas, vegetables and wines. There are plenty of organic recipe books in print to get you started.

Try to buy fresh produce locally, and avoid re-thawed foodstuffs. Ask for home-grown fruit and vegetables, and try to find where food has come from so you can avoid any that has been sprayed, artificially ripened or coloured. Gradually build up your list of organic food suppliers and shops, including health food and farm shops that specialise in organic products. In order to encourage fresh, genuine, local organic production you should avoid supermarkets when buying fresh produce, as much of their stock will be thawed from what has been frozen for storage. Their purchasing power and centralisation of production and distribution works against the interests of small, local producers, whom modern pagans should endeavour to support. Above all, be wary of advertising claims such as 'full of natural goodness', 'wholesome', 'energy-rich' and 'prevents heart disease' accompanying packaged foods as they are too ambiguous to be taken literally.

Non-organic food

If forced to purchase non-organic food, try to assess the condition and enquire about its origins. Chemical residues on the surfaces are a particular concern, and a waxy feel may indicate their presence. Fruit and vegetables are best peeled or scrubbed to remove any surface residues, or at least washed well.

Preparing organic food

Changing to organic food is both culturally and metabolically desirable, but using organic ingredients in cooking methods that do not preserve their flavour, texture and nutrients is pointless. Organic food requires simple, appropriate cooking so its abundant flavour can be fully appreciated and its nutrients remain undecomposed.

Steaming is the preferred method of cooking vegetables and fish, as it preserves nutritional value, flavour, texture and colour well. Boiling causes leaching of vitamins and other vital nutrients, and should be used only when a high temperature and thorough cooking is essential, as with red kidney beans. Grilling is quick and a good way to cook meat and fish. Use a rack or griddle that allows excess fat to drain away. Roasting meat in its own juices on a rack, allowing excess fat to drip into the pan, is also a satisfactory way to cook it, especially high-fat meats like lamb. Shallow frying with no oil or just a little, in a heavy pan, is a good method of cooking foods that don't release their own juices. Another way of preserving nutritional value, texture and flavour is to stir-fry, preferably with cold-pressed virgin olive oil or sunflower oil. Deep frying is not an advisable method of cooking, especially for potatoes, as large amounts of fat are absorbed. Coating with batter first is equally unhealthy. Baking is another acceptable means of cooking, for your own bread and cakes especially. These six – steaming, grilling, roasting, shallow frying, stir-frying, and baking – are the recommended ways for modern pagans to cook their food.

Prepare foods containing vitamin C by steaming, as near as possible just before eating, because vitamin C is easily oxidised and leaches out quickly when the food is cooked in water. Deep freezing and deep frying destroys vitamin E, as does storing vegetable oils, its main source, other than in a cool, dark place, in tightly stoppered containers.

As microwaving food involves molecular changes in foods that are not fully researched, it is not known what the long-term effects of eating microwaved food are. Modern pagans are advised not to become reliant on the microwave as a regular means of cooking.

Preserving your home-grown food

Natural harvest seasons are short, and can only be extended a little way by staggered planting. You can, of course, prolong the season of almost anything by embalming it in the freezer, but the thawed-out tastes and textures can be disappointing, and the joy of seasonal eating removed if all foods are available all year round. It matters not that you can afford not to preserve and store, for there is much to be gained by storing and preserving your own food. It keeps you out of shops, provides you with different tastes, and is a pleasurable activity that gives you a sense of achievement, even if winter survival is not the point of doing it. Not only that, fresh spring tastes are all the more exciting if winter tastes have been different. The commonest preserving techniques have always been bottling, pickling, chutneying, smoking for meat and fish, salting for meat and a few vegetables, jam-making and making into alcoholic beverages or cordials.

Fruit, including tomatoes, bottles well, but generally not vegetables because they are not high enough in acid. The principle is basically heat sterilisation in boiling water, then immediate sealing. Fruit preserves well in jams, too. Runner beans can be well preserved by salting.

Chutneys and pickles are made by flavouring fruit and/or vegetables with spices, and then preserving in vinegar. For chutney the ingredients are spiced and sweetened, then cooked in vinegar until excess liquor has evaporated. Pickles are put down whole, or in chunks, in vinegar and not heated. Excessively moist ingredients are salted first to remove a lot of the moisture. Eggs, onions and apples pickle well.

Fruit wines, particularly elderberry, parsnip and other root wines, coltsfoot wine, rhubarb wine and the refreshing nettle wine are all old country favourites. Excellent flower wines include broom, cowslip, dandelion, elderflower, gorse, and rose. Mead can be made at home, as can cider, perry, and wine, beer and cider vinegar, provided you have the right equipment. Special varieties of apple and pear are used to make cider and perry respectively, picked ripe and left for a few days to soften. They are crushed in a press, and the juice fermented in vats. About 10–14 lb (5–7 kg) of apples/pears will make a gallon (4.5 l). Sweet cider/perry has about 8 oz (250 g) of sugar added per gallon (4.5 l). To make cider vinegar, the cider is poured through a perforated, wooden plate inset into a barrel of beech shavings, and drawn off through the cock after about a week.

The following old country recipes may be tried.

Mead
4 lb (1.8 kg) of honey is poured on to 1 ¼ gallon (5.8 l) of water in a deep pan and heated sufficiently to melt. The juice of three lemons and some crushed crab apples, for a little tannin, are added. Cover and leave to ferment, adding a dash of rosehip syrup if very slow. Rack and bottle in the usual way.

Dandelion and Burdock Beer
2 lb (900 g) young nettles
8 oz (250 g) dandelion leaves
8 oz (250 g) fresh or 4 oz (125 g) dry burdock root
1 oz (25 g) ginger root, grated
Brewer's yeast, amount according to instructions
4 lemons, juiced and peeled
2 gallon (9 l) water
2 lb (900 g) plus 8 tsp Demerara sugar
2 oz (56 g) cream of tartar

Put the nettles, dandelion leaves, burdock, ginger and the lemon peel into a large pan. Add the water and bring to the boil, then simmer for thirty minutes. Put the lemon juice, 2 lb of sugar, and the cream of tartar into a large container in which fermentation can take place, and strain the liquid from the pan, pressing the plants well to extract all the juices. Stir the contents of the container to dissolve the sugar and cool to body temperature. Sprinkle on the yeast, cover and leave in a warm place to ferment for three days. Filter and bottle, adding ½ tsp Demerara sugar per pint. Leave until the beer is clear, normally about a week, before drinking. Don't count on having any of this beer left if I should happen to call.

Elderberry Wine
12 lb (5.4 kg) elderberries on stalks
6 lb (2.8 kg) sugar
2 gallons (9 l) boiling water
4 oz (125 g) lemon juice
yeast

Put the berries in a deep bowl, pour on the boiling water, and mash the fruit with a potato masher. Cover and leave for twenty-four hours. Add the sugar and yeast, the latter according to manufacturer's instructions, and leave to finish fermenting. Rack into bottles.

Sparkling Elderflower
24 heads of elderflower, picked on a hot day in full bloom and scent

3 lb (1.4 kg) white sugar
Juice of two lemons
2 gallons (9 l) cold water
4 tbsp white wine vinegar
No yeast is needed as the flowers have sufficient natural
yeast on them.

Put the flowers and lemon juice in a deep bowl. Remove the
pith from the lemon rind, slice and add. Add sugar, vinegar and
water, cover and leave for twenty-four hours. Strain into bottles,
lightly cork and leave for two weeks. Drink within a month.

Culinary herbs and their uses in the kitchen
The use of herbs for flavouring is an ancient tradition recorded
in this country as early as Roman times. A herb is simply a
plant, a part of which, whether it be root, stem, leaves, flower
or fruit, is used for flavouring food, or for its scent, or for its
medicinal properties. It is the first and second properties that
concern us in this chapter.

Growing, harvesting and storing herbs
Most herbs are easy to grow. They are annual or perennial,
and generally like light, sunny, well-drained soil that is nourished
but not too organically rich. A few prefer shade, and many are
quite drought-resistant and unfussy. Rampant herbs like mint
are best grown in a container or otherwise confined.

Herbs are either eaten fresh or dried by the best method of
keeping their colour, aroma and flavour. They can be stored in
the refrigerator for a few days, wrapped in damp kitchen paper
or in bunches in water. Normally, herbs are harvested before
flowering, on a fine, warm morning after dew has evaporated,
but before the leaves heat up too much. Pick lavender before
the flowers open. Try not to over-handle as herbs bruise easily.
Every minute counts as the aromatic oils start to evaporate as
soon as you have harvested. Initially, tie them in bunches and
hang in a cool airy place, then put on a drying rack in a strong
draught of air, at 70–80°F (21–27°C). If damp, lay in a cool
oven on its lowest setting overnight. Rub the leaves off the stem
when dry and brittle, crumble and store in labelled, sealed glass
or pottery jars in the dark. For herb mixtures such as parsley,

thyme and bay for bouquet garni, a traditional additive to casseroles and stews, store together.

Dried herbs are more pungent, so only about a third of the quantity of fresh herbs is generally needed for the same intensity of flavour. Freeze-dried herbs are said to have more flavour than air-dried. The higher the essential oil content, like rosemary and bay, the more flavour is retained after drying. However, all dried herbs lose character quite quickly, so don't overstock indoors.

Preparing fresh leafy herbs for immediate use

Wash under running water, press gently between sheets of paper towel and spread on a rack. Remove from woody stems with fingers or fork. Tear with the fingers if loss of delicate flavour is to be avoided, as with basil. Strong flavours like chives survive plenty of chopping with a knife, others will take a little, like lovage and sorrel. For quick release of flavour in a dish with short cooking time you can bruise the herb first with a pestle and mortar. Handle garnishes as little as possible.

Preparing herb bulbs, flowers, seeds and fruit for immediate use

The amount of flavour you want determines how you prepare the herb. Lightly press a garlic clove with the flat blade of a knife to break the skin, and peel. Slit onion skin and peel by hand, and slit the bottom of shallots and blanch in boiling water for three minutes to release skins. Then slice the clove or bulb for a mild flavour, chop for a stronger flavour, and crush or pound for the strongest release. Roasting garlic gives the sweetest, least pungent flavour. If you tend to weep when preparing alliums, immerse them in water, or chew on a bread crust to prevent or relieve tears. If you get bad breath after eating them, then rub peppermint oil on the soles of your feet (yes, feet!) beforehand.

For peppers, broiling (roasting under the grill) brings out the natural sweet flavour best.

Seeds and nuts have their flavour released successively more powerfully by using them whole, lightly crushed, flaked, then chopped, up to grinding into powder. Gentle roasting or dry-frying also releases more flavour. Almonds are normally flaked.

Caraway, coriander, cumin, fennel and mustard seeds can be lightly roasted before crushing. Hard seeds like coriander are best ground in a pepper mill. Nutmeg is grated as required, and ginger root, after peeling, may be chopped, grated or squeezed.

Saffron is infused in warm water for five minutes to release the flavour, and vanilla pods are infused in milk or sugar to flavour custards or desserts. Infusing is also the method for herbs like parsley that are used to flavour sauces. Flowers can be infused in a similar way, either whole or as individual petals. Remember to sterilise all bottles used to store aqueous or oily herbal preparations.

Preparing teas or tisanes

The leaves, flowers or fruit of many edible plants can be infused in hot or boiling water to make a tea. Strain and serve hot or cold.

Preparing herb cordials

In a similar way to teas, you can infuse herbs in syrups to make cordials, or in alcohol to make punches. Rosehip cordial is an old favourite:

2 ¾ lb (1.25 kg) rosehips
4 pints (2.4 l) water
granulated sugar – 12 oz (350 g) for every pint (600 ml) of syrup made

Bring the water to the boil in a saucepan. Finely chop the rosehips, add to the water and reboil. Cover and simmer gently for ten minutes. Remove heat and stand for fifteen minutes. Strain through a jelly bag previously sterilised with boiling water. Cover and leave to complete. Measure the syrup volume and weigh the requisite amount of sugar. Gently heat the syrup and add the sugar while stirring until dissolved. Boil until syrupy; about five minutes should be enough. Pour into bottles and cork. Store in the refrigerator, in which it will keep for a few weeks.

Herb condiments

Herb salt is simply made by adding a mixture of dried herbs to coarse salt in a mortar and crushing with the pestle until thoroughly mixed. Good choices are bay, dill, fennel, oregano, rosemary, tarragon and thyme. Such salts are traditionally rubbed into meat, poultry or fish as a dry marinade before roasting or grilling, and stirred into casseroles, stews or soups.

An old favourite condiment is horseradish mustard, the classic accompaniment to roast beef:

1 oz (25 g) mustard seeds
4 oz (125 g) dry mustard powder
3 tbsp (45 ml) grated horse radish
4 oz (125 g) light muscovado sugar
2 fl oz (50 ml) olive oil
4 fl oz (120 ml) white wine, or cider, vinegar
1 tsp lemon juice
8 fl oz (250 ml) boiling water

Put the mustard seeds in boiling water for one hour. Drain, and put the seeds into a blender with the rest of the ingredients. Blend until perfectly smooth. Put in jars and store in the refrigerator.

Herb butters, creams and cheeses

Herb butters can be readily made by beating the butter to a cream and then beating in the herb mixture. Chill until needed. Herbs to choose from include basil, chives, coriander, marjoram, parsley, rosemary, tarragon and thyme, to which can be added lemon rind, salt and black pepper to season. A similar method is used for cream cheeses. When flavouring milk or cream with herbs, bring to the boil, remove from the heat and allow the herb or herbs to infuse until cool and to taste. Chill and strain. Sweet herbs like bay, lavender, rosemary and thyme work well.

Herb sauces

Dips, gravies, mayonnaises and sauces can all be made with herbal flavours. To make a herb dip, fold finely chopped herbs into crème fraîche, fromage frais, mayonnaise or yoghurt. Other ingredients can be blended in to taste, like lemon juice, garlic, ginger and other spices, with salt and black pepper seasoning if desired. For a gravy, add your herb mixture to the basic gravy stock and simmer gently until the intensity of flavour is what you want. For a rich gravy for meat roasts, offal or sausages, try a mixture of chopped or sliced onion, parsely, sage and thyme, with black pepper seasoning.

To make honey and mustard salad dressing, whisk 1 tbsp runny honey with 1 tbsp Dijon mustard and 4 tbsp white wine or cider vinegar. Season with black pepper to taste. Herbs are what the well-dressed salad wears in the modern pagan kitchen.

A traditional bread sauce is made from cloves and bay leaves:

1 peeled onion
4 oz (125g) breadcrumbs
8 whole cloves
2 bay leaves
1 pint (600 ml) milk
½ oz (15 g) butter
3 tbsp (45 ml) single cream
salt and ground black pepper to taste

Press the cloves into the onion. Put the milk in a saucepan and add the bay leaves and onion. Bring to the boil and remove from the heat to steep for fifteen minutes. Remove the bay leaves and onion and stir in the breadcrumbs. Simmer gently until thickened (about ten minutes), then stir in the butter and cream. Season to taste.

Preparing herb oils and vinegars

These are simple to make by adding the selected herbs to the oil or vinegar. For oils, choose strongly flavoured herbs like basil, bay, marjoram, oregano, sage, tarragon, and thyme, and combine as desired. Light oils allow the herb flavour to dominate, so choose grapeseed, olive or sunflower. Wash herbs, dry, remove bruised parts and push into bottles. Fill with the oil and cork, and allow to stand in a cool place for two weeks for the flavours to be absorbed. Strain through muslin into bottles. Herb oils normally keep up to six months.

For vinegars, the herbs above may be used too, and also dill and mint. Avoid strong red wine vinegars likely to mask the herb flavour, but use light red or white wine vinegar or cider vinegar. Boil vinegar in a saucepan, not made of aluminium, pour on to the herb or herbs – chopped for stronger flavour – and leave to infuse for two to three days. Strain through muslin into a jug and pour into bottles. Cork, and it will keep for six months.

Preparing herb pickles and preserves

An old established herb pickle is made with dill, popular in times past with cold meats and cheese:

1.5 lb (675 g) ridge cucumbers
large bunch of fresh dill
3 tbsp (45 ml) coarse salt
3 bay leaves
2 star anise
5 peeled, sliced garlic cloves
1½ pint (500 ml) white wine vinegar
2 tsp (10 ml) mixed peppercorns
13 fl oz (375 ml) water

Trim the ends of the ridge cucumbers and cut into 2 inch (5 cm) pieces. Cover with cold water and chill overnight. Drain and pierce with fork, and pack into jars with the dill and garlic. Into a saucepan put the vinegar, water and the rest of the ingredients, and boil for five minutes. Pour over the ridge cucumbers and seal.

Another classic recipe is for mint sauce:

Large bunch of finely chopped fresh mint
¼ pint (150 ml) white wine vinegar
7 tbsp (105 ml) boiling water
Up to 2 tbsp (30 ml) caster sugar

Put the mint into a bowl, add the boiling water and leave to infuse. Cool to lukewarm, then add vinegar, and sugar to taste. Bottle, and store when cold in the refrigerator.

Some ideas to conclude

If cooking a barbecue, you can sprinkle herbs on the coals to use the vapour to flavour the food, scent the air and help keep flying insects at bay. Any dried herbs that no longer have the intensity of aroma to indicate sufficient flavour for cooking can be used to make pot pourris for air freshening. Dried herb mixtures in a bowl freshen and scent the air, and in bags, based on lavender, keep drawers and cupboards fresh and insect-free. Lavender sprinkled on a summerhouse floor will achieve the same effect. And after all that labour you deserve a herbal bath. Hang a herb mixture, dried or fresh, in a muslin cloth bag under the hot tap to create a relaxing or invigorating bath. A good mixture to relax in is chamomile, jasmine and valerian, whereas an invigorating mixture would be lavender, lemon balm, mint and rosemary.

The herb recipes above are simple but tasty examples of what can be done with home-grown herbs, to add interest and flavours to basic meal ingredients. You can so easily corrupt your healthy eating plans by starting with fresh basic foods and combining them with purchased, processed accessories like sauces containing synthetic additives. It is but a short step from simple recipes to experimenting with your garden herbs, singly or in mixtures, and preparing them with various degrees of flavour release with your chosen basic foods so that you get the complement and intensity of flavour and aroma you are seeking. This creative approach is the modern pagan culinary way.

Once you have experience in the culinary uses of herbs, you will be well placed to move on to the more precise methods of preparation required for the production of medicinal herbal products introduced later in the book.

Diet and lifestyle

A modern pagan attitude to food and lifestyle should mean that dieting is unnecessary, save in terms of quantity as related to changing activity and for physiological conditions requiring medical guidance. Over-indulgence of any kind, beyond that accompanying special occasions, is in pagan terms undisciplined and anharmonic. Beyond basic guidelines for moderate, healthy eating, balanced nutritional intake and consumption of adequate water there is no modern pagan diet as such, for that would be just another fad diet, of which there are rather too many these days. Modern pagans can eat whatever has been naturally and humanely produced or processed in acceptable ways without unnecessary adulteration, variety being nutritionally better for you than monotony. However, given the tempting abundance of food of poor quality and low nutritional value today, it is wise to consider some basic nutritional and physiological guidelines carefully before planning a healthy eating regime, so that you are equipped to make sensible choices. The guidelines that follow shortly refer just to day-to-day eating and not to special celebratory meals. A natural diet is not, and is not intended to be, in any way austere, and occasionally you can eat whatever you fancy.

The sort of nutritional advice that has come from governments, scientists and the food industry during the last forty years has been conflicting and often tainted with vested interest, such as of the food manufacturers, whose dietary suggestions should always be studied critically. For some people, like vegetarians and vegans, diet is fashioned by personal conviction. However, we must be wary of adopting a diet when we no longer have the lifestyle that is suited to it. Food is now abundant, concentrated and heavily advertised, and we can so easily override the natural constraints on appetite and imbalanced diet found in the wild. We live twice as long as our ancestors but commonly suffer from a range of diseases and complaints that hunter-gatherers rarely suffer from – for example, behavioural disorders, certain allergies, diabetes and obesity; coronary heart disease, stroke, hypertension, and other heart complaints; and disorders of the intestine and associated organs, like gallstones, constipation, piles, cancer of the colon, and diverticular disease. Now that these are regarded as at least partly diet-related, chief suspects are high fat consumption in the case of coronary heart disease and lack of fibre in the case of diverticular disease, to give but two examples. They are termed 'diseases of affluence' but are better styled as 'diseases of indulgence and nutritional ignorance'.

Fortunately a consensus is emerging among dieticians, physiologists and biologists towards what constitutes a diet that is practical, predominantly natural, nutritionally balanced in terms of all essential components (protein, fat, carbohydrate and fibre, vitamins, minerals and water), and biologically sensible in relation to our evolutionary history. Changing to a healthier diet does not just mean broadening the variety of foods consumed to prevent deficiency of nutrients, it means eliminating some foods, replacing others with more acceptable substitutes, changing the proportions of certain types of food, and preparing and cooking foods appropriately to preserve nutritive value. One objective should always be to maintain optimum body weight.

There is a growing body of learned opinion that we should all drink more fresh water to avoid dehydration and the problems known to be associated with it, such as periodic lassitude. Moreover, feelings of hunger, leading to daily over-eating, are often just feelings of thirst, and may be better relieved by taking water. Even moderate consumption of caffeinated drinks like tea and coffee is dehydrating, and there are sound physiological reasons why drinking water regularly can be helpful in the prevention of, or relieving the distress of, arthritis, asthma, high blood pressure, stomach ulcers, and stress and anxiety states.

The 'monkey diet' is an interesting natural example of the way in which diet and lifestyle can be mutually regulating. An omnivorous monkey will eat fruit in the morning, for a quick energy conversion before the most active period of the day; then meat for protein and essential minerals in the middle of the day; and cellulose, which takes a long time to digest, before the night's rest. Perhaps there is a message for us all in this observation.

Fad diets abound, sometimes making a lot of money for their inventors, but are usually nutritionally unsound and should be avoided. A fad diet that is drawing interest is based on the alleged link between metabolism and blood group and the conviction, drawn from supposed evolutionary evidence, that people with specific blood groups need a particular balance of nutrients. There is no physiological evidence to support the claim that at different stages of the evolution of *Homo sapiens* dietary changes necessitated by changes in habitat, climate and food availability have, in parallel with alleged related haema-tological changes, led to a relationship between blood group and nutrients necessary for a healthy body containing that blood group. Modern pagans do not need fad diets if they stick to natural foods as far as possible and physiologically recognised nutritional balance.

The omnivorous human

The ideal diet might seem to be the natural diet of *Homo sapiens*, but there is no way of knowing what this is; and anyway diets have to change in nature as climate, terrain and competition change. One thing has remained consistent: the superiority of breast milk over cows' milk or formula milk. Babies fed on formula milk tend to overfeed, get immune responses, and can contract infections through poor sterilisation, and their mothers fail to lose the weight normally lost during lactation and suffer psychological problems through lack of bonding with their babies. As with all animals, the human body has evolved in nature and has adapted to its food sources. Just a glance at our teeth alone seems to indicate that *Homo sapiens* is an omnivore, and given the abundance of plant food and the difficulty all carnivores have in catching regular prey it is reasonable to assume that *Homo sapiens* is adapted principally to a plant diet with enrichment by meat.

If true, such dietary versatility explains how *Homo sapiens* tribal groups were able to exploit the globe for food, which they did in variety except for a few hunter-gatherers like the virtually carnivorous Inuit of polar North America and the nearly herbivorous Ainu of northern Japan. Generally, variety in the human diet has, until relatively recently, ensured a broadly nutritious intake. The meat of wild animals is lean compared with fatty farm meat, and wild plant material highly fibrous compared with farm crops. Fibrous plant material would have had to have been eaten in quite large quantities to get sufficient nutrition from it, so there would have been a shortage of energy-giving components unless fat was consumed in reasonable amounts, which it could be if extracted from brains and bone marrow, a practice early humankind is known to have pursued. The diet of early *Homo sapiens*, therefore, had no refined carbohydrate, plenty of unrefined carbohydrate, especially fibre, a reasonable amount of protein, was low in fat and adequate in vitamins and minerals, and on the face of it this was healthy and sustaining.

Vegetarianism, veganism and modern paganism

Vegans will eat no animal or food derived from an animal, such as eggs, milk, cream and butter, whereas vegetarians do often eat dairy produce and eggs. Many pagans may choose to be vegetarians or vegans because their fondness for animals dictates their choice of diet, but there is no conflict between carnivorous eating and paganism. The issue of whether it is truly pagan to aspire to a natural lifestyle, including diet, and yet by conscience become vegetarian or vegan, is one that traditional pagans have considered at length. Dental and archaeological evidence suggests strongly that the human species is an evolutionary omnivore, and true pagans maintain this biological tradition, not least to ensure maximum bodily constitution. But modern paganism is about making lifestyle choices, and matters of conscience are important in that they support these choices. Vegetarianism and veganism are therefore not at variance with modern paganism; indeed, the compassion of vegans and vegetarians towards animals is a strength that we could all draw from to moral and practical advantage. The most serious nutritional problem vegans have is in obtaining vitamin B12, which has only animal sources, so a supplement is necessary. Vegans also lack the best dietary sources of calcium – milk, yoghurt and cheese – so must watch calcium intake carefully. Both vegetarians and vegans lack the best sources of iron, which is haem iron from animal blood and offal, but can compensate because ascorbic acid (vitamin C) enhances the absorption of non-haem iron from plant sources.

Fats and fatty acids

Fats are generally classified in three categories: saturated, mostly animal fats but some are in coconut and palm oils; monounsaturated, mostly in nuts and fruit; and polyunsaturated, mostly in vegetable and fish oils. Generally, solid fats tend to be saturated and liquid oils unsaturated, although there are some exceptions as noted above. Fats provide essential fatty acids for specific bodily functions so cannot be eliminated from the diet. Although the prime energy source in food, fat has become notorious because excess of it, unlike carbohydrate and protein, is stored in the body, including places like the lining of the arteries, but mostly in adipose tissue beneath the skin. Mammalian stored fat tends to be saturated, and is a source of energy twice as good as carbohydrate or protein, but if an animal is deficient in fat or stores little, as applies to deer, then they burn muscle protein for energy when needed in an emergency, and therefore lose body weight sharply when food is scarce.

All essential fatty acids for humans are polyunsaturated and their principal sources are from seeds and green leaves, both of which are needed to get all that we require. Liver is rich in essential fatty acids, but particularly so is breast milk as it contains those essential fatty acids necessary for the proper development of babies' brains. Cows' milk does not contain the right essential fatty acids for human babies, but has the advantage of being high in protein.

Good polyunsaturated fat sources, with the highest content first in the list, are safflower seed oil, soya bean oil, sunflower seed oil, walnuts, brazil nuts, peanuts, and soya flour.

The relationship between fats, fatty acids and good health

Deficiency of essential fatty acids is suspected as being related to the high incidence of multiple sclerosis and schizophrenia, and as a factor in the incidence of blood clots. Diseases common in high-fat consuming societies are breast cancer, colon cancer, and coronary heart disease. Cholesterol appears to have a role in the accumulation of fatty and other deposits in the arteries. The three most significant risk factors in coronary heart disease are smoking, hypertension and high concentration of cholesterol in blood. Keeping cholesterol levels down appears to be desirable, and it is important that as much cholesterol as possible is high-density lipoprotein cholesterol, whose proportion is increased by exercise and taking fat in polyunsaturated form, but in modest amounts. Blood cholesterol levels are partly determined by diet as well as genetically on an individual basis. Mono-unsaturated fatty acids, for example in olive oil, seem to have a neutral effect on cholesterol, neither raising nor lowering it. Statistically, lowering total fat intake to no more than 20 per cent would make coronary heart disease rare, so at least some saturated fat should be replaced in the diet by polyunsaturated fat. Egg yolk and liver are the principal high-cholesterol foods, and should therefore be eaten in moderation.

In order of significance, the risk of heart attack is greatest if blood cholesterol is high, then if blood pressure is high and smoking occurs, then lower risk factors like diabetes, obesity, stress, sedentary lifestyle, and drinking soft water, because it is deficient in metal ions. All are difficult to quantify, but all are risk factors. Although common sense tells us that prevention is better than cure, changing one's diet and lifestyle probably increases one's chances of avoiding coronary heart disease and the other conditions mentioned, even though some damage already done may not be reversible.

Purveyors of foods use facts and statistics selectively to protect their vested interests, especially where the now notorious fat is concerned. Some margarines have comparable amounts of saturated fats to butter so on this basis alone would seem to be no healthier. Only polyunsaturated margarines can reasonably make the claim to be healthier than butter. Vegetable oil contains no cholesterol, so is healthier from that point of view, but vegetable oil can be highly saturated, for example, from palm oil, so this tips the scales the other way. In terms of calorific value there is little difference between margarine and butter, but this is not the main issue in the health debate. Much consumed fat comes from dairy products (milk, cream, butter, cheese, and cakes, pastries, biscuits, etc., made from them) and meat, especially sausages and meat pies as these come from the less lean parts of a carcass. Just changing to skimmed milk would mean a significant reduction in fat intake, which overall should consist principally of polyunsaturated fish oils and oils from plants like maize, safflower and sunflower, with minimal amounts of animal fats. Fat should constitute no more than 30 per cent of energy intake, of which no more than a third should be saturated fat.

Carbohydrates

Another energy source, carbohydrate, needs to be eaten sufficiently to compensate for reduction in fat, and in protein too.

Babies obtain most of their carbohydrate from lactose in milk, but thereafter nearly all consumed carbohydrate comes from plants. Important carbohydrates are the monosaccharides glucose and fructose, the latter common in fruit, the disaccharide sucrose, and the polysaccharide starch, and they are all easily digestible sources of energy. Dietary fibre, or roughage, are carbohydrates that are structural materials from plant cell walls. There are five types of fibre: cellulose and hemicelluloses from plant cell walls; lignin, a woody fibre from roots, which may help in prevention of varicose veins, haemorrhoids and rectal cancer, and which stimulates saliva when chewed to help prevent the acidity that contributes to tooth decay; gums exuded from plants, which help reduce cholesterol intake; as do pectins from fruit pulp, which do the same for fat as well as for cholesterol. Cellulose is not digestible by enzyme action, only by bacterial assistance, for example, in the rumen of cattle. For humans these fibrous carbohydrates are not energy sources, but we should still eat plenty of our carbohydrate as unrefined plant material with its cellulose and other cell wall materials intact, because this will fulfil our fibre needs. Suitable carbohydrate foods are raw or lightly cooked vegetables, fruit, cereals, pulses (peas, beans and lentils), potatoes, flour and wholewheat bread. Cereals, pulses and potatoes also contain good amounts of protein and the full range of fibres may be taken from eating all of fresh fruit, fresh vegetables, whole grains and beans.

Refined carbohydrate, commonly sugar and extracted starch as opposed to the starch that occurs naturally in unbroken cells, is undesirable as it is pure carbohydrate and easily over-consumed, and is not accompanied by anything else of nutritional value. Sucrose, then, is not a nutrient, save for its part in energy production, and generally we should eat fewer foods containing simple sugars and more containing starches and fibre.

Good digestible carbohydrate sources, with the highest content first in the list, are:

- Rice, oatmeal, wholewheat flour, split peas, lentils, and butterbeans

Good fibre sources, with the highest content first in each list, are:

- Grains – bran, soya flour, wholewheat flour, oatmeal
- Pulses – haricot beans, chickpeas
- Fruit – dried apricots, prunes, blackcurrants, dates, raspberries, blackberries, sultanas, currants, raisins
- Nuts – desiccated coconut, almonds, fresh coconut, brazil nuts, peanuts
- Vegetables – peas, parsley, spinach, sweetcorn, and celery

The relationship between carbohydrates and good health

The amount of carbohydrate we eat and whether it is refined (freed from fibrous cellular materials) or unrefined (containing that dietary fibre) affects our susceptibility to coronary heart disease, diabetes, gallstones, obesity, and intestinal disorders like constipation, diverticular disease and cancer of the colon. Honey is one of the few naturally occurring refined sugars, but is not eaten in large enough quantities to be a problem, whereas sugar, which is pure sucrose extracted from sugar beet or sugar cane, and molasses, treacle and syrup, are problematic components of many people's diet. Sugar is not only easily metabolised, but is the principal cause of dental caries, by feeding the bacteria whose acidic secretions dissolve tooth enamel. Equally serious is sugar's contribution to obesity, as it is added to food as a sweetener, a preservative and to produce a smooth texture. Also, brown sugar is just as dangerous as it is refined to the same degree as white sugar. Sugar has only half the calorific value of fat so is not even the best energy food available. Ideally a diet should contain no refined sugar at all, but certainly no more than ten teaspoons per day. White flour is largely refined starch, and therefore so is white bread, which makes both easily digestible, but they are reasonably good foods because of their fibre and protein content.

Diets in which most of the energy foods are unrefined carbohydrate do not lead to obesity – that is to say, diets low in fat and low in refined carbohydrate. As such a diet makes you feel full sooner, because of the fibre, you eat less, and it also takes longer to eat. Also, the presence of fibre slows down the rate of absorption of sugars from the small intestine, making the onset of diabetes less likely over a period of time as the concentration of blood glucose is maintained within acceptable bounds. A high refined carbohydrate and low-fibre diet appears strongly to be linked with diabetes that starts in middle to old age. It is known that pectins, which are found in fruit preserves like jam, have the effect of reducing the rate of absorption of glucose. The fibre itself is not absorbed from the small intestine but passed on into the colon. Minerals and water are absorbed into the blood stream from here, and the fibre is bacterially broken down, to give amongst other things volatile fatty acids, which provide a minor source of energy. More fibre causes more bacterial reproduction as they thrive on it and it is the dead bacteria that make up most of the bulk of faeces. Faeces of people on a high-fibre diet are greater in mass but softer and passed through more quickly and easily than those of people on a low-fibre diet. The former therefore rarely suffer from constipation and rupture of the gut (diverticular disease). A low-fibre, high-fat diet is linked to cancer of the colon, which in turn is related to the length of time faeces remain in the colon.

Gallstones are crystallised cholesterol and form in the gall bladder. People on low-fibre diets are more prone to get them. Fibre prevents bile salts, which help emulsify fat during its digestion, from being reabsorbed, passing out in the faeces instead. In response, the liver must make more, and to do this it uses cholesterol, thus using it up. Any process like this involving the use of cholesterol helps to keep its concentration down, as does any process promoting its excretion. Fibre thus helps lower the risk of coronary heart disease. Fibre intake should be no more than thirty grammes per day; good fibrous foods include cereals, wholemeal bread and pasta, fresh fruit, dried fruit, vegetables and nuts.

Proteins and amino acids

The foods you eat to give you balance in all the components except protein will almost certainly supply your protein needs too; so strict protein accounting is seldom necessary. Proteins supply most of the amino acids the body requires, but not all. Of the twenty or so amino acids needed in the body from metabolism of protein, eight are essential from foods because the body cannot synthesise them. They can be obtained from animal sources such as meat, milk and eggs, whereas vegetable protein sources often lack one or more essential amino acids so a mixture is advisable, for example, from wholegrain cereals and pulses, not one or the other. Cereals tend to lack the essential amino acid lysine, but soya beans have all essential amino acids. Generally speaking, all cereals, pulses, roots and tubers are good sources of protein.

Good protein sources, with the highest content first in each list, are:

- Yeast extract – probably the best source
- Grains – soya flour, wheatgerm, bran, wholewheat flour, oatmeal
- Dairy produce – cheese, cottage cheese, yoghurt, soya milk, skimmed milk
- Eggs
- Nuts – peanuts, pistachios, almonds, walnuts, brazil nuts
- Pulses – chick-peas, lentils, tofu, split peas, and haricot beans
- Meat – pork, chicken, fish, beef

The relationship between proteins, amino acids and good health

Although vital for growth, cell repair and enzyme manufacture, protein is not stored in the body so must be eaten regularly. We need a minimum amount of protein and extra amino acids to maintain the body and it must be balanced against energy foods, as enzymes are needed to deal with such foods. Without energy foods (carbohydrate and fat) the body converts protein to carbohydrate and therefore muscle wastage occurs. Because the plant sources of protein mentioned above must have the nutrient needed for seedlings and new shoots to thrive they contain good amounts of both protein and carbohydrate. Taking in too much animal protein normally means extra animal fat too, which is undesirable, and the excess protein tends to be used for conversion to carbohydrate, rather than utilising fat, which is then deposited.

Vitamins and their role in maintaining good health

A basic diet of vegetables, fruit, cereals, pulses, potatoes, a little meat and a little fish, all in variety, will also supply your mineral and vitamin needs. Unlike most fats, carbohydrates and proteins, the functions of these components of the diet are highly specific and individual. None can therefore be omitted from the diet. Although serious vitamin deficiency is rare in developed countries, partial deficiency may be more common than is realised, partly through destruction of vitamins in food preparation or processing. Vitamins are only required in small quantities, but the body cannot make them so all must come from food. The vitamin content of foods is seriously reduced by careless preparation, cooking, storing, and commercial processing. Water-soluble vitamins are easily destroyed by cooking, especially the B group, folic acid and vitamin C, and are not retained in the body for long, whereas fat-soluble vitamins (A, D, E and K) are more stable and stored in fatty tissues and the liver. Your vitamin requirements are higher if you are a baby, child, pregnant, breast-feeding, elderly or ill, and your intake should be more frequent if you drink alcohol, smoke, drink coffee or take regular medication.

Vitamins are required in a variety of metabolic reactions, but some have certain specific and well-known functions. Vitamin A and its precursor ß-Carotene are essential for proper vision. Alone of the vitamins, vitamin D, essential for formation of bones and teeth, is synthesised by the body, if the skin has sufficient exposure to sunlight, so in temperate climates this is not a reliable method of making it. Vitamin E is an antioxidant protecting against free radical damage, and vitamin K is needed for blood clotting. Vitamin C, another antioxidant, is easily oxidised and destroyed by heat. Stored potatoes and fruit will tend to lose their vitamin C content, and mashing cooked potatoes incorporates air, which oxidises some of the vitamin C that has survived the cooking.

Regular vitamin C is essential as it is an antioxidant and helps to prevent oxidation of polyunsaturated fatty acids, and may help prevent the onset of some cancers. Spina bifida has been linked to deficiency of the B vitamin folic acid during pregnancy, good sources being liver and green vegetables, especially endive, fresh peas and chick-peas. The custom of boiling green vegetables in sodium bicarbonate decomposes folic acid and other vitamins. Dairy foods should in general be taken in modest quantities. Cows' milk is designed for calf nutrition, not human, and it is high in saturated fat and protein. It does, however, have good amounts of the vitamin riboflavin, but so do liver and green vegetables, and of calcium. Calcium deficiency can mean proneness to high blood pressure as well as osteoporosis. Excessive doses of vitamins can be harmful, so vitamin supplements are not necessary if you have a healthy diet, unless under medical direction.

Good vitamin sources, with the highest available content first in each list, are:

- Vitamin A: eggs, butter, milk and milk products, liver, fish and fish oils
- ß-Carotene: sorrel, carrots, parsley, margarine, spring cabbage, broccoli, red peppers, tomatoes, apricots, peaches, mangoes
- Vitamin B1 (Thiamin): yeast extract, wheatgerm, brazil nuts, peanuts, bran, soya flour, millet
- Vitamin B2 (Riboflavin): yeast extract, almonds, wheatgerm, cheese, egg yolk, milk and milk products, liver, red meat, green vegetables
- Vitamin B3 (Niacin): yeast extract, liver, red meat, fish, bran, peanuts, wheatgerm, wholewheat flour, dried peaches, mushrooms, potatoes
- Vitamin B6: bran, yeast extract, liver, wheatgerm, walnuts, soya flour, red meat, poultry, hazelnuts, banana, salmon, green leafy vegetables, potatoes
- Folate/Folic Acid: watercress, bran, yeast extract, liver, green vegetables (especially endive), peas, chick-peas, orange juice, wheatgerm
- Vitamin B12: liver, beef, lamb, egg yolk, cheese, yeast extract, cottage cheese, other dairy products, fish. There are no plant sources.
- Pantothenic Acid: red meat, cereals, vegetables
- Biotin: egg yolk, liver, grains, legumes (peas and beans), red meat, milk

- Vitamin C: red pepper, blackcurrants, rosehips, oranges, mangoes, papayas, kiwi fruit, parsley, sorrel, strawberries, green pepper, lemon, broccoli, Brussels sprouts, potatoes, milk
- Vitamin D: butter, margarine, egg yolk, cheese, milk, liver, fish and fish oils
- Vitamin E: unrefined vegetable oils (wheatgerm, safflower, sunflower), hazelnuts, almonds, peanuts, margarine, brazil nuts, wholegrains, green leafy vegetables, poultry, fish, egg yolk, potatoes
- Vitamin K: cabbage, lettuce, soya beans, cauliflower, spinach, Brussels sprouts, peas, liver, red meat, dairy products

Minerals and their role in maintaining good health

The seven major minerals, so-called in dietary parlance, are sodium, potassium, chlorine, calcium, phosphorus, magnesium and sulphur. At least nine are known to be needed in small amounts (trace elements), iron (required to make haemoglobin for oxygen transport in the blood), zinc and copper, which mainly come from meat, and manganese, chromium, cobalt, selenium and iodine (required for manufacture of thyroid hormones). Fluorine is needed to harden tooth enamel. As plants absorb minerals from the soil they are a good source. Mineral balance is also important and can be upset by taking in too much of one, for example, too much sodium from salt in processed foods, or excess phosphorus from phosphate fertilisers absorbed by crops.

Good mineral sources, with the highest content first in each list, are:

- Calcium: milk, yoghurt, cheese, cereals, spinach, parsley, dried figs, almonds, watercress, soya flour, brazil nuts, hard water
- Chlorine: most foods
- Chromium: spices, brewer's yeast, red meat (especially beef), wholegrains, legumes, nuts
- Copper: fresh yeast, liver, shellfish, bran, brazil nuts, egg,

dried peaches, desiccated coconut, parsley, currants, whole-wheat flour, broad beans, bananas, potatoes, tomatoes, mushrooms
- Fluorine: tea, seafoods
- Iodine: milk, seaweed, seafood (especially haddock, whiting, herring, with less in plaice and tuna)
- Iron: cockles, black pudding, liver, oatmeal, beef, lamb, bran, wheatgerm, parsley, soya flour, dried peaches, millet, egg yolk, dried figs
- Magnesium: bran, brazil nuts, wheatgerm, almonds, soya flour, peanuts, millet, wholewheat flour, walnuts, oatmeal, legumes, green leafy vegetables, seafood
- Phosphorus: red meat, poultry, fish, eggs, dairy products, cereals, nuts, legumes
- Potassium: yeast extract, dried apricots, soya flour, bran, dried peaches, parsley, dried figs, wheatgerm, sultanas, nuts, potatoes, dairy products, red meat
- Selenium: brazil nuts, red meat, fish, eggs, grains
- Sodium: most foods
- Sulphur: egg, milk, most protein foods
- Zinc: offal, lean meat, seafoods, bran, brazil nuts, cheese, pecans, garlic, almonds, peanuts, walnuts, wholewheat flour, oatmeal, pulses

Dietary support for your immune system

It is hardly surprising to learn that the foods that keep our body supplied with essential nutrients are the same foods that ensure that our immune system is able to keep infection at bay. You know if your immune system is coping because you fall prey to infection infrequently, and when you do you recover quickly and fully. But many people today complain that they seldom feel really well, and suffer from a string of disorders, many of them minor in effect but irritating and persistent. Examples of such disorders, which could indicate insufficient nutritional support for the immune system, are allergies, digestive problems, thrush, skin infections, and joint stiffness and pain. As if we don't expect enough from our overworked immune systems to fight bacterial, fungal, parasitic and virus infections, they are put under further pressure by environmental toxins, over-reliance on antibiotics, mild painkillers and other drugs, poor nutrition, lack of exercise, stress, shock, and emotional imbalance. Conditions known to deteriorate with emotional stress include irritable bowel syndrome, tension headaches, migraine, eczema and psoriasis. To give our immune system a fighting chance it needs the body to have a balanced nutritional intake, and a few particular components from foods.

Skin care is very important, for the skin is the first line of defence against micro-organism invasion, backed up by the action of antibodies for anything that gets through. The second line of defence is both acquired and adaptive immunity, a defence that is built up by the body's experiences in dealing with previous invasions. A complex biochemical system like the immune system works best in its natural state, not undermined by a succession of mild pharmaceutical preparations from the chemist. For example, mucous discharge from the nose is the body's way of clearing out toxins, yet many people take medication to dry it up.

Certain lifestyle changes can positively affect the performance and robustness of your immune system. They include cutting down on alcohol and caffeine intake; giving up smoking and avoiding passive smoking; avoiding exposure to radiation and too much sunbathing; and taking care in environments where chemicals are used, such as in dry-cleaning or exposure to car exhaust fumes. Other important changes that will give positive support to your immune system are changing to a diet of natural foods, for which modern pagan eating is ideal; avoiding dehydration by taking regular water; avoiding processed foods and those containing chemical additives; regular exercise; and relieving stress. The immune system works less well as the body ages, but it still needs the same level of support. Passive resignation as you get older, and a nonchalant attitude when young, will only ensure that you miss the chance to keep it in the best possible shape for your age.

Food components known to boost the immune system are vitamins A, B6, C, and E, ß-Carotene (the precursor of vitamin A), the minerals selenium and zinc, lycopene, reservatrol, and co-enzyme Q10. Vitamins A, C and E and selenium are antioxidants, which eliminate harmful and excess concentrations of free radicals. The latter will almost certainly build up if you do not make the lifestyle changes advised in the previous paragraph. Sources of these components not already given are:

- Lycopene: tomatoes, watermelons, guavas, grapefruit. Cold-pressed olive oil improves the body's ability to take up lycopene.
- Reservatrol: grapes, especially red.
- Co-enzyme Q10: oily fish, offal, peanuts.

Good composite sources of several components are green tea, live natural yoghurt, and shiitake and reishi mushrooms.

Dietary-related disorders and diseases

High blood pressure is the normal precursor to stroke, the bursting of a blood vessel in the brain, and one of the factors contributing to risk of coronary heart disease. As we age, our blood pressure normally rises. For some people part of the cause is obesity, but in everybody the two prime factors in increasing cases of hypertension are thought to be stress, which is an individual reaction, and sodium levels, mostly from salt (sodium chloride). Morever, there is evidence that the cell membranes of those prone to hypertension handle sodium differently, and that the relative proportions of sodium, potassium and calcium are important. One of the functions of sweating is to get rid of surplus salt, but sodium deficiency, if it occurs, is generally signalled by muscle cramp. It is common in developed countries for people to eat at least ten times as much salt as they need, partly through over-eating of processed foods. A reduction in salt intake is advisable for us all, and if the purpose of adding salt is to flavour food then a walk round the herb garden should provide you with plenty of alternatives. High blood pressure is also linked to potassium and calcium intake, so the existence of low sodium, potassium and calcium together is a balance that is physiologically necessary for low risk of hypertension. Vegetables are good sources of potassium and vegetables and fruit for calcium, as well as non-fatty dairy foods like skimmed milk.

There is no single cause of obesity, and to a certain extent proneness is individual, but there are strategies which are preventative for many. Being obese is having excessive stored fat, and is the main cause of being overweight. Fat people die sooner on the whole. Obesity itself is only a moderate risk factor in hypertension and coronary heart disease, but it often accompanies higher risk factors. People differ in how efficiently they utilise energy foods just as much as in how much fat they store, so burning off the fat is only part of a strategy. Eating habits must change, because eating a little too much day after day eventually adds up to obesity. Reversing the trend, in theory, should occur if a little less is eaten than is needed, and more exercise taken. But your individual rate of metabolism may complicate this logic. Reducing energy food intake may cause rate of metabolism to temporarily respond by decreasing, just as more intake can temporarily speed up the rate of metabolism. Therefore, a consistent strategy of reducing proportional intake of energy foods by changing to a balanced diet, maintained over a period of time, with increased exercise (which does increase rate of metabolism, though not dramatically) is the most likely to be successful. One can only wonder why governments do not tax salty, fatty processed foods heavily, and it would be a worthy lobby on the part of new pagans to strive for price differentials through taxation to ensure that it is not commercially attractive to make and sell unhealthy foods.

We expend energy from foods in maintaining body temperature, maintaining bodily cells, structures and organs, and movement of all kinds, but only a small excess of energy foods over a period of time can have a marked effect on weight by fat storage, and what is 'small' is individual because of differing rates of metabolism and propensity to store fat. Being virtuous in spurts of enthusiasm is pointless. Light to moderate exercise does, after a while, increase your appetite, whereas heavy exercise does not, at least not for an hour or two afterwards. Unfortunately, even the latter doesn't of itself cause the loss of very much weight, but regular exercise is an important factor in a weight-losing strategy as it keeps the wheels of metabolism turning and converts some fat into muscle tissue.

Fat is the body's long-term energy store, whereas glycogen is the short-term store and far less calorific than fat. If you go on a crash diet, and this is not advisable unless you are under medical supervision, it is the glycogen store that is used up, and you lose the large amount of water that accompanies it. This loss of glycogen and water may inspire temporary delight at the apparent success of the diet but it is easily put back when your old habits return. Also, as fat is called upon to be metabolised to replace the glycogen and water far less is needed weight for weight, so the initial dramatic weight loss is not sustained. If a crash diet is maintained for too long then muscle tissue degrades too, and that may have serious physical consequences. Therefore, a modest energy deficit per day over a long period, with regular exercise, is the healthiest plan.

Towards a healthy eating strategy

A general healthy eating strategy may be summarised as follows. Eat planned meals and not a series of snacks, so you are always in control of your intake of food. The proportion of vegetable protein should be increased at the expense of animal protein. Derive most calories from unrefined carbohydrate, which is fibrous so you feel full more quickly. At least thirty grammes of fibre, with an increased proportion from wholegrain cereal, should be consumed per day, and no more than nine grammes of salt per day, preferably less. Try to take in no refined carbohydrate, but certainly eat no more than fifty grammes of sucrose (refined sugar) per day, and preferably much less. Reduce fat intake, no more than a third of which should be saturated. Moreover, no more than 30 per cent of your total energy food intake should be fat and no more than 10 per cent of total energy food intake should be saturated fat.

It is clear that many foods appear several times on the lists above and are therefore highly nutritious. To these vegetable staples you may add meat and offal, with the fat removed, fish, shellfish and fungi, all in moderate amounts, and fresh fruit. Water should be your normal drink with and between meals. With a good diet you will not need supplements of any kind. For the actual nutrient content of each food and the recommended daily intake you should consult specialist books on diet, and your family doctor too if there are medical reasons why you need to diet or avoid certain foods.

Bringing up a baby to enjoy life on natural foods

Before conception

The healthiest maternal body is the one fed on a balanced diet of natural foods since long before conception. As folic acid concentration is so important in pregnant women it is wise to ensure you are already eating suitable foods before you conceive, good choices being green vegetables, milk, oranges, potatoes, wholegrain bread and cereals, yeast and meat extracts, and yoghurt.

When pregnant

It is best to avoid soft ripened cheeses like Brie and Camembert, blue-veined cheeses, goats' or sheep's milk cheeses, unpasteurised milk and products, pâté, raw or undercooked meats, and re-heated cook-chilled meals, all because of the danger of the *Listeria* bacterium. Eat only cooked eggs with the white and yolk solid, and only thoroughly cooked meat.

Breast is best

Modern pagans believe that the natural and preferred food for a baby from birth is its mother's breastmilk, from which it is weaned onto a varied diet of fresh, natural foods. This biological strategy, for that is what it is, activates the whole body's metabolic biochemistry and ensures that all pathways are supplied with the nutrients required for all-round health. Human breastmilk is not only a balanced, whole diet for the human baby, it is the medium through which antibodies to infections are passed from mother to baby. Breastfed babies are less likely to suffer from infections, such as in the stomach, ears and respiratory system, and less likely to have allegic symptoms such as colic, runny nose, eczema and wheezing. They also smell nicer! Babies fed otherwise have more body odour, more pungent breath and malodorous stools. Breastmilk is convenient, uncontaminated, and available automatically at the right temperature, and is given in an intimate way that is emotionally and physically bonding for both mother and baby. A mother on a natural diet, including sufficient water each day, will produce the best possible quality milk for her baby, and normally she may breastfeed safely for up to two years from birth.

Being alert to allergies

It is wise for nursing mothers to avoid cows' milk for the first few days of breastfeeding, as it is one of the commonest foods to cause allergies. If the baby reacts when you resume drinking cows' milk then stop drinking it and seek immunological advice. The foods that most commonly cause allergic reactions are, in order of the most numerous reactions first: cows' milk and cows' milk products, wheat, food additives, fish, soya, citrus fruits, coffee, and synthetic sweeteners. Nursing mothers are advised to avoid all food additives and synthetic substances, and to drink only a little coffee. Otherwise, there is usually no reason why they cannot continue with their own varied diet, including the other items in the list, unless there are reasons to suspect an allergy.

Weaning on to solid food

When indications are that a baby is ready to be weaned, planning a varied diet from the start is most important. One reason is that it will help guard against food fussiness or even addictions; chocolate, caffeine and fizzy drinks having often been cited in the latter respect in young children. At about six months old is the time when babies are generally ready to start to have solid food, because the gut will be mature enough to digest it, its gagging reflex will be under control, the first teeth will probably be erupting, and it will have the posture, co-ordination and jaw flexibility to cope. 'Solid' here means natural food you choose and prepare. There is no need at any time to purchase jars of proprietary baby food, however 'healthy' the labels claim they are. Babies not ready for solids at six months can just continue to be breastfed.

Introduce solid foods one at a time. If you get a response such as a runny nose, rash, wheezing, or sore bottom, withdraw that food temporarily and try it later. Not all a baby's digestive processes are fully functional for all foods immediately. If later introduction sees a repeat of the reaction, especially after another six months, seek advice. After a week or two of single foods at a time you can try mixing one or two together. Normally, a baby's metabolism is mature at about a year old.

It is not advisable to give coffee, tea, colas and other fizzy drinks, or fruit drinks to babies. Give milk, water, and solid fruit and water instead of fruit drinks. Remember that commercial baby foods may contain thickening agents, salt, sugar or other sweeteners, colourants and preservatives, all of which could be harmful. Babies should not be given sugar (sucrose) to start a life towards obesity and tooth decay, and that goes for processed foods containing sugar such as biscuits (including teething biscuits), cakes, fruit drinks, jellies, puddings, soft drinks, sweets, and tinned fruit. For much the same reasons, it is better not to give honey to babies under one year old. Try to resist using food as a teething or other comfort, but resort to the teething-ring idea instead. Avoidance of excess salt is as important as avoiding sugar, so babies should not have the likes of crisps, relishes and sauces. As tea and coffee interfere with iron metabolism in babies, these should not be given either, not even in decaffeinated form.

Good starting foods for weaning, appropriately steamed, stewed or mashed, are avocado, banana, chicken, ground rice, meat, offal, potato or sweet potato. Later you can follow with low-acid fruit, green and root vegetables, and mushrooms. Then introduce pulses, wholegrain cereals, wholemeal pasta, other fruit, chopped nuts, fish and dairy products. Give water or pure fruit juice to drink. It is not advisable to feed a baby cows' milk while it is still taking breastmilk. Any extra calcium that a baby may need for good development of teeth and bones can come from oily fish, wholemeal cereals, greens, pulses and dried fruit. As infants are slightly more prone to anaemia than older children, meat and egg yolk are valuable as good iron sources, as well as wholegrains, green vegetables and dried fruit.

When fully weaned, the modern pagan child then eats what the whole family eats, not what advertisers and friends recommend. Parental control of diet now will set the most healthy pattern for childhood.

How to change your diet and preparation of food

Audit what you grow, buy and eat

To audit your food intake, first look at your current diet and decide what is healthy and what is not healthy. Then decide what you must not eat and resolve to do without or find replacements. Examine your food growing, purchasing, and preparation techniques, and your methods of cooking.

Change your purchasing strategy

Try to grow and make more yourself, and change your shops from supermarkets to health food or farm shops selling fresh, organically grown food. Be adventurous and investigate what you have not eaten before, as variety is very important, and many old varieties of fruit and vegetables are reappearing in the shops. Edible seaweed, for example, is high in protein, vitamins and minerals and after a short soak to soften is ready to cook. Check all labels carefully, especially for long lists of additives. Wash all fruit and vegetables to remove any residues of chemicals, and generally be prepared to spend more time in the garden and kitchen. You will be repaid by less time spent ill in bed, or in surgeries and hospitals. You may end up spending more on your food purchases, but better health is cheap at the price, and you will spend less on medicines and other pharmaceuticals. Organic farming does not employ hormone growth accelerants; unnatural animal feed; animal feed laced with antibiotics; insecticide, fungicide or herbicide sprays; or artificial fertilisers. Organic fruit and vegetables may not be as large or nicely shaped, whatever that means, but they will be delicious, and organic meat is incomparable in its flavour and texture. As organic food will not have lashings of preservatives added it must be used up in the recommended time and you will have to shop more often. Buy early in the day so your purchases are more likely to be fresh.

Prepare your food in a more healthy way

After changing your purchasing regime, the next step is to change how you prepare the food to preserve its nutrients, flavour and texture. Make your own meals from fresh ingre-dients, and sometimes replace cooked fruit and vegetables with raw. Pulses and whole grains should be washed and beans and peas soaked to save cooking time. Pulses do cause an increase in flatulence, but that is a small price to pay for their nutritional value. Dried fruit can also be reconstituted by soaking in water, but remember that soaking leaches out nutrients if done for too long, so dry afterwards and keep in the refrigerator until required. Replace frozen food by the fresh equivalent as often as you can. Look back at the section 'Preparing organic food' and read again about preferred cooking methods.

Avoid peeling and cutting as this causes many nutrients to be lost, although to some extent this can be countered by sprinkling with lemon or vinegar. Root vegetables may be lightly scrubbed, but fruit needs to be handled with care as it bruises easily. Wash, dry and keep soft fruit in the refrige-rator to avoid vitamin loss, and don't cut it until you are ready to use it as oxidation of vital components starts as soon as the flesh is exposed. Fruit should not be sweetened, but cooked slowly in its own juice, with the skins still on. Drink water and eat fruit instead of fruit drinks, as this will give you fibre as well as quench your thirst. Dried fruit is very nutritious and the higher proportion of fibre to fresh fruit means you will feel full up sooner and not over-eat. Figs and prunes are natural laxatives, not that you should need them for that purpose if you have a healthy diet. They are good foods in their own right.

Reduce sugar intake

If you can, change your taste to do without sweetened products, but if not, buy the equivalent with non-sugar sweetener, reduced sugar or natural juice. This applies especially to sugar-free cereals, drinks and canned food. Instead of buying sugar-coated cereals make your own from wholegrains, dried fruit and nuts, or porridge from rolled oats. Avoid putting sugar on cereals, but try fruit or dried fruit instead. Similarly, avoid adding sugar to tea or coffee, but try fruit or herb tea. Proprietary cakes, biscuits and other such foods made with sugar are best not purchased at all, as you can bake your own and control the ingredients. Start to change over to decaffeinated coffee and low-tannin tea, and reduce alcohol consumption.

Reduce salt intake

On no account add salt or sodium bicarbonate when cooking vegetables. Replace salt normally added in cooking with herbs and spices, or use a low-sodium salt or baking powder, and avoid processed ingredients, as they contain salt as a preservative, especially if canned. Resist adding salt to your meal, or eating salted snacks.

Reduce fat intake

Fat, especially saturated and hydrogenated vegetable fats, can be reduced in a number of ways. Use skimmed or semi-skimmed milk instead of full-fat milk, wholewheat bread or flour instead of white bread or flour, and brown rice instead of polished white rice. Replace cream, evaporated milk, condensed milk and salad dressings with natural low-fat yoghurt. Instead of fruit yoghurt add your own fruit to natural yoghurt. Try mature cheeses or reduced-fat cheese. Replace luncheon meat, salami, etc, with lean ham. Remove skin from fish and poultry. Topside beef is less fatty than sirloin and leg of lamb less fatty than shoulder. Replace milky drinks, fizzy drinks, squashes, etc, with water or fresh fruit juice. Replace butter with polyunsaturated margarine, or just do without it, for example, in sandwiches. Switch to low-fat spreads.

Cook only with polyunsaturated oil or margarine and keep the temperature low to moderate to avoid conversion to saturated fat. Use non-stick pans as they need less oil. Drain all excess fat. It is better to grill, steam, roast or poach than to fry. Replace fried potatoes in their many forms with jacket potatoes, fish in oil with fish in tomato sauce, and flaky and shortcrust pastry with choux pastry. Avoid processed foods, or replace those containing additives with their natural equivalent without additives. Finish a meal with fresh fruit instead of puddings, tarts and the like. Try not to eat snacks, but if you must, eat fruit, nuts (fresh, not salted) or raw vegetables.

Be responsible

Looking after your health is not only important for your own sake, but for the sakes of those who care for you and about you, and for those who depend on you and for whom you are in some way responsible. This is all part of the modern pagan holistic way of looking at personal health.

The modern pagan culinary calendar

Recipes for dishes for pagan festival days and folk celebrations may be found in books on folk customs, and are traditionally made from seasonal ingredients gathered from nature's harvest. Sadly for non-pagans nowadays, through commercialisation and creeping loss of family and community focus in people's lives, especially when families have become scattered, the excitement of the build-up to calendrical festivals and the preparation of their special foods has largely disappeared. Many formerly special seasonal foods are now available all year round and people tend to buy things like Easter eggs, simnel cake, Christmas cake, Christmas pudding and Yule logs instead of making their own with all the family joining in. The long commercial lead-in to festivals like Christmas and Easter has removed their special calendrical status and turned them into just a tedious period of over-indulgence and monetary waste. Neither is on a pagan festival day so this sort of corruption and commercial manipulation spoils no new pagan's year, but you should be aware that the same could happen to your commemorative days unless you restrict your attentions to their proper place in the annual seasonal cycle. Many traditional Celtic recipes survive, and some had nine ingredients as this was a sacred number. Buy and prepare the food specifically for the occasion and make it a part of a short, exciting build-up with children fully involved. They love to go into the garden and countryside to collect whatever has just become available. One relatively easy way for modern pagans to help re-establish their connection with Mother Nature is to re-institute these forays into her realm at such times.

It is but a short time ago, well remembered by the elderly, that with the exception of staple foods, it was the weather and tides that determined what you ate and when. As an expression of their oneness with the natural cycles, modern pagans value this connection with the past and the seasonal cycles of produce. To have freshly caught mackerel, people had to wait for the shoals to arrive, and some had to risk their lives to catch them; to have fresh, succulent cherries, the trees had to be tended, protected from birds and the fruit picked; to have fresh eggs and poultry regularly people had to put in long-term effort and care; but the products of their labours were, in terms of taste and nutrition, always worth it. Satisfaction was both sensory and in terms of emotional and physical attachment to the natural world. The last is still very important to modern pagans, and is why seasonal eating remains a tradition, even though they can easily buy or freeze produce all year round like anyone else. There is an element of nostalgia in this desire, but it is more than that, as it includes humility; a desire to go with nature; the wish not to ruin the delight of patient antici-pation, especially for children; and the strong urge to maintain the interest and pleasure of variety through the culinary year.

Sharing your company and food is sharing part of your way of life. It also gives you a chance to show off your culinary skills, experimenting perhaps, using creative presentation with herbs, flowers, segments of fruit, arrangements of seeds and nuts, dustings, wrapping in fresh leaves, and choosing interesting containers and dishes. And good presentation means taking the same care with the production of side dishes too. You can decorate the table with folded napkins, flowers, wood or stone sculptures, origami, or other artistic ideas. Entertaining allows you the luxury of foods you can afford only on special occasions, but the basis of the meal will still be good, wholesome ingredi-ents. With a little imagination you can recreate the old moods of the seasons, using the foods and their presentation, without letting commercialism do it for you or filling your celebrations with artificial things and sentiments that have no place in modern pagan seasonal family traditions. The latter are described in the sections that follow, in the hope that you will recreate them.

Winter

The onset of winter evokes memories of privations and shortages to be expected and endured, and the advancing darkness and cold made them seem inevitable. It was a time for hot food, putting candles on the table to keep the gloom at bay, and lively conversation to keep spirits up. After the meal it was an occasion for storytelling, divination and round-the-table games. At Samhain it was traditional to have what some call Hallowe'en room and table decorations, with turnip or pumpkin lanterns. The colours violet, black, gold and brown were in evidence. At the Winter Solstice, with the sun at its lowest point, all means of light were used, and the decorations were of evergreens, holly with red berries, ivy and mistletoe, and a decorated log.

In times of self-sufficiency, freshly slaughtered farm meat, and shellfish like mussels, were early Winter fare, notably goose and pork, but after that it was salted meat and what could be caught in the countryside. The meat would be eaten with the growing variety of root crops and winter greens becoming available. The temptation with a hot meal was to make it strongly tasting, which meant spices, herbs and condiments. Parsley was a popular addition or garnish, and so were stronger-tasting herbs like garlic, mint, and rosemary. There were always the perennial herbs to fall back on, such as marjoram, sage, savory, and thyme, but as Winter set in dried herbs would become the norm until Spring. To round off the meal, something made from the hard fruit crop, generally apples and pears, would be served, or imported grapefuit, bananas, or grapes, which were at their best. And it was marmalade time, as the Seville oranges had arrived in port. Baking bread was a popular Winter activity in the kitchen, as was making honeyed cakes.

Spring

After the end of Winter shortages, as both daylight and optimism increased in equal measure, children visited their mothers and helped prepare the table and food. Tables were adorned with pussy willow, spring flowers and blossom, as sap rose and plant life awakened. At Imbolc, candles still lit the scene, and colours used were white, pale green for the first young shoots, and blue for the brightening sky. As the first lambs were born, lamb and ewes' milk cheese were eaten. Around the vernal equinox the weather is often fickle, but it was seed-planting time, and that could not be delayed. Seedcake was made, and painted eggs joined the spring flowers and catkins as decorations. As light overcame darkness, and the sun grew stronger, yellow, especially flowers, appeared in abundance. It was a Spring custom to decorate chairs with ribbons and to strew rushes or hay on the floor.

Good weather at Ostara was family picnic time, often the first outdoor meal of the year. The last of the Winter vegetables was enjoyed – carrots, parsnips, swede, turnips, cabbages and leeks – and the first of the Spring fare – greens, cauliflowers, purple-sprouting and white-sprouting broccoli – appeared, and later spinach, and the first salads, watercress, radishes, spring onions, and cucumbers from the greenhouse. As the air freshened, so did the tastes from the herb garden. Fresh for the first time were basil, chervil, dill, lovage, mint and tarragon, going well with tender young vegetables, fish and lamb. The old favourites sage, thyme and marjoram were available, and later on chives, a change from Winter's onions and garlic, parsley, and sorrel. Early rhubarb was a delicacy, and the last apples and pears from Winter storage were finished up. From the dairy came curd and low-fat cheeses, soured cream and natural yoghurt, and there were eggs in abundance, from hens, ducks, geese and quail. Other seasonal foods, some reflecting times when fishing or gaming seasons started, were salmon, eel, herring, shellfish, seaweed, chicken, hare and rabbit.

Summer

Summer brought feelings of warmth and plenty, and of indoor and outdoor eating, and picnics including the traditional cake and ale. At Beltane there was always a fire or bonfire to herald the start of Summer and of the light continuing to gain dominance over the darkness. Poles decorated with ribbons, hawthorn and other blossom, and flower crowns adorned the room and table, with pastel colours of the early Summer flowers – white, green, pink, yellow and blue. By the time of the Summer Solstice, when the sun was highest in the sky, stronger colours seemed to match the strength of the light and heat. Oak leaves, roses and hay were used in decorations, and the colours yellow, red and green were in evidence.

The new asparagus was boiled plain and served with melted butter, and the first tender broad beans were eagerly devoured.

Mange-touts, peas, new potatoes, onions, and beetroot all appeared, as well as crisp, light summer cabbages and lettuces. Tomatoes and courgettes were ready, and later, red and green peppers, runner beans, French beans and marrows. The first strawberries and gooseberries did not last long, neither did the raspberries and currants a little later. The short cherry season came and went, as did the crops of peaches, nectarines, plums and greengages. Chilled soups, salads, pasta dishes and barbecue grills cry out for fresh summer herbs, like basil, dill, coriander, summer savory, lovage and chervil. Stripped rosemary stems make good kebab sticks, and herbs sprinkled on barbecue coals make an inviting aroma while cooking. Pan-fried meat and fish were topped with herb butter, and marigold and nasturtium flowers were a favourite garnish. Other seasonal foods were oysters, cockles and pilchards, and fruit cheesecakes.

Autumn

By September there was a chill in the evening air as nights began to draw in. In the mornings there was mist and dew on the cobwebs, to tell us Autumn had arrived. Although evening meals would now often be warm, lunches would still be light, including salads, and taken outdoors. Thoughts were on the harvest, and at Lughnasadh newly cut wheat, corn dollies and sickles were the decorative themes, with colours of yellow and orange. The aroma of freshly baked bread filled the kitchen. When the Autumnal Equinox arrived, harvest would be done, and darkness overtook light unchallenged. Colours of gold, orange, red and brown were used in decorations, and particular seasonal foods were apples, grapes, hops, pine cones, and, at the time of the rutting of stags, venison. Harvested also were hazelnuts, blackberries, and crab apples. Whitebait was caught, there was cider to make, and goose was ready for the table.

The Autumn mushrooms and other fungi were collected in large numbers, and from the kitchen garden came pumpkins, sweetcorn, good potatoes and carrots, Autumn cabbage, and calabrese. Watercress was abundant. The last of the plums and greengages was picked, and then came the short damson season, followed by the first of the decent apples, and in October, pears. Chestnuts were roasted in hearth and bonfire, potatoes baked and sausages grilled. In Autumn, with grains, nuts, orchard fruits, fungi, and the first of the root vegetables, there was a lot to prepare with herbs. Bay, marjoram, rosemary and thyme came into their own.

And so, the annual culinary wheel moves round again.

7

Pagan, Heal Thyself

There is a body of opinion that after decades of stress, antibiotics, unnatural foods and relative inactivity, the body is losing the ability to heal itself. After a sustained period of pollution, interference and destruction, the natural environment is similarly losing the ability to regenerate. The answer to both crises is that each must heal itself of this apparent inability to heal itself. There is no cure as such that either can take to magically revivify, for 'cures' are just another form of human intervention. Just as to combat stress individuals find that the only realistic approach is to change their attitudes and outlook, so the same applies to how we approach the global problems of the natural world. But our first priority is to relearn how to heal ourselves, for it is an ancient art whose time has come again.

Your personal health audit

Your personal health audit needs careful thought, and total honesty, embracing as it should your physical, mental, and emotional conditions as you are aware of them. A total mind and body audit is more than just a list of aches and pains. Do you seem particularly prone to infection? Are there recent circumstances that may be contributory? Are there lifestyle choices exposing you to vulnerability of certain kinds, mental or physical? Are you moody or otherwise mentally or emotionally fragile? Is there a pattern to the behaviour, or a link with your changing physical condition? What comments and observations have others made about your attitudes and condition, and do they strike a chord? The answers to these questions are related to your own personal definition of wellness, and whether healing strategies of appropriate kinds are needed to restore you to it.

Defining wellness

Wellness is a personal, holistic state of equilibrium between mind and body, where your physical, mental and emotional conditions are balanced and working positively, smoothly and in an integrated way. Healing is the process of restoring this delicate balance, your balance, and knowing from your personal health audit what you are striving towards determines the strategies you adopt. It all depends on what you see as the ideal state of wellbeing for you, physiologically, psychologically and emotionally. This assessment will include how you see and feel about yourself; how you relate to others; your balance of work and play; where your life is now and where it is going; and what you need to make you happy. These are all elements of wellbeing, so how do they stand with you? What in essence is your sense of self?

Personal vulnerability

Elderly traditional pagans have contributed much to this chapter, for theirs has been the responsibility of guiding their families through life in and on the edge of non-pagan society as well as among true pagans. In an alien society, any group faces difficulties of adjustment and adaptation, of unfamiliar expectation, of discrimination, condemnation and rejection; all of which is potentially stressful and creating of vulnerability to physiological and psychological reaction. Traditional pagans have in turn reacted by developing equilibrium maintenance and restoration strategies over time, and these have been remarkably successful in allowing them to preserve their identity and yet co-exist where they have to interact and to make a living. These strategies are offered to modern pagans as the basis upon which they may compile their own programme to achieve and sustain their personal states of wellbeing.

It is a modern pagan act of faith that any mental or physical condition can be healed by activating the appropriate mechanism. Identifying the mechanism comes from listening to what your mind and body are telling you and that means loving and caring for them unceasingly and being philosophical and flexible to circumstances. Any form of mental and physical abuse to your own body loses you ground in the quest for equilibrium. Maintaining your health is your responsibility solely; doctors and therapists just carry out occasional repairs.

Unrelieved stress depresses immunity, so after a major life trauma illness often follows in an unhealthy person. 'Dying of a broken heart' is also in this category, as feeling unloved, or hating oneself, are also factors that depress our immune system. By contrast, love is a healing emotion, and regularly interacting with a supportive family and with a pet raises your immunity.

Negative thinking and activity also depress immunity. Happy people have less illness. Disturb the mind and you disturb the body. Relax the mind and you relax the body, allowing healing to proceed. Often, healing needs us to change to be successful, usually in the form of replacing negativity with positivity. Such a sensible pronouncement is easy to say, but it needs a good deal of honest self-analysis and strategic planning to identify our negative thoughts and actions and turn them into a positive, fulfilling health-producing formula.

Illness is the body's way of telling us its needs are not being fulfilled. This may be our fault, or it may be external. It is better to pre-empt from childhood and prepare the body for a healthy life. Determination to combat illness is an important mental tool in the fight to restore good health, because being positive stimulates natural reserves. The fact that disease affects us physically, mentally and emotionally tells us that all these must be brought back into balance for a full recovery, not just curing the physiological symptoms as conventional medicine would have it. Our bodies have the self-healing mechanisms, we just need to find the means to stimulate them, and successful strategies for a variety of circumstances are offered in the sections below.

Restoration and maintenance of health

Once you restore your personal equilibrium, that is not the time to return to your old ways. Balance and harmony are part of a dynamic relationship between mind and body, and having restored that dynamic equilibrium you will only stay healthy if you maintain it. Maintenance strategies and restorative strategies in holistic healing are one and the same thing. You can vary the formula as the occasion suggests, but the approach should remain an integral part of your lifestyle.

Good health means taking responsibility

The prospect of lifelong good health is very appealing to all but incurable hypochondriacs, but we are not so keen on what it takes to get it. If you have re-orientated your life in the ways described so far you will have already taken steps to improve your health, especially in terms of better diet. But there are other dimensions to your wellbeing, not least your responsibility to your dependants and extended family, upon whom your state of health will have an impact. You owe it to them to honour your obligations of care, and to pass on your wisdom and experience, none of which you can effectively do whilst struggling to cope with your own health problems. By today's standards, most of these are statistically likely to be self-inflicted.

And you have a wider social responsibility too, not to divert limited medical resources towards disorders that are caused by self-abuse, through eating junk food, through over-indulgence in food and alcoholic drinks, and through taking stimulants of various kinds. You should regularly observe personal and sexual hygiene, and, indeed, it is highly significant that the overall health of the populations of developed countries improved dramatically in the nineteenth century because of greater environmental cleanliness, such as clean drinking water, better personal and food hygiene, proper sanitation and sewage disposal, and cleaner air, rather than through improvements in medical treatment. Indeed, the latter have contributed to the deterioration of the health of the populace by weakening, or causing the neglect of, the body's natural healing mechanisms.

Another dimension to your good health, after personal habits and social responsibility, is caring for your immediate environment, ensuring it is clean and safe. Such an environment, and the calmness and sense of belonging that it engenders is itself part of your wellbeing, for it enables you to detach yourself from the conditions that aggravate the factors leading to self-inflicted disorders and the expensive, complex systems of care set up to deal with them.

Support from family and friends

One hopes your sense of responsibility will be reciprocated by support from loved ones. On the psychological and emotional levels love is a front-line agent in the fight to activate the link between mind and body, and to provide an enduring sense of purpose in restoring wellbeing. Those who are loved have more self-worth and a more responsive immune system.

The healing power of touch

Healing is always done within, not from without, but there are powerful means of energising a body's natural healing mechanisms, one of which is the loving touch. Feelings of being loved, cared for and reassured are especially reinforced by touch and are part of bonding from birth, and babies deprived of them may grow up to have problems forming relationships. Even in the elderly, tactile support is appreciated and therapeutic, part of a lifelong need we all share for emotional security, confidence in the future, a feeling of safety, acceptance as an individual, and a buttress against distress. In Western society these facts tend to be undervalued, and touch is not encouraged, or is misinterpreted as over-familiarity or as a sexual prelude. Because it has been so misconstrued the value of the healing touch has largely been lost, except amongst true pagans. It is something modern pagans are strongly urged to revive as an aspect of family togetherness and mutual health support.

Within the family, hugging, caressing and touching are expressions of love that allow the conditions to be established for mutual healing to take place. Touching the affected area of discomfort is a natural reaction, of long-standing habit, and hearkens back to former times when it was appreciated that comforting through touch stimulated healing. If there is a pet in the family, then fondling that pet and curling up with it is very therapeutic too, and pet owners who spend time close to their pets generally have less stress and illness than those who do not or who do not have a pet.

Massage is touch-based, and it eases muscles and tendons, calms the nerves, stimulates circulation, regularises digestion, and soothes constricted muscles and nerves. All of these promote healing, and elements are part of the therapies that employ touch, such as Reiki, Shiatsu, Therapeutic Touch and Polarity Therapy. Reiki is a 'laying-on of hands' technique, originating in Japan, which seeks to disperse 'energy blocks', or 'hot spots' causing disharmony. Shiatsu comes from Chinese medicine, and aims to rebalance a subject's 'energy' using pressure applied with the elbows, hands and fingers, and stretching and tapping of limbs and joints. Breathing techniques and meditation are also employed. Therapeutic Touch is a technique to rebalance disruptions in the body's 'energy field' by mutual exchange of 'energy' between the practitioner, patient and environment. In Polarity Therapy, practitioners use their hands to influence the flow of 'vital energy' round the body and balance the human 'energy field'. They also advise stretching exercises. In the hands of experienced practitioners these techniques are regarded as safe.

Positive thinking and action

From principles to thoughts to deeds

The modern pagan way of cultivating an attitude of positive thinking and action derives from the traditional pagan strategies of adapting to non-pagan society. They are pre-emptive in the sense that they avoid a lot of effort and soul-searching to overcome emotional problems, because these are less likely to arise. Personal control over your mental health is the objective. Your thoughts, feelings and decisions can then give rise to positive, helpful actions, whose consequences you are more likely to approve of and feel comfortable with. If your beliefs govern your thoughts and actions, it follows that you will maintain a logical consistency between thought and deed, for that is what gives you conviction and satisfaction. Inconsistency and perfidy are the roots of much anxiety and cause loss of control of a situation, necessitating remedial action later. Modern pagans have a fundamental set of lifestyle objectives, and this is the key to their positive strategy.

Being positive also means letting go of negativity, so you may forgive, cease to brood, and stop nursing old wounds, grievances, guilt and resentment. Negativity is like a self-fulfilling prophecy, the more you have the more is thereby generated.

Taking control of your actions

When faced with an adverse situation, it is how you choose to think of it, positively or negatively, that determines whether it causes you anxiety or not. 'Positively' in this context does not refer to the situation, which may not be regarded by you as desirable, it refers to your determination to deal with it constructively. You and your principles determine how you think, the situation should not be allowed to do it for you. This also means that you accept responsibility for your actions, in the modern pagan way, even if some consequences turn out differently to your initial expectations. You learn, and are wiser next time. Blaming the situation, and this may mean blaming the people involved, simply harms your own mental health. This leads to a personal victim culture, which is psychologically damaging for you as you lose control of one aspect of your life after another. Blaming events in your past for perceived present inadequacies is another aspect of victim culture, for you are keeping past events alive in your mind instead of taking immediate responsibility for your current thinking about current situations. A mind and body in control and determined to shoulder responsibility is in a healthy state.

Be philosophical and flexible

The more you demand the less you may turn out to be in control, especially of yourself and probably of the situation also. Being rigid and demanding is likely to use emotional energy in becoming frustrated and anxious, rather than using your energy in taking a flexible approach to problem-solving that will reduce anxiety.

Getting your own way is not necessarily the end of your troubles, because you then have to preserve that situation to keep anxiety at bay, and you may worry about losing the hard-won gains. Being flexible, however, means being able to cope with the fact that nothing ever stays the same, and you are able to deal with that. Desire and preference are positive, and good catalysts for considered action, but insistence and demand are negative, for their rigidity can leave you devastated and unfulfilled when you find you are not entirely in control, and vulnerable if you do achieve your objective and worry about sustaining the position. You will feel like the old dominant lion constantly under threat from aspiring pretenders to the leadership of the pride. There is only one way out of absolutism, and that is retreat. Being philosophical and flexible gives you a choice of paths, and the chance to compromise and obtain a working solution that you are mentally happy to adjust to. Such an approach is far healthier than being single-minded and demanding.

Accept reality and adapt

Accept positively, not with resignation, because this is a negative attitude, implying that you are powerless to make changes to your situation. By accepting reality you are better able calmly to assess and make a constructive attempt to find a path through that you are comfortable with. It may be a compromise, but the important thing is it works. The alternative is to become weighed down by your apparent helplessness and in your mind to blow the situation out of all proportion to its real significance. There is always another day, an alternative, and another path to tread.

Accepting reality does not just apply to tragic events. It can apply to something like perceived unfairness. There is no universal standard of morality in society, and adapting to this is as important as coping with personal tragedy. Modern pagans will find that many of their standards of interpersonal conduct are not shared by society at large, but they have to deal with this by learning how things are done, and adapting to them, even exploiting them to find a way forward. The more certainty you demand in a complex society the more disappointment you are headed for. Accepting change and uncertainty and adapting to them is the positive way. The same is true of opinion. Pluralism is part of a complex society too, and this also calls for adaptation so that you accept multifarious views and perspectives. Expecting to be right all the time brings the same frustration as expecting certainty. Accepting an imperfect world and learning to weave in and out of its obstacles is a vital part of positive thinking. Avoidance and procrastination, in order to offset frustration and possible failure, is negative thinking and simply leads to more avoidance, and an unhealthy state of mind.

Self-esteem

It is hard to live harmoniously with others if you are not at peace with yourself. To be at peace with yourself, as with society, you must accept your imperfections and fallibilities and allow for them in your lifestyle. Some you may successfully change, others you may not. Striving for perfection makes you vulnerable, whereas accepting your own idiosyncrasies and those of others makes you feel normal and in control.

One of the joys of humanity is the uniqueness of the individual. You are unique, and it is something to celebrate, not examine minutely and feel ashamed of what you find. You have a special combination of characteristics, and the art of positive living is to recognise that and turn them to your advantage. Whatever your passions in life, if they harm no one then enjoy them, whatever others may think. We all have to find our niche in society, where our unique characteristics blend and work successfully for us. That is the skill of turning your individualism to advantage.

Balance your own interests with those of others

Look after your own interests by all means, but don't dishonour obligations to others, or incommode them while you pursue your path. It is a question of balance again, flexibility in different situations. Selfishness and narcissism eventually bring about social isolation, whereas balanced self-interest establishes particular boundaries that may be movable in specific circumstances. A good example is working for a demanding employer, and not allowing time for the family, pleasure, and relaxation, and thus being overwhelmed by work. This means deciding priorities and quality-time allocation and sticking to them. You only live once, so don't allow others to take away your time. You deserve time for your own and your family's interests.

An absorbing activity is very healthy, as long as it doesn't become an all-encompassing obsession or addiction. If you haven't got an absorbing interest, try to find one, experiment and have a go. And just as you should unashamedly pursue your own personal interests, regardless of what others might think, so you should be tolerant of the idiosyncrasies of others, and their chosen interests.

Protect your integrity by not allowing compromise on your personal ethical standards, moral principles and values, for that works against emotional wellbeing. In a job, you may feel your working life is just role-play, but if you cannot be genuine it is probably the wrong job for you. If you are not honest with yourself as well as with others, and project a false image for short-term gain, the real you will eventually come out. If being honest leads to your rejection, that is better than struggling in a relationship in which you try to maintain the false image you initially created.

Negative, healthy and negative, unhealthy

Negative emotions are healthy if you are philosophical about them, deal with them and move on. This is healthier for you than indifference, for that implies lack of determination or sour grapes, or being positive about everything, which is just self-deception.

These are healthy negative emotions:	These are correspondingly unhealthy negative responses:
concern	anxiety
sadness	depression
annoyance	anger
remorse	guilt
disappointment	self-pity

So, accept you are fallible and try to keep your negative emotions constructive as in the left-hand column instead of destructive to yourself as in the right hand column.

Be constructively critical and creative

People who think positively are often critical in the constructive sense, and creative. They think for themselves and make their own judgements without being prone to naivety and gullibility, for example at the hands of advertisers and the media and other vested interests. This is positive thinking, giving you control. You are also less prone to accept stereotypes, but take things and people as you find them.

Typical examples of uncritical negative thinking are looking upon situations as black or white, with no shades of grey; jumping to unwarranted negative conclusions; focussing on the negative and assuming the positive is just flannel or sweeteners; assuming an action or comment is directed at you personally instead of at what you may represent, as in your job, or have no control over, for example your children's errors in their adult life. You can resolve these negative thoughts by weighing up evidence that supports or contradicts your way of thinking, and reaching an alternative standpoint. This is a healthy problem-solving approach, which allows positive decision-making rather than indecisiveness and ultimately self-defeat.

Improving your relationships with others

This is a vital part of positive action and contributes towards feeling good about yourself. Letting a driver out of a junction does as much for you as for that other driver by making you feel good about doing a good turn. Accept tolerantly how other people are, within reasonable limits, especially their differences to yourself. This allows celebration of everyone's uniqueness, not just your own. Once you accept openly, suspicion of others lessens, and trust is more likely. Lack of trust leads to fear of betrayal or letdown, and blocks the development of a relationship. Developing trust means genuine, honest communication of your positive and negative feelings, and listening as well as talking, rather than communication punctuated with obfuscation, deceit, subterfuge and euphemism. Developing trust means being trustworthy and honourable yourself, keeping promises, and doing what you say you're going to do. Then you will have self-respect and respect from others, a health-giving combination.

Prevention as a health strategy

No-one reasonably disputes the good sense of, and necessity for, fire and safety regulations and expecting action in accordance with them, but talk in similar terms about food, drink, alcohol, drugs and smoking and it seems that different standards obtain, and that whilst being burned to death or electrocuted are properly regarded as serious fates to avoid, contracting disorders brought about by over-indulgence and substance abuse are not, perhaps because they are not instantaneous in their effect and the body's remarkable resilience allows life to go on for a time. The need for a preventative regime is especially difficult to get across to teenagers, whose active bodies seem to them to be indestructible, but their reckless bodily disregard puts them among any nation's least healthy group, whereas regular exercise, drinking plenty of water, eating organic food, looking after personal hygiene, being safety-conscious, and having a community and environmental orientation to their lives would set them up for a long healthy future.

Vested interest versus your health
The reason why harmful substances like tobacco, alcohol, excessive salt and refined sugar in foodstuffs, and fossil fuels are not banned or restricted in most countries is because many voters enjoy or use them, governments take huge tax revenues from their sale, and there is a great deal of commercial and industrial vested interest in keeping them on the market. Similarly, the reason why our local environments are an obstacle course of hazards and severe pollution, and no provision is made for less dangerous, cleaner alternatives, is again down to vested interest, official financial priorities, and supine indifference on the part of the majority of consumers.

The remedy is in your hands; if you want to be able to walk, cycle or use public transport you must deny yourself the convenient but more polluting and hazardous alternatives and follow your conscience. By making an informed choice between drug medicine and folk medicine you and others of like mind will eventually have the same commercial impact as that of choosing natural foods instead of processed foods.

Drug testing
As with other manufactured products, it is wise to inform yourself about all drugs and cosmetic preparations that you contemplate using. In addition to investigating the production

and marketing strategies of drug manufacturers you should pay particular attention to how drugs are tested, what the short- and long-term side effects are, and whether cheaper generic versions are available.

Unlike natural preparations that have been tried, tested and available for centuries, drugs must legally undergo a rigorous, scientific test regime, and rightly so. Testing cosmetic products on animals is now widely regarded as wholly unacceptable, but the use of animals in testing medicines is a difficult issue for new pagans, deciding what to do when folk medicine has no effect or answer and recommended conventional medicines have been tested on animals. For all but would-be martyrs the latter will have to be chosen until there is an alternative, for you will have, as stated above, responsibility to or for someone else close and dear to you. Martyrdom is a complex reaction to your convictions, but to surviving dependants it has the consequences of selfishness.

Pride in the natural self

The only so-called cosmetics that would be of interest to modern pagans are those with a cleansing or other dermatological function. It is part of the modern pagan image to avoid cosmetics whose function is solely to change appearance, however they are tested, and thoroughly in keeping with modern pagan ideals, as they can be used to mask the true self and create an artificial countenance, and become part of a false personality. If you have had the good sense and willpower to adopt a natural, healthy-eating regime then you should consider the value to your self-esteem of looking natural too. If you are dissatisfied with the body you were born with, or with your partner's, you may care to ask yourself by whose criteria you are making such a judgement. In all likelihood it will be based on the media image of film stars, models and other so-called celebrities, when a more objective judgement of an individual would focus on personality and character. A combination of modern image-processing of digital photographs and cosmetic applications can remove all the blemishes that such people really have, so the basis for the comparison is probably false anyway. However, it is the damage it does to the self-image of impressionable youngsters, especially girls, that is most worrying, as it causes them to embark upon unhealthy, starvation diets and the liberal application of make-up in order to meet what advertising tells them is society's expectations. It certainly is not the expectation of modern pagans, for whom natural appearance is what appeals most, for it shows the true self through an expressive, unplastered face and the charm of an unpretentious personality.

The media image of a desirable male can be attained by a normal healthy-eating programme and keeping the muscles in tone, whereas females have a less forgiving image to aspire to and must risk anorexia, experiment endlessly with make-up, and examine every bodily protuberance for possible plastic surgery enhancement or modification of shape. And the regrettable outcome of this male-inspired image projection is that many women, of all ages, feel depressed about perfectly normal bodies and actually go to some or all of the lengths described. It seems to matter more to men what women look like than it does to women what men look like, especially in middle age, when image-conscious women feel they are past the stage when they are likely to be seen by men as being attractive, whilst men claim they are still regarded by younger women as being attractive, so they don't worry nearly so much about how they look. It matters not to modern pagans at all, so 'be only what thou art'.

As any chess player will confirm, only a physically fit body can cope adequately with a high degree of mental activity, and it behoves all of us to recognise and understand the interdependence of diet, exercise, lifestyle, and bodily and mental health. The example from China of employees taking time out to meditate and exercise is an illustration of the recognition of the complementary relationship between physical and mental harmony, and is a good example for you to follow. Achievement of inner harmony is a vital factor in the re-establishment of your self-esteem and confident display of your natural, individual personality. Technology, commerce and advertising, with their customary symbiotic association, have never been short of producing ways of artificially moulding superficial personalities, through a never-ending range, or perhaps cycle is a better word, of hairstyles, make up, clothing and accessory fashions, and the like, all with the aim of controlling your tastes and determining when you should change them to meet what they deem are society's expectations. 'Be only what thou art', be proud of your own character, and use your natural self to project your personality, for you are unique, not a clone created by commercialism.

Enjoy yourself and laugh

This simple advice has been shown time and time again to be linked to good health. It has been demonstrated in the course of research that happy, laughing people are healthier than those who are weighed down by the serious side of life.

Affirmations

An affirmation or mantra is a positive statement that you deliberately choose to make, in this case to regularly remind you of a key element of your health strategy. You can choose more than one if you wish, but all should be in the affirmative and in the present tense to emphasise your present situation and desire. It is a practice in auto-suggestion. The most famous published affirmation is that proposed to his patients by the French healer Emile Coué at his clinic in Nancy: 'Every day, in every way, I am getting better and better.' But for you the mantra ought to be personal and relevant to your circumstances and projected path, repeated as and when you choose.

Establish a healthy sleep pattern

Insomnia is a common reaction to stress, so try to get up early, exercise regularly through the day, and don't eat late in the evening. Keep your bedroom cool and sleep on a firm bed. A hop-filled pillow is an old cure for insomnia. Try to relax before going to bed; tryptophan helps, and its synthesis in the body is assisted by eating cereals and milk. Another suggestion is to listen to quiet music or read in the evenings, but don't watch television or listen to the radio as these promote too much mental activity. Smoking, drinking alcohol and drinking caffeinated drinks are all bad ideas. Get your partner or a family member to massage you, especially the feet if you are subject to cramp. A routine of exercises, according to your needs, before the evening relaxation period is a good preparation for winding down.

Natural holistic medicine

So far, strategies discussed have been personal or involving family and friends, but it may be that you will need to invite more specialist help, including medical practitioners and therapists.

The terms 'conventional', 'complementary' and 'alternative' are widely applied to specific medical practices today, but to traditional pagans, natural holistic medicine, of which herbal remedies are a part, is conventional medicine. To non-pagans, however, conventional medicine means the treatment that they receive from their family doctor or the National Health Service. The term will, therefore, be used here in the latter sense, to avoid confusion. To traditional pagans, natural holistic medicine is their alternative to conventional medicine, and some will not resort to conventional medicine, although some will. Both conventional and natural holistic medicine have been successfully used for conditions that the other has been unable to influence, and therefore it seems prudent for modern pagans to view the two as complementary, so that they may acquaint themselves with the characteristics and scope of both, in order to choose the most likely to be efficacious in their case. A large range of alternative medical practices has grown up over the centuries, some highly specific in their application, some comprehensive in the breadth of conditions treatable. Collectively here, these will be known as complementary therapies. Healing for modern pagans, therefore, consists of complementary choices between natural holistic medicine, comprising selected complementary therapies, herbal remedies, and holistic strategies for mind and body, and conventional medicine, or combinations of the two.

Complementary therapies differ considerably in their approach, the better-known ones involving direct contact, such as manipulative and structural therapies, postural techniques, touch-based therapies, energy therapies, use of natural extracts, or interaction with the mind. But they all share the characteristics of being based on the belief that mind and body constitute the whole person, and should be considered and treated together, that is to say, holistically. Conventional medicine, on the other hand, regards each symptom as having a specific cause that is capable of isolation and treatment, usually with drugs. Natural holistic medicine tailors treatment to the individual, whereas conventional medicine tends to regard treatment as rectifying malfunctioning physiological and biochemical systems.

Modern pagans recognise that psychological factors influence bodily condition, including immune response. Stress is one such factor, hence the emphasis on relaxation and self-control in modern pagan holistic health strategies. Some pagans believe that the whole body and mind is permeated with an 'energy' or 'vital force', and that it is in a balanced, dynamic state in a healthy person, and depleted or unbalanced in an unhealthy person. Some complementary therapies aim to rebalance the vital energy of the body and mind system. Energy in conventional medicine is equated solely with the product of cellular metabolic processes, being interconvertible with matter. So far, there is no known scientific proportionality between the two concepts of energy. What is known, however, is that measured energy transfer within the body is affected by mental state, as with the heart and brain, and restoring this transfer to normality is one of the aims of a holistic approach to medicine.

The interplay of the mental and the physiological is easily illustrated, for we all know that our mental state influences our endocrine, nervous and immune systems, in turn affecting our moods, sleep pattern, reproductive cycle, metabolism and other functions and organs. Stress, negative thought patterns and emotional disharmony thus upset the body's physiological and biochemical balance as well as its mental state. This is the holistic view of health. Restorative measures can replace these disharmonies with positive, life-affirming ones, examples being relaxation, meditation, positive thinking, visualisation. They all stimulate the body's natural healing mechanisms. Meditation and relaxation particularly are known to improve circulation and breathing, help to balance hormone activity, lower blood pressure, release muscular tension, and stimulate the immune system.

Natural holistic medicine aims to stimulate a person's natural healing capacity. Disease, unwholesome diet, lack of exercise, stress, and other factors produce disharmony, which affects the body's self-regulatory mechanisms. The same factors can produce different incapacities, to different degrees, in different people, which is why we all require a unique strategy for restoring the balance. This is not to say that everyone is capable of being in sparkling health. Genetic predisposition to certain debilitating conditions and permanent physiological malfunction through whatever cause can mean that some will not enjoy the all-round good health of others. And we are all prone to the occasional temporary infection. But it remains a modern pagan belief that despite an individual's imperfections they can take steps to promote their body's natural healing and maintenance resources through the lifestyle they choose.

Choosing a conventional medical practitioner and complementary therapists

The ideal family doctor for a modern pagan is one who is interested in, or at least open-minded about, what natural holistic medicine has to offer, and can assist you to choose the best strategy for restoring your health. Many complementary therapies have professional bodies, and some are regulated, so there are some that particularly offer the opportunity of proper appraisal with respect to your needs. You should not turn to any form of healing merely out of disillusionment or dissatisfaction with another. Your reasons should be positive and based on relevant information about the techniques contemplated. The most common complementary therapy practitioners consulted, with the most common first, are those specialising in acupuncture, chiropractic, homoeopathy, hypnotherapy, osteopathy, aromatherapy, reflexology, and therapeutic massage. Years ago, complementary therapy had the reputation of a last resort, particularly for the elderly, for long-standing conditions, but now maintenance and enhancement of health are factors, as well as early referral for other conditions. The most common conditions referred are muscle and joint problems, stress-related conditions, arthritic and rheumatic problems, cancer, HIV, psoriasis, eczema and multiple sclerosis.

If there is a professional body, or a voluntary body if not, that represents a complementary therapy, then do get information and lists of approved practitioners, and inform yourself about accreditation, validation of training, and registration procedures. You will also want to know about codes of practice and ethics, complaints and disciplinary procedures, and requirements for indemnity insurance of practitioners. Remember that if a complementary therapy is unregulated, then even though a professional body exists, someone struck off by that body can still set up on their own and continue practising. So, always go through channels you are confident about before using a complementary therapist, just as you should always be certain that a conventional medical practitioner is properly qualified and legally entitled to practise.

Many conditions and ailments respond to more than one complementary therapy, and it may be advisable to consult with more than one practitioner as well as your family doctor. Some therapists use more than one technique, such as combining their main therapy with herbal preparations. Get an idea of the programme of treatment, how many sessions may be required, what techniques are used, whether your condition is likely to respond, and how much it costs.

Conventional medicine has so far failed to treat many chronic conditions such as arthritis and eczema, or find cures for conditions like the common cold and influenza. Also, there is a body of opinion that conventional medicine has failed patients on a number of counts, including practices and attitudes like over-prescribing; long waiting times; lack of consultation time and the liberal use of the prescription pad to empty surgery waiting rooms; impersonal manner and poor rapport, including the neglect of the needs of carers; declining standards of hygiene and perceived care in hospitals; paternalistic doctor-knows-best attitudes; and a mechanistic and reductionist approach to medical diagnosis. There is a widespread opinion that most drugs are less effective and have worse side effects than their manufacturers claim; are often tested with insufficient thoroughness, in order to launch on to the market as soon as possible, and in ways decent people would disapprove of; that incentives are offered to promote their use; and are sold at arbitrary prices around the world, the highest of which seem hard to justify. It seems not to have dawned on many conventional medical practitioners yet that patient-centred consultation, notions of holistic mind–body balance, and encouragement of self-healing, resonate well with people today.

Exercise both mind and body

Think about posture during the day and spend short periods on the floor with body straight and hands by the side, and try to clear the mind. If posture problems or muscular pain accompany your stressful period then ditch the high heels and take advice on footwear; standing, walking, and sitting correctly; and on lifting and carrying. This is worthwhile at all times, not just because you have stress pain, and others can observe and advise you. The Alexander Technique is designed to correct bad postural habits and teach you strainless standing, sitting and moving. This can be extended to include safe ways of bending, lifting and carrying.

Regular exercise helps to dissipate tension, prepares the body for both rest and concentration, and keeps the heart and circulation in good running order. Fit, healthy people find it easier to relax and sleep. A number of reactions to stress affect muscles one way or another, the back being one of the first places to give you twinges, so look after it and strengthen it with exercises. Before exercise you should relax the body by lying on your back, with your head supported, say on a book, knees bent, feet flat on the floor, arms relaxed by your side, palms down. Breathe normally and regularly, then your internal organs, ribcage and muscles will all relax. Your chosen exercise routine should then follow and be monitored regularly. If you feel pain then stop and seek advice. Exercise out of doors if possible and counter any dehydration with sips of water. Start modestly and gradually build up the length of time you spend on your routine. Smooth, harmonious movement is better than jerky, vigorous movement, and you should include swimming and exercising in water. Test your suppleness with stretching and flexibility exercises. Check your waking pulse rate first thing in the morning; it should fall from an unfit 80–100 pulses per minute to under 70. Test several times after exercise; the fitter you are the faster your pulse rate will return to normal. Brisk walking and cycling help improve stamina and are an important complement, like swimming, to your basic exercise programme.

Maintain a healthy diet

A regular, healthy diet is essential to equip the body to combat stress and other conditions that cause mind–body imbalance. Some foods produce symptoms that are similar to stress reactions. Sugar is one such, as it increases blood-sugar level and therefore affects your mood, which can plummet to depression when the level falls. This can tempt you to eat more sugar. Coffee, tea and colas containing caffeine can cause heart palpitations, raise blood pressure, stop you relaxing and sleeping, and make you anxious. Saturated fat will raise blood cholesterol. By keeping to the dietary advice in chapter six you are well prepared to cope with stress. Chamomile, valerian and peppermint teas have a calming effect, and you should make sure you have enough vitamin B6, which is thought to help combat stressful reactions, and vitamin C to boost resistance to infection.

You are advised to read again the sections in chapter six on dietary advice.

Boost your immune system and detoxify your body regularly

You are referred to the relevant sections in chapter six, which you may wish to re-read in connection with your personal health strategy.

De-stress your life

The nature of stress

Stress is a personal reaction to your environment, not something that the environment causes you. No-one is to blame for stress but yourself.

Non-pagans refer to coping with the pressures of life as stress management, but modern pagan techniques of establishing and maintaining personal equilibrium are integral aspects of their lifestyle, for a peaceful state of mind is highly regarded for its own therapeutic value and for the way it enhances the personality. To be at peace with the world you must assume that the pressures of life will fall upon you, and prepare yourself to deal with them in a purposeful and practised way. Waiting until you feel stressed may be too late, so incorporate self-healing strategies into your lifestyle. However, for the purposes of this section of the chapter, it is easier to present a strategy to restore and maintain equilibrium if it is assumed that you do not currently employ these therapeutic techniques. Of course, stress is not the same thing as a challenge, for the latter is inspiring and motivating, and the individual feels in control, whereas the former is characterised by a feeling of powerlessness, even paralysis. Some common events in our lives, like moving house or school, seem stressful at the time, but most people react positively to them and get through what is really a finite period of challenge, whereas ceaseless accumulation of unwanted everyday occurrences is the most significant contributor to chronic stress.

Stress is the ultimate self-inflicted wound, but it is one that you can take responsibility very successfully for healing, using safe, natural methods. Of all the approaches you could take to deal with your adverse reactions to the pressures of life, for that is what stress is, the one least likely to be to modern pagan advantage is to go and see a medical practitioner or pharmacist, for drug medicine and orthodox medical techniques generally can be very damaging to a mind and body experiencing stressful situations. Some types of complementary medicine, however, have a great deal to offer. Your goal should be to find a safe, natural approach that has a permanent or controllable effect.

The way to start tackling a particular problem is to try to put it into perspective and identify those situations that you are reacting to in a way that is affecting your demeanour and health. If you are annoyed by a neighbour's dog barking you can close the window, or remonstrate with your neighbour, but that may only bring temporary relief, for the dog will almost certainly bark again. Even if it doesn't, you have done nothing to help yourself, because next time a crying baby will elicit the same sort of reaction from you. Stress is serious business, because even a non-existent but perceived threat could cause it. You can't control the world around you, but you can control your response to what happens in it.

If you talk to others who dislike such situations you will know that each individual reacts differently. Some reactions are psychological, like anxiety, reduced concentration and restlessness, sleeplessness, low self-esteem, anger and resentment, and inability to cope; whereas others are physiological such as indigestion or ulceration, heartburn, comfort eating or loss of appetite, unexplained muscular twinges, and sweaty palms. If the latter consequences persist your physiological state will deteriorate and you may become more prone to illness because your immune system is depressed; new conditions may develop, and existing conditions may be aggravated, notably asthma, sexual dysfunction, depression, migraine, high blood pressure, heart problems, eczema, ulcers and forms of cancer. Your mental and physical conditions are both at stake if you ignore the importance of regulating your personal equilibrium.

It may go against the grain, but it is not helpful to look for someone else to blame for your feelings. You must resolve to heal yourself. The most obvious and most natural counter is relaxation, which is highly individual and may take many forms, according to what is best for you. Its purpose is to wind the body down and divert the brain or use a different area of it. This is why playing a musical instrument, both a creative and an aesthetically pleasing experience, which therefore engages different regions of the brain, is so successful in promoting relaxation.

Most of the dangers our pre-Stone Age ancestors faced were physical, and many of those dangers had big teeth, so the usual response was either fight or flight. The body's reactions to these responses, namely tautness of the muscles, adrenalin flow, blood-pressure rise, heartbeat increasing in frequency, are still with us, which is why we have so many physical and physiological responses to situations in everyday life that are not physically threatening, such as the loss of a relative or pet, the break-up of a relationship, redundancy or dismissal from employment, loss of financial investment, or cancellation of a public transport service. Fighting and escaping are no longer the simple alternative answers. Kicking the cat never worked anyway, but stroking it might.

Understanding the body's reaction to stress

You may need to remind yourself several times when feeling under stress that it is your reactions to events you are dealing with, and these reactions are therefore connected to your personality and current demeanour and circumstances. A sound proposal in the early stages is to cement relationships firmly within your extended family and ask for help from them, and at the same time resolve to rebuild any fractured relationships. Your relatives, pets, neighbours, friends, and colleagues are valuable allies in that they represent stability and companionship in troubled times. Make positive efforts to be accommodating and pleasant to others; give way to others in various respects, such as deliberately being courteous to other drivers; keep to your normal diet; avoid alcohol; take more exercise; keep occupied, especially creative pursuits as these raise self-esteem, and arrange regular social engagements; avoid loneliness; develop a relaxation regime if it is not part of your lifestyle already; and generally try to bolster up your feelings of wellbeing in as many areas as possible. If you recognise the onset of stress you should act on these suggestions immediately, for they will be the bedrock of your strategy. Don't take any orthodox medication, as that is designed to relieve symptoms not causes. Holistic approaches to stress management recognise the interconnection of mind and body in producing the reactions to stress, and therefore in formulating a strategy, which must be an active strategy, to relieve it and restore inner harmony.

Whatever your chosen strategy, you will need to adapt and hone it to your own needs and responses, for we are all different in how we react to stress. You will learn a lot about your body and what works for its individual physiological reactions to stress, but you will only come up with an effective stress-beating regime if you try a number of approaches and stay positive in the belief that one, or more in combination, will work for you. In this way you will not dissipate your anxieties on to those people or events you think are the cause. If thousands of insects are buzzing round you, are you going to try swiping at them all, or are you going to develop ways of controlling your own reactions and ultimately to change your demeanour? Which do you think is the most realistic strategy in the long term?

The body's physiological reactions to stress, notably increased heart rate, faster breathing, rise in blood pressure, trembling of muscles to prime them for action, decrease in production of saliva, rise in levels of blood sugar and cholesterol, increased perspiration, increased sharpness of vision by dilation of the pupils, reduced inflammation, increased production of blood-clotting factors, all initiated by the hypothalamus in the brain directing the production of adrenalin and noradrenalin by the adrenal glands when the brain perceives threat, are not under conscious control. The survival advantage of many of these involuntary reactions is obvious, but they are a disadvantage when it comes to chronic stress. To counter this disadvantage you have to develop ways of conditioning your brain not to regard the body as under threat.

The perception of threat by the brain produces the same bodily reactions whether the threat is physical or psychological, so an individual undergoes the same sort of stressful physiological reaction to anxiety as if it had come face to face with a hungry tiger. If the tiger turns away your body will return to normal, but anxieties may persist, causing your body to remain in its tensed-up state and liable to suffer serious, even permanent, malfunction. This is the danger your personal relaxation strategy is designed to avoid. The consequences of stress-induced physiological malfunction are highly individual, so the strategy must be suited to yourself, not borrowed from someone else. Support from others is very valuable, but the strategy must be your own. Crying and laughter are two reactions known to help the body restore its equilibrium after stress, but with chronic stress, also known as burn-out, they can't do the job on their own. Always remember that a fit, healthy body of normal weight, which is rested each night, copes far better with the effects of stress than an abused one.

Identifying your signs and symptoms of stress

Common life-cycle changes such as death in the family, a birth, a parting, are stressful for a time, but they are generally expected and we prepare for them and cope with them. Reactions to everyday events tend to be more connected to individual temperament, particularly to lack of patience or understanding. The first signs may be fidgeting, or other nervous mannerisms like biting nails, preening hair, constantly smoothing or straightening of clothing, or tapping fingers or feet. This phase may be followed by some of the following: headaches, indigestion, back pain, diarrhoea or constipation, rapid breathing or asthma-like symptoms, dermatological problems, dry mouth, clammy hands, and many others. Some reactions are hereditary – for example, psoriasis. It tends to be easier to control your reaction to stressful events that need ignoring, because you are powerless to stop them, such as traffic noise, than events requiring your intervention, such as a bullying boss.

If you are objective and honest with yourself you will be able to identify stressful events and your physiological and physical reactions, with help if necessary, and you need then to analyse your consequent behaviour. In addition to the responses mentioned already, you may start to rush everything you do, including speech, or feel listless yet be unable to relax or sleep, or cry a lot, or lose your interest in sex, or become indecisive or reckless, or look to comfort eating or excessive drinking or other substance abuse. Auditing these events and your reactions, in the form of a diary if you choose, is a very difficult thing to do, requiring extreme frankness and humility, but easier with the help of family and friends. Achieving it is a vital step in planning your relaxation and coping strategy.

The value of a mentor in combating stress is incalculable, especially if you feel depressed or over-anxious. Feelings of shame, embarrassment or inadequacy are common, as is the fear of being thought neurotic or feeble-minded. The fear of 'losing face' can prevent people from seeking assistance or unburdening themselves, so early on seek a willing mentor, meet regularly and share feelings and ideas. Strong modern pagan family ties are invaluable here.

Equilibrium restoration strategies to consider

Relaxation

Learning to relax is complementary to learning good posture and movement and putting together an exercise routine, and similarly should be a daily undertaking. Sitting in front of the television with an alcoholic drink, a packet of cigarettes and a bottle of tranquillisers is the antithesis of relaxation as many parts of the body and brain are put into overdrive. Some strategies are good for short-term relaxation such as a change of scenery by leaving your place of work during a break and going for a walk, sitting down to write a letter, having a bath or shower, or doing a job in the garden, but for long-term effectiveness you need a personal, regular routine.

Deep rhythmic breathing should be part of this routine. Place the hands flat on your abdomen just above the navel, and inhale so that your stomach rises and pushes your hands out. Then exhale to deflate the expansion of the abdomen. Repeat. Try to duplicate this expansion and contraction each time. Now lie on your back with legs outstretched and arms outstretched by your side and commence deep breathing. Clear your mind of active thoughts and after a few minutes tense each part of the body and allow it to relax. This sequence of progressive muscle relaxation puts both mind and body at ease and is a good unwinder. If it helps achieve a greater sense of tranquillity then accompany with your choice of music, recordings of natural sounds like birdsong or whale calls, visualisation of a pleasant scene, or quiet repeating of a mantra – which may be a sound without meaning or a word or phrase that you have chosen as an affirmation. You will find your breathing slowing as you relax, and as your heart rate, blood pressure and muscular tension decrease your circulation and digestion will improve. You will feel calmer and more composed, and better able to concentrate and remember; your mood will brighten, resolve and resilience strengthen and problems appear more in perspective. Clearer thinking means more sound appreciation and assessment, leading to greater confidence in solving your personal problems.

Acupuncture, originating in China, is a technique to consider for the relief of pain caused by stress, but the pressure points used by its practitioners to ease pain can be engaged with the fingertips, by pressing firmly but gently and precisely. Under guidance you can relieve pain like headaches. Another Chinese technique is t'ai chi ch'uan, or t'ai chi for short, a form of relaxation in motion, with deep, slow breathing, which can alleviate stress, induce calm and dispel negative thoughts. By focussing on the balances of the body in movement excess muscular tension is released.

Visualisation

Visualisation is a way to distract yourself from stressful thoughts and focus the mind on what you consider to be calming and restful. A scenario is constructed, either from the imagination or from happy memories, in order that you experience it physically, mentally, emotionally, sensorily, and in a positive, relaxing and highly personal way. By clearing your thoughts and substituting your scenario, you can lose your senses in the visualisation. Choose a quiet, cool, dimly lit spot in the garden or house; wear comfortable clothes; lie down on a firm bed or lounger, or the lawn, supporting the head as advised before, or sit in a high-backed chair. Relax the muscles and close your eyes. Successful imaginings may include a place where you have been able to relax before, such as a beach, wood, lakeside, mountain plateau, or sailing on a calm sea. Imagine the sights, colours and shapes. Then extend the visualisation to other sensory imaginings, like smelling the sea or woodland air; hearing the sounds of birds, surf or rustling leaves; feeling the breeze or sun on your face; touching rocks or bark, or trailing the hands in water; or stroking your dog, cat or horse. Visualisation is a very personal experience, but all the more effective for it.

Meditation

Bodily processes and mental activity can both be slowed by meditation, which involves concentrating the mind on a single thought, word, mantra or object, or by contemplating through focussing the mind on a philosophical concern. You can combine meditation with your relaxation strategy and choose to engage your mind in positive thinking, taking a new look, perhaps from various angles, at situations that you feel stressed about. This is partly about self-esteem, self-confidence and self-control, but also about replacing over-reaction with perspective and balanced judgement. Analysis in a relaxed situation is more likely to be reasoned, and more likely to highlight your good qualities and achievements rather than result in you running yourself down. Being positive is being in control, but a negative demeanour means others are in control of you, by influencing your decisions and behaviour.

The stress therapies in this chapter have evolved as part of a holistic approach to stress, addressing both the causes and its physiological manifestations. Therapies like acupuncture, acupressure and homoeopathy work on the principle that stress causes imbalances in the body and if these are restored then the body's natural capacity to heal itself is given a fighting chance. Homoeopathy uses highly diluted tinctures of substances that induce similar symptoms to the ones a person is suffering from. Thereby, homoeopaths believe, the body is stimulated to heal itself. Most of the substances administered are of natural origin. Homoeopaths claim to be able to tailor a course of remedies to an individual's stress symptoms. Relaxation techniques help to regularise the cardiovascular and digestive systems as well as the musculature and thought processes. Aromatherapy uses the soothing scents and penetrative properties of natural oils to aid relaxation. This may be by way of massage, such as with chamomile, rose or sandalwood oils; or placing the oil in your bath water, or in water to soak the feet in; or in a face pack; or by vaporising over a burner, as with jasmine or lavender, or in a bowl of hot water. Three groups of oils are generally recognised: those that invigorate the body and raise the spirits, including basil, bergamot and rosemary; those that induce calm, particularly cedarwood, jasmine and neroli; and those that tone the skin or otherwise enhance the health of other organs, as do lemongrass and myrrh.

Techniques such as massage, reflexology, the Alexander Technique, osteopathy and chiropractic focus on reducing muscular tension and relieving stress-induced pain through manipulation or posture correction. Massage allows two partners to explore the sense of touch, which humans tend to under-use as they do smell. With a range of essential oils mixed with base oil, both senses can be fully engaged, enhanced by the use of a vaporiser and aromatic candles. Caressing with fabrics of different texture like silk and velvet, or with feathers, is another possibility, all of which is designed to make this part of your strategy pleasurable, especially if shared with your partner. Reflexology aims to treat bodily ailments or stress symptoms by massaging areas of the underside of the foot called 'reflex areas'. Osteopathy is the manipulation of the skeleton, and chiropractors relieve the compression of nerves caused by stress-related tension. They do this by applying controlled pressure with the hands to the muscles, bones and joints. In particular they seek to correct misalignments of the vertebrae, which can pinch the spinal nerves and cause pain anywhere along the path of the nerve. A full examination is needed to detect skeletal or muscular problem areas. Neuralgia and arthritic and rheumatic consequences of stress can also be treated by chiropractic. Practitioners use techniques such as heat therapy, ultrasound, ice packs and traction to assist realignment.

Our mental resources are brought into play to assist our other natural healing mechanisms in techniques such as t'ai chi ch'uan, meditation and yoga. Yoga hails from ancient India and combines meditation and exercise, using deep breathing and stretching to reduce muscular tension and blood pressure, and induce a feeling of tranquillity.

Not one of the methods above employs drugs, so you may feel confident in trying the ones that appeal after consultation with an experienced practitioner.

Make your home a haven

Stress in one member of the family can bring about a chain reaction of disharmony in the immediate family; so all members benefit from being brought together for a frank discussion and appraisal of the situation early in the formation of the stress-reduction strategy. They have a valuable part to play in the strategy as they have a stake in the wellbeing of the stressed relative, and it may be their turn next if heredity has anything to do with it. A stress-free home is a safe, relaxing place with good security measures; attention to accident prevention and hygiene; plenty of fresh air and as chemical- and pollution-free as possible; a minimum number of 'house rules' of conduct; and with colour schemes, lighting and furniture arrangement that all find both functional and aesthetically pleasing. Plants help to clean the atmosphere of poorly ventilated spaces by converting your exhaled carbon dioxide into oxygen, but also they will remind you that outside is the tranquillity of the natural world. Such a home will be a retreat from stress if the whole family is part of the strategy.

Choice of colour is very personal, but some themes are regularly claimed to be able to influence mood and sense of space. Dark shades are said to make a space seem restricted and light shades give a roomier look. Blue and turquoise are held to be relaxing, calming colours and in light shades seem to enhance feelings of spaciousness. They could be considered for rooms where peace and communication are important, such as areas where both talking and relaxation take place. Green and brown, nature's colours, are thought to be harmonious and calming, and to offer a comforting natural presence. They may suit a room like a study where concentration and creativity are common activities. Blues and greens may also make a sunny room seem cooler. Yellow, orange and white are said to be cheerful, stimulating colours, suited to areas where you welcome visitors and socialise. Reds are regarded as warming and arousing, but can reduce the feeling of spaciousness and make you feel enclosed. They are said to suit places of sensuality and stimulation. Reds, oranges and yellows warm up a cold, north-facing room.

Opinions obviously differ about such things as colour, décor, lighting and furniture arrangement, so there are no hard and fast rules, only what pleases the family, and the ideas herein are only suggestions for your consideration. You may wish to achieve some measure of balance, such as keeping walls and flooring light-to-medium in shade and tone, and being flamboyant in moderation such as on upholstery, curtains, fittings and accessories. Lighting enables you to enhance or tone down the mood of a room in different ways. You can employ dimmer switches or use spotlights to pick out certain features. Experimenting with light bulb colour can produce some pleasing effects; pink may give an appearance that you feel is warmer than white, and blue more subdued.

Good sound-proofing in your house allows rooms to be used for individual pursuits without anyone disturbing others, and keeps external noises out if you so choose, although circulation of fresh air is important as is an acclimatisation strategy if external noise is a cause of your stress. Keep rooms on the cool side, especially bedrooms, and guard against central heating drying out skin and respiratory passages. Bowls of water strategically placed, and regularly sprayed and watered plants, will help maintain a moderate humidity.

The odours in your home can affect your mood too, for the area of the brain that interprets what the nose smells is linked to the area dealing with emotion. Some scents bring back childhood memories, as though somehow they are stored in long-term memory, while others are ambient in the house through the operation of appliances, choice of finish and decoration, and degree of ventilation. The vapours of basil, peppermint and rosemary oils are all said to enhance mental alertness. Put a few drops onto damp cotton wool in a saucer and place near a radiator or in a sunny spot, so that the vapour is released. The essential oils of rosemary and geranium are used to help alleviate the effects of jet lag or other disorientation of the biological clock. By the use of plants with scented flowers or leaves, pot pourri, candles, and natural fragrances you can create odiferous regions to your taste in any room.

The Chinese practice of feng shui is the creation of an environment held to be harmonious and emotionally enhancing by attention to the position and arrangement of a room's structures and furnishings. The objective is to go beyond what is merely aesthetically pleasing and physically comfortable to create an environment that itself actively promotes wellbeing.

The bathroom is one room that naturally appeals as a place of health, with no artificial preparations therein, to relax and revitalise as well as cleanse. Hot baths are not a good idea if you are under stress as your blood vessels dilate and the heart must work harder. A cool bath reduces the heart rate and has a calming effect on mind and muscles. You can practise your relaxation techniques whilst soaking, and then finish off with a shower, firstly with the water just warm, then a few minutes under cold water to finish off. Dry yourself, and the body will be in a receptive state for massage to be very effective. According to the outcome desired you could add essential oils to the bath water. A few drops of lavender oil in an evening bath have a calming effect and help with sleep. A lavender- or hop-filled pillow does likewise. But there are a number of other bathroom preparations of long standing. Adding a mixture of whipped cream (one tablespoon) and lemon juice (six drops) to bath water will help to moisturise dry skin. Epsom salts in the water will help to cleanse the skin and reduce swellings. A mixture of equal parts of oatmeal and honey is a good exfoliating mixture, which may be rubbed on gently with pumice or a loofah. Cucumber slices help to reduce the smarting of tired eyes. These are useful in their own right, but also enhance general wellbeing.

As at home, so at work

Your programme of renewal and relaxation can be continued at work when duties permit, during breaks and in between tasks. Regular stretching exercises and attention to posture and the dangers of repetitive strain injuries are important in sedentary jobs and those requiring the deployment of tools, as is the occasional change of scene and rotation of tasks. Don't skip meals, however busy you may think you are, and sip water to counter dehydration, not tea or coffee. Keep your room cool and keep the air circulating. Make use of the journey home if you can to begin the process of unwinding – rather than talk shop or take the troubles of work home. An audit of a typical day at work will reveal where appropriate aspects of your strategy can be incorporated. If you have the freedom to do so, try to apply to your office the same principles of colour, odour, and arrangements that have been successful at home.

The healing garden

The garden as a place of healing

Aside from the nutritive benefits of the kitchen garden, there are other obvious healing benefits from the garden, such as the beauty of plants, their juxtaposition and association, and the joy of working amongst them and their natural animal associates. Then there is the fresh air, the exercise, the scents, tastes, touch and sounds of the garden. Every plant is converting carbon dioxide to oxygen, thereby helping to replenish the atmosphere.

Just walking into a garden aimlessly, to unwind and relax and see what comes, is itself therapeutic. To slow down to the pace of the natural world is to uncoil the tensions that an unnatural lifestyle has created. Gardening activities are very varied, requiring concentration, muscular co-ordination, dexterity, reasoning, and many other skills, both mental and physical, and this makes gardening an ideal displacement activity for the person under stress. The garden is a productive, rehabilitative place, giving a positive sense of achievement to counter the low self-esteem often characteristic of stress. Its tasks are elemental, to do with nurture and care, and they have beginning, development and maturity phases, and a satisfying conclusion.

We have been on intimate terms with the natural world for most of human evolution, urban dwellers only relatively recently, so it may be we have a deep-seated need, as well as a desire, to recharge our mental batteries in nature. As nature runs to its own schedule, so then must those in intimate contact with it, and therein lies another aspect of healing, returning the body to natural pace and rhythm. Plants sprout, mature, flower and fruit when conditions are right – no amount of human impatience, bred in the material, commercial world, will change that. You can make small changes to your garden's seasonal cycles with respect to individual crops, such as by forcing, but by and large, you must go with nature. Learning this is invaluable education, for you may have to learn to live with aspects of the material world too, and find you are better for being able to adjust. Sharing your garden with wildlife rather than battling to exclude it teaches you to be inviting and accommodating. Losing your obsession with 'pests' and 'weeds' breeds perspective that all have their place and uses, just like people in society. Using natural methods of control teaches you co-operation, delegation, trust, and that hospitality is repaid. Gardeners learn patience, that investment in the future pays off, that hard work brings rewards. The flexibility and adaptability of nature means that you can experiment, and try again if it fails. Nurturing a living thing brings out caring instincts, feelings of being needed and of value, and the ability to see a project to conclusion. The garden can indeed be a training ground for society at large, for where else can so many social skills be honed without another person in sight?

The physic garden
The physic garden provided the means by which the natural culmination of millennia of accumulated herbal knowledge could be put to systematic medicinal use.

Grave contents 60,000 years ago have included known medicinal herbs. Since ancient times, comfrey was so effective at aiding the healing of battle wounds it was called knitbone. Yarrow was carried by soldiers as a quick-acting astringent and antiseptic, and called woundwort. The number of lives saved by these two herbs alone is incalculable.

Chinese records of herbal medicine date from about 2,500 BCE, and about 1,500 BCE the Egyptian Ebers Papyrus of herbal prescriptions was written. Successively we then have the publication of Babylonian, Indian, Greek, and Roman pharmacopoeias. About 950 ACE a monk called Bald, at the time of King Alfred, asked a scribe Cild to write a herbal, and it is the earliest English herbal to survive, called *Leech Book of Bald*. The next was *A New Herball* by William Turner in 1551; then *The Herball of Generall Historie of Plantes* by John Gerard in 1597; then *Herball* by Nicholas Culpeper, a work full of astrological references, about the middle of the seventeenth century. The first known physic garden was laid out at Pisa, Italy, in 1543. The first to appear in the UK was the Oxford Physic Garden in 1621, followed by the Chelsea Physic Garden in 1673, founded by the Society of Apothecaries to train apprentices.

The rational science of the Age of Enlightenment in the eighteenth century saw doctors start to prescribe chemicals instead of herbs. The idea became current that humankind was somehow separate from nature and had special needs, in particular, that the mind and body were separate. Thus the holistic approach to medicine was gradually abandoned. Specific compounds were extracted from plants instead of using the whole plant. Helping to fight or prevent disease means boosting the immune, hormonal and nervous systems to encourage the body's healing mechanisms, and often whole plants have these capabilities within them, and they do it with relatively few side effects. Meadowsweet (*Filipendula ulmaria*) contains salicylic acid, so is an analgesic and anti-inflammatory, but it doesn't cause bleeding in the stomach or digestive problems like aspirin because of other chemicals in the plant that counter acidity and ulceration. Medicine continued along this path until the return of green consciousness and holistic philosophies in the 1960s.

The dung-enriched raised beds of traditional physic gardens were made from elm planking, but nowadays old railway sleepers are a more easily obtainable substitute. In a physic garden it was always one herb per bed, and there were many traditional patterns, such as a chess board pattern with alternate paving slabs, or a cartwheel or clock design, or a ram's horn. Containers were also used, particularly for rampant herbs like mints. By considering both culinary and medicinal uses a combined area can be a very useful feature of any domestic or communal garden.

Herbal medicine

Opening the herbal medicine chest

For those willing to search, there are thousands of years of herbal wisdom and tradition to draw upon, with many associations between herbs and bodily imbalances being of long-standing application. Examples include products from the foxglove that relieve the effects of heart failure and dropsy (water retention), and act as heart stimulants, not to mention the flowering tops of hawthorn, which also help in the treatment of heart disorders; derivatives of quinine, extracted from the bark of the Peruvian cinchona tree, that have been effective against malaria; the ability of tannins to help wounds to close and to reduce infection; ingestion of water and glucose to offset the effects of altitude sickness; an infusion of a peeled slice of ginger in hot water helping to settle the stomach of someone suffering from travel sickness, and also the anti-inflammatory and anti-coagulant properties of ginger and its stimulation of the circulation; the application of arnica cream to aching muscles and of a cream made from a mixture of arnica and calendula to sore nipples; herbal remedies for stress relief from skullcap, a woodland plant; preparations from valerian root to reduce nervous tension; a poultice of cabbage leaves and potato juice to relieve tenderness, a mixture that also aids digestion, soreness and swelling; relief of headache and migraine by use of feverfew; the antibiotic properties of nasturtium; the soothing effect of strawberries on sunburn, cucumber on itchy skin, lemon juice on chilblains, and onion on bee stings. Mould, lichens, mosses and spiders' webs have all been used successfully to dress wounds, on account of the presence of natural antibiotics, and the British Army used sphagnum moss as a dressing during the First World War. Then we have the use of St John's Wort and fennel to treat depression; marigold tincture to help wounds heal; the ability of liquorice to contribute to the treatment of stomach ulcers; easing the discomfort of over-eating with an infusion of chamomile; the relief of chesty coughs with thyme and of sore throats with honeysuckle syrup; peppermint to relieve nausea; marjoram and rosemary to stimulate the circulation, the latter also helping the recovery from fatigue and moodiness; echinacea to boost the immune system; sage antiseptic throat gargles; chewing parsley to combat bad breath; and many more too numerous to record here.

Pharmacies and drug manufacturers charge high prices for preparations that vary in their effectiveness and extent of side effects, whereas natural remedies can often do better for little or no charge. Literature on herbal preparations contains some that work for everybody, some that seem to work for some people and not others, perhaps reflecting the fact that there are individual as well as species dimensions to physiology, and some that appear to have no efficacy at all. There are some herbal preparations that are very powerful and have dangerous side effects if misused or taken in large doses. You must be prepared to do research and seek guidance to help you find what works for you. Herbalists have a holistic approach to healing, considering causes as well as symptoms, and general wellbeing and prevention. Nevertheless, you should inform your family doctor about your intended use of herbs if you are currently undergoing treatment under her or his guidance.

Choosing the right method of herbal application

To be efficacious herbal ingredients must be properly extracted or the herb as a whole properly prepared. Simply picking a plant and chewing it may be dangerous. A water-soluble component can be extracted as an infusion or decoction, whilst alcohol-soluble ingredients would be prepared as a tincture. Many medicinal herbs are also used in the kitchen as flavourings, but their medicinal dose will generally be more than that used for culinary purposes. The first step in preparing a herb is often to dry it for preservation, ease of storage and to concentrate the active ingredient, but you must know which part of the plant contains the latter, for other parts may be poisonous. Potato tubers are edible, and used in herbal medicine, but the rest of the potato plant is poisonous.

Essential oils are concentrated and are normally used highly diluted. For massage they are added to a base oil, such as soya, sunflower, grapeseed or almond oil, although carrot or jojoba base oils are preferred for the face. Keep them away from your eyes and don't take internally. Children should only handle them under guidance, and you must use approved formulae so as not to use too high a concentration, especially if using as an inhalant to induce relaxation, stimulation, emotional reactions, memory recall or other types of mental stimulation. A typical quantity to add to your bath water would only be five to ten drops. The physiological effects after absorption through the skin must also be considered when selecting oils, and you may need to change the treatment according to the body's reaction. These are just a selection of cautions to exercise when choosing herbal applications.

Homoeopathy is based on the 'like cures like' principle. If it looks like a duck, walks like a duck and quacks like a duck, then it will cure a duck. The smaller the dose of the diluted ingredient the more effective homoeopaths claim it will be. Homoeopathic medicines are commonly prepared as an alcoholic tincture before dilution. Usage in tiny concentrations distinguishes homoeopathic medicine from herbal medicine and renders properly prepared homoeopathic remedies non-toxic.

Bach Flower Remedies are based on the belief that certain plants or combinations of plants can influence emotional states according to one's personality. The freshly picked flowers are floated on the surface of pure natural water in a glass bowl, according to prescribed rules.

Chinese herbal medicine stems from the ancient belief that the body has a vital energy flowing through it called chi, which is controlled by the balancing forces of yin and yang. If the yin–yang equilibrium is upset in a particular way then administering an appropriate herbal medicine can restore the balance. Chinese herbal medicine has caused the near extinction of large numbers of animals and plants, and should not, out of conscience, be used by modern pagans. At present the Amazon forests are being plundered for medicinal plants, and the products of the companies involved should similarly be boycotted.

Choosing the right herbal product

If, for example, you are considering a skin preparation, your first thought should be that the natural skin can normally look after itself, and so it is with other parts of the body. But if you need to cleanse or moisturise the skin then you must choose appropriately. Put a mixture of equal parts dried nettles and chamomile flowers in a bowl and pour on boiling water and you will produce a general cleansing steam for the face, but specific combinations of herbs or essential oils suit specific facial skin types – dry, oily, sensitive, and so on – and are applied as massage oils, steams, face packs, or cleansing solutions accordingly.

Herbal skin preparations can also have a toning effect, and tighten the skin according to their degree of astringency, varying from the soothing rose oil to the astringent sage. Some preparations have both a cleansing and moisturising function, unlike soap, an example being cucumber extract. The latter also soothes mild burns. Wheatgerm oil is a therapeutic skin oil, as it is rich in vitamin E, nourishing the skin and helping to tighten wrinkles and stretch marks, although it is not recommended for use simply to counter the natural effects of advancing years. Comfrey extracts are good for repairing damaged skin and relieving irritation and soreness.

Herbal face packs can serve a variety of functions, to cleanse or enhance skin texture in desired ways according to whether the skin is dry, oily, etc. They may be based on waxes, gels, plant gums, egg white, milk protein, clay or other natural base, to which is added the essential oils or herbs to achieve the desired outcome. Fennel creams, for example, are commonly used for dry skin. Herbal creams and lotions for other parts of the body have a variety of purposes, such as the relief of irritation or inflammation, to treat bruises or swellings, as an embrocation or liniment, as a bactericide, as a coolant, to improve circulation, and to treat blackheads or other dermatological conditions. Rather than buy shampoos with synthetic, ecologically damaging ingredients, try nettle preparations for a hair rinse, and rosemary and lavender preparations for cleansing the scalp.

Herbs providing pain relief have been known for centuries, an ancient example being oil of cloves for instant relief of toothache. Other examples are feverfew or lime blossom tea for headaches; peppermint to aid digestion; chamomile flower tea for indigestion; willow or meadowsweet extracts for general pain relief; and lemon balm tea, preparations from guelder rose bark, or lavender infusion for period pains. Many new ones are under investigation in various parts of the world, presenting a strong case for preserving biodiversity.

Harvesting herbs from the wild

There was an ancient belief that the medicinal properties of herbs would be at their most potent if they were harvested at full moon. To harvest when the moon was waxing was to risk weak or no efficacy, and on the waning moon, the herb would be malignant in its effects. Ingredients for potions designed to harm were thus harvested.

If you collect your own herbs from the wild they should be carefully identified, and smelt and examined for freshness. Put them into plastic bags and put in the freezer for a few days to kill any hidden larvae. When you are ready to prepare them, shake and wash them. Active ingredients are found in different parts of the plant according to the species, so you may find yourself collecting the seeds of one, the flowers of another, the root of a third, and so on. Remember to harvest thinly in any location. Once the parts have been dried, divide into portions for storage, in case deterioration affects some of them; the usual agencies are heat, light, oxidation, moisture absorption and microbiological infestation. Date the containers, which could be dark jars or bottles, or brown paper bags, and keep them dry and cool (below 15°C/60°F).

Choosing the right method of herbal preparation

The method of preparation depends on the intended usage as well as the characteristics of the ingredients. For internal use, herbs are prepared as infusions, decoctions, tinctures, syrups and juices, commonly, always taking care to prevent loss of volatile components. For external application it is more usual to employ creams, ointments, aqueous lotions, or infused oils. Preparations are further classified according to their therapeutic purpose, such as analgesic, astringent, diuretic, expectorant, laxative, styptic, and so on. However, there is a further dimension to consider, namely the age and physiological condition of the recipient. Caution should be exercised, and advice sought, if you are pregnant, if you are currently undergoing medical treatment, or if you are considering administering to young children. Herbs really work, as their old country names often vividly relate. Nowadays the diuretic dandelion is known by a corruption of its French name, meaning lion's tooth; possibly because its English name is piss-a-bed.

In case of allergy or adverse side effects always start a course of herbal medicine with a small dose or application and gradually increase to the recommended amount if all is well. Check in the literature, or with an expert, to see if a maximum dose is recorded, in which case it may indicate toxicity in large amounts. However, the majority of herbs are safe and their effects and doses well known and easy to find in herbal literature. You may be in a position to be able to choose a family doctor who is sympathetic to the practice of herbal medicine, which would be fortunate, but there is little to be said for most of the over-the-counter products obtainable from pharmacies, which are just heavily sweetened mixtures of flavourings of dubious efficacy.

Harvesting from the physic garden

Your best introduction to herbal medicine is through those ingredients that come from plants you can grow in the garden. No identification will normally be necessary, and they are always available fresh. Those herbs with a preventative use can simply be eaten as a normal part of the diet. Every modern pagan garden should have herbs for both culinary and medicinal use, conveniently near the house if you wish, but there is no reason why you can't interplant other plants with herbs to lessen the risk of concentrations of herbivorous insects and to give each herb its ideal position. Don't grow them near a road, as traffic exhaust fumes will contaminate them.

Fresh herbs are essential if you are to have both enjoyment from them and confidence in them. If purchasing, buy them labelled from reputable sources, and propagate them yourself if you are pleased with their quality. Only grow in pots if you have no garden, as they dislike drying out or having their roots restricted. In both circumstances quality will be reduced. Planting several different herbs in one pot is not a good idea, as the more vigorous will deprive the others of root space and nutrients. Your horticultural methods should be strictly organic if you are growing herbs to eat or to make into medicinal preparations.

When you have chosen the appropriate part of the plant to harvest, water the plant if necessary and wait until the next day after any dew has evaporated so that the part you want is dry. Harvest, dry and store in a dark place without delay. Leaves, especially from plants with essential oils, are best picked just before noon, when the oil content is highest, as they tend to scent the air in the early afternoon sun as the oils evaporate. Leaves and shoots should be young, unbruised and not yet in flower. Don't wash them at this stage unless you have to, so that mould is discouraged, and take indoors to dry. From the drying stage onwards the herb should be out of direct sunlight. The best conditions for drying leaves, stems and roots is very dim light or darkness, a temperature of 20–24°C, good ventilation, on plain paper on a wire rack, or hung up in small bunches. Pick flowers when the weather is dry, late morning, and just after bud opening. Do not wash or damage the petals, and spread thinly on paper or muslin, in a temperature of 18–20°C.

Roots are best harvested in autumn after they have stored their natural constituents for winter, and the plants selected should be at least two years old. Ease them up carefully, and only take a portion of the root of a perennial so that it can resume growth. Clean the root with brush and water, then dry, but be gentle with roots whose active part is in the surface layer, like valerian. Thick roots will dry better if cut into strips, and a higher drying temperature can be used for roots, up to 50°C. Other conditions such as good air circulation and dark conditions still apply. Harvest seeds on a warm, dry day when the seed head is fully ripe but before the pod bursts. Shake into a paper bag and dry in a dark, warm, airy place as quickly as possible. Avoid temperatures above 40°C for seeds containing essential oils, as these will evaporate. Harvest berries when ripe. Bark should be peeled from young branches when damp so that it comes away easily. Do not remove a complete ring of bark from the trunk or the tree may die. Remove mosses, lichens and insects, break into several pieces and dry as for roots. You can also cut off a branch in late Spring or early Summer and strip it.

Making your herbal preparations

Before you start, make sure all equipment and containers are sterilised. Preparations for internal use are normally in aqueous solution and the simplest form is the infusion, or tisane, of which teas are an example. For teas/infusions, take 1 oz (25 g) of fresh herb (or half the amount of dried herb), put in a jug and add water that is just off the boil. Infuse for ten minutes and strain. Any not used immediately can sometimes be kept in the refrigerator for one or two days, but no longer. If an ingredient is likely to be decomposed by heat then make a cold infusion. This type of preparation is normally employed for the softer parts of plants (flowers, leaves, young stems), but for tougher parts (root, bark, seeds), even when broken up, a decoction is prepared. To make a decoction, grind up the herb with a pestle and mortar. Take 2 oz (50 g) of fresh herb (or half the amount of dried herb), and pour on 1 pint (650 ml) of water. Bring to the boil, simmer covered for ten to fifteen minutes and strain. Add water to make up to the desired concentration. Like infusions they can be stored in a refrigerator for one to two days, but use immediately for maximum potency. Gargles and mouthwashes are normally made as strained infusions.

Many teas have medicinal uses. Peppermint tea is drunk for indigestion; lime flower and chamomile teas to help you sleep; rosemary tea to improve circulation and relieve migraine; and an old cold relief tea is made from a mixture of hyssop, lavender, marjoram and thyme.

If you soak a cotton cloth in an infusion or decoction it can serve as a hot or cold compress for inflammation, swellings or bruises. To make a poultice powder the herb in a mortar with a pestle, and mix with a little hot water to form a paste. Spread on gauze, or sandwich between layers of muslin, and apply to the skin and cover. Bandage if necessary. This method is effective in drawing out pus or splinters or for treating abscesses.

Tinctures are made when the active ingredients are soluble in alcohol. Usually their concentrations are higher than infusions, so doses tend to be smaller, and they keep longer in storage. To make a tincture, soak the fresh herbs in an aqueous alcohol mixture. For meadowsweet you will need 50 per cent alcohol, for calendula 70 per cent alcohol. Raspberries and cider vinegar make a tincture for coughs and sore throats. The container is sealed, kept in a warm place and shaken twice daily, relieving vapour pressure if necessary. Strain and store in a dark bottle in a cool place.

To make a cream or salve, mix essential oils or tinctures with a base cream or natural wax. Their usual function is to treat large areas of skin requiring moisturising or soothing. Creams made with waxes and no aqueous content are usually called ointments. They are thick and form a barrier, soaking in slowly. A basic salve can be made as follows. Melt 16 fl oz (450 ml) olive oil and 2 oz (50 g) beeswax in a bowl. Mix in the herb, heat over a pan of simmering water for two hours. Cool to the touch and squeeze through a muslin jelly bag into jars. Leave to solidify and store cool.

Liniments are made by mixing oils with tinctures, adding drops of essential oils or powders as required, to give a consistency suitable for massage. The application of a liniment stimulates blood flow. Infused oils – that is, vegetable oils infused with herbs – are also used as massage oils. Infusion can take several weeks, then strain and store in a dark bottle. A lotion is made like an infusion but applied externally, for example, as an eye, ear or mouth wash.

Syrups are made like decoctions but often sugar is added. Such preparations are damaging to the teeth and may upset daily carbohydrate intake, so either control of concentration is advisable or perhaps avoidance of their use. A basic syrup mixture uses equal amounts of runny honey and unrefined brown sugar, say 12 oz (325 g) of each. Mix, bring to the boil, and skim off the scum. When thickened, leave to cool, bottle and cork.

Inhalants help to relieve nasal congestion and inflamed sinuses. They can be rubbed on the chest, spread on a cloth for direct inhaling, or made in aqueous form in a bowl to breathe in when a cloth is placed over the head and bowl. Rubs are simply made by mixing drops of essential oils with Vaseline as a non-active base.

There are other types of preparation, but the list above covers the commonest ones made in the home. Some powdered herbs can be taken directly, by sprinkling on food, or put in hollow gelatine capsules available from suppliers of herbal medicine. Sometimes no preparation is necessary. Just a leaf on the skin can be enough, as with lemon balm on a cold sore, which soon gets the swelling down.

As to the question of which herb treats which condition, you should be guided by experienced herbalists or their literature, and take careful note of concentrations and doses. The list of conditions that respond to herbal medicine is a very long one and well documented, but you must inform yourself fully before proceeding, for only then will you have the successes that will nurture the confidence to pursue herbal medicine further.

Herbal remedies you can make

Press a fresh yarrow (*Achillea millefolium*) leaf on a cut or bruise to sooth and stop the bleeding.

Dab an infusion of the leaves of Lady's Mantle (*Alchemilla vulgaris*), or a root decoction, on to insect bites.

Stir the petals of *Calendula officinalis* into a pot of aqueous cream until coloured orange. Remove the bits and apply to burns, grazes and sores.

Take an infusion of chamomile flowers for headaches, indigestion and insomnia.

Take a decoction of elecampane root (*Inula helenium*) externally for acne and cuts.

An infusion of mint leaves aids digestion and eases heartburn, nausea and diarrhoea.

An infusion of the leaves of lemon balm is good for allergies like eczema and hay fever. Externally, a leaf reduces the swelling of cold sores.

Basil leaves may be rubbed on stings and bites.

An infusion of rosemary leaves and flowers, or a decoction of the leaves, or an infusion of sage leaves, makes a good mouthwash.

An infusion of nasturtium leaves is a good blood cleanser and detoxifies the liver. It is a diuretic and high in iron and vitamin C.

An infusion of stinging nettle leaves detoxifies the kidneys.

For foot massage, pour base oil into a bowl and add two drops of oil of peppermint. Mix well and massage all over the foot. This feels cool and improves the blood circulation.

For a face massage, warm the skin over a bowl of boiling water with a towel over the head and bowl for five minutes. Dry the face. Mix 3 per cent oil of lavender and oil of rose, and add two drops to wheatgerm oil. Massage the face and neck. You can also use oil of peppermint for a steam facial, by putting five drops into the boiling water.

Fill a pillow with dried hop flowers from late Autumn, with some lavender flowers if you wish, to help you sleep.

Herbs were strewn on medieval floors to scent, including basil, balm, chamomile, costmary, hyssop, lavender, meadowsweet, sage, thyme and the scented rush *Acorus calamus*, and you may like to revive this practice. Fumigation was done with angelica, elecampane (*Inula conyzae*), juniper, pine, and the roots of *Rhodiola rosea*.

The healing power of colour in the garden

Members of our society tend to have an instant reaction or association when certain colours are seen, such as red meaning danger, stop or ripe, or green meaning go, unripe or natural. Colour reflects emotions, as when someone 'sees red', or goes 'green with envy', or 'feels blue'. Someone with an uninspiring personality is termed 'grey', and language or personality that is vibrant is 'colourful'. If we are unwell we are 'off colour'. Individuals, however, often have very personal associations with colour. They have likes and dislikes, and favourites that can dominate their moods and purchases.

As the wall of the womb is translucent, the foetus is bathed in a golden glow, the first colour a baby is aware of. After birth, the exposure to artificial colour and light begins for many babies, and so does the effect on their health and wellbeing of hours in the unnatural artificial interior light of buildings, especially fluorescent light, which contains more blue, green and yellow than natural daylight. Over-exposure to artificial light produces a condition similar to Seasonal Affective Disorder (SAD) that is found in northern Europe during winter when natural light levels are low. The only effective counter is to expose babies and children to as much natural light as possible.

There is more to our perception of colour than just the visual image. Exposure to red light increases blood pressure, heart rate, breathing rate and muscular activity, so it is a colour that excites and stimulates. Blue has the opposite effect, that of calming these functions and reducing tension.

Also, our perspective is different with different colours. Red flowers in the garden appear closer, blue further away, so the brain perceives them differently. Blue flowers may be planted on boundaries to make them appear wider. Green neither recedes nor advances visually.

Traditional pagans have contributed the following reactions to colours in nature and in the garden:

- Red areas of the garden (those that absorb other colours and reflect red) stimulate and excite, pick you up and boost vitality, create a feeling of warmth. It is a joyful, vibrant and dominant flower colour. Red is good for active areas such as a child's play area. Pink has a milder effect, and is warm, inviting and soft, the effect retained into the evening.
- Orange is warm, optimistic, joyful, and invites movement. It is good for an eating area. Its richness goes well with purple and bronze. Peach is milder and more relaxing.
- Yellow is mentally stimulating rather than physically like red. It aids concentration and reasoning, and helps to clear the mind. It is also a cheery colour in the garden, like the sun. It is a very reflective colour, lasting into the evening. Pale yellow, apricot, stone and beige can make light, warm walls of colour.
- Green is peaceful, relaxing, contemplative, regenerative, hopeful, emotionally optimistic and de-stressing. It is a restful colour that does not tire the eye, being a mixture of warm yellow and cool blue. Green, along with silver and grey, is a good neutral shade in the garden. A tapestry of shades of green has great charm and subtlety.
- Blue areas calm and are contemplative, more so than green. They slow the individual down to nature's pace, invite patience and encourage dreams. True blue is not common in plants, violet and purple being seen more often. It is alluring with yellow, and in combination with silver and white, blue is very cool. A walk in a bluebell wood is very calming and therapeutic.

- Violet is meditative, nostalgic, philosophical, sleep-inducing and invites creativity.
- White plants reflect all colours, so lightening an area in dim light. Generally, dark colours absorb light, light colours reflect more light. At different times of the day in different atmospheric conditions shades change, and at dusk it is a world of monotones, except for the ethereal quality of white. Some white flowers are night-scented and attract moths. White flowers with grey-green foliage is a pleasing combination.
- Pastel colours work well in the soft light of northern Europe, and light to the north shows up the true shade of colour. Morning light has a cool, blue tone, midday a golden glow, and evening the red tone of the setting sun.

In nature in northern Europe, certain combinations of colour are common at different seasons. Spring brings an explosion of colour, and is full of greens, yellows and blues, and some white and pink. In Summer, bolder colours emerge, including strong yellows, reds and mauves, and in Autumn, we have more fiery shades – oranges, gold, russet, reds and purples. By Winter browns and greys abound, with bark and berries providing colours like red, yellow and gold. Whether the colour is continuous or broken up is determined by the habit of each plant, and of course as the seasons progress changes in colour groupings and contrasts occur naturally.

Some colours seem to complement each other, such as the pairs red/green, orange/blue, and yellow/violet, and they can be near one another, or one dominating and the other within in a lesser amount. A mixture of 70 per cent healing colour and 30 per cent complementary colour works well.

The healing power of scent in the garden

It doesn't take much for scent to pervade a garden. Jasmine, rose and honeysuckle climbers, a carpet of thymes and chamomile for all to walk on will soon transform the atmosphere. Like colour, scent evokes reactions and associations. We all have memories of how familiar places used to smell, such as our childhood home, school and neighbourhood. Tasting also actively involves the sense of smell, and this is evocative in a similar way.

When planting scented plants, choose a warm, sheltered place, or the wind will simply disperse the perfume and the coolness will mean little vapour release. Plants with scented foliage, such as chamomile, lemon balm, mint, rosemary, thyme and scented-leaved geraniums can be placed where you will brush past or walk over them.

Perfumiers distinguish five broad groups of odours:

- Citrus: lemon, mandarin, orange.
- Floral: jasmine, lavender, lily-of-the-valley, mimosa, rose, rose-scented geranium, violet.
- Green: basil, chamomile, clary sage, eucalyptus, lemon balm, marjoram, mint, pine, rosemary, thyme.
- Spicy: bay, carnation, cypress, fennel seeds, hops, juniper berries, pink, stock.
- Woody: angelica, birch, cedar, cedarwood, yarrow.

Scents in the same group can be grouped together, or you can concentrate individual scents. Consider the seasons so that you don't have scentless areas at certain periods, particularly Autumn and Winter, when choices are fewer. If you have colour groups in the garden, for the red area choose appropriate revitalising scents like basil, citrus, eucalyptus, fennel, lemon verbena, peppermint, rosemary, roses, scented-leaved geraniums, summer jasmine, and thyme. For the blue area, calming scents would include chamomile, clary sage, hops, lavender, marjoram and some other scented-leaved geraniums.

Feeling uplifted by scent promotes wellbeing, and it is known that what we smell passes into the bloodstream via the lungs. If you put an odiferous substance on the skin, it will be detectable later on the breath. Aromatherapy relies on the use of essential oils in massage to relieve physical and mental stress, and also uses inhalation, soaking, and some other means of impregnation. Planting and enjoying garden plants is your home-grown aromatherapy. The use of incense to cause drowsiness, mood alteration or trance is partly aromatherapeutic.

Essential oils, distilled from plants, can be used in the same way as herbal medicines, although their concentration is much greater so care should be exercised. They should not be given to children. Lavender oil heals burns with little or no scarring. Chemically, essential oils are often aldehydes, ketones, alcohols or phenols. They should be kept in amber (not blue) glass jars, stoppered and in a cool, dark place. Once opened, they have a shelf life of no more than three years. For massage, mix with a carrier oil – that is, a nut or seed oil like grapeseed oil (especially good for pregnant women), sweet almond oil, or apricot kernel oil. Mineral oils or baby oils are not suitable.

Different oils stimulate or relax different parts of the brain, producing different responses. The oils also get carried by the bloodstream to various bodily organs and muscles where they produce responses. They can be vaporised using ceramic burners or rings. Eucalyptus oil can be used thus as a decongestant for someone with a cold. Although distillation to produce essential oils needs special equipment, you can make usable oils by collecting petals, such as of the rose, putting them into a jar and covering with a carrier oil. Leave for one to two weeks, strain through muslin and bottle. This is concentrated enough for massage.

The healing power of touch in the garden
Exploration by touch in the garden is a neglected, yet very enjoyable, way to lose yourself and life's cares. Each bark and stem has a unique texture; each leaf a unique surface, whether it be rough, smooth, prickly, downy, sticky or otherwise distinctive; and each seasonal change brings something else to feel – catkins, seed pods, fruits, fern fronds, mosses, liverworts, lichens, pond plants, and much, much more.

The healing power of sounds in the garden
Moving water has a soothing sound, and it not only cools the air but seemingly the emotions too. Water breaking into droplets produces negative ions, which have a positive effect on the circulation, so that we feel refreshed and invigorated.

Still water, although silent, promotes relaxation and contemplation in the garden. It provides a mirror to reflect light and the changing patterns of the day and night sky. The mind is released to wander while the eyes gaze into water. Watching water plants and pond life is an engaging activity.

Other healing sounds in the garden are the wind in the trees; the rustling of leaves, particularly the sounds of aspen, willows and poplars trembling in the wind; the swaying of bamboo and other grasses in the breezes; and of course birds and their wildlife companions.

Mazes

Mazes are to some a pleasurable pastime, but to others an expression of a psychological need to solve puzzles and undertake a quest. The latter involves choices, meditation, reasoning and review, just like one's whole lifestyle, and so the labyrinth becomes in the mind a microcosm of life itself. The path to the centre can be the route to an individual or communal goal, and the presence of seven rings in the ancient circular mazes implies magical use.

If you have the space, then you could create a turf maze inexpensively. A longer-term project would be a hedge maze, usually planted in slow-growing evergreens like yew, cypress, eleagnus, holly or laurel, but these need clipping annually. A maze would make an ideal addition to a communal garden so that a sizeable project could be undertaken.

8

The Extended Family

Finding your place in the natural world

We have seen in chapter five how to bring nature closer and communicate with our fellow living organisms through the senses. Close contact with animals, including pets, and plants in childhood is an important preparation for engagement with people, and to prepare children fully, you need to go beyond the recommendations in chapter five, namely to observe and study, to smell the scents of flowers and leaves, to feel the textures of bark and rock, and so on. Dealing with all sorts of people requires tolerance, understanding and self-control, and these qualities can be developed in home and garden in a number of ways. In the kitchen, use the hands as much as possible in the preparation of food. Similarly, in the garden, try to use the hands rather than tools, even for jobs like cleaning out an overgrown, silted-up pond. Get the whole family involved and do the job from in the pond. Getting used to feeling the raw flesh and internal organs of a fish or chicken, or soil, mud, compost, slime, algae, tangled roots and the like, and not recoiling from the experience, which in most cases is learned behaviour from others, is important conditioning for both adults and children, as is experiencing insects, spiders, centipedes, crustaceans, etc, crawling over one's skin or alighting on oneself without having the urge to crush them or brush them off. Instead of swatting flying insects, keep still and observe. Whether it be wasp, fly or crane fly, allow them to buzz round you and to settle on your skin. If you are indoors, just open the window and let them out. When a beetle crosses your path, get on your knees and watch it. Soon our invertebrate friends become just another part of the natural scene, and you will realise that they are simply going about their daily business and not in any way trying to interfere with you, just like strangers you pass in the street. By such self-discipline and understanding, you, and more importantly, your children, will learn the forebearance that makes interaction with fellow humans so much more dignified and fulfilling.

Whilst it is reasonable for health and hygiene reasons to keep organisms posing a genuine risk out of the house, the 'tread-on-it' and 'swat-it' syndromes outside the house, where every creature that flies or crawls by is crushed, are totally against new pagan oneness with the natural world. If you find a spider in the house, you can leave it alone as a useful predator or put it outside, but to kill it is barbarism, as there is no survival issue at stake. We have no trouble with the concept of loving our immediate family because we live and share our lives with them. But the same is true of our extended family in the wild. The modern pagan concept of the extended family demands that the criteria that govern one's actions towards one's fellow human beings apply also in one's dealings with animals, both domesticated and wild, save in so far as matters of survival are concerned, but including the humane slaughter of animals for food.

Through contact with wild creatures you can emphasise to your children the necessity of the roles of both predator and prey, but do not vilify the predator nor pity the prey, for a child must understand the difference between survival killing and murder, and between hunting for food and hunting for pleasure, the latter deemed unacceptable in modern paganism. We gather from or fell plants for survival, as we slaughter animals, but in all other respects a child should be taught never to harm or disturb wild animals and plants – indeed, not to do to a living organism what would be unacceptable to do to a member of one's immediate family, a message effectively projected only by example. Even survival issues are necessarily tempered by degree. The practices of picking wild flowers, digging up naturalised bulbs, or transplanting wild plants to gardens are frowned upon by new pagans, but picking wild fruits and harvesting them by taking modest bounty from each plant is perfectly acceptable. As powerful members of every global ecosystem it behoves us to take our responsibilities towards our fellow planetary inhabitants as seriously as we take responsibility for our immediate families. Ecological imbalance in nature and ecologically unsound attitudes create a situation like a disharmonious household, adversely affecting all who live there, without exception.

How you treat animals is a pointer to how you may treat people. Tread on an insect, and you may become someone who 'treads on' or 'squashes' people in your dealings with them. This is more than a semantic comparison. Merely keeping a pet – as opposed to treating it as part of the family, studying it and learning about its behaviour and needs – is not engaging with an animal, as is revealed by the widespread ignorance that leads to cruelty to pets. Similarly, if you allow your children to break branches off trees and thrash them against trunks and undergrowth on the grounds that plants don't have 'feelings', you are condoning destructiveness, which may then be turned on public and private property.

Pets and how to relate to them

Pets and other animals are part of the extended family too, but it is not acceptable new pagan practice to have exotic pets, which necessarily are kept in cramped and unsuitable accommodation, fed unnatural food and are unable to enjoy even an approximation of a natural lifestyle. Similarly, new pagans should refrain from keeping any other pets in restrictive conditions; this applies to birds and rodents in small cages, rodents in hutches without substantial runs, fish in tiny bowls or tanks, and reptiles and amphibians in small vivaria. Children can, under expert guidance, learn a great deal and have much pleasure from keeping pets, but only if the animals are kept, treated and trained appropriately, and considered as a member of the family. This applies to working dogs as well as pets, and does not imply that pets should be cosseted. Much ill-treatment of pets, especially dogs, is caused by regarding them as child substitutes or status symbols. Unfortunately for the chastised pet, it doesn't behave like a child nor understand complex sentences of admonition; it behaves as its animal instincts tell it to.

Those who ill-treat pets, especially children who have learned to do so from their parents, may transfer their behaviour and act insensitively or cruelly towards their own children, siblings or others outside the immediate family. It is essential, therefore, that, before having a pet, you learn about its care, and make sure you can provide fully for its needs. Read books by reputable experts, talk to experienced breeders and owners, and offer to look after someone's pet for a short time to see if the family's routine can be adjusted adequately to accommodate its needs. When you then decide to have a pet, bring it up with species-specific care, involving the whole family, so that all interaction is consistent, thereby avoiding the anxiety caused by confusion. Never strike a pet, particularly not as a punishment, as they are unlikely to link what you consider to be a punishment with what you consider to be an offence, and will simply learn in future to be wary of you – and you will never have their full confidence again. Helping to bring up a pet with gentle methods and thorough socialisation is both a joy and an education for a family, and the child learns that responsiveness does not require threat or force. Threats advertise inadequacy and weakness to people as well as pets. Learning not to underestimate the intelligence and capabilities of people is made easier if a child brings up a pet, for animals are much more intelligent than humans generally give them credit for, and pet owners soon find this out.

A wolf in human clothing, or a dog?

Train yourself before you try to interact with a dog

Pagan dog training is not training your dog to become a model pagan, but using modern pagan philosophies and your bond with nature to bring a dog into the immediate family whilst still retaining its canine characteristics. This section is not intended to be a comprehensive dog-training manual but an exploration of how a modern pagan should seek to interact with a dog that is taken into the family.

Before we look at how you should prepare yourself for the responsibility of having a dog in the family, let us assume for a moment that you have completed your preparations and acquired your dog. Your first action should be to sit the dog in front of you, and say, 'This is no dumb animal. This is a highly intelligent, adaptable sensory creature. If we were both lost in wilderness, I would be the one to die first.' Repeat it over and over again until you believe it. You may think you are bringing a dog into your family, with you in command, but the dog thinks it is incorporating you into its pack, and it is in charge. A dog is of a different species, so it does not understand you, your language, or your notions of family and obedience. So, to return to the subject of preparation for having a dog, it is a priority for you to learn about canine ways and social interactions, the wolf pack being a good example, on which there is excellent research and literature.

If you try to treat a dog as though it were a human child – for example, by shouting at it, giving it instructions in sentences, or by smacking it – you will never have a contented, trusting dog. It will always be wary of you and only as responsive as its survival dictates. If you bring it up as a dog, using approaches that recognise its canine upbringing, intelligence and instinctive reactions, then you stand a good chance of having a happy, well-adjusted dog that is fun to be with. A confused dog is a troubled and troublesome dog, so plan your methods consistently and appropriately.

Select a breed that suits your lifestyle

Before you purchase a dog, which should only be from a reputable breeder or rescue centre, so that either you are able to see the puppy in the litter with its mother or you are able to learn about the dog's life history, you should consider carefully what breed suits your accommodation, circumstances and daily pattern of life. If you buy a breed that requires several miles of exercise every day and you are housebound in a high-rise block of flats then you are not going to be able to provide properly for the dog, who will be miserable, bored and troublesome. Talk to experienced dog owners and breeders, and get the right breed for your lifestyle. Even small dogs need regular exercise and stimulation, more than you probably realise. Seek advice also on selecting the temperament that suits, and visit the dog several times before agreeing to buy.

A mongrel makes as good a pet as a recognised breed, but if you prefer the latter, remember that each breed was selected for a task, whether it was to hunt by running down prey, to dig for quarry, to retrieve game, to fight, or another purpose. This means the dog will have certain inherited dispositions that will influence its behaviour, and you will be wise to take this into account when planning your training strategy, and the word 'training' refers to you the owner as well as the dog. How a dog looks is not as important as how it is likely to behave. An inappropriately brought-up dog will dominate, manipulate and train you instead of the other way round, and you will only have yourself to blame. Keep repeating, 'This is no dumb animal . . .'!

Socialising a puppy

Let us now assume that you have chosen a puppy, that it is inoculated and ready for introduction into your home. Having learned about the breed characteristics – and a mongrel may inherit traits from either parent – your training strategy must take them into account, for most breeds were not intended originally to be pets. A sheepdog, or a dog that has successfully competed in sled races across tundra, is hardly likely to make a good pet for an urban family. And, incidentally, if you just want a pet then a dog is probably not a good choice at all, but if you want a fellow pack member to share your life with, then a dog is a strong contender and may really turn out to be your best friend, humans included.

A puppy bred in a home environment will probably be partially socialised by the sights, sounds, smells and comings and goings of people and other dogs that are typical of a home. It will be used to being handled and inherited traits are more likely to be spotted in a busy environment, such as nervousness, as will behaviour learned from the mother such as fear and aggression. Nevertheless, you should plan to continue socialisation after you have taken the puppy home. Puppies need to be with their mother for six weeks, for during that crucial time they learn methods of canine communication, especially body language, and without it they may get into difficulties when meeting other dogs. It is part of their communicative upbringing to be able to give the appropriate signals on the one hand, and learn to interpret them on the other, or they may get into scrapes or spats because they have unwittingly provoked aggression. Moreover, the bitch will use this time to stamp her authority on the litter, so the puppy learns to accept discipline, but unless you continue with a form of discipline the puppy understands your attempts at training will cause confusion and suspicion. If a puppy stays too long in the litter it may have problems relating to humans, so six weeks is about right, or up to eight weeks if you know it is being well socialised.

Canine pack hierarchy and behaviour

A dog's ancestors were co-operative pack hunters, and a group of feral, or even domestic, dogs can revert to this behaviour if led by a dominant member. Each member finds and remembers his or her place in the pack, and it may take a challenge, or show of strength, or even a fight, to achieve and maintain their place or progress. Showing the teeth is a warning signal, whereas we show our teeth when we smile. This is just one example of how human–dog communication can go wrong. Dogs don't use sounds in a linguistic way like humans, so it is pointless talking to a dog to communicate, although the tone of your voice and your demeanour will be associated and noted. Teaching a dog single word commands works well, but hand signals are better because body language is the dog's way. They communicate with position and movement of body parts, especially eye contact, facial expression, ear movements, body posture and tail movements. Making eye contact normally denotes consent or approval, so merely turning your head away communicates firm disapproval. Staring, however, is usually threatening, more so if accompanied by a growl.

In the litter, jostling and wrestling are ways that dominance is asserted and submission learned. Holding the head up is a sign of confidence, whereas lowering the head expresses caution and lowering the whole body is submissive. In the battle for food in the wild the order of eating is important, the most dominant normally eating first, although the dominant dog can choose to vary this rule in special circumstances. Guarding and placing a paw on an object is a dog's way of advertising his possession of it, and this would in the wild often include food. For the most part, hierarchical order is important in canine society so that dogs do not step out of line, or they may get punished or down-graded. Similarly, the dominant go first into the hunt, so the order of walking and stalking is important too.

As a lowered body is submissive in the eyes of a puppy, it may find your large, erect body intimidating, so if you are not displeased and there is a possibility of confusion get down to the puppy's level and open your arms in welcome. Puppies are confused to begin with by the way humans use eye contact and smiles as a sign of friendliness, whereas to dogs, as mentioned earlier, eye contact if short denotes approval, but a long stare disapproval. You can emulate the way the bitch disciplines a puppy by rolling it over on to its back to expose its vulnerable stomach, staring at it and growling. This is all you have to do to give a dog a ticking-off. Once again, smacking is ineffective and counterproductive towards building up a companionable relationship.

Your dog's senses and how they are deployed

A dog has a sense of smell that is over a hundred times better than ours, and more sensitive than its powers of vision. They learn the body odours of those in their pack, including yours, and can tell if a pack member is young or old, healthy or unhealthy, ready or not for mating, just by scent. They locate and track potential prey by scent, and will familiarise themselves with their home area by creating a scent map in their brains, refining it on each walk. Such behaviour is strongly indicative of the territorial imperative of their ancestors.

Hearing is another sense with which dogs can far outstrip their owners, by at least four times in terms of sensitivity. As they can hear higher-pitched sounds than we can, it explains why they suddenly dash off in woods and along hedges looking for rodents, whose squeaks are of high frequency. But dogs can be distressed by sounds like fireworks because to them they are very loud indeed.

A dog detects shape and movement well, but would be no good at an identity parade, for its perception of detail is not good, neither is its colour discrimination. In dim light they can see better than we can, and will continue at dusk to chase after rabbits, squirrels and the like long after we have ceased to see them. The heat from a mammal's body helps to radiate its scent, which a dog cannot fail to pick up, and when you consider how powerful is the combination of its hearing, scenting, sight and perception of movement, it is no wonder that dogs miss very little that happens around them, which is probably one of the reasons they were domesticated in the first place. Nothing you do can change their sensory awareness, so recognise and adapt to it, and put it to good use.

Helping your puppy fit into the family pack

Dogs watch their pack members, particularly their movements, reactions and body language, for this is how they assess mood and personality. They will learn your habitual routine and soon they will know what you intend to do when you have barely twitched your muscles to start. If you are a boring, sedentary family your dog will settle into the same lazy routine, but if you have lively children your dog will join in the fun, but will of course be less inclined to be the relaxed dutiful companion you may have wished for. Emotions displayed to others in the family, like anger or excitement, will be picked up by the dog, and it will assess relationships by behaviour as it tries to fit everyone into the pack hierarchy.

Should you wish to bring up your puppy in a particular way you must involve the children in its training as well, so that it responds to consistent expectations from all the family. Once the puppy learns that it is bottom of the heap it will be content to know and keep its place. If any family member is inconsistent in their actions, the puppy will exploit them and manipulate that person's generosity and weakness to its advantage. It will then consider that person to be below it in the pack hierarchy. Eventually it may dominate the pack, getting all of you to fondle it or feed it on demand, or take it for a walk on its terms, or even to keep everyone out of the corner it considers to be solely its own territory. You ought, for the sake of harmony, to avoid this at all costs by being pack leader yourself from the start, however cute and cuddly your dog is.

Distraction is a very effective strategy instead of what you consider to be punishment. A dog's memory is short for day-to-day incidents, but long when it is smacked or pampered. Your notions of 'naughtiness' are not theirs, and they don't connect a smack with 'punishment' for being 'naughty', save as a consecutive action. Trying to 'punish' a dog several minutes after an alleged 'offence' is pointless as their memory span will not enable them to link the two. Encouragement, praise and reward are the ways forward. What you term 'obedience' can be looked upon as simply an intelligent animal's successful manipulation of your affection for it. It learns that jumping through the hoop gets it a titbit and an excited reaction. It enjoys athletic exercise and enjoys the taste of the titbit, so it can't lose. It isn't so much doing your bidding as showing its survival skills. The more you look approvingly at the dog and get excited about what it does the more comfortable it feels with that action. The same can be true of barking. If you give it attention when it barks, it may be taken as approval, whereas ignoring it, or distracting it, is a better strategy to eliminate the tendency.

Consider this example of common sense canine training. Your puppy has just messed on your carpet, but it is not feeling 'guilty' because it has simply performed a natural function. If you react angrily, and you are the pack leader, the puppy will lower its body in submission to try and appease you, but it won't connect your anger with what it has deposited on the carpet. It may look guilty, but it isn't feeling guilty. In fact it is feeling both downtrodden and confused. This is where you can be as cunning as a dog and learn to spot when it is preparing to relieve itself, for example by sniffing for a suitable spot, and then distract and encourage it to go into the garden. After the deed is done, praise it, and it will soon learn how to please you and get praise again. You think you have house-trained the puppy, it thinks it has manipulated you into reacting approvingly, so all are pleased with themselves.

Forestalling dominance

In packs, the right to breed, the choice of the best places to sleep, and other privileges are the right of the dominant. If you bring up your puppy to be bottom of the pile it will be more willing to please you and more trainable and biddable. Allow your dog to be dominant, male or female, and it will use canine ways, including aggression, to frustrate your wishes, so a dog's training must be reinforced regularly and consistently so that it has no aspirations of leadership. To a dog, in addition to those matters already mentioned, the following are significantly hierarchical: winning games of strength like tug-of-war, so make sure you win more than the puppy; claiming ownership of toys, so keep more than 50 per cent to yourself and bring them out to play with at a time of your choosing and then take them away; claiming your personal possessions or territory, so never allow it to have them or to go into your private spaces like bedroom or study; biting or growling and getting away with it, so stop playing or doing whatever has elicited the behaviour, and ignore the puppy for a little while.

Sleeping places for dogs should be low down and on the ground floor if you sleep upstairs. Dominant dogs in a pack like to hold the high vantage points. Never let a dog on your bed or even in your bedroom. Keep your dog on the floor, off the furniture, unless you invite it onto a particular place like a settee to groom it, or to cuddle up together and bond. Go through a doorway or gate first to emphasise your position as pack leader. If the dog is lying across your path make it get up and move out of the way; don't step over it. If you allow your dog upstairs, make it walk behind you, but still keep it out of your bedroom. Sit in the dog's basket sometimes to emphasise your right to oust it from its favourite place of repose. Your dog should see you eat first, as befits your position as pack leader, then be fed afterwards. Don't give it any of your food as titbits, as this is seen as a privilege, and remove any uneaten food from its bowl so it doesn't get the choice of eating when it feels like it.

If a puppy craves attention, turn your head aside and ignore it. A pack leader controls interaction, and one way to emphasise this is to call the puppy to you when it is engaged elsewhere and make a fuss of it or play with it as you wish. Don't give treats for nothing, only rewards for doing your bidding. This way the dog learns that being what you term obedient pays, even though it doesn't look upon its behaviour as obedience but clever subservience to the pack leader. All attention-seeking behaviour is best ignored, for shouting or otherwise responding is giving recognition back. Handle, examine and groom the puppy regularly, to show it you can touch it anywhere, anytime, anyhow, but also as part of your pack bonding. Continue this assertion of your dominance outside the home so the puppy knows you're boss everywhere, and get the rest of the family to maintain their dominance similarly. Puppies are very appealing and hard to resist, so you may have to steel yourselves at times and take the canine way.

Forestalling aggression

Aggression towards pack members by a socially adjusted, contented dog is very rare. Aggression outside the pack, towards strangers or other dogs, is also rare, and only occurs when the dog feels threatened by aggressive body language or by feeling cornered in a stressful situation it sees no way out of. It will send appropriate body signals, but most humans don't know how to interpret them, and so risk getting bitten. After the body signals the fearful dog may growl and show its teeth as a further sign of stress. To smack it now is very foolish; instead, the tension is better defused immediately. A dominant dog that gets away with aggressive posturing may become dangerous. Dogs rarely become fearful if they are properly socialised and exposed to common sounds and experiences in their local neighbourhood. If you are aggressive towards your dog it will learn that aggression pays and will regard it as acceptable pack behaviour; after all, the leader uses it. It may then try to defend you aggressively, because you have shown the way by your own example. Instead of saying to your partner, 'Not in front of the children,' you should be saying, 'Not in front of the children or the dog.' A puppy expects protection from a pack leader, not exposure to unpleasant experiences, teasing by children, or being forced into frightening situations. If you constantly pull the puppy away from other dogs or people who are non-threatening, which will be the vast majority, it will assume that you fear for its safety, and when it is older and more confident it will have the urge to see them off.

Dogs have a territorial instinct, and are more confident on their home patch because they instinctively think a dog or person from elsewhere will respect their territory. They will see them off only if they regard them as a threat. So, take the puppy to meet visitors, even delivery people, and get them to make a little fuss of it. Dogs become especially fearful in cars because they are confined in a small space, so never leave them in a car on their own, even in cold weather when there is no danger of them overheating. If a puppy play-bites, don't over-react, but utter a mock scream of pain and turn away. A puppy that thinks it has hurt the pack leader will feel contrite and behave submissively. Now distract it with another game. Generally speaking, avoid rough and tumble games, for a dog that is inclined to be dominant can have its confidence excited to the point of aggression. By socialising your puppy with plenty of mature dogs it will learn the body language that precedes aggression and therefore learn not to overstep the mark. Guarding food is another feature of pack life that can cause aggressive posturing if you approach its food bowl, so get it used to you handling the bowl while it is eating, such as by moving it slightly, and putting your hand in and out of the bowl so it is not anxious about having its food taken. You can then take the bowl away and give it back, reinforcing your authority and ability to dictate when it feeds.

Use your dog's canine instincts to advantage

Dogs bred for hunting or retrieving will instinctively chase other animals, especially small, nimble ones like rodents, for they make the chase exciting. Plenty of play involving chasing and retrieving toys will help you to keep control, as you can train the dog to respond to a recall when it is on the way to retrieve. It is difficult to so train a retrieving dog to suspend this instinct and come back to you, but it is necessary if you are to have total control when you need it – for example, when it is heading for a busy road. Generally, when a dog is doing what it was bred to do, your training routine will undergo its severest test, and will reveal where more work and bonding is needed.

The key to successfully bringing up a dog in a modern pagan pack is to 'think dog' and 'act dog', and to not treat a dog like a substitute child. A wolf pack is a fearsome fighting machine, like a well-organised commando unit, whose hunting strategy betrays considerable intelligence, but the pack also has a high degree of social cohesion, mutual care and organisation. If you want a wolf's cousin in your pack, you will have to be more cunning and astute than the dog is, in order to become and to stay top dog. If you're not up to it and not prepared to think and act dog then don't be so cruel as to bring one into your family. But if you are so prepared, you will have a wonderful time sharing your life with one of nature's truly intelligent and versatile animals.

The human members of the extended family

Encourage your children to watch with you how a dog approaches another dog, and you may all learn something about interacting with your fellow humans. The shape, size, colour, etc, of the other dog do not matter; it is how the approaching dog perceives intent and mood, through body language and expression, that determines the success of the meeting. A wagging tail is the equivalent of our smile, and every agreeable dog met gets a wag, regardless of its appearance. How many people do you know who have a smile for every agreeable person they meet? Or do they make visual judgements first, and never get round to deciding if they are truly agreeable? Perception of threat is a strong emotion, and a barrier to forming trusting relationships and tolerance. For example, when a dog barks, a baby cries, or a hay fever sufferer sneezes repeatedly, do you judge that they are annoying you, or is it your intolerance that causes you to be annoyed? Can such circumstances really be considered a threat?

In the same way that you can learn that other living things with whom you share space are, in the vast majority of cases and instances, no threat to you, so you can learn that most of your fellow humans aren't either. They want primarily to go about their daily business like the buzzing insect or the scuttling crab, and not to upset you. There are those who do so selfishly and aggressively, as we all know, but learning to engage as success-fully and tolerantly as most dogs comes only from a premise of trust in the good nature of most of our fellow inhabitants. A bad experience is more important in that it allows us to put it behind us and move on, than it is in reminding us that caution is sometimes needed and that we must remain alert. Most scars acquired through interaction are mental, not physical, and often arise through our own perceptions and prejudices.

Once you have concluded that you are not under threat from those who you suppose are different in some way, the differences become irrelevant in your dealings with them. Perceiving that differences of race, religion, sexuality, mobility, dexterity, etc, are threatening is learned behaviour. Watch children of different physical capabilities, races and religions playing together. They mix wonderfully well, until they learn their parents', friends' or society's prejudices. Then the camaraderie is replaced by superficial misjudgement and stereotyping. The strength of the notion of extended family is that all have the same rights to equality and to a dignified natural life, and no living thing is excluded. The goal for modern pagan parents is to bring up children to respect the primacy of this notion throughout their formative years, a path from which there are many enticing sidetracks for them to avoid.

Your immediate family

Now that we have summarised the modern pagan vision of the extended family we can focus on the human members of it, starting with our immediate blood relatives and dependants. The modern pagan immediate family is first and foremost a caring, mutually supportive unit of different generations. Traditionally, this would have revolved around a male and female partnership with their children, extended to include dependent grandparents and possibly other relatives in need of support, care or protection. Nowadays, the term 'family' has widened in scope to include adopted children and even adopted grandparents, same-sex partnerships and communal friendship groups of various compositions, but these are all viable and reasonable arrangements under new pagan philosophy if they meet the criteria of mutual care and support. It is primarily attitude, commitment and naturalness that make a twenty-first-century new pagan family successful, not conformation to an institutional norm or expectation. In this book, the terms family, community and environment are really points of reference in that they are three words that provide focal points for descriptions of objectives for changes of attitude and behaviour. But in essence they are just parts of a global whole, our world; indeed they could actually be regarded as tautological. Those who regard their neighbours as part of their family, their community, and their environment, for the three amount to much the same thing in terms of how the parents should behave towards them, have taken a vital step towards their own and their children's character development.

Children are alert, perceptive, intelligent beings, who study those around them, and naturally tend to assume that what their elders do and say is acceptable and may be imitated. Whatever the composition of the family, those within it who give the love, support and care that a child needs will be looked upon by the child as parents, whether biological or not. There is undoubtedly a special bond within the biological family, but blood kinship alone is no guarantee of competent parenthood. If you are acting like a good parent, then a child will bond with you as though you are one. Fostering is common in the animal kingdom, and it works. The old adage 'not in front of the children' makes good sense up to a point, but why are you having to restrain yourself? Preparing to be the centre of a family means taking a long, hard look at yourself, at your attitudes, habits, behaviour, manner of speaking, philosophies, and particularly whether you tend to betray your prejudices and intolerance. You may do well to consider reshaping your own life before assuming the responsibility for another, for sooner or later the real you will be shown to your children.

You are not alone in the modern pagan family, for it is a partnership, a pooling of strengths and ideas, of talent and wishes, of means and ends. It provides opportunities for all to blossom as well as to share, to fulfil others' needs and be fulfilled in turn. One significant new pagan family philosophy is essentially very simple. What you look after will return the compliment in some form. Your offspring, your pets, the wild inhabitants of your garden, your fruit trees and vegetables, your flowering and non-flowering plants, your house, your neighbours, your fellow inhabitants of the village, town or city, even the soil and rocks, may all be considered part of your extended family. If you care for them, they will in turn provide for you, whether it be care, help, courtesy, sustenance, visual beauty, interest, warmth and comfort, or other pleasure or utility. If the only freedoms you allow yourself are those which harm or disturb no-one, you will have enormous scope for a productive, enjoyable life for yourself and family, and if such restriction of freedoms becomes widespread, then the human species will have an assured, secure and harmonious future. No-one has the right to claim an action to be a personal freedom if it harms or disturbs another.

Who are your neighbours, and how do you approach them?

The key to loving your neighbour is your perception of your neighbour; seeing your extended family members for what they truly are, so that you can lovingly embrace them as they are, not as you may initially have viewed them. The human personality is unique and complex, and those who are interested only in a preconceived, idealistic notion of it are doomed to a lonely existence and much disappointment. Possibly the most extreme public reaction towards someone who did not conform to standards of expected appearance, because of facial and bodily deformity, was that suffered by Joseph Carey Merrick, known as 'The Elephant Man'. His name was not John Merrick as erroneously used in David Lynch's celebrated film of his life. One day, towards the end of his tragic life, he was expressing his gratitude to the staff of the London Hospital for providing him with a room, board and daily care, and he included an apology for their having to observe his gruesome appearance, but added, 'The mind's the standard of the man.' Indeed, he proved to be a man who was as gentle and dignified as he had been deprived and tormented, and he had a most attractive personality, but only the kind and perceptive staff of the London Hospital were ever able to find this out.

Are you able to look beyond the mask to find the inner person? Do you study features and mannerisms and make judgements from stereotypes, or do you allow yourself time to discover the real person, who may be a slow starter socially and give the wrong impression at first? What are the significant ways in which you make an initial assessment, such as facial appearance and expression, body language, style of dress, make-up and adornments, manner of speech, and are they fair?

Are superficial aspects really important and worth rejecting someone for, who could be a nice person underneath? Associations, whether personal or business, are so often founded on first impressions, on cultural signals and populist markers such as using approved buzz words or mannerisms, but these are all veils that can cover a body so thoroughly that its mystery is preserved, until one perseveres and persuades the wearer to draw them back one by one.

Taking a long hard look at yourself and how you approach people can be very revealing. Is it your upbringing, or a dominant parent, that is acting or speaking, or is it you? Is this how you want to be? Are they really society's norms you are claiming to uphold, or your own? Are you more interested in one-upmanship than comradeship? Our use of language and metaphor often betrays our genuine feelings. Do you, for example, use 'he/his' for all references to a person or position that may be male or female? Whom or what do you describe as 'it' – a child, or an animal perhaps – and why change the pronoun at all? There are differences in the choice of language that males and females make that come from their different upbringings and natural characters, but we can all take care with our language. Are you blunt or do you soften the blow with euphemisms? A smile is so simple and effective, but once you start using language you must remember that it's no use meaning what you say if you don't say what you mean. We have words for every circumstance, so make sure you choose appropriately and endeavour to discern what others really mean, instead of jumping to conclusions.

In a hectic lifestyle where fleeting interactions are all too common, the consequences of superficial analysis and careless words can be very damaging to relationships or even stop them forming. If it needs time to get to know someone then give it time, and your friends will be better chosen and more endearing and companionable. Look upon a meeting, like our wagging dog, as an optimistic prelude to the discovery of a new friend, but give her or him a chance. You can fail to discern the inner self by being thoughtless, for example, in the way you formulate questions, or the responses you ask for when designing a form or questionnaire, responses that betray your prejudices and handicap the respondents. Are you perhaps an interviewer who is looking primarily for candidates like yourself, or do you have functional objectives principally in mind? In any situation where you are making an assessment, you should ask yourself if your ground rules automatically exclude any section of society.

Presumption should never be a substitute for a positive approach, for the way you perceive others, categorise them, seek to mould them to your idealised template, or the extent to which you are prepared to adjust, determines how far you have to travel to feel comfortable in your community, and how much adaptation you will need to feel a part of the human extended family. Waiting for others to change to your specifications won't work; it is for you to set the example.

Modern pagan parenting: an instinctive, biological and traditional role

It is often said that the human species has departed so far from the natural state that its behaviour is conditioned by society, not by natural instinct. It is true that amongst different social groups certain norms have evolved, but the role of the parent in human society remains to a large extent biological, and for modern pagans that fact is crucial. It helps the anxious parents-to-be realise that they have the natural instincts to cope admirably, if only they allow themselves to use them instead of listening to society's mixed, confusing exhortations. Your primary aim as a parent is to bring up a child, or children if you desire and can manage, to be a nice person and to interact in a natural way with nature's extended family. Those in different social groups will have slightly different ideas as to what constitutes a nice person and how they should interact with their fellow living organisms, but the differences are slight. Instinctively we all know a nice person when we meet one, for all humans belong to the same species and we have the same basic natural reactions, despite the different local environments to which we have adapted.

So, as you prepare for parenthood it is a time to rely as much as possible on your human instincts. They will be honed, of course, to a small degree by your individual character, but it remains true that underneath we all know in our consciences what broadly constitutes a sound preparation for life in our global village in the natural world. How successful you are in shutting out the siren voices of those who would steer you in other directions determines whether you will become a successful modern pagan parent. This book does not contain a tick list of desirable parental attributes, nor does it describe the perfect model offspring, for the designs are in the genes, but millions of years of evolution would scarcely have been spent creating a human stereotype that matches any of the aggressive, destructive, arrogant, selfish, anti-social individuals that plague every society the world over.

What should be the individual roles of mother and father, apart from their specific procreative functions? Is there a masculine and feminine blueprint? Once again, your natural instincts will interpret your feelings and a baby's behaviour and responses, if you allow them to be the dominant factor rather than the messages of macho male and subservient sex-object female that emanate from the world's media machines. The old adage 'use your common sense' is still a good one, but use *your* common sense, not the claimed good practice of gurus and advertisers. Follow *your* instincts, not the advice of commercial and other vested interests. Again, there is no tick list needed, just a natural focus on a natural process.

Modern pagan parenthood and the extended family

The value of the global notion of family lies in the application of what commonly happens in the home to the extended family beyond, where what are generally referred to as traditional family values are far less frequently applied. Are you someone who is caring within the immediate family and less so without? How many people do you know who have different attitudes and ways of treating people outside the family to those displayed inside? Protective we may be of our offspring and close relatives, but are others so much less important to us that we adopt almost a different personality towards them? This barricade between the immediate family and the rest of society is one for modern pagans to dismantle. As a parent you will want society to graciously welcome your offspring into the fold, but what sort of welcome do you give others? You bring up a child and encourage it to develop its natural aptitudes, but are you as keen to recognise the strengths and talents of others, or do you judge them by other than their equal worth as fellow humans and the contribution they can make to the extended family? Do you encourage your child particularly to be competitive, even to the extent of brooking no opposition, or is your primary objective to help your child embrace the value of co-operation and appreciation for the abilities of others?

Whether to encourage competitiveness or co-operation is not a mutually exclusive choice by parents, but a consideration of how you achieve a balance between the two. How well you as a parent can look through the veneer of appearance, social status, race, language, religion, and sensory and physical capability, will largely determine how your children perceive their global family members in terms of worth and valued contribution. Your degree of self-esteem has been greatly influenced by how others treated and regarded you; the degree of tolerance of your children of the idiosyncrasies of others will be learned from those who are the most influential where your children are concerned. Who is it that you wish to be responsible for determining your child's adult personality? Is it your children's friends perhaps, or their school, or teenage magazines, or the exploits of media personalities, or advertisers and purveyors of fashion and merchandise, or will *you* be in control? Who do your children turn to first for help and advice? Who is their most influential role model? To have control you must take control, for there is a queue of vested interest ready to usurp your parental authority if you do not.

Nobody likes being the victim of today's 'blame culture', but the citizens of the developed world who are most likely to wear the cap because it fits are parents. Many have lost control of their children because they have delegated their upbringing to influential forces outside the immediate family, namely peer pressure and commercial and vested interests promoting aggressive, discriminatory attitudes; passive entertainment; self-indulgence and consumption. This has happened partly because parents have delegated their own lives to these forces too. Instead of being in a family unit in their early life to the extent that they recognise it as the prime influence, young children are increasingly finding themselves and their inspiration on the outside of the front door to the family home. When such children talk about being 'left out', they are referring to the world outside the home, but members of a modern pagan family would be far more concerned about being 'left out' of the family circle, for only there will their natural character be developed. It is your circle; try always to ensure that your children feel an integral part of it.

Togetherness in the extended family

A feeling of togetherness for our extended family comes naturally, but not inevitably, out of togetherness in the immediate family. Many families give mutual support to one another, but how many put up the shutters rather than be willing to accept the need for a contribution from the extended family? Or is pride and a display of independence more important than valuing and embracing the experience and assistance of others? Being in control means you can from time to time with older children admit valuable influences from outside the family without fear of the consequences. Of course it is right, as a family, to find time to be together, especially for meals and celebrations, but also to discuss the myriad matters of mutual interest, matters that affect young as well as old. But the recognition by a maturing child that there is experience, expertise and information elsewhere, and that the wider the range of opinions sought and received, and the skills and knowledge acquired, the easier it is to synthesise its own perspectives, is a valuable milestone to reach along life's journey through the global village. Your child cannot find the middle of the road if he or she can't see the edges, or has them shielded by blinkers that you fit. It is a wonderful achievement if a child feels loved and cared for in the home, but the real prize is for your child to feel loved and cared for by the extended family, and this means reciprocating by contact with it and loving and caring for it in turn.

How is this to be done? A child will only learn togetherness with all sections of human society if it has contact with them, just as it can only appreciate its position in the natural world by interacting with both its wild and domestic inhabitants. The growth of leisure activities like diving, whale-watching, bird-spotting, and wild flower expeditions, is a boon for the modern pagan parent wanting to encourage children to so engage away from the local environment, but beneficial interaction with our fellow humans needs to be part of our everyday life, and to go far beyond the interactions made with family, friends and work colleagues. Travelling is a common pursuit now, but it would broaden the mind far more if the tourist got off the beach and sightseeing trail and spent the time experiencing as much of genuine local life as safely possible. A tour operator specialising in Latin America has had the inspired idea, for example, of offering a choice between a day sightseeing in Quito and a day spent visiting prisoners in Quito prison. Even if such an option doesn't appeal, you can certainly take your family to local festivals and events, shop in local markets, and visit as many places off the tourist trail as time allows. Of course there are considerations of personal safety and security of property, but usually local advice is obtainable. Ask local people for assistance whenever you need it, so that your children can see that language is no barrier. Smiles, gestures and mimes go a long way to persuading both parties of the universality of helpfulness and good nature.

The modern pagan view of social structure has no place for segregation by age, sex, sexuality, aptitude, appearance, intellect or philosophy, neither segregation in the mind nor in physical reality. It regards education, rehabilitation and atonement to the victim as more important for wrongdoers than incarceration and the notion of punishment for punishment's sake. But to develop fully in the mind the significance and benefit to human society of propagation of these views, modern pagans, adults and children alike, must empathise with all sections of it, and must continue to do so until the sectional boundaries no longer exist in fact or thought. The opportunities are many and varied, but you will need to enquire about them and seek them out locally. No child or adult should be so preoccupied with entertainment and self-indulgence in their leisure time that they cannot spare some time to meet and help others.

In a true community to give is to receive

Charities of all kinds depend on voluntary contributions and assistance, so if you have a little time to give, they can fill it. Fundraising is vital, and the more ideas and contributions received the better. If you have specific trade or professional skills then you would be helping the disadvantaged to acquire independence by passing them on. Even if you don't have a specific skill that could be utilised, just visiting and assisting the sick, the elderly, the housebound, and those in prison can bring immense pleasure, and fulfilment for you. Take your dog along if allowed. An hour spent being read to by a child and receiving affection from a dog is a joy to an elderly person, and they in turn can delight a child with tales of long ago and with their incomparable wisdom. And do you know the nearest elderly people to your family home, and whether or not they are coping?

Pooling resources and labour for communal projects was commonplace years ago in developed countries, and it is high time this practice was revived, especially in deprived urban areas where co-operative local initiative is so important in revitalising run-down neighbourhoods. Communal projects where all local people take part are an excellent way for participants to learn how to organise, to use tools, for adults to pass on skills to the young, to co-operate and share in a common purpose, and to get to know the folk you see regularly but never seem to have time to become acquainted with. By involving your child early in life in community service you will probably not have to witness their shying away from 'something for nothing' commitments in favour of the instant payback of self-indulgence, for the pleasure of helping a needy recipient will be thanks enough. Although in most cases helpers have to do the travelling to offer their help, the housebound or restricted helper can provide valuable administrative service by writing letters, making telephone calls, and general organisation, or by offering temporary sanctuary to a tired carer.

This might seem like the usual list of laudable objectives for the altruistic, but there is a higher aim, to reorientate your own mind and to encourage your children to regard such activities as lifelong pursuits. If you had always wondered how to bring up a child not to be selfish, arrogant, narrow-minded and grasping, then look seriously at these caring activities. Insularity tends to breed egocentric ways of thinking and behaving, but communality is unique in that it leads unswervingly to vision, perspective, compromise, adaptability and, above all, consideration and tolerance. Reaching out into all corners of human society is, on a larger scale, like walking into the natural garden. Just as you engage with and learn to love and cherish the inhabitants of your garden, so you can achieve the same pleasure and fulfilment from engagement with your extended human family, for they are but the denizens of nature's world plot.

Children brought up with passive entertainment, which all too often is encouraged by parents as an impersonal child-minding service, will find it harder to establish a niche, for they are just like the masses. Active pursuits, deliberately chosen for their variety, will exercise their skills and mental capacity. They will pursue some and reject others, but the parents' role is to facilitate and encourage, rather than steer and dictate, during the experimental years of youth. Individuality can be expressed in so many different ways if the opportunities are provided, and these should be social, physical, mental, co-operative, competitive, so as to exercise both mind and body. In this way the child is prepared for their parental and social role, knowing herself or himself, and knowing what contribution she or he can make with confidence. Passive popular culture is the dustbin of natural aptitude. Don't allow your child to jump in and be unable to raise the lid.

Femininity, masculinity and sexual equality

Having guidance and role models from both males and females is very important for the socialisation of the new pagan child, but their concepts of masculinity and femininity are not entirely governed by their genes and hormones. There is an old joke that to tell a male from a female you simply pull its genes off.

But a child soon learns that in human society many aspects of male and female behaviour are conditioned by social expectations rather than by genetic instincts. In the modern pagan home, children are shown that femininity and masculinity form a complementary partnership, not a contradictory or competitive one, and from here it is to be hoped the example will pervade the extended human family.

In the animal kingdom males and females normally have defined roles in the reproductive cycle, care for the young, hunting, defence of the group, and so on, and because males are often larger and stronger and better adapted to hunt for and defend the family, it is assumed that masculinity is equated with aggressive, macho behaviour in human society. On this assumption, parents commonly bring up boys in such a way that encourages and shows approval of such behaviour. Similarly, the caring, maternal role of females in the wild is used to imply that human females alone should be caring, and that they should be subservient to males. The upbringing of girls has traditionally reflected the prevailing desire that they should typify this role and have the attitudes, and only those, that go with it. This delineation might be appropriate if we were still living a natural hand-to-mouth existence, but such simplistic analysis does not stand up in the complex society that humans have created. Moreover, it ignores the fact that the male–female partnership in the wild is a co-operative one, and by no means all parental functions are exclusively conducted by one or the other. Also, even in the wild, masculinity and femininity are difficult to define in a social sense. Their reproductive functions are indisputable, as is the choice of who breastfeeds the baby, but what roles are definable strictly on gender lines after that? If you think males alone are the aggressive sex, then try threatening a lioness that is protecting a cub.

If you examine your and your partner's or opposite sex sibling's attitudes and capabilities you will probably conclude they are much the same, save where anatomical factors give one or other the advantage. The essence of a successful modern pagan partnership is, therefore, how well the partners pool their talents on behalf of the family. Machismo and subservience are highly destructive socially, as they represent a denial of the need to be co-operative and resourceful on behalf of dependants. In human society, physical defence of the family and the use of aggression to provide for it are seldom required of males, most aggression being nothing to do with these functions. Similarly, subservience and suppression of females' aptitudes and abilities is a waste of talent, which in some societies represents an enormous untapped resource.

You and your partner can provide best for your family by pooling your strengths and resources, and agreeing a division of labour, or sharing tasks, whichever is appropriate. Once you descend to the level of biological male and female stereotypes then some of the talents of one or the other, or both, will be suppressed and wasted. If you decide that mother staying at home to care for the family and father going out to work to provide financially for it is the best arrangement for you both then you will ensure it is a success, but all manner of variations can work well in different circumstances, if the will and spirit of co-operation are there. As a partnership, you can easily audit your aptitudes by examining your strengths and weaknesses and deciding together how best to deploy your talents and to improve and develop where needed. Pooling of contributions is a strategy that can work productively in the extended human family too, where the common good is served best by wherever the most valuable contribution comes from, not by defining roles as customarily male or female and perpetuating gender discrimination and denial of talent to the community. Meritocracy sits very comfortably with modern pagan social philosophy.

The traditional family unit of male and female parents with their own offspring and grandparents provides the greatest biological diversity in terms of male and female generational input, but it is no more likely to succeed as a stable family than a non-traditional arrangement if the group dynamics are unfavourable and the desire to adapt and compromise is lacking. Two people in a relationship have to constantly work to make it succeed because times change, they change, and change needs understanding, adaptation and compromise. Two apparently compatible people can have a failed relationship because they put their selfish interests first and stop trying to make the union work, but two very different characters can have a successful collaboration because they put their particular likes and dislikes aside, or relegate their importance, and work hard to dovetail their lives through give-and-take.

You may have felt socially restricted, even imprisoned, by gender expectations in your upbringing, and if we are to avoid producing another generation of aggressive males and unfulfilled females, parental expectations will have to change to reflect the needs of both the immediate and extended human families. 'Boys will be boys' no longer, but civilised, and you will know what that means with respect to the social circles you move in. You know instinctively what characteristics in your children will make them worthy and valued citizens; you don't need a list, only your natural good sense and social perspective.

With regard to worth in the extended human family, sexual equality is as important as generational equality, but it has taken a long time for such a philosophy to become socially accepted as a truism. There is no evidence to support the contention that women had equality, even matriarchal authority and matrilinear succession, in old Celtic society, but in the evolution of twentieth-century paganism, sexual equality became an essential feature of any community claiming to be pagan, and this state of affairs is an indissoluble part of new paganism. Pagan cultures through the ages have always recognised the importance of skills and qualities commonly demonstrated by women, partly through traditional upbringing and partly as a result of natural female character and aspiration, notably family care, healing and divination, but male dominance of the upper echelons had been the norm in ancient societies, a state of affairs that men have tried desperately to perpetuate. Modern pagan society is founded on equality and merit, and scorns the waste of talent and opportunity that arises through discrimination on the grounds that the notion of equal worth is compromised, that the self-esteem of the individual is reduced, and that this talent is denied to the community, which is thereby the poorer and doomed to make slower progress.

Modern pagan life ceremonies

Legal union or personal commitment?

The establishment of a modern pagan family unit and the degree of failure or success of a relationship or partnership are not related to whether or not the pair have gone through some sort of institutional union like marriage but to personal intention to make the association mutually fulfilling. Whilst it is a matter of choice whether or not a couple enter into some form of legally recognised association, this decision will not itself change the basic problem in failed partnerships, which is lack of unfettered commitment to lifelong mutual care and support, to the perception of a family as a mutually dependent unit, and to the value to all of the extended family principle.

Handfast

The commitment to partnership is known as handfast, traditionally done by clasping hands through a holed stone. Any form of words and accompanying ceremonial is for the partners to decide, and the ceremony is normally witnessed and celebrated by the whole of both partners' families, and any friends they wish to invite. It is not intended that handfast itself has any legal basis, but partners may choose to draw up a legal contract determining how the ownership of joint property is to be dealt with if the bond is broken, and how children, elderly dependants, pets and other domesticated animals are to be cared and provided for in that event.

Handparting

Breaking the bond is known as handparting, and it is wholly unpagan if, after mutual attempts at reconciliation and consultations within the family, it becomes an acrimonious affair. The choice of words and ceremonial actions is again individual. The point of parting is not to hurt one another but to stop hurting one another, and any member of the family affected by the weakening of the bond. No arrangements for children and other dependants can possibly match the togetherness and security of the family, but the issue has to be resolved, and all the better if done sensibly and amicably. Those who cannot part in peace and understanding put themselves outside the bounds of modern pagan harmony and should re-examine their commitment to its philosophies.

Naming the newborn

The naming of a newly born child and its presentation (wiccaning) to all relatives gives the opportunity to welcome the newcomer into the family fold, and in keeping with new pagan dislike of creed there is no formal ceremony or recommended form of speech, only what the parents choose to include. The birth must of course be registered if that is a legal requirement. The gathering is a chance to renew contacts and express joint feelings and responsibility for the child, as no member of an extended family is without the commitment to care for the child in the unfortunate circumstance that one or other parent is unable to do so. In return, those members have a right to be consulted and to have their opinions heard over matters to do with the child's development and future, but the final decision always rests with the parents. The sharing of views within the household, and with more distant relatives, is extremely important, especially for the first child. There is a strength in the collective experiences of older members of the family that trendy ideas commonly abroad within any one generation cannot match for consistency and proven worth, save of course in matters where general and scientific understanding has genuinely superseded what the previous generation held to be advisable. This is the sort of filtering that parents have the responsibility to do, but sensitively and with gratitude for the advice.

Same-sex partnership

A same-sex relationship can have the most important ingredients of a modern pagan union just as a traditional relationship can. There is no primacy of one sex over another in the new pagan world. Males and females are biologically different for reproductive and parental reasons. Their mental and physical attributes would logically have evolved to be complementary to one another in order that the baby would have the highest chances of survival and to thrive whilst in the care of, and able to learn the skills from, both parents; the normal way amongst primates. In order that the modern pagan child has the best opportunity to benefit from the maximum number of parental skills and to be able to adjust emotionally to both masculine and feminine attitudes, it would seem biologically sensible to be brought up by a male/female partnership. Whether the male and female are married or not is irrelevant as it is the stability and commitment of the partnership that makes the difference to a child. A same-sex partnership committed to new pagan ways can still give a great deal to a child in terms of care and values, and by regularly socialising the child with members of the sex not represented in the partnership, perhaps on a basis of mutual assistance, the child can still become a well-balanced individual. It is values and fond care that are at the root of the modern pagan approach to parenting; as modern paganism is a set of attitudes, it can be embraced whatever someone's sexual orientation, as long as the importance of a child growing up in a world populated by both sexes is realised and acted upon in its upbringing so it can relate readily to both.

The family elders

No modern pagan extended family of relatives is complete without the oldest generation. The elderly are our cultural repositories, our bridge to the past, our storytellers and founts of wisdom, but they have in many developed countries been marginalised, even neglected. As in so many instances the so-called developing regions show the way forward, by continuing to respect the contribution of the elderly, in both consultative and practical roles. But families everywhere can once again benefit from their unique experience and range of skills, if they can change their attitudes to them to respect and inclusion, but of course respect has still to be earned. It is hard for elderly people who have struggled to bring up their children, been through the stresses of a career, and coped with life's vicissitudes, to change roles when taken into the extended family. It requires a willingness on their part to release the reins of authority, especially when they themselves were not brought up as part of an extended family. So the same adaptation and commitment is required of the elderly when joining the extended family as was required when they first entered into their partnership, or the extended family will not be a harmonious team.

Fundamentally, the extended family of relatives is a survival strategy, so that the skills and wisdom of the old are not lost when their hunter-gatherer ability and physical fitness have waned. 'Survival of the fittest' is not acceptable in its Darwinistic form in a caring society, for it is part of new pagan philosophy that 'charity begins at home', but it doesn't end there. Care for the family is every family member's concern and responsibility, as is maintaining contact with family members living elsewhere. Any intolerance shown by one generation towards another will not be eased by isolation of family members, nor by infrequent contact between grandparents and grandchildren with all the harmonising benefits that that contact brings. The elderly are being too readily consigned to care homes instead of being taken in by the family, which may be a consequence of family breakdown, so characteristic of the last three decades of the twentieth century, but it is also a consequence of the elderly being seen as a nuisance, a drain on barely adequate income, and an interference with the enjoyment and established routine of their children's lives. The generation gap widens when both sides have failed to adapt, and this failure is more pronounced when families drift apart. Close families learn to accept one another's idiosyncrasies and to live in harmony with 'give-and-take', with everyone feeling valued and that their contribution is appreciated and worthwhile.

Taking in an elderly relative needs the same sort of planning and discussion, of needs and contributions, as the parental partnership. With their vast experience, the elderly can share in the running of the home, but should be seen as more than just convenient baby-sitters. They have a unique perspective on life that youngsters cannot match, and in addition to their contribution to collective analysis of the family's requirements they are part of society's checks and balances when they make their recollections and experience available, and it is taken notice of. The elderly can delight the whole household with folk tales and recollections of life long ago and how it has changed through their long lives. It is important for children to sit and listen and to be encouraged to enquire further of those who are the seat of a nation's wisdom, and the bearers of its traditions, values and social history, as well as a valuable counter to relentless modernisation, change and pace of life. With no close link to the past, a child cannot easily tread the bridge of history and appreciate what is worth preserving and what valuable lessons may be learned, unless they engage with their elderly relatives. For want of a little patience and respect a lifetime's experiences are theirs for the sharing.

Crossing the bridge to the Otherworld

With the exception of complying with any laws on matters appertaining to registration of death, inheritance and committal of the body in an approved place, the family may devise their own ceremony when a member dies in this world and crosses the bridge to resume life in the Otherworld. The best option for modern pagan burial, where burial in the wild is not permitted, is in an approved green burial ground such as may be found in many countries nowadays. They are landscaped, free of wind chimes and other inappropriate noises and intrusions, planted in keeping with the surrounding countryside, with memorial plaques to mark the graves. They offer closeness to nature, a refuge for wildlife, and enable the land to be preserved for future generations. Similar green sites have become pet burial grounds, although there is no modern pagan objection to a site being used for burial of both pets and pet owners. In memory of the life of a relative it is fitting that all family members should be present at the committal and that they share reminiscences of the life of the deceased, principally so that younger members are apprised of their contribution to the family.

The family saga

It is every modern pagan's duty to the continuance of family tradition to record their personal memories in the form of a saga, which is their contribution to a cumulative archive that all future members can have a copy of to read, reflect upon and identify with. A saga takes the form of chronological recollections of one's life and those who have been key influences within it, starting with one's earliest memories. As many relatives as possible are brought into the evolving story, their contributions being noted. Any form of visual presentation may be used, including the incorporation of scrapbooks, photographs, art and design work, and anything else of personal archival value. The family may also wish to draw up and regularly update their family tree, so that all may see each relative's saga as part of the full ancestral picture. Once completed, the individual saga is handed to the family's appointed keeper, to be read after the committal of the body. Committal may be by burial or cremation as the closest relatives decide, for both traditions are present in pagan history. Thereafter, the honouring of dead relatives and ancestors should be done at least annually, traditionally at Samhain. The tradition of saga within the family is an effective way of instilling an appreciation of generational continuity, and through it, and through close contact with the elderly during their latter years, the young can come to terms with death as that which follows the fulfilment of life.

To know your ancestors is to understand yourself

We are all in some ways a product of our past, even those who deprecate living in it. Knowing your ancestors is knowing the answers to some important questions about yourself, such as about the traditions you were brought up with, the human attitudes and skills passed on through the family, the influences upon it and ultimately upon you. Your ancestors may no longer be with you in body, but various facets of their life in this world live on. Your looks and some aspects of your behaviour are genetically inherited, others are copied and passed on, but whichever it is for a particular attribute it is part of the uniqueness of your family line. It isn't always possible to know if a physical defect or mannerism is congenital, but there should be no shame in one's genes or one's looks, so be proud of their uniqueness and the long generational march that produced them. In many societies today people have been conditioned to believe that looks and mannerisms should conform to standards invented by the media, and in consequence they spend huge amounts of time and money, and dissipate a great deal of anxiety, because they don't conform to these artificial commercial standards. Look in a mirror instead of in a fashion magazine, and there you will see true beauty, a unique product, not a fashioned clone, of biological evolution and a natural lifestyle. Thousands of years of family history are etched on that visage and on the body below it; your history and therefore your personal heritage. The more you find out about it the more expressive and meaningful it becomes.

Tracing your ancestral line and the details of your ancestors' lives is a superb exercise in detective work for adult and child alike, and brings rewards for a methodical approach rather than leaps of faith, assumption and guesswork. There are many obstacles, such as discontinuous records, inconsistent spellings and use of aliases, but overcoming these is part of the thrill of the quest.

Start your enquiries with your immediate family and then visit more distant relatives, and pay particular attention to the older members and their recollections. Keep careful written records, in chronological order, of what you learn and find. It is normally straightforward to track down civil registration documents such as certificates of birth, marriage and death, and they often contain names of parents and spouses, family addresses and occupations, and can lead you to the places where civil and parish records can be consulted. Local cemetery records usually include locations of graves. Knowing occupations will enable you to consult documentation held by professional or trade organisations. Military records are often comprehensive, including photographs and descriptions of appearance, so if an ancestor was in the armed forces you can learn much about this phase of his or her life. Knowledge of educational qualifications and the institutions where they were gained can lead to further information, as can business and financial records. Wills often include full names and addresses of family members who have been beneficiaries or executors, and, like civil registration documents, copies may be found in public record offices. Other well-documented events include arrests for criminal activity and court proceedings, official change of name and immigration.

Family photographs of unnamed relatives contain various clues, especially if family likeness leads you to believe that presently unknown faces are actually relatives. Someone in military uniform wearing medals will point you towards useful information in regimental records. The style of dress and room furnishings in the photographs can help to date them. If you can find letters, diaries, bills and other paperwork they can provide further clues, so ask relatives if you can search in attics and other storage areas, and keep elderly members of the family informed of your progress as this can jog memories and elicit further reminiscences. Note these down and put in chronological order, as your own memory may fail you later. Relatives are usually very keen to share their reminiscences, and telling children about their forebears can help to bridge the generation gap. Episodes from a murky phase of the family's history may be enthusiastically related, even embellished, by those who revel in their notoriety, but ignored by those who feel a sense of shame, so great tact and delicacy may be needed. There is great benefit for a child to be involved in the research, for it may be the first time they have really been able to have a lengthy conversation with a relative they see little of. Children only lose their sense of fairness and open-mindedness when adults pass on their prejudices, so don't warn children about what they may or may not learn from any of your relatives, and try not to let your own preconceived ideas intrude either. Only the facts are relevant to the task; hearsay and handed-down invective can tell you more about the informant than about your ancestors.

There is much in a name, particularly a trade surname, and research may already have been done on it, possibly by one of your distant relatives. This can be checked in the genealogical directories that are published in many countries, and on the Internet, but you must beware of names arising out of changes of spelling convention, or misspellings, or through morphological changes to the word over time. If national census information is published then this can provide valuable information, although coincidences of names, occupations and place of residency are possible, particularly with regional surnames. Church records of parishioners, baptisms, confirmations, marriages, and burials may be useful. In association with information about the places of residence and occupations of your ancestors you may find old maps revealing, and back copies of newspapers in library archives may contain articles about an ancestor. In some countries property and taxation records are available, and also electoral registers and local government records.

Having completed as much of your family tree as you can, what might you find and what are you to make of it all? Does it matter if one of your ancestors was beheaded for treason or was the illegitimate offspring of a transported horse thief? You can't judge a book by its cover, nor a character by the way the individual is treated by society. There are no universal norms of virtue or justice, and no single section of society has a monopoly on goodness or evil, for both are found across the social spectrum of any age past or present. Privilege and opportunity usually stemmed in the past from birthright and connections, not from experiential or professional qualifications, or suitability, so the good person and worthy citizen can never be found simply by examination of historical records detailing someone's circumstances or fate at the time the details were compiled. Often it was the entrepreneur, inventor, adventurer, champion of the disadvantaged or exposer of injustice who fell foul of conservative society laws, and probably they did much that you could be proud to be associated with.

Above all, your ancestors, warts and all, are your kin, and you their scion, and they allow you to extend your family back through time to create an intangible ancestral bond. Strengthening this bond is one of the joys of genealogy, which can not only identify your ancestors and their relationships, to enable you to construct a family tree, but tell you what sort of characters they were and what kind of lives they led. Learning history by monarchs, prime ministers, presidents and the wars they initiated is to neglect the stable unit of society, the ordinary family. Studying family history, on the other hand, takes you to the heart of life in a past time and place; the ideas, beliefs and values of your ancestors; the structure and organisation of their communities; their rural, urban and industrial environment; their working lives and their modes of transport and communication; and the personalities of each individual. These are all at the core of what is important to modern pagans, and to understand and learn from them, and to appreciate how your own life was thereby influenced and perhaps even shaped, should represent your ultimate genealogical aim.

Your house is more than just an inanimate part of your home

A building is a palimpsest on to, and in to, which every former resident has left an imprint. It is an individual matter how this is perceived and experienced, and some would seem to be more sensitive than others to the characters that have lived, and the events that have been played out, within the boundaries and walls. You may be lucky enough to still live in your ancestral home, but even if not, it will have evidence of its past occupants. Somewhere they have left their mark, and it is for their interested successors to find what traces remain. Some claim to see them as ghosts, or to hear their actions and movements, and occasionally their voices. Signs of their presence are claimed when objects are inexplicably moved or damaged, and a chill in a part of a house has also been regarded as evidence of their presence. Whilst some activities, like eating, drinking and smoking, can certainly give rise to the absorption of spillages or smoke into the fabric of the house, it is claimed that sounds and even emanations from what we see as a visual image can be absorbed by materials like wood and stone, producing the so-called 'stone tape'. How the alleged contents can be released or replayed has yet to be discovered, but the very existence of the supposition indicates a belief that a house is more than a mere structure, and contains hidden as well as visible evidence of the dramas once played out between its walls. A house that is a place of tranquillity, consideration, mutual respect and togetherness will leave a stone tape that could be replayed with no embarrassment. Even if you do not have the sensory perception to become aware of past events, or you just don't accept the hypothesis, you might care to reflect upon the legacy you will leave behind you when you move out, however that legacy is manifest.

There is much of interest to be gained by tracing the history of your house and its former occupants. If for no other reason, the research involved engenders a sense of belonging to a place that has been cherished and lived in. It may be, of course, that the house has been abused and used for purposes you would disapprove of. Whichever it is, the history of the house is an indelible part of its character, to be shaped further by you. Memories and information probably exist somewhere, and it makes an absorbing family pastime to try and tap into them. Furthermore, once you know all about your house you will doubtless approach any projected modifications or decorations with particular care, for you now have known heritage to protect for the future.

The best place to start is with the exterior of the house, and you should seek advice and information to help you date it by architectural features and constructional techniques and materials. It may be a reproduction of an older style, but the more recent building materials will give this away. Later additions are usually obvious, as they disturb the proportions and homogeneity, sometimes the symmetry, of the original. Large or important features such as doorways or chimneystacks tend to stay in their original positions, whereas walls can be re-rendered, re-faced, or even re-sited in the case of interior ones, and windows can be moved or bricked in.

The older the house the more likely it is that its building materials will be local. If it is near known transport routes such as major roads, railways, rivers or canals, then the materials could have come from elsewhere. The earliest houses will probably be timber-framed, with walls of materials like wattle and daub or of cob (made from straw, mud and chalk), the latter replaced by plaster or lath and plaster. Large stone blocks used for construction indicate a more expensive house, whereas stone rubble or flint was more typical of humbler dwellings. Rubble houses were often lime-washed for weatherproofing. Brick-built houses can be dated by the shape and size of the bricks and the bond – the pattern used by the bricklayer to lay the bricks.

Any interruption to the principal construction, such as extra layers on top of walls to increase ceiling height of upstairs rooms, or extensions, should be discernible. Doors, door frames, window frames, and roof substructure can be dated by the type of timber; the cross-sectional shape, style of carving if present, and jointing methods; the overall architectural style; leading, type of glass, and the method of opening in the case of windows; and type of metal fittings. Early roofs had steep pitches because of the need to get the rain and snow off quickly before it penetrated the shingle or thatch. Tiling and slating enabled shallower pitches to be employed without leaking. Styles of chimneystacks and pots, guttering, downpipes and other external fittings all help in the dating of the exterior of the house. House insurance records, if available, are valuable guides to the property and contents at the time the policy was taken out, often including plans and detail like colours and styles of furnishings.

Looking inside the house, the area least likely to have changed is the roof space, where clues abound in the form of type and cut of timber, methods of jointing and tieing, and the overall structure. Plastering of walls and ceilings is useful for dating, as the earliest plaster was a thinly applied mixture of lime and sand, and both thickness and composition changed over the years in recognisable ways. Places where former windows or cupboards were filled in and plastered over are usually noticeable, as are other signs of internal alterations. Important rooms might have had wooden panelling on the walls, of oak in older houses, but when scarce later, of pine. Styles of ornamental plasterwork are indicative of the age, and with the advent of wallpaper in the nineteenth century, one layer often being applied on top of another, further help with dating was unwittingly provided. Early floors were normally of compacted earth covered with straw or rushes, to be followed by flagstones, then brick or tiles. Timber floors came later, and as with all carpentered structures these are dateable by the techniques of construction. Features such as fireplaces and staircases are also indicative of a particular period, and in the case of the former in determining possible earlier uses of rooms.

After a full inspection, take a comprehensive set of photographs of your house, inside and outside, including the roof interior and all interesting features. Take the photographs square on and from the side, but not at an angle. Draw up a detailed plan, scaled and using the same units of measurement as would be found on old plans, so that a direct comparison can be made. Measure thicknesses as well as lengths, breadths, heights and angles of pitch. Note changes in floor level and disposition of roof timbers. Make at least one copy of the plan so you can take it to a land registry or local records office or archive to aid in your investigation. Finding your property on old maps is not always straightforward because of possible renaming or renumbering, and the fact that it may have replaced an earlier, now demolished building.

Having identified the earliest mention of your property you can try to determine the names and occupations of former occupants. Your research may lead you to title deeds; census returns; street directories; electoral registers; trade directories; local rate or tax records; church records for parish or diocesan properties, and tithe maps; private estate records of tenancies; records held by professional bodies of surveyors, architects and builders; and so on. If you manage to trace former occupants you could try to find out more about them through research in biographical dictionaries and national portrait and photographic museums and archives. Newspaper obituaries are often quite detailed, as are publications about titled persons and those following particular professions or who occupy other stations in society. At this point you are really following the same leads as if you were tracing your own family history, and the final pieces of the jigsaw can similarly be sought.

Abilities and disabilities; we all have both

Returning now to the extended modern pagan family, the disabled and other discriminated groups have an equal and valued place in it and in new pagan society as a whole. Nobody is perfect or good at everything, but some people think they are or act as though they are. Communal living came about because people realised that by pooling resources and making an individual's particular skills available to all, great mutual benefit was possible. Such a skilled person was valued, whatever his or her other imperfections, because it was the communal good that he or she served that alone was important. By being prepared to offer this skill for the benefit of others, such a person earned respect and felt worthy of it. But anyone less than fully able-bodied in today's demanding, self-serving developed world knows that it is what people can't do that matters more than what they can do, and being conspicuously different in ability than the perceived norm invites impatience, disregard and even contempt. One single incapacity can cancel out the worth of a multiplicity of skills in the minds of selfish discriminators, as in the case of someone using a wheelchair. A sane, intelligent, educated person with partial paralysis has much to contribute, but cannot break through the barrier of negative thinking that pervades like a miasma the air above the self-proclaimed normal individuals, whatever normal means. In the same way, being female, having a physical or mental impairment, coming from an ethnic, religious or cultural minority, or having a minority sexual orientation are disadvantageous in that these people similarly cannot readily overcome the prejudice of negative thinking. What is worse, ignorance and bigotry towards incapacity can take on importance as essential attributes for identity in tribal sub-cultures, particularly amongst the youth.

There are biological reasons for this negative thinking, connected with survival and the drive to maintain exclusive reproduction to preserve the species and protect food sources. An albino of a species is often mobbed and driven off by the other 'normal' types, because it is different and therefore perceived as a reproductive and survival threat. But communal living has created a different, more serious threat – internecine conflict – and this is fuelled most vigorously by negative thinking. Moreover, a species like our own under so much social and environmental pressure needs positive thinking to pool talent co-operatively for the communal good, for consideration of talents, instead of incapacities and differences, establishes people's worth, and generates the dignity we all deserve to feel. People with dignity and a sense of worth seldom commit crimes. Once upon a time it was unthinkable to commit a crime against one's neighbours because you lived with them and depended on each other. Ostracism could mark the end of one's respect, wellbeing and prosperity. Positive thinking reduces crime for similar reasons, for someone who feels part of the community instead of alienated from it has too much to sacrifice by being anti-social.

If you see someone disfigured or disabled, make a point of greeting and talking to them. Offering assistance or solicitude to the elderly and disabled without a patronising tone is a skill for us all to learn by example. If you are on appointment panels, committees, boards, or other steering groups, speak up for all sections of society, and give everyone a fair chance by being positive and objective, and try to ensure that there are provisions for all in your local area, particularly access by way of wheelchair ramps and through wide doorways. Be prepared to lobby where legal obligations are not being carried out, for only when there is widespread vocal concern from the whole community will we get more executive action on behalf of the disenfranchised. Try to support, with your children, functions, fêtes and other activities to raise funds for care homes. In one sense the disadvantaged are very lucky, for they have the community's kindest people looking after them, but these good people are often elderly, or have suffered, themselves. If you are a parent, try to make it your goal to add your children to the list of contributors and supporters, even if only in a small capacity. We can all spare a short, regular time to help others, however busy we claim to be.

Rehabilitation of the criminal

New pagan attitudes to fellow humans extend equally to wrong-doers. Consideration of one's fellow humans as part of one's extended family makes crime against them less likely, but there will still be those who commit crime and among them some who are a sufficient threat to need imprisonment. No other institution cries out more for imaginative rethinking in most countries than the penal system, which tends to punish crime by humiliation, degradation and desensitisation, leading to despair and inadequacy, and the continuance of criminality on release through inability to make a living any other way. The modern pagan notion of imprisonment is an opportunity for education and rehabilitation, and those who are not perceived as a threat to others should receive education and training in the community, along with more imaginative community service tasks, particularly engagement with the disadvantaged and the victims of crime. The compensation of victims, either financially, or in kind, or through personal service, is also an objective modern pagans can identify strongly with. Only when both sides consider the debt to be paid can the extended family harmony be truly restored. So, be prepared to offer your services in whatever capacity you can, by visiting, offering educational or training opportunities, or providing or supervising community service. There could be scope for involving older children in the latter, and it would be a very acceptable outcome if they came to appreciate the value of retaining the majority of wrongdoers actively in the extended family so that they can be rehabilitated rather than embrace the widespread view that they should be locked up and the key thrown away. It is the perfect opportunity for an impressionable young adult to realise that the factor most commonly found to underlie the drift into aberrant behaviour is lack of the love, guidance and stability that a caring family can provide.

Equality of worth

Notions of sexual equality, self-esteem, communal worth and freedom from discrimination arise naturally from a modern pagan upbringing and the embracing of society as part of an extended family. The modern pagan parents who take it upon themselves to ensure their children engage on equal terms with the opposite sex, the elderly and with minority and disadvantaged groups are nurturing the capacity to live comfortably in the world as it is, not as the pretentious, the idealistic and the discriminating might like it to be. No amount of opposition can quell the human spirit nor remove human dignity permanently. Children are indeed worthy who see themselves as defenders of everybody's worth in the global village and the niches of all living things in the global garden, but this can only arise if the parents lead them through by example and introduce them to their fellow inhabitants as equals. With this aim firmly entrenched in its experience the young modern pagan can avoid having many of society's negative and discriminatory attitudes, and be disinclined to accept entrenched institutionalised norms and expectations, but instead follow natural instincts and social good sense.

9

Upbringing and Education

Your culture, or somebody else's?

It is a fundamental and ancient conviction that children have a right to their indigenous culture, and it is to be hoped that modern pagan parents will ensure their children's heritage is passed down. Throughout human history, social groups have borrowed various aspects of culture from their neighbours and remodelled them, so all societies are cross-cultural to a degree, and the process of multicultural cross-fertilisation will continue unabated. What matters to a child is a sense of belonging to the place where their family resides, and this feeling of attachment comes from knowing, understanding and practising local culture. The sharing of inheritance is part of the bond that holds the fabric of society together, the society that is the hub of the extended family. Eventually when the children have matured, they will be in a position to make their own cultural choices, and these choices are more likely to be informed, wise and relevant to their circumstances if their upbringing is consistent, reasoned and grounded in their own local culture. Any child's heritage is rich and diverse, but for many children today all they are brought up with is popular, international culture, which may be experienced all over the world, transmitted and maintained by multinational media organisations for vast profit rather than for people's cultural edification.

Cultural models and icons

When asked who are their society's greatest and most influential figures, children brought up only in popular media culture will normally choose a current celebrity from sport, pop music, cinema, television or fashion. Such a choice is undoubtedly a

genuine one from their limited perspective, but modern paganism regards the whole range of indigenous culture, past and
present, in all its aspects, as the field to choose figures from, and
then perhaps the choices would stem from a rational assessment
of worth to the wellbeing of the extended family, the actual
circles in which it lives from day to day, and the direct influences
upon its lifestyle and its natural environment.

Modern pagan icons whom you may wish your children to
emulate can just as readily be drawn from the fields of science,
technology, conservation, social reform and care in the community, as from the literary, visual, dramatic or musical arts,
or physical endeavour, and in any one of these from across the
whole spectrum, for breadth is as vital a part of indigenous
culture as depth. There are, for example, virtuoso musicians,
dancers and composers in folk music, jazz, and musical theatre,
just as in classical music, opera and ballet, for cultural snobbery
has no place in modern paganism. It does not matter if the
iconic people chosen are themselves pagan or non-pagan, it is
their value as purveyors of culture that is most important. Our
choices are our own, and are of equal worth if informed and
drawn from exposure to the whole cultural spectrum, the
spectrum one hopes you as a parent will introduce your children
to. It is the narrowness of exposure and the rejection of other
cultural fields that is so disturbing about popular media culture
and the fact that so many children are influenced by it from a
young age and trapped within it by a monocultural upbringing.
If the day comes when selfless, community-spirited local people
are included amongst our children's icons, then they will have
truly grasped the cultural significance of the concept of the
extended family and its accommodation of cultural breadth.

Living your culture by taking pride in your heritage

In daily life we draw upon our heritage constantly – for example,
in the linguistic sense by quotation, simile and phraseology; or in
the artistic or scientific sense by drawing upon and extending or
modifying the achievements of the past – but if these threads
are broken or allowed to wither then our education will no longer

flow from our own roots, it will be determined solely by the most powerful and influential aspects of popular media culture. One of the sharpest knives that seeks to sever these threads is political correctness, one of whose purposes is to make us ashamed of our indigenous roots and their values and to get us to adopt cultureless amorphism in our communication and actions, and eventually in our thoughts. To deny your children the link to their cultural past is to risk leaving them without moral or aesthetic authority or foundation.

Wherever you live, try to learn about both your cultural history and its relevance to your everyday life and about the history of your locality. Take a pride in where you live as well as pride in your language; your folk music and dance; your traditional dress, arts and crafts; your folk tales, nursery rhymes, sports, games and children's stories; your culinary traditions, and other day-to-day cultural aspects of life; but remember when you pass them on to your children that you are part of the global pagan family with all the communal and environmental responsibilities that that implies. Your community can evolve with changing times and yet retain respect for the past. Always support restoration of old buildings, for example, rather than demolition and rebuilding in modern style, and be proud of the epithet 'old-fashioned' if it is applied to your preference for what has proven worth.

It is a sharp weapon in the armoury of the purveyors of political correctness and those who seek to replace indigenous culture by popular media culture to condemn the passing on of folk music and folk tales because they portray images and attitudes of the past. Of course they do, and it is part of the interest and pleasure in handing them down to explain how and why times have changed. Any sensible parent can readily ensure that their children don't take them literally.

Language as a cultural binding force

Encouraging your children to be proud of their language and how they express themselves will help them fend off the growing demands for quick, flexible modes of communication by an increasingly complex and impatient society where time is more of the essence than quality of expression. Bringing up your children to read regularly and to play word games is an enjoyable, tried and tested way to increase their linguistic competence and flexibility. Language has always evolved to meet people's needs, and will always do so, but the trend towards regarding anything that happens to be understood as being acceptable, and some even regard it as therefore correct, seeks to discard yet another aspect of our heritage. Moreover, it is removing another element of choice to fail to teach children the rules of pronunciation, spelling, grammar and punctuation so that the individual cannot have the basis upon which to choose the most appropriate means of communication or usage of language. And when one hears a teacher of English language reprimand a pupil for incorrect 'pro*noun*ciation', to quote a consistently mispronounced word, one knows at least one source of the problem, the current lamentable knowledge of the English language demonstrated by teachers, and indeed broadcasters.

Your linguistic and literary heritage is expressed through your language, and whatever it is it will be an extremely rich and valuable one, containing as it does so many windows to your cultural past. If the necessary language skills are lacking your children have no access to that past, and if they cannot converse with their grandparents they cannot connect with their ancestral heritage. Without the stability and models from one's own culture children are exclusively in the hands of the media, with its alien messages and values, and disregard for grammar and spelling. No language can be put in a glass case and protected from such influences, any more than we can put our children in the same glass case to protect them from values and attitudes originating from elsewhere. But parents and teachers can do their jobs properly and connect children with their own cultural roots, to enable and equip them as young adults to make their own considered decisions from then on, rather than, by default, leave them to be manipulated freely from outside the home, school and community.

Heritage is the foundation of the family

A family without a firm foundation of cultural heritage is like a house built on sand, prone to shifting, swaying, cracking and possibly even crumbling or collapsing. But by a family proudly retaining and passing on the full breadth and depth of children's indigenous cultural heritage, they can make informed choices when they decide for themselves how they wish to shape their lives and what cultural influences they are comfortable with. If they don't choose then the media barons and their narrow-minded disciples will choose for them. Along with the rediscovery of our cultural roots comes a reassessment of the debt owed to true pagans of the past and the aspects of traditional pagan culture that they clung on to. Our way of life, in both thought and deed, is still infused with paganism, and many daily routines, habits, sayings, games, calendrical rituals, folk songs, folk tales, morals, attitudes, and behaviour have discernible pagan origins. A modern pagan upbringing is simply reclaiming the rest, rejecting what is no longer appropriate for our times, disentangling some of it from a corrupted state, and recovering what has been forgotten or nearly lost through the march of time. Making this process relevant and meaningful by applying it to the way that modern pagan children are brought up and educated today is a strong thread in this chapter.

The aesthetic and sensory dimensions of a cultured upbringing

Telling your children about their cultural roots is not enough, as culture is for the experiencing by being actively involved in it. If your own knowledge and experience has lapsed then as part of your preparation for parenthood you could seek out local resources and reacquaint yourself, but it is also great fun for parents and children to explore and learn together. Within the words, music, dance steps, practical techniques, and artistic designs of folk heritage lie the human experiences of your ancestors, many of them very similar to what we experience today. Just as a plant flowers more profusely from strong, deep roots, so will your children prosper in terms of their more deeply rooted intellectual and aesthetic appreciation. The bedtime story and lullaby is an institution the world over; a valuable, impressionable time to pass on folk tales, nursery rhymes and songs. Encourage your child to learn how to play a musical instrument, and include folk music in the repertoire. For a full aesthetic experience, take your children to recitals and concerts to hear live music and see the musicians in action, for witnessing and experiencing performance is so much more enriching than just listening to sounds from a recording. When developing artistic and practical skills, use traditional designs and techniques as examples, whether it be painting, modelling, wickerwork, ceramics, textile production, or a host of other exciting, challenging crafts. To develop dexterity and artistry at the same time as absorbing one's indigenous culture is both satisfying and nurturing to a child. If you are not familiar with a particular artistic form then seek out classes locally, or get together with parents who are. In any case, some skills have wider scope if practised communally, such as dancing and singing, and they allow the child to share aesthetic enjoyment with others.

Another important outcome for the cultured members of the next generation is that they will be able to draw upon traditional sources for their artistic inspiration as well as contemporary ones, an opportunity that urbanisation and industrialisation have denied to so many in the recent past as people have lost contact with their rural roots. As in the natural world, your culture is all around you if you care to seek it out, and by encouraging your children to be active in learning about their folk heritage you will be enhancing their creativity and expressiveness in a meaningful way and combating the greatest deficiency in academically biased school education programmes, namely the downgrading or neglect of the development of the senses and their aesthetic appreciation.

If you are blessed with the five senses, you and your child can look, but do you see and intelligently interpret all that is there? You can listen, but do you hear and assign all that there is to discern? When you smell, do you really discriminate, and similarly when you taste, do you savour all the ingredients or just the most pronounced? Do you explore and respond when you touch, or just make fleeting contact? The senses, and your interpretation of what they pick up, both require exercising if full aestheticism is to be developed, and the joys of aesthetic sensitivity and discernment are precious lifelong gifts for children and adults alike.

Formal education all over the world has veered away from assigning high value and social status to the aesthetic, that is to say, to our 'feelings' as opposed to our tutored 'thoughts' and 'actions'. Folk culture relies heavily on the senses and on our instincts, rather than on the rational and logical ways of the scientific and technological age. Reclaiming the instinctive, the impulsive, the sensual, the rhythmic, the humorous and our senses of both individuality and togetherness, is a vital part of the revival of paganism. This is not to say that formal composition cannot be of great aesthetic value. Of course it can, and it should be part of every modern pagan child's education to experience all artistic forms, but an appreciation of one's own traditional folk heritage gives a child more than just an artistic experience, it passes on the richness of collective aesthetic inheritance.

Young children have abundant energy and curiosity and an innate sense of rhythm. Making music and dance with them is a declining activity in homes, where all too often someone else's choice of music and sentiment is listened to passively. As with all artistic endeavours, aesthetic development can only occur fully by active involvement, so start by encouraging your child to use its senses, particularly hearing and touch, to find music in nature and in everyday activities. Sounds are all around us, and many are rhythmic. The old favourite of the noise of the wheels of a train is still a good example, and sitting in the garden on a breezy day will provide many more, as things sway, rustle, clatter and creak in the wind. The songs of birds, the varied sounds of insects, mammals and amphibians, all provide inspiration. When children are working with you in the house or garden, create a work song to match the rhythm of your actions. This is a centuries-old technique to relieve the monotony of tasks like paddling a boat or using tools repetitively such as when chopping a log or turning the soil. It is quite easy for children to make their own instruments, and to do so from scrap materials promotes the virtue of recycling. With help a child should be able to make instruments of different types – percussive, plucked or wind. A young pear leaf between the thumbs makes a reed instrument of surprising capability, and even the two hands can form a rival to the ocarina. In this way, the same hands-on approach as is successfully used for visual arts and crafts can be applied to music, and together they constitute vital aesthetic development of the young senses. Music-making, sketching, painting, sculpture, and other constructional projects are often regarded as mere play, and of inferior educational status to 'academic' pursuits, but such an opinion is profoundly ignorant of the importance of an aesthetic sense in the maturing young person.

Countering anti-aesthetic attitudes

The abundantly energetic behaviour of young children and their innate sense of rhythm are endearing characteristics that, unfortunately, many regard as tiresome and unseemly. Such opinions cause parents, and later teachers, to tell the children to 'behave', in the same way that dog owners 'punish' dogs for behaving precisely as their natural instincts tell them to behave. Moreover, those who hold such opinions then try and channel children's energies into prescribed, 'approved' actions. Thus begins the sensory and emotional deprivation of children and the start of a lifelong confusion about the social acceptability or not of various types of instinctive behaviour. Like all young animals, children are bursting with exuberance, but if they have to stop and think at every juncture the containment makes for easier manipulation, thereby condemning their aesthetic faculties to under-use and to being under-valued, although it does make them more socially agreeable and less embarrassing company for social-climbing parents. Of course, anarchic abandon is no more productive than extreme caution, but society and its educational arm can with great benefit redress the balance between prescription and aestheticism more towards the aesthetic, to give children a genuine chance of being well-rounded. A home that encourages aesthetic and sensory engagement is a vibrantly absorbing place for young, eager, receptive minds.

Restoring pride in the folk who gave us folk heritage

A common nineteenth-century reaction to traditional arts and crafts was to denigrate them, then 'modernise' them and adapt them to more 'acceptable' standards and techniques. Far from considering folk songs to be educational, for example, they were often bowdlerised by removing their earthy content and their tunes made chromatic in the name of propriety and order and for ease of parlour piano accompaniment. But modern pagans may reclaim the originals from national archives, and are encouraged to do so through local libraries and folk clubs. In this as in all aspects of culture modern pagans are free to take their inheritance back, and with the receipt generate again the feeling, spontaneity and release that comes from true aesthetic involvement and appreciation. Folk music, it must be said, does not have the military precision of much composed music, and folk arts are often the product of expression rather than adherence to the rules of geometry, but they have an individual vitality that conformation to a formula cannot achieve. Whereas classical dance forms move to the music, the opposite is true of folk dancing, where the music arises from the moves, and indeed all folk art forms develop from instinctive and sensory motives.

Explain to your children that folk songs had, and still have, a valuable social purpose, and reading the words together will make this clear. They bear witness to people's contemporary trials and tribulations as well as to occupations now gone, many of them requiring both brain and brawn, both rural and industrial, and to the whole gamut of life's emotions, relationships and social expectations, all surprisingly familiar to us today. The realisation that human aspirations and trials are much the same in one generation as in the next is a compelling part of a child's historical perspective, as one can learn from history through the medium of records like songs, poetry, and other contemporary writings. These songs were functional in their time as well as entertainment, for they were a way of expressing the singers' place in the natural order and how they viewed their lot. As a form of communication, folk song allows those who share the singers' sentiments or experiences to identify with their common strands of life. Subjects common in folk song are those which are prominent, and therefore highly exploited, in popular culture today, but as a means of making money rather than cementing a common bond. Traditional folk song may have lost some of its contexts, but just as many new ones have arisen, and the folk medium can survive in any age as a contemporary window on life as well as a significant influence in family and communal upbringing. Like all artistic creations it is a much under-used and underestimated way of imparting to a child the relevance of their cultural heritage.

In summary, your children's artistic achievements are uniquely theirs, in a way that their academic achievements are not, for the latter are produced largely by conformation, the former from the heart and soul, so praise them and treasure the results, and please encourage active aesthetic pursuits throughout their childhood.

Who is in control of your children's upbringing at home?

Although this chapter concerns the upbringing and education of modern pagan children, it will inevitably continue to explore modern pagan attitudes to our fellow human beings and to the social and environmental problems we all face, for children will be exposed to them throughout. It is scarcely necessary to make a long, comprehensive list of society's ills, and the difficulties of bringing up a child to cope with them: it would make depressing reading and we all know what those ills are in our own society and how our lives are adversely affected by them. The value of modern pagan philosophy to global society as it is now evolving is that it offers all of us, who so choose, a way to a happier, healthier, more fulfilling lifestyle with hope for a genuinely contented future, and it does so without the need for a peasants' revolt. Such a revolt is not in most people's natures to participate in, but quiet revolution works if the collective will is there and also the stamina and conviction to stay on one's chosen path within, not without, our social community.

Parents-to-be are especially important in the implementation of modern pagan ideals. You are the bearers of humanities' future and this chapter is directed particularly at you. The objectives of a modern pagan parent are very simple and obvious, and have been alluded to already: to bring up a child to become a nice person, a devoted integrated member of the family, a good citizen of the community and a responsible inhabitant of the planet. There is no need to define the adjectives used here – 'nice', 'devoted', 'good' and 'responsible' – because we all know in our hearts what they mean. All parents make mistakes, and unfortunately we can't press the rewind button and re-record an episode in a child's life to get it right second time, but if you face these setbacks with humility, honesty and dedication, the natural resilience of children and their sense of security within a strong family unit will enable you and your child to get back on track. If you are not committed to these objectives then you really ought not to become a parent at all. Bad parenting is the bane of society and the most important cause of wayward behaviour in young people, and the most obvious form of bad parenting is not the consequences of the parents being bad people, for most are not, but a direct result of the parents relaxing their control of their children's upbringing and allowing people and forces outside the home to become the dominating influence instead. The modern pagan parent stays in charge, and relaxes control only in concert with the developing maturity of the child.

New parents, then, do well to study the opposition and plan their campaign, and it is a strength of modern pagan principles that they provide a consistent, objective framework for such planning of a child's upbringing.

Modern pagans and the media

Media and advertising forces and peer pressure are powerful influences that can't be avoided altogether, but you can equip your children to make appropriate choices by explaining the reasons for your guidance and providing more meaningful and fulfilling alternatives. In order for parents choosing a modern pagan lifestyle and upbringing for their children to prepare for the task ahead, it is worthwhile taking a look at some aspects of the global media-consumer society, or 'the media', and its powerful advertising techniques through pagan eyes.

There are several sides to the media, which we all learn to filter and select from. It can serve by promoting public awareness; it can be self-serving by representing vested interest; and it can be a destructive force in society by encouraging the grasping, aggressive aspects of human nature. While giving guidance to your children on how to filter and select, you the parent will have many a battle with the media and their converted disciples for control of your child's health and welfare. The gangs of the media's proselytising disciples are collectively known as 'peer pressure', which will be a powerful manipulative force tugging at your children to make you relinquish governorship of their upbringing. The media have no choice; either they win the fight for your children's hearts and minds or they lose customers and eventually go out of business. From birth, children are to the media the next generation of consumers, but your parental strategy and values stand in their way. They will therefore strive to replace your values with their own. You can't isolate your offspring from the media, for its tentacles will creep into every corner of their lives, and you will want to guard against your children becoming social outcasts. Your best strategy is probably to control their exposure to it initially while you gradually equip them with the personal standards, values and objectives that will enable them to make sensible, informed choices for themselves. Consistent family standards impart a foundation that is difficult even for the media to undermine. Those standards may be temporarily overlaid by adolescent preoccupations, but they will almost certainly resurface in early adulthood and continue to be significant from then on.

The media will adopt the following tactics, to which new pagan responses are appended in italics:

1. They will insult your intelligence, claim that they know better than you, and that their advice is well founded, approved by experts and thoroughly tested, although you will have no way of verifying these claims.

   Your experts are your natural instincts and good sense, backed up by generational wisdom through the extended family. Take control and make your own

*choices. It is a new pagan ideal that advertising be
restricted solely to adults, to demonstrable fact, and is
stripped of all claim, opinion and temptation, and you
may care to lobby towards this end. It is also advisable
to find the time to check claims, lists of ingredients,
recommendations for use, etc, so that you remain in
control of your purchasing and usage. Abstinence and
prevention mean fewer remedies to seek.*

2. They will use emotional blackmail by suggesting your
   children will lack peer status and be left out if they
   don't buy their products and services and change their
   lifestyle in recommended ways. To achieve these ends
   your children will be made to feel insecure, discontented,
   unfulfilled, inadequate and deprived if they don't follow
   their exhortations.

   *A child who is loved, feels secure, has an interesting
   and varied lifestyle, and has positive experiences of
   the advice you have given, will be a contented child
   and will continue to turn to you for guidance and
   support. Children can only be wrapped in cotton wool
   for so long; eventually they need to acquire sufficient
   media awareness and powers of discrimination to be
   equipped to make their own choice of lifestyle, and
   that can only be successful if you have discussed and
   rationalised the differences between your chosen path
   and that of the followers of the media, together with
   the consequences of taking either path.*

3. They will proclaim the ascendancy of manufactured
   and processed materials, goods and food over the
   natural and additive-free.

   *An active healthy child on a natural diet, brought up
   in surroundings as natural as possible, has every
   incentive to continue with what is worthwhile and
   fulfilling. Your children will be aware that they have
   fewer health problems, and greater variety in their*

diet. They may also have fewer possessions, but they will be well-made, responsive to touch and treasured.

4. They will try to impose their own promoted role models and lifestyle values and claim that they, not you, set the standards.

   Your family role models will be ones that personify your perceptions and principles, and so promote them and their example as vigorously as the media's. The advantage for you is that you can demonstrate the worth to society of your role models, whereas the media's are promoting only vested and self-interest.

5. They will forcefully suggest the new and denigrate the old and the tried and tested as old-fashioned; and they will elevate style above functionality.

   Valuing the past and its heritage, and respecting the elderly, help to counter the claims that everything of old provenance is unsuitable for today's 'modern', technological world.

6. They will exhort your children to strive for the media's own ideals of perfection in terms of excitement, 'looking and feeling good', financial and material gain, and heightened sensory experiences, and all with as little planning, waiting, effort and pain as possible, ignoring all obstacles and opinions to the contrary. Actions that don't achieve any of the results above are not deemed worthwhile; they are not 'cool'.

   The rejoinder to this arises perfectly from closeness with the natural world, where the senses are amply fulfilled and patience and care greatly rewarded; bonding within the family; socialisation within the community; and varied physical and mental stimulation during the formative years. Thus fulfilled, a child will not fall easy prey to such temptations.

7. They will encourage consumption and serial purchase and disposal, and competitiveness to maintain the cycle. Your children will be urged to replace old, much used, and well-made articles by new items with built-in obsolescence, although no child will readily part with a much loved, knocked-about toy unless it learns to do so from its parents.

    In the new pagan home the child will be brought up with the principles and practices of sustainability; mending, adaptation and recycling; instead of consumption, disposal and destruction.

8. They will use linguistic manipulation, patronising deceit, and sexual and violent imagery to capture the attention and gain the obedience of impressionable young minds.

    The modern pagan family is not interested in bland cultural uniformity but in translating its philosophies for the common good of the extended family in the natural world. It is more concerned with selflessness and responsibility than exercising 'rights' and claiming 'freedoms'. The vulgar, egocentric, foul-mouthed, aggressive, sexually obsessive, drug-taking images of media personalities are no example for new pagans.

9. They will implore your children to leave their childhood, with its protective parental regime, behind as quickly as possible in order to become fully-fledged consumers and media disciples.

    A child that enjoys its childhood is less willing to abandon it than a child who feels that all the excitement is outside the home. But don't plan to bring up another Peter Pan, for maturity should develop naturally out of your efforts during the adolescent years, and when to start releasing the reins only parental instinct can determine – but not too soon, or those precious childhood years will be all too few.

10. They will use glossy packaging, propaganda, and exaggeration to justify their overblown prices for little substance. In this way, a desire is created for what is not needed, and that article quickly becomes redundant. Whether the article has any real purpose is irrelevant, for its purpose is so that the consumer acquires status by having it and impresses others so that they in turn will buy one. Also, a great deal of knowledge formerly learned from grandparents and parents will, if unchecked, be replaced by advertising-laden, superficial snippets in picture books, videos and on the Internet, and gradually the next generation of parents becomes a generation of slaves to advertising because it has no other ready sources of information.

Materialism and greed are not part of new pagan lifestyle, which seeks satisfaction in simplicity. There are issues here too about litter and recycling. Litter campaigns would not be needed if nobody dropped litter, or better still, nobody purchased articles sold in unnecessary packaging, or even better, if nobody manufactured the packaging or even the item, which everyone could probably do without anyway, in the first place.

In our propaganda-saturated consumer society, actions which are worthwhile in themselves are deemed less important than those which earn money or result in consumption. If the product of an action is regarded as more important than the process then creativity and employment simply become chores, in contrast to the days of the craftsmen when the process of manufacture was as fulfilling and satisfying as the finished item. Improving oneself is seen in terms of its link to wealth and possessions, not personal, artistic, technical or community achievement and the satisfaction to be derived therefrom. For modern pagan children, values are more valuable than valuables. Key elements of modern pagan upbringing are an appreciation of humankind as part of a global ecosystem; care and love for other living things and for all other components of the natural environment; redirected focus onto the family and community rather than on the self and towards greater internationalism; preference for long-term good health instead of the instant pleasures of over-indulgence and self-abuse; acceptance of technology only as far as it serves a need without undesirable consequences; and sustainability and simplicity rather than relentless growth, consumption and complexity.

Modern pagans as informed consumers

Parents-to-be preparing for the media onslaught on their future children are better able to raise and maintain consumer awareness if the family as a whole informs itself and audits its commercial and technological consumption. Consumer power tends to be greatly underestimated as it is only occasionally a highly organised phenomenon, when a particularly significant development ignites a popular movement for or against it. In most cases consumer power derives its magnitude and effectiveness only by the collective desire of individuals to act. If you convince yourself that a problem is too big to be solved by popular action, and do nothing out of a feeling of individual impotence, then you are underestimating the importance of your contribution, for you may inspire many others to follow. Whatever action seems appropriate, whether it is a campaign of information, protest or boycott, it should always be lawful and informed. The gathering of information about, and in support of, consumer issues is essential to buttress the chosen action with a considered and properly researched framework of facts to justify the cause. The general public is normally sharp and intelligent when it comes to consumer issues, but also wary of vested interest and ignorant agitation. But even if you don't wish to publicly take part in or acknowledge your support for action, your private action is still worthwhile on behalf of your family, and simply the exercise of responsible choice is important, and one of your credentials as a modern pagan.

Industrial production from raw materials creates a demand for what must inevitably get scarcer and therefore be offered at a higher price later. It is economically profitable in the short term for industry to exhaust natural supplies, and then it moves on to create demand for new products, most of which were probably never really needed in the first place, but advertising persuaded the gullible that they were essential. Armed with your list of audited commitments as a responsible consumer, you can refine your intentions by fully informing yourself of the background to the products and practices that you intend to do without. Ignore the siren calls for you to 'be there or be square'; your new slogan is 'boycott and be in control', and it is an empowering initiative. Once you know the manufacturing history, from extraction of raw materials, through stages of production to retail sale, of every item you have decided to audit, you have empowered yourself as a consumer. You can share this knowledge with others of like mind, just as their findings can be passed on to you.

Some decisions will be easy for you – for example, if you find that the raw materials include products from endangered species; those hunted, felled or collected indiscriminately in the wild rather than from sustainable harvesting or farming; those produced inhumanely, or processed by child or slave labour or by other human malpractices; those extracted with no programme of environmental reclamation, replanting or pollution control; and so on through a long list of practices which every modern pagan can boycott without conscience. So, boycotting fur coats to save endangered wild cats is straightforward, but if you disapprove of whaling and want to boycott whale products, do you know what they are? This is where Green pressure groups can help, for they produce literature with just this sort of information. As things stand, people are still buying leather treated with whale oil, pet food containing whale meat, soaps and candles made from whale products and perfume from the sperm whale extract ambergris. It seems that with the remaining intransigent governments of countries refusing to cease whaling, the only course of action is to boycott not just all whale products, but all products and services from the countries allowing whaling, or from those supporting whaling countries through trade in whaling products.

If your family and its environment are to have healthy futures, passive acceptance of unsustainable consumption is no longer a viable option. Furthermore, there is far more at stake than first meets the eye. The depletion of wood and mineral resources is a case in point. Hardwoods are harvested unsustainably from rainforests and temperate forests alike; we all know it perfectly well, but we continue to purchase hardwood products and thus encourage more felling of hardwood trees. Making furniture from mahogany and teak and replacement window frames from mahogany are not the only ways to make these products durable and attractive. It is not only the loss of beautiful forests that is the consequence, but loss of biodiversity, shrinking of the gene pool for agriculture and husbandry, disappearance of potential medical ingredients, soil erosion, flooding, distortion of weather patterns, and the forced abandonment of an ancient way of life by indigenous people. But the reverse is also true, in that every positive ecological decision brings about a chain reaction of improvements. Buying organically grown, additive-free foods, if one can prove that they are, will have the effect of reducing the use of pesticides, herbicides and other chemical residues.

However, there are dangers in being too trusting of so-called watchdog organisations and consumer councils that are financed by, or have a close association with, the organisations whose activities they should be investigating and monitoring on the public's behalf. They will not represent consumer interests, so decisions are best made on the basis of information and incli-nation. Whenever you can, try and shop locally, as making fewer vehicle journeys to out-of-town supermarkets reduces pollution and makes it less likely that more green-belt land will be given over to such developments. It is also important to buy direct from producer groups in developing countries so that local sustainable production is supported and not the rape of the environment by exploitative, greedy, multinational companies. Purchase of the latter's cash crops, such as coffee, tea and sugar, from developing countries means that large areas of land are not available to indigenous people for local sustainable agriculture and for nature reserves, which employ local guides and provide facilities for paying tourists. These are just some of the many issues to be considered by the modern pagan family desirous of bringing up children in a home where there is balanced consumer awareness.

Pregnancy and motherhood: only as fashionable as nature intended

After the previous discussion of a number of matters for parents-to-be it is time to consider the joyous times of pregnancy and birth. When your pregnancy is confirmed resolve first and foremost to enjoy it, and feel proud of your condition rather than worry about losing your youth or figure, or some of your freedoms or ability to work in certain capacities. Some look upon pregnancy as an infirmity and will treat you like an invalid given half a chance, but just let your doctor and your own feelings and bodily reactions tell you what is best in any situation. When preparing for the duties and responsibilities of motherhood, focus your considerations on the natural aspects of body care, birth and caring for the babe in arms. There is no need to spend money on stylish maternity clothes and cosmetic preparations, when what the baby will most appreciate is a maternal body in as natural a state as possible, in preparation for a natural birth. Try to avoid undergarments that may damage the nipples or constrict the abdomen; and, provided you are posturally comfortable, it is better not to wear a bra at all and to wear loose clothing.

Upon the assumption that pre-natal checks and consultations with family doctor and midwife reveal a healthy prospect for the pregnancy and birth, the preferred option for modern pagans is a natural birth at home, so that the baby emerges straight into the home environment. Ideally this will not be a home obsessed with the ultra-cleanliness and sterility that was once characteristic of our hospitals, and which nowadays is suspected of being responsible for the failure of the young to acquire a range of natural immunities. Most 'special' baby toilet preparations are unnecessary and merely start the lifelong exposure to chemicals that has blighted the lives of the last generation. You may be a proud mother, but try not to be fastidious about cleanliness. Too much bathing causes loss of skin oils and texture, and a return to terry nappies will mean that they are only changed and washed as required, and your dustbin will have fewer disposable items to tip into landfill sites. Nappies are best left off as often as possible, and certainly when your baby is in the garden, in a warm, shady spot. Bleaches and ecologically unsafe detergents are not suitable for the washing of nappies, nor indeed for the washing of any baby clothes.

As with toiletries, most baby furniture is unnecessary, cots and playpens often being used as cages for the convenience of the busy mother. A baby carried by its mother in a sling, as may still be seen commonly in sub-Saharan Africa, is a more contented child than one left to cry itself to exhaustion or planted in front of the television. You may like to think seriously about re-establishing this tradition, as one of the delights of visiting an African village is to be greeted by happy, lively, sociable children. When your baby is eager to become mobile allow the little chap to crawl. Crawling is a very important pre-walking activity and should not be denied a baby by the use of a 'baby-walker'. Get your baby used to being in the garden as much as possible to attune its senses to nature, but beware of exposure to sun and cold as babies lose and gain heat rapidly. A baby can be over-stimulated, denying it those important quieter moments for reflection, observation and recollection of its experiences, and for relaxation prior to sleeping.

Your baby's health

Starting your baby on a natural diet
It is an opportune moment to read again the advice already given in chapter six on breastfeeding and weaning a new baby. Note that vegan diets are not advisable for babies as they can result in malnutrition, and vegetarian diets will have to be carefully thought out for nutritional balance. Eating is an important communal occasion for the whole family, so try to allow the baby to share meals with you whenever its sleep cycle allows.

Obsessive and over-protective mothers resort to drugs when it is better to look holistically at the baby's condition and consider the strong reserves of self-healing and survival that all babies naturally have. No drug should be administered to a baby without qualified medical approval, as its general physical and mental wellbeing will not get a good start in life if it becomes used to knee-jerk medical responses to symptoms. An active, outdoor baby will be healthier than one kept indoors in a scrupulously sanitised and overheated house. As has been alluded to in chapters six and seven, there seems to be a relationship between modern lifestyle, stress and environmental pressures on the one hand and complaints such as heart disease, arteriosclerosis, arthritis, cancer, allergies, certain mental illnesses, pre-menstrual tension, diabetes, and, in children, glue ear and hyperactivity, on the other. The new pagan style of parenting offers an opportunity to break this cycle. Your baby needs you and your partner far more than drugs and technology, for it is not a patient and should not be treated as such. A natural upbringing is a stress-free, healthy upbringing, but of course every mother can usefully learn basic first aid, and tried-and-tested folk remedies for day-to-day complaints that would respond to them.

Choosing toys and entertainment

A baby that is brought actively into the family from birth has plenty to engage its eager senses, without armfuls of plastic toys of dubious value and physical aids of no value whatsoever. Toys made from natural materials invite engaging exploration by touch, and are durable and valuable heirlooms. Playing with water and a variety of natural items of various textures is also just as stimulating as some so-called educational toys. Whatever toys you select should as far as possible promote the physical and intellectual development you and your principles support.

Rather than be lured by toy manufacturers' claims that their product is essential for your baby's development, there is more to be gained by letting the baby explore the house and garden and be involved in the family routine. Sensory experiences gained inside and outside the house have an important influence on their perception, reasoning and judgement. The exploring baby will have accidents and mishaps, but it must learn from these so that it accepts that its actions have consequences. Try to clean up spillage without fuss, and not make it the subject of admonition or, worse, retribution. Your reactions will be studied and copied by the child, so if you are impatient and quick to lose your temper then your child will learn this behaviour. If you as a mother adopt an over-tidy, over-clean mentality it can make your child reluctant to follow its natural exploratory instincts and lower its self-esteem, as well as prevent exposure to dirt and micro-organisms that help attune its natural defences. Talk to your baby regularly, as just the sound and tone of your voice is reassuring, and, when it is able to understand, tell it your own stories rather than constantly read someone else's, so that your culture and values are the most important influence. Select television and radio so as to conform to your values while you have the control. Later in life when your offspring get into some difficulty or other it will be the strength of the values you imparted that will get them through the crisis with, one hopes, minimal lasting damage.

The highly mechanised, beautifully decorated showpiece home, with its well-manicured garden, is an uncomfortable place for a growing, mobile child. It cannot share in your family life and make a contribution towards cooking, cleaning, decorating and gardening, for example, if these tasks are automated or done by outsiders, and unless you are tolerant of mess and mistakes. Cooking from natural ingredients, making things for the home from non-toxic materials, and helping with tasks in the garden, are enjoyable activities for a child, who will come to regard its new pagan household as an interesting and educational place, whether toys are available or not.

Early years at school for modern pagan children

There are few institutions in countries where pagans live today that evoke so much concern amongst them as the way schools are constituted and managed. This is certainly true for modern pagans, who currently only have a choice of pre-school playgroups and schools established along lines that do not meet the perceived educational needs of their children. Generally, there is a desire amongst modern pagan parents not to institutionalise their children too early by sending them to pre-school playgroups. This is so as not to expose them to those habits and behaviours of non-pagan children that people who follow the modern pagan path disapprove of and wish to delay contact with until their own children are more mature and self-assured. The preference is to keep the family together, where, in the home, your child can learn language properly and acquire the habits and norms that you desire for it, and socialise with other children and learn social skills under your guidance. In any case, too early a diet of pre-packaged schooling can work against your children's natural development and creativity. If you have taught them to make their own toys and amusement they will grow up to appreciate the value of recycling, with useful craft skills, understanding multiplicity of use with a flexibility of mind. A longer time at home will also enable you to focus more on their aesthetic and sensory development, and to explain your own philosophies. A more mature child can more readily be prepared for the inevitable problems associated with peer pressure to conform with tribal behaviour and become 'one of the gang'.

The test of a good school for a new pagan parent will generally be small size, and how far it determines and develops a child's natural abilities and capabilities. Unfortunately, conformity and prescription are more usual in schools than individuality and addressing particular needs. Published material is followed with unquestioning obedience, and too little development is based on a child's own experience, and the results of its own senses, thoughts and judgements. A child might be forgiven for thinking that schooling, particularly in large schools, sees no place for lateral thinking, imagination, hands-on dexterity, craftsmanship and pride in handiwork, or co-operative as opposed to competitive attitudes. A holistic education is more valuable to modern pagans than a compartmentalised one based on centralised establishment rules of conformity, linked to a product and onward route which it alone perceives to be appropriate and worthy. There is in many countries a growing disenchantment with institutional schooling, and a growing interest in schooling conceived, established and managed wholly by co-ordinated groups of parents themselves. For modern pagan parents this is an attractive prospect as things stand.

During your child's first year at school you may be worried that your happy, lively, helpful, polite, interested, well-adjusted offspring, who has been the centre of attention with some regularity, is now part of a large institution where she or he is one of many and facing daily assaults on the values and habits that you have carefully imparted and nurtured. But you are still the final arbiter, although not without a struggle from now on against those forces which seek to remove individual choice, foremost among them bullying and pressure to follow the crowd in matters of popular culture. Popular culture may also seep into school activities with the aim of making them more enjoyable, but what can happen is that they simply encourage triteness and superficiality. Whatever tendencies your children pick up, whether it be from pupils or teachers, you the parent have the right to decide upon what is harmless, what is just a passing phase, what is likely to compromise their values and beliefs, and what may well lead them seriously astray. No two sets of parents are likely to reach the same decisions, for they are driven by their individuality, the same as that which they are trying to preserve in their children, but what you decide should be upheld consistently. While your children are at school, the wheel of their ship of destiny still needs your hands tightly upon it, or their peers will steer it for you.

Children do not so much need protection as help to equip themselves to understand and cope with the situations they meet so that they keep their self-esteem and sense of pagan purpose. They may learn for the first time to lie, deceive and respond aggressively, and these will be stern, early tests for your determination to insist that their modern pagan values are not going to be cast aside. The behaviour of other boys will be a particular source of concern, for far too many headteachers and teachers, especially males, follow the example of bad parents and allow uncivilised behaviour by boys to go unchecked. You are entitled to expect that no person in the school, nor the school as an institution, treats your child in an undignified way or in a way that compromises your personal beliefs and values, and there is no just cause for reluctance to inform the school of what you expect from them in these regards.

When your children come home each day they may seem hyperactive because schools inhibit free expression. What is not a good idea to help them unwind is to put them in front of the television, stereo or computer, or push them out of the door to play a tribal game like football. After enquiring about their day, read them a story, or get them interested in reading to themselves, or making music, doing gardening, cooking or taking the dog for a walk. Recreation and enjoyment generally is better for a child if it does not involve a marketed activity or mindless entertainment, in which other people's values are being promulgated, but does involve genuine creativity and scope for the imagination. When children are refreshed is the time to start them on any homework they have been set.

During the years of schooling from about seven to twelve, a child begins to develop independent thought processes and to question. Its balance, co-ordination and dexterity are also maturing, so physically and mentally children of this age-range welcome activity and the chance to be involved in discussion about the ups and downs of life, the dos and don'ts of personal and social interaction, and a range of physical and problem-solving challenges. What is undoubtedly worth preserving is a child's sense of wonder, love of nature and generosity of spirit, by not pushing a child to grow up too quickly. Child-centred advertising and peer pressure will become an intrusive element, and a child will also start to become aware of the rat race of school, college/university, employment and retirement, and perhaps start to forget that there is more to life.

The imitation of adults and attempts to adopt their ways and lifestyle are principally what deprive children of their precious childhood, self-esteem and independent character, not to mention the trials of not being emotionally mature enough to cope with such a lifestyle at an early age. Once trapped on such a course, a child will become a willing subject for commerce and the media. With opposition from the media to a value-driven style of upbringing, the new pagan parent can only stagger on, and must do so with undiminished interest in the child, cleverly juggling control and choice, while discussing contentious issues and continuing to set a good example. It is a time for clear choices of friends, toys, and forms of entertainment, and delicate, reasoned discussion, as it is a difficult balance for a new pagan parent to strike, to ensure that the new pagan child is well-adjusted to the real world and not a social outcast, and that it understands popular culture but does not adopt cultural norms that you the parent disapprove of. New pagan children must of course know the modern pagan philosophy intimately to be comfortable with like-minded friends and appreciate the differences with popular culture, but they must also, in order that they are not alienated from society at large, be encouraged to mix with, and avoid isolation from, non-pagans.

Guiding modern pagan children through the maze of popular culture

There will be some pupils at your child's school who spend most evenings watching television or playing computer games, not even pausing for a meal at the table, but having it from a tray on their laps, and the scope of their conversation at school, reinforced by publications that mainly deal in celebrity gossip and scandal, will reflect this. Unfortunately for modern pagan parents, television and computers have spawned a growth in passive, mindless entertainment, which is watched then forgotten, as an escape rather than as an enriching, aesthetic, intellectual experience. Escaping from time to time is one thing, but hours each day is a damning indictment of the individual's lifestyle, and it is a lifestyle that is of no benefit to modern pagan children. Entertainment can become more important than being informed or intellectually stimulated, and entertainers can become stars and public figures with a standing out of all proportion to their talent and social worth. This constant disguising of the real world makes its problems, such as individual and communal deprivation and ecological pressures, less prominent in the minds of maturing children, and illustrates the way the entertainment industry fritters away vast amounts of human and material resources.

People of all ages benefit from activity and creativity, rather less from passivity, although we do all gain restoratively from quieter, ruminative periods. Children brought up as modern pagans are unlikely to get so bored that they need to be force-fed entertainment, because their enjoyment arises naturally from a varied, creative lifestyle. In any case, children don't have to have fun all the time, and they like to amuse themselves as much as to be amused. Their own games will promote discussion and arguments, and all sorts of other interplays, and it is important that they learn to resolve issues themselves.

You as parents will have to decide which models and icons you want your child to look up to, which forms of entertainment are just harmless frivolity, and which have damaging implications for your child because of the language, images, attitudes and temptations they project. To do this means taking the trouble to keep in touch with popular culture, to watch children's programmes, to read children's books, to monitor what children do on their computers, and generally take a close interest in what will become your child's world if you are too busy or uninterested to take notice. You can't steer their ship of destiny from the cabin, you have to be on deck at the wheel watching the sea and weather and making adjustments accordingly.

By the time your child is a teenager you may feel you really want to ban much that he or she is being exhorted to do by friends and by the media. How far you should take diplomacy and compromise will be your sternest challenge. The lure of teenage tribalism, despite its tendency to breed anti-social and selfish behaviour, is a strong attraction to a child without secure family ties and a fulfilling lifestyle. So, you have twelve years to put these firmly in place, and to know your children intimately, how best to approach them, how to reason with them, how to balance advice against self-discovery, and how to insist upon your objectives without damaging self-esteem or the family bond. If you have achieved all this in their formative years you are in with a chance of steering them along the middle of the path through adolescence. This is where parental instinct and a consistent set of values score over formulae and lists of dos and don'ts where raising children is concerned.

The release of abundant energy, emotions, rebellious ideas and claimed 'rights' with no thought of the consequences for others or themselves, and no appreciation of the social limits of free expression, and impatience with parents and prescribed or orthodox ways, are characteristic of the teenage years, but this release can be channelled. Channelling teenage energy is made easier by your choice of role models during the formative years, and by the demonstrable denial that individual personalities are misfits. Your role models most usefully include the unsung, such as those who care for others; the selfless who give service to the community beyond the call of duty; the arbitrators and others who promote togetherness; the researchers and creators – whether they be artists, craftspeople, scientists or technologists; the deployers for the common good; conservationists and environmentalists; and as many local people as possible. Few, if any, of the current national and international celebrities would make it onto this list, as devoted voluntary service or intellectual achievement are deemed too dull to make good media transmission, as is good news generally.

The modern pagan family is characterised by good communication, especially listening, and shared family values, beliefs and interests, all of which helps to smooth the way through the turbulent teenage years and negotiate a path around harmful subcultures. The teenager equipped with a consistent set of personal, community and environmental values is better able to make the transition to independence, and those values should eventually resurface and reassert themselves after any period of going astray. A family which has constructively encouraged togetherness and sharing of problems; extended caring from the home to the community; valued all honest effort and contribution however modest; avoided waste and unnecessary purchases; repaired rather than discarded; saved energy, recycled and composted; eschewed products with unnatural additives and avoided chemicals in the garden and home; made rather than bought; walked, cycled, travelled by bus or train rather than used the car; and encouraged both intellectual and healthy physical development, will have laid a solid foundation. In such a family, competition, aggression, demand, materialism and self-aggrandisement are less likely, and co-operation, synthesis, reason, care and self-fulfilment are more likely. But however coherent the family philosophies are, and however consistent their implementation, the parents still have schools to contend with.

A modern pagan reaction to institutional schooling

The belief that schools extrapolate what is begun in the home is naivety of the most expansive kind, and probably modern pagans constitute one of the community groups that is least well served in that their intellectual, social and environmental objectives are least likely to be met. But in most countries schooling is compulsory, although many other harmful experiences are banned. Not for nothing do people quote the apocryphal advice 'Never let your schooling interfere with your education'. The institutional oppression of the cultured individual, prescribed syllabuses and schemes of work, and the suppression of individuality, amount to a straitjacket that prohibits youngsters from their early years from developing a solid foundation of natural aptitudes, knowledge and practical skills before embarking on man-made, academic pursuits, such as they might need to be able to pursue a chosen career, let alone the even heavier responsibility of citizenship and future parenthood. No new pagan could possibly be happy with schools in their present state, for the attitudes they want to see in the growing generation, as outlined in this book, are not, with the best will in the world from teaching staff, going to be instilled under the present highly institutionalised state education regimes.

Schools most likely to appeal to modern pagans, namely small community schools, are being closed in villages and small towns in the name of economy of scale, whereas a better strategy would be to keep them open and properly resource them, and to split large schools into smaller, more manageable units. The basic philosophy in education at present is competition, and that creates losers as well as winners, failures as well as successes, based on institutional criteria that mean little to individual parents who just want to see their own child's potential maximised. Children are ever in danger of being swallowed up in the rat race within large, impersonal schools, where anonymity, alienation, disruption by unruly pupils, persistent, unchecked bullying, and the other consequences of the current epidemic of bad parenthood in the developed world have just as serious an influence on them as prescriptive teaching programmes. Modern pagan parents are more interested in their children learning practical skills and developing their intellects than in being on the receiving end of these influences and programmes. Not only are some of the non-academic parts of these programmes of little relevance to modern pagan children and their parents' aspirations, but there are serious deficiencies in the training of teachers to deliver them. Many reputable organisations and educational institutions have produced teaching materials on social, health, environmental, and economic awareness, but these are little used as they are branded as propaganda by the politicians who regulate curricula. All is tightly controlled, regulated, and assessed, with little or no room for an alternative imaginative and creative approach. But, if educational law allows, modern pagan parents can take matters into their own hands.

The Folk School

Parental control of schooling

Parents, not schools, are better placed to be legally responsible for their children's behaviour and education, free as they are from the constraints of politics and the temptation to engage in mass social engineering. They have only what no government can claim to have, a direct personal interest in their own children's education – as individuals, not as components of national examination statistics. In many countries of the world, where legislation permits, lifestyle and religious groups, and local communities, have successfully set up and managed their own schools. They have drawn upon natural parental instincts and aspirations, and the tenets of their personal philosophy, rather than centrally directed prescriptive didactic programmes. Initially, such parents may have worried about whether they would meet society's educational expectations, but far more important for their children is that they meet their own expectations and give their children what state institutions have singularly failed to give them.

In no measure do modern pagans wish to opt out of the educational routes to sound academic and vocational qualifications and the careers that these open up. But to them, schools are best confined to being examination factories for academic and vocational qualifications, and are not seen as an extension of social services provision. Teachers are best employed solely to teach the subjects they are qualified to teach. All other aspects of a child's education, especially matters concerning personal attitudes and relationships, sex education, healthy lifestyle, the family, community and citizenship, religious education, and the natural environment, modern pagans prefer to be in the hands of parents, using either an expanded home education scheme, with the necessary financial assistance, or small, parent-managed Folk Schools. The term Folk School is used for a school run by modern pagans for modern pagan children whose parents wish to be in control of those curricular aspects just mentioned, and who wish to have the freedom to introduce others of their choosing. Children of non-pagan parents demonstrably in sympathy with the aims of the Folk School would be welcome. Schools managed by other local interest groups are referred to herein as Local Community Schools.

The organisation of the Folk School

The New Folk Year
(• indicates the nine national holidays)

The Folk School Year
(• indicates national holidays)

Winter
1 November to 31 January
21 December • The Winter Solstice
31 December/1 January • Twelfth Night

Winter Holiday
12 December to 2 January
Winter Term
3 January to 11 March
31 January •, 1 February •, 2 February •

Spring
1 February to 30 April
31 January/1 February • The Spring Festival
21 March • The Vernal Equinox

Spring Holiday
12 March to 1 April
Spring Term
2 April to 8 June
31 April •, 1 May •, 2 May •

Summer
1 May to 31 July

30 April/1 May • The Summer Festival

21 June • The Summer Solstice

Summer Holiday
9 June to 2 July

Summer Term
3 July to 10 September

31 July •, 1 August •, 2 August •

Autumn
1 August to 31 October

31 July/1 August • The Autumn Festival

21 September • The Autumnal Equinox

31 October/1 November • The Winter Festival

Autumn Holiday
11 September to 1 October

Autumn Term
2 October to 11 December

31 October •, 1 November •, 2 November •

A number of organisational possibilities present themselves, according to local preference and custom. A split of four days in academic/vocational school and one day in Folk School, or three days and two days respectively, or a long morning in academic/vocational school and a short afternoon in Folk School each day, could all be organised on a suitable local basis. The Folk School Year is based on the New Folk Year, and has terms of approximately equal length and holidays spaced out at regular intervals. The establishment of national pagan holidays ensures that the Folk School is not in session on modern pagan festival days.

Parent-managed Folk Schools would normally have to be state-funded. Their size would necessarily be limited, in order that they remain local and reflect local wishes, including keeping to the folk calendar. In keeping with modern pagan philosophy on the extended family, the Folk School should be so constituted, and access to, and facilities in, the buildings so arranged, that all children in the community, irrespective of physical or sensory disability, can attend. In the long run it is more expensive to keep children apart, as the soaring cost of inequality, discrimination and segregation testifies. In the Folk School, those who do have a certain capacity would be responsible for assisting those who do not, and they would do so in rotation so that all come in contact with the spectrum of capacities and incapacities that exist in the local community. Whilst the career value of learning a foreign language is undeniable, it is deemed important for modern pagan children to also learn sign language, Braille, and any other means of communication used by the sensorily disadvantaged groups in the community. This would remove one of the most significant barriers that isolates these discriminated groups from those who use only vocal and written communication, and promote friendship and understanding within the Folk School.

The organisation of the Folk School on a mutual help basis within the student body is complemented by voluntary service within the community, where each is assigned to help someone without one of their capacities or incapacities. A normal-sighted adult in the community being assisted by a blind student is an imaginative idea for community service, but it is necessary to pursue it in order that positive recognition of talent and equal worth can be achieved.

Parents of children attending state or private schools five days a week may choose to set up Folk Schools at the weekends. These could serve a dual purpose as meeting places for modern pagans as well as provide the opportunity for them to pass on their skills through the folk curriculum. Associations could be developed with local organisations, charities and care homes sympathetic to the objectives of the folk curriculum, with mutual benefit in terms of expertise and voluntary assistance.

The Folk School curriculum

The broad sweep of the Folk School curriculum has already been referred to, but there are certain specific issues to address.

In the new pagan mind there is no difference in worth between academic and vocational subjects, as craftsmanship and applied science and technology are as highly valued as intellectual achievement. Elderly craftsmen and craftswomen like stonemasons, thatchers, furniture makers, seamstresses, etc are disappearing with no successors to follow them because of their lowly status in society and limited earning potential. Restoration of historic buildings is severely hampered already by shortage of experts with the necessary craft skills. It is time for a concerted effort to reverse in people's minds the lowly position of practical expertise, but to deserve accolades craftsmanship must be skilled enough to merit them. Bad workmanship is as much a blight on a country as a population unable to communicate and to handle numbers, but it is not brought so frequently to public attention. Perhaps one job of the Folk School might be to resurrect traditional craft skills and raise their social status before they disappear, as well as ensure that all young people have the practical life skills to complement the personal, social, health and environmental aspects of their education.

In order to make progress towards ending religious discrimination and discrimination against the non-religious, modern pagans would be in favour of academic/vocational schools' curricula having no religious components, nor compulsory acts of worship, save for examination courses in Religious Studies on an optional basis. Although modern paganism is not a spiritual lifestyle, modern pagans live amongst people who have religious conviction, and it is a vital step towards fraternal harmony that each understands the basic tenets and philosophies of the other. A broadly based religious awareness programme is therefore deemed important in Folk Schools, for to understand religion, undeniably a force in the shaping of cultures around the world, should be part of every child's education, including that of modern pagan children. But compulsory denominational Religious Education would in academic/vocational schools not be acceptable to modern pagans. There is no reason whatsoever why religious groups interested in setting up Local Community Schools with a religious ethos, and modelled on the Folk School, should not do so.

It would suit early risers like modern pagans to start the daily Folk School programme early to make full use of the morning, the most intellectually productive time of the day, with community service and other off-site activities to follow. A practical approach is envisaged wherever appropriate. Many suitable elements for the Folk School curriculum follow naturally from topics introduced and discussed in this book, namely personal holistic health care and natural remedies; basic first aid; natural diet and cookery; organic gardening and nature conservation; ecology and sustainable harvesting; pet care; folk singing, folk dancing, folk arts and crafts;

sexuality and sexual health; personal finances and financial management, including debt avoidance; voluntary service; understanding paganism and world religions; and specific topics of local interest.

All-age schooling

Adult and continuing education fit very comfortably into the modern pagan philosophy of lifelong learning, so the Folk School could also take on a role similar to that of adult education evening classes. Such a role would further promote the ideals of new paganism and empower people through friendships and sharing of contacts and information. Folk Schools admitting all ages could be run on a commercial basis like adult education institutes, with the fees paid by adults subsidising the free classes provided for children. Those who may be interested in adopting certain elements of modern pagan lifestyle, such as a natural diet, or creating a natural garden, would be welcome to enrol. There is a great deal of scope and communal momentum possible in the conception of the Folk School, and modern pagans are strongly urged to consider setting them up in their localities.

Educational standards amongst modern pagans in mainstream schools

Modern pagans value education highly, and their children need little prompting to strive for the most exacting intellectual and ethical standards. Theirs is an image to change, in a society that has all manner of unwarranted attitudes towards them and their lifestyle, and progress towards acceptance will only come when modern pagans earn influential positions that enable them to influence events, and when popular and proven aspects of modern paganism advance from people's consciences to official policy-making and official action.

10
Folk Ways in a Technological Age

From natural past to technological present

This chapter is about principles and choices, and about compromising neither. To live comfortably as a modern pagan within a technological society will require you to reassess your capabilities, versatility and degree of independence. Your body has enormous reserves of stamina, healing power and physical dexterity, but you may well underestimate them greatly, and imagine you cannot complete or even attempt various tasks without technological help. It is likely that as you have matured into adulthood you have become increasingly dependent on technology, with its attendant manual and sensory de-skilling and lapsing physical fitness, and suffered a consequent lowering of self-esteem and loss of independence. There is in all probability nothing wrong with your senses or muscular co-ordination, just lack of exercising them, trusting them and reliance on them. Regaining use and control of your body is a vital step in relieving stress in our noisy, hectic world. The simple act of walking is so much more relaxing and personally empowering than relying on the technical and organisational complexities and vast consumption of resources of a transport service, which is almost certain to let you down some of the time, thereby causing avoidable problems. You may of course have no choice but to use public transport or a car, but if walking is a choice you will be all the better for taking it.

If you examine each facet of your life you will probably be surprised as to the degree of technological intrusion into it. Some very important aspects have virtually been taken over by technology, an example being the way that people have been replaced by automated telecommunications.

A logical first step to reducing your dependence on technology would be to learn more about your body and how to keep it fit, and then to use it rather than employ technological devices. In all likelihood you will not be able to manage the sort of manual labour that was common in the days of the industrial revolution, or match the quick-thinking, strength and stamina of the hunter–gatherer, or even the explorers of previous centuries. But you may still be eating the amount and type of food that physically active people ate before the days of labour-saving devices, even though your daily exertion is minute by comparison. In so doing you risk obesity and its attendant physiological problems.

Such developments as the revival of folk medicine, the employment of more natural materials, promoting whole body fitness, and a simpler and more personally fulfilling lifestyle have all happened because they can co-exist with technological change in other aspects of our lives. Continued co-existence in harmony requires the recognition that individuality and lifestyle are more important than technical advancement and commercial gain. Walking to the North or South Pole is still an achievement and a communion with nature despite the modern communications equipment, satellite navigations systems and backup teams with powerful transport that now accompany it. Preparing technically for such an expedition is nowadays straightforward, whereas the physical and mental preparation and control are much more worthy of admiration. Doing without any technology in your daily life and going completely 'back to nature', although very nostalgic and romantic, is unrealistic these days. It is certainly not a suitable preparation for your children who must face life in a technological world, learn to deploy technology responsibly and understand what is good and what is bad technology in terms of natural sustainability.

There are six key concepts to the modern pagan approach to life in a technological society: these are choice, personal empowerment, simplicity, practicality, need and sustainability, and they can readily be applied to each technological application you contemplate making. Moreover, as part of your commitment to re-examining your relationship with technology, you could adopt the practice of constantly reviewing your use of it. Is it your choice to use a device, or have you been persuaded by advertising or peer pressure? Is it of necessity you have decided to use it or is it just that you haven't considered the non-technological alternatives? Does it give you the same feeling of being in control, or are you likely to become a slave to such devices and therefore adopt them unnecessarily or more frequently? Is it depersonalising? Does it take over decision-making, intervention and adjustment? Are you consuming resources and damaging the environment, and are the inevitable environmental consequences irreversible? Are you happier doing without it? These are very important questions to ask yourself before applying technology to any process over which you have choice.

It will be easier for you to appreciate the dexterity and ingenuity with which non-technological societies cope with the exigencies of life if you take an interest in how your ancestors performed everyday tasks. They understood the real meaning of words like 'necessity', for they had neither choice nor leisure time in any amount. But with their limited resources they made remarkable achievements and deserve respect and admiration for being the founders of the technological age, even if their developments were not always wisely or humanely deployed by politicians and entrepreneurs. The more you and your community can rekindle respect for your heritage the easier it will be to accept the moral obligation of preserving it for future generations to learn the lessons of history. One of these lessons is the ascendancy of evolution over revolution. An example of the devastation to cultural heritage and attitudes towards it caused by revolution was the desire to 'sweep away the old' in the aftermath of the two twentieth-century world wars. This critical period saw the end of tried and tested ways; durable, functional, craftsman-made articles; and closeness to nature and community; to be replaced by cheaply made mass-produced items with built-in obsolescence, fashion, style, and fancy gimmicks; and the swamping of local dependency by regional, national and international commerce.

But you are not powerless to resist being carried along with these trends. Keep the six key concepts constantly in mind, and forget trends and keeping up with the latest fashion in this or that. By allowing yourself to be persuaded to increase the pace of your life and change things more frequently you are accepting that commercial profit, superficiality and consumption of precious resources are more important than durability, functionality and efficiency. The most significant and far-reaching of the six is simplicity, for no other determination will rid the world of unnecessary, wasteful, polluting technology faster, and allow you to take full control of your life. Using these fundamental observations as a basis, we can now expand on the practices of what might be termed eco-paganism.

Technological pollution

There is a form of pollution that currently has no recognised name, but which may be called technological pollution. It is the use of precious material and human resources for the manufacture of short-lived, unnecessary devices. This is the easiest form of pollution for you to avoid. Look in your garden shed at the number of tools that consist solely of blade and handle. If one part breaks it can be replaced. Furthermore, your use of these tools exercises your muscles, develops your dexterity and co-ordination, and produces little noise, no fumes, and results in no consumption of the fossil fuel resources that generally produce electricity. Compare that with a power tool, powered lawn mower, or electrical gadget. They may save you time, but at what cost? Repetitive strain or vibration injuries, a higher electricity bill and depleted resources, noise, disempowerment of your manual skills, few possibilities for recycling, and problems with disposal, are some of the costs. If, as in most countries, the manufacturer is not liable to a surcharge on the principle that 'the polluter pays', are you happy to purchase the item at all? Are you also happy to buy a device that has been marketed without any environmental audit of the consequences of its use and without any form of technological licensing to guarantee that it is safe, quiet, energy-efficient, non-polluting, recyclable or biodegradable, and actually needed?

These are choices you are free to make. Instead of tolerating the noise and fumes of your power mower, you might consider changing your garden design ideas and getting rid of the lawn, or using a low-growing alternative to grass. Instead of throwing away and replacing blunt tools, learn to sharpen them. If you can, turn screws with a manual screwdriver, and return to using other manually operated tools as far as is practical. Undoubtedly, many power tools allow jobs to be done quickly and cleanly, which would otherwise mean a long, exhausting, uneconomic, and perhaps impossible haul with manual tools, so this issue is one of balance, and it is the consumer's choice how the scales tilt.

Every time you return to a hands-on approach to a task you are taking charge of the technique, its outcome and its consequences. Moreover, you are putting your personal stamp on it, and you can feel justly proud of your achievement. Automation of a process, where your intervention is not only unnecessary but can also be denied, means you have no power of control or adjustment, and no chance of putting your own mark on the process. All you can do is select from someone else's choices and chance to luck that a malfunction will not occur. You must ask yourself if you are content to see the need for your contribution eliminated and for paralysis to be the inevitable consequence of malfunction. If you have been trapped inside a vehicle when the central computerised control of various devices like locks has been damaged in an accident you will have some idea of the health, practical, logistical and financial problems that denying human intervention can create. The deployment of automation does not have to be automatic, it is another decision to be consciously made, not done purely in the name of technical advancement.

Depersonalisation of communication

Even your choice of appropriate style of communication can be taken away from you by the depersonalised use of combinations of statements from computerised comment banks to compose, for example, educational reports or business references. If you have the choice, personalise all communications. Write letters by hand whenever you can, and instead of emailing or telephoning colleagues in a nearby room go in and talk to them. Not only does person-to-person communication sit more comfortably with new pagan togetherness, your linguistic skills will be better developed and regularly honed, so that precisely the right nuance can be found and employed, and face-to-face contact gives you far more chance of developing an open and understanding relationship where facial expressions, gestures and body language can be beneficially used and interpreted. This approach is especially important for your children, who belong to a generation often described as poorly communicating, semi-literate, and manually de-skilled.

Environmentally auditing your use of technology

Technological achievements are not going to be abandoned, but they can be conceived, developed and used more sensitively, more safely and with more control. Science and Technology are not incompatible with paganism; indeed they have many of the aspects of paganism, such as practicality, intellectual honesty, and the understanding and harnessing of nature's forces and resources. But technological inventions are only compatible with paganism if there is not an unacceptable cost in developing and using them. One person's noise or waste is another person's torment, because for every freedom there is a consequence and therefore a responsibility, and when pollution of all kinds is regarded as an individual as well as an industrial and govern-mental concern then consumer choice can bring its awesome power to bear.

As a modern pagan consumer you will want to take the opportunity to do an environmental audit on each item of technology that you contemplate buying, having established a genuine need. Look particularly at how and with what human and natural resources it was manufactured; how safely it can be disposed of; what potential it has for recycling; what power consumption normal use requires; what pollution in the form of noise, fumes, and waste output is likely to result from its use; and what adverse health factors may compromise its long-term use. Such an audit should be done as consistently as reading the lists of ingredients on packets of processed food.

Conservation of natural resources

Conservation is a central theme in paganism, and it is a basic tenet of modern paganism that the human species is not a special creation but just a very numerous and demanding one, and the demands it makes on the natural environment have been evident since early recorded history. Only when the human species began to shed its arrogance did it learn that it was part of all natural cycles, and that pressure on the environment meant pressure on all of us. Learning country ways is to appreciate when this pressure is starting, and what interdependencies need protection. If the environment is shaped in unnatural ways there will doubtless have to be an unnatural response to the problems caused, and it is a consequence of urban living and corporate control of resources that many no longer understand what is or is not a natural, safe, sustainable response. The water suppliers in developed countries, for example, have taken the responsibility away from the user, who therefore has largely lost interest in the management of this natural resource. Natural resources of several kinds are now remote from consumers, who no longer link them directly with their needs, but expect to have them on tap without having to take responsibility for them.

Just as you are urged to audit technology before you purchase, so there is an equivalent obligation to monitor your own usage of natural resources and those produced technologically, so that you can cut down, cut out, save and reuse, or find more acceptable alternatives as appropriate. Saving and reusing household water; switching off unnecessary electrical devices or replacing them with manual alternatives; walking and cycling instead of using powered transport and using public rather than private powered transport are all well-known examples. An audit of your own lifestyle will reveal many more.

Communal responsibility for the local environment

In the same way we are dependent on natural equilibria we are dependent on each other. Doing things communally, with everyone making a contribution of labour and resources, is far more efficient than individuals all trying to do essentially the same thing on a small scale, and consumes fewer resources. Communal labour, without power tools and heavy machinery, can achieve a great deal in terms of rubbish clearance and environmental enhancement and restoration, as well as undertake new projects. Communal initiatives also make the local environment safer because everyone has a stake in it and is proud of their contributions. Society at large is only a safe environment if we all take responsibility for it and if we can trust that this is the case. Just as a local act of pollution can have far-reaching effects, so crime in general affects not just the victim but everybody. Once upon a time no-one dared to commit a crime in a village, as it meant ostracism and lasting consequences for the perpetrator and family. If we had this pressure back on a larger scale to suit conurbation living and mixed communities in both towns and countryside, with nobody minding their own business in the face of anti-social behaviour, then the considerate majorities could reclaim their communities.

This section of the book is not concerned with global ecological problems and the promotion of action groups of eco-warriors, although many pagans may choose to support such groups in various ways either actively or morally, and is not about using consumer power for political change. It concerns the everyday aspects of lifestyle that offer scope for protecting and improving local environment and encouraging children to do likewise. Some people show despair and helplessness in the face of huge environmental problems, but the collective will to tackle them can only be generated initially by individually successful contributions, however small, to local environmental consciousness and protection. Pressure on any ecosystem eventually affects us all, in what is global interdependence, but to bring about global equilibrium there must first be local equilibria, and that is where eco-paganism most effectively starts. Eco-paganism was laughed at once upon a time as retrograde simplicity, but now it is widely recognised that such a lifestyle is as morally enriching as it is healthy and materially harmonious with nature, and the only foundation for future generations that we can responsibly bequeath.

Waste and recycling

It is part of the new pagan philosophy to simplify life and reduce clutter, to buy only what is really needed, and to think about possible reuse rather than disposal. It is often an easy decision to make to forego buying an article when it is heavily, gaudily packaged and supported by a big and unconvincing advertising campaign, as neither of these accoutrements would be necessary if the quality and usefulness of the article spoke for itself. Before the issue of recycling arises, consider carefully how you can cut down on purchases, especially those that are packaged. The use of too much packaging, and far too much complex packaging, for small consumer items, especially food, is part of the deliberate deception of the consumer by manufacturers and their advertisers into thinking there is more in the package than there actually is. We can all think of a packet that has stayed the same size for years while the weight of the contents has gone steadily down. When we have been reconditioned to paying more for less, we are then offered a 'giant' or 'bumper' sized version for even more money, although it is probably to the original specification. Up to a third of household rubbish can be packaging, so by supporting the use of returnable containers, buying in bulk, and unwrapping excessively packaged goods and leaving the packaging in the shops, you will be making an important contribution towards ending this practice. Packaging is also a contributory factor in generating a 'throw away and buy new' mentality instead of encouraging people to recycle by reducing the amount of unnecessary packaging that they are burdened with. Recycling means less environmental damage, lower demand for virgin resources, and reduced consumption of energy on reprocessing than on making items from raw materials.

Once you have streamlined your purchasing strategy you can organise the recycling of those containers and other items whose purpose for you has been fulfilled. Sort the items carefully according to the recycling facilities available, but typically these might be paper; cardboard; plastic; iron and steel; aluminium; other non-ferrous metals; and white, brown, green and other coloured glass. You can add textiles for recycling through charity or remanufacture outlets; sump oil from car engine maintenance; items made from rubber; batteries; refrigerators and other household appliances; unused constructional materials and unwanted timber or branches. Garden waste, household peelings and leftovers are best composted. This is just a basic list to get you started, and there are additional specialist disposal facilities for particular items or chemicals. Your local authority or public library will be able to give you a list.

It is not true that saving on paper wastage helps reduce the felling of rainforest trees, for such trees are normally hardwood species and used for furniture, window frames and the like. It is true, however, to say that recycling paper allows land to be left in its natural state or set aside for regenerated forest, rather than used to plant more pines for wood pulp with the lower biodiversity that their forests have and the periodic need for felling and replanting, if the latter ever happens. Glass, which is made from sand, limestone and soda ash, requires quarrying and landscape destruction as well as energy for its high-temperature manufacture. Recycling glass uses less energy, and bottle return schemes and standardisation of sizes and shapes would help reuse. Much the same applies to metals, and their recycling is even more desperately needed because of severely depleted metalliferous deposits. Reducing energy consumption is most critical for aluminium, whose extraction consumes vast amounts of energy, but also important for copper, tin and iron. As steel cans are magnetic they can easily be sorted from aluminium ones in preparation for their return.

The list of environmentally damaging items to avoid grows ever longer. Most consumers now know about aerosols containing chlorofluorocarbons (CFCs) and their contribution to ozone depletion, and non-biodegradable plastics whose sheer volume is rapidly filling up landfill sites, but it behoves all new pagans to keep in regular touch with industrial and commercial practice and its consequences and take appropriate consumer action. But remember, recycling on its own is not enough. By simplifying your habits, limiting purchasing, leaving packaging in shops, as well as recycling, you will be playing your part in giving the regenerative powers of the natural environment a fighting chance.

Pollution

Regulating your practices and purchases to minimise pollution requires both research and planning. Much local pollution is basically litter, packaging or containers of various kinds, and it is to be hoped you have already taken steps to avoid the purchase of packaged items and to recycle what is unavoidably acquired. But the consequences of human activity produce local pollution that is of international concern, namely to the atmosphere, watercourses, and soil, so it is imperative that all activities are examined that result in any form of emissions, run-off or disposal.

The biochemical cycles of the elements, especially of nitrogen, sulphur and lead, have all been radically changed from their natural state through pollution of the air, rivers, ponds, lakes, seas, forests and soil, and we are at present trapped in a progressive and accelerating sequence of combustion, tree felling and land clearance, leading to a serious gaseous imbalance in the atmosphere's natural composition. The latter is gradually changing, with the percentage of compounds like carbon dioxide and sulphur dioxide increasing through the burning of fossil fuels. What combustion, especially of fossil fuels, can you do without, or can be saved by changing your consumption habits? Instead of bonfires, compost your household and garden waste. Minimise your use of the car in favour of walking, cycling or public transport, and make sure central heating and other household devices employing combustion are as efficient as possible by maximising insulation and rationing their use. Disposal of chemicals into the environment is equally serious, and the amount of permanently fouled land continues to grow. Local authorities provide guidance on disposal or recycling of all chemical substances and appliances containing chemicals, like refrigerators, to guard against dumping in landfill sites where the chemicals can seep into the ground.

The build-up of greenhouse gases limits the amount of heat that can escape from the atmosphere, and this contributes to global warming. According to meteorological scientists, it requires only an average rise in temperature of a few degrees to bring tropical conditions to areas that are currently temperate, with melting of polar ice and a rise in sea levels, and an average fall of a few degrees would bring on another Ice Age. Associated weather changes will disrupt current agricultural and constructional practices, sharply reduce survivability of crops and farm animals, and cause building techniques of all kinds to undergo expensive revision. All of this will take resources away from ordinary people. The causes of the greenhouse effect are a catalogue of environmental neglect and abuse. Fifty per cent of the effect comes from generated carbon dioxide (CO_2), 80 per cent of which is from burning fossil fuels and 20 per cent from deforestation and other vegetation clearance and erosion. The more land is returned to a natural state, particularly if replanted with local species of trees and shrubbery, the greater will be our chances of restabilising the atmosphere. Local and national replanting schemes are urgently needed throughout the world, as is a return to natural farming, and you should use your influence at whatever level you can. Then there is emission of methane gas from decomposition of buried waste, coal mines and gas leaks; chlorofluorocarbons (CFCs) from aerosols, refrigerants, air-conditioning units, plastic foam used in upholstery, solvents and sterilants for medical equipment; nitrous oxide (N_2O) from fossil fuel burning and land clearance; and ozone (O_3) from electrical equipment and chemical reactions caused by the effect of sunlight on hydrocarbons and nitrogen oxides.

Simplicity of lifestyle is a significant response to the accumulation of these pollutants. Many of these contaminants, or the devices containing them, are not necessary, and could either be dispensed with or replaced by biodegradable or more ecologically friendly alternatives. Electrical aids of various kinds can be replaced by mechanical or manual devices, or just by more tolerance and adaptability. Once you focus your mind on a simpler lifestyle the list of what you can do without will begin to grow, and a further examination of the present consequences of pollution will emphasise the wisdom of this strategy.

Certain components of the atmosphere are either under serious threat of depletion or are increasing in concentration alarmingly. Ozone protects us from solar ultraviolet radiation, which causes skin cancer and cataracts, kills phytoplankton in the upper zones of the ocean, which are at the start of food chains, and retards crop growth. This vital molecule is depleted by reacting with chemicals, such as CFCs, released into the atmosphere, so it is not only unwise to use aerosols, but unnecessary when pump-action sprays or roll-ons are available. The presence of sulphur dioxide (SO_2) and nitrogen oxides in the atmosphere, put there by emissions from industry, coal- and oil-fired power stations, and vehicle exhausts, is the principal cause of acid rain, as these two chemicals are converted into acidic products, including sulphuric and nitric acids. A proper level of investment would see these emissions cleaned up, for the technology has been in existence for some time. Acid rain damages all plant life, poisons waterways, acidifies soils (thereby lowering crop yields), corrodes stone and metal, and causes all animals respiratory problems. Hydrocarbons in exhaust fumes are a serious hazard, for some are carcinogenic, and some combine with nitrogen oxides to produce ozone. Catalytic converters partially remove these chemicals, and you may choose to have one fitted if you need a car, but the devices are neither a perfect nor a long-term solution. These problems are all soluble, if the international will and co-operation, and national investment, could all be brought to bear on them. Your contribution to public pressure to this end is vital.

The sea is equally badly polluted, and to upset the sea's ecological balance is to upset the world's largest ecosystem, with its enormous protein food stocks, its importance in the world's rainfall and other weather patterns, and its part in the global sulphur and sodium cycles. Radioactive and other toxic waste, untreated sewage, industrial effluent, run-offs of farm chemicals like fertilisers and from silage and slurry, waste and discharges from ships, oil spillage, and detergents all find their way into the sea and inland waterways too. Bacteriological levels in the coastal waters of developed countries are still too high for safety, and birds continue to die in large numbers from oil discharge. Detergents and fertilisers cause eutrophication (excessive growth of micro-organisms leading to reduction of levels of oxygen, light and food for aquatic life) of waterways, particularly nitrate and phosphate components, so the case for buying phosphate-free detergents is very compelling. The illegal dumping or burial of drums of toxic waste continues to pose hazards when the drums corrode and leak, the seepage ending up in our watercourses.

Pollution on an industrial scale is a problem for governments rather than for householders, but your reaction as a consumer at the end of the commercial chain is very important, as it sets off a chain reaction that goes back to the commercial source. What you and others do not buy or use will eventually cease to be produced; what you recycle does not need to be remade. Every natural fertiliser and phosphate-free detergent you buy will reduce production of environmentally damaging ones, and if you can use only natural fertilisers and cleansing agents then so much the better.

Fossil fuels are finite resources, their extraction environmentally damaging and disposal of waste products difficult. Electricity generation by fossil fuel burning produces greenhouse gases and acid rain gases, and generation by nuclear power stations produces radioactive waste whose disposal presents a hazard that will last long into the future. Light and heat are forms of pollution, the former all but preventing astronomy in urban areas. You can help in many ways with energy conservation by responsible household management, turning off what is not needed, using low-consumption fluorescent tube lights, instead of high-energy incandescent bulbs, and buying low-consumption appliances. Cavity walls and lofts can readily be insulated, pipes lagged, openings sealed against draughts, and windows and doors double-glazed – but not with hardwood frames – or protected with secondary glazing. Check to see that elderly relatives and neighbours have these improvements, if necessary by helping them apply for local authority grants if these are available. Materials such as CFCs and urea-formaldehyde polymers should be avoided, as they are known to be environmentally toxic. It is a pity that wind and wave power have not progressed satisfactorily; the former is unfortunately noisy, and wind farms tend to be regarded as an eyesore, and both have insufficient output currently for even modest needs. It is, nevertheless, worthwhile to support further research into alternative power generation.

Transport and travel

How far you are prepared to modify your travel arrangements is a serious test of your modern pagan commitment to a cleaner, quieter, safer environment. Vehicle travel has become highly individual and a convenience around which human society has increasingly revolved. People have come, by their chosen commitments and the expectation by themselves and others that they can travel anywhere, to depend upon their cars, but they burn fossil fuels; require large amounts of metal to construct; pollute the air with exhaust fumes containing oxides of carbon, sulphur and nitrogen, not to mention lead compounds and carcinogenic by-products from hydrocarbons; take up a lot of space; require vast areas of land for roads and parking; are noisy; encourage laziness; cause accidents; and are costly. More roads and facilities for car travel seem to lead to more car production and use. The reduction of road noise is an achievable objective that has been neglected on cost grounds, yet would add enormously to the quality of life for millions of people. No amount of speeding, drunkenness by drivers, bad driving, stress, congestion or injury seems to lead in developed countries to a significant return to public transport, which is still regarded as unreliable, slow, expensive and having a limited number of routes and destinations. Furthermore, too little progress has been made in providing access for disabled people. It does not seem to matter that town driving is not cost-effective for a single car driver as average speeds are low and fuel usage high, or that more use of public transport would reduce road accidents, pollution and noise.

There would be clear health benefits and an improvement in the quality of our lives if there were more use of rail, with more electrification schemes, and of buses. A network of cycle paths, better safety and security for cycles, and consideration of cyclists by other road users, would encourage cycling, just as adequate personal security on public transport, and at train and bus stations, would encourage women and children to use it in greater numbers and with greater frequency. Putting freight back onto the railways would reduce the number of heavy lorries on roads, and with it the vibration damage they do to the roads themselves, buildings, underground service pipes, and bridges, not to mention the noise and diesel pollution produced. One goods train can carry the loads of many lorries, but such an obvious point has consistently been lost on successive governments in developed countries, where traffic pollution is highest.

The message is clear for ordinary folk: take the initiative yourselves. Waiting for improved public transport services before deciding to use them is a policy that has got us nowhere, so perhaps we should all be prepared to use them immediately in very large numbers, and suffer overcrowding and inconvenience until transport providers respond. Any provider with any business sense will not fail to do so. By studying public transport routes and being prepared to consider working and living near to them, a start could be made towards a strong lobby for integrated, reliable public transport schemes. Travel by public transport can be a very productive time for you, for reading, writing, studying, composing, and so on, whereas car travel is simply movement, and stressful movement at that. Cycling and walking are wonderful exercise in the fresh air, and will help to slow the pace of life for you as part of your drive towards stress-free simplicity.

In Conclusion: The Joy of Modern Paganism

Modern paganism is a journey of discovery for some and of rediscovery for others, but for everyone who embarks upon the journey there are many new joys to be experienced. You will learn a great deal about yourself as a person, about your body and what it needs to stay healthy, and how much there is to be gained by using all your senses to the full to explore the beauty and interest of the natural world. Non-pagans treat a woodland walk like a thoroughfare, as a convenient way to get to their destinations, but new pagans take the trouble to observe the wildlife and the rich tapestry of colours; to appreciate the variety of scents that emanate from the plants and animals and which are carried on every breeze; to listen to the sounds of the wind, the rustling leaves, the birdsong, the rodents scuttling away through the undergrowth; to touch the bark and leaves and to taste the dew and nectar; to gather fungi, nuts and berries to eat; and then to arrive later but greatly fulfilled. You will also have the opportunity to try new foods and different methods of preparation and cooking, all of which will soon enable you to benefit from the boundless opportunities that good health and a physically fit body allow you to grasp.

Changing your lifestyle offers you the chance to take a fresh look at your natural abilities, your intellect, character and personality, and to begin to take more pride in them and develop them positively and usefully. Gaining fulfilment includes feeling good about yourself as well as about your relationships with others. Being in control of your thoughts and actions and setting worthwhile standards you are comfortable with as an individual, and which strengthen your ties with the family and community, allows you to make sensible, informed choices as you tread life's meandering path. The simpler your lifestyle, the more prosperous and carefree you will feel, and this feeling of prosperity has nothing to do with your finances but with the enrichment of your life.

Connecting with other people, especially family members you may have lost touch with or fallen out with, in a caring, supportive and understanding way will bring reciprocal rewards. The more family bonds are strengthened by togetherness, carefully thought-out guidance, consistent standards of upbringing, and an educational programme that is relevant and true to modern pagan ideals, the more productive and pleasurable the mutual dependence of the family unit will be.

Making a contribution towards your community and environment gives you a sense of ownership and belonging which no transient, factional or self-centred lifestyle can ever give you. By offering more than you take, and considering how your choices affect others, you will receive more and more favourable responses, and come to understand the real meaning of community spirit. The value of considering the whole natural world as your extended family will enhance both your control over your own life and your ability to make the right decisions based on your lifestyle audit. By coming to terms with accepting only useful, sustainable technology you will feel confident in the modern world yet comfortable with the responsible stance you have taken. Through the adoption of the modern pagan calendar, your new lifestyle will have a day-to-day focus and periodic celebratory days on which to fully engage with the most important aspects of modern paganism and significant aspects of pagan heritage that still have relevance today. You will also be sharing a way of living that has no social, ethnic, religious, political or other factional boundaries or exclusions.

Perhaps most crucially for some, you will find out, or renew your acquaintance with, what enjoyment really is, and learn not to confuse it with excess, over-indulgence, or forced excitement because you have the impression the occasion demands it. If you make responsible choices in your life and are in control of yourself, your body's health requirements, and your relationships, and you feel comfortable in your environment because your mind is attuned to it, you will not look upon enjoyment as something you derive from a change of routine, or as a relief from the pressures of life, but as a natural and nourishing experience to be gained from any or every aspect of your existence.

The purpose of the preceding pages has been to explain the essence of modern paganism and encourage readers to absorb it and restructure their lives in the new pagan way, for new paganism means old harmony regained. Encourage others to buy and read this book, and to achieve the aims it espouses. Above all, seek to explain, reason, demonstrate, and rely on the infection of your good example. No modern pagans should feel deprived because of their chosen path, for there are new pleasures to discover and new satisfactions to acquire from alternatives you feel more comfortable with. But sharing experiences within an alternative lifestyle is also important, because making the most satisfactory choices for your lifestyle can profitably come from being informed and from discussing options with others.

Modern paganism is both an individual and a communal movement, and it draws some of its effectiveness from the openness of its adherents and their readiness to discuss, consider and adapt, for the movement is not hidebound by any creed or bible, but driven only by basic survival philosophies and the desire for a fulfilling yet sustainable quality of life. You may meet opposition, but deal with it in a calm but determined way, for any aggressive response is against the spirit of new paganism and counter-productive. Your destiny is linked to that of your fellow planetary inhabitants, for you share the same living space, the same finite resources and thus have an unbreakable interdependence. No other association can productively influence your and your family's fate. Under modern paganism, the care, stability and future of those near and dear to you, those you live amongst, all your fellow living organisms and the ecosystems we all share, will be the essential objectives for the quality of all our lives and for our survival as a species.

Sources and Contacts

The following list of organisations is offered to readers seeking further information about some of the lifestyle activities and techniques mentioned in this book. Inclusion in the list does not necessarily imply recommendation by the author.

Chapter 5

Organic Farmers and Growers Limited, 50 High Street, Soham, Ely, Cambridgeshire, CB7 5HF, tel: 01353 722398, website: www.organicfood.co.uk

Scottish Organic Producers Association, Suite 15, Software Centre, Stirling University Innovation Park, Stirling, FK9 4NF, tel: 01786 458090, email: contact@sopa.demon.co.uk

Organic Food Federation, 1 Mowles Manor Enterprise Centre, Etling Green, Dereham, Norfolk, NR20 3EZ, tel: 01362 637314

For advice on organic gardening and organic outlets for fruit and vegetables:
The Soil Association, Bristol House, 40–56 Victoria Street, Bristol, BS1 6BY, tel: 0117 314 5000, website: www.soilassociation.org

For organic certification schemes and advice on genetically modified crops:
Soil Association Certification Limited, Bristol House, 40-56 Victoria Street, Bristol, BS1 6BY, tel: 0117 929 0661, email: info@soilassociation.org, website: www.soilassociation.org

Friends of the Earth, 26–28 Underwood Street, London, N1 7JQ, tel: 020 7490 1555, website: www.foe.org.uk

Greenpeace, Canonbury Villas, London, N1 2PN, tel: 020 7865 8100, email: info@uk.greenpeace.org, website: www.greenpeace.org

World Wildlife Fund for Nature, Panda House, Weyside Park, Godalming, Surrey, GU7 1XR, tel: 01483 426444, website: www.panda.org

For advice on encouraging wildlife:
The Royal Society for Nature Conservation, The Kiln, Waterside, Mather Road, Newark, NG24 1WT, tel: 01636 670000, website: www.rsnc.org

The Royal Society for Protection of Birds, The Lodge, Sandy, Bedfordshire, SG19 2DL, tel: 01767 680551, website: www.rspb.org.uk

Butterfly Conservation, Manor Yard, East Lulworth, Wareham, Dorset, BH20 5QP, tel: 0870 7744309, website: www.butterfly-conservation.org

Pesticide Action Network UK, Eurolink Centre, 49 Effra Road, London, SW2 1BZ, tel: 020 7274 8895. email: admin@pan-uk.org, website: www.pan-uk.org

Compassion in World Farming, Charles House, 5A Charles Street, Petersfield, Hampshire, GU32 3EH, tel: 01730 264208, email: compassion@ciwf.co.uk, website: www.ciwf.co.uk

For advice on how to change to organic farming:
Elm Farm Research Centre, Hampstead Marshall, Newbury, Berkshire, RG15 0HR, tel: 01488 658298, email: efrc@compuserve.com

For advice on humane treatment of livestock:
The Farm and Food Society, 4 Willifield Way, London, NW11 7XT, tel: 020 8455 0634

For advice on dealing with pesticide misuse, and on GM crops:
Green Network, 9 Clairmont Road, Lexden, Colchester, Essex, CO3 5BE, tel: 01206 546902, website: www.green-network.organics.org

For advice on organic gardening and farming, to both consumers and practitioners:
The Henry Doubleday Research Association, Ryton Organic Gardens, Ryton-on-Dunsmore, Coventry, CV8 3LG, tel: 02476 303517, website: www.hdra.org.uk

For advice on city farms and community garden projects (all organic):
National Federation of City Farms, The Green House, Hereford Street, Bedminster, Bristol, BS3 4NA, tel: 0117 923 1800, email: farmgarden@btinternet.com

Sustain, The Alliance for Better Food and Farming, 94 White Lion Street, London, N1 9PF, tel: 020 7837 1228, email: sustain@sustainweb.org, website: www.sustainweb.org

For advice on woodland management:
Forestry Commission GB and Scotland, Silvan House, 231 Corstorphine Road, Edinburgh, EH12 7AT, tel: 0845 367 3787, website: www.forestry.gov.uk

The Centre for Alternative Technology, Machynlleth, Powys, SY20 9AZ, tel: 01654 702400, website: www.cat.org.uk

For rare varieties in cultivation:
The Royal Horticultural Society, Wisley, Surrey; administrative offices at 80 Vincent Square, London SW1P 2PE, tel: 020 7834 4333, website: www.rhs.org.uk

Chapter 6
For details of retailers of free-range and organic meat:
'Q' Guild Limited, PO Box 44, Winterhill House, Snowden Drive, Winterhill, Milton Keynes, Buckinghamshire MK6 1AX, tel: 01908 235018

For literature on special dietary problems, allergies and food intolerance:
Berrydales Special Diet, New Berrydale House, 5 Lawn Road, London NW3 2XS, tel: 020 7722 2866

British Society for Allergy, Environmental and Nutritional Medicine, PO Box 7, Knighton, Powys, LD7 1WP, tel: 01547 550380, website: www.jnem.demon.co.uk

For literature and recipes for allergy or sensitivity to gluten:
The Coeliac Society, PO Box 220, High Wycombe, Buckinghamshire, HP11 2HY, tel: 01494 437278

A non-profit making organisation that campaigns for the right to safe, wholesome food, and is unconnected to the food industry, advertising or government:
The Food Commission (UK) Limited, 3rd Floor, 5–11 Worship Street, London EC2A 2BH, tel: 020 7628 7774

For advice on the benefits of breastmilk and breastfeeding of babies, and of bringing up children on a varied diet of natural foods:
La Leche League (GB), BM 3424, London WC1N 3XX, tel: 020 7242 1278

British Dietetic Association, 5th Floor, Charles House, 148/9 Great Charles Street, Queensway, Birmingham B3 3HT, tel: 0121 200 8080, website: www.bda.uk.com

The Vegetarian Society of the United Kingdom, Parkdale, Dunham Road, Altrincham, Cheshire, WA14 4QG, tel: 0161 925 2000, website: www.vegsoc.org

The Vegan Society, Donald Watson House, 7 Battle Road, St Leonards-on-Sea, East Sussex, TN37 7AA, tel: 01424 427393, website: www.vegansociety.com

Chapter 7

British Complementary Medicine Association, PO Box 2074, Seaford, East Sussex BN25 1HQ, tel: 0845 345 5977, website: www.bcma.co.uk

British Holistic Medical Association, 59 Lansdowne Place, Hove, East Sussex, BN3 1FL, tel: 01273 725951, website: www.bhma.org

Council for Complementary and Alternative Medicine, 63 Jeddo Road, London W12 6HQ, tel: 020 8735 0632

Institute for Complementary Medicine, PO Box 194, London SE16 1QZ, tel: 020 7237 5165, website: www.icmedicine.co.uk

Natural Medicines Society, PO Box 134, Chessington, Surrey, KT9 1HP, tel: 0870 240 4784, website: www.the-nms.org.uk

Research Council for Complementary Medicine, 60 Great Ormond Street, London WC1N 3JF, tel: 020 7833 8897, website: www.rccm.org.uk

British Acupuncture Council, 63 Jeddo Road, London W12 9HQ, tel: 020 8735 0400, website: www.acupuncture.org.uk

British Medical Acupuncture Society, 12 Marbury House, Higher Whitley, Warrington, WA4 4AW, tel: 01925 730727, website: www.medical-acupuncture.co.uk

Society of Teachers of the Alexander Technique, 129 Camden Mews, London NW1 9AH, tel: 020 7482 5159, website: www.stat.org.uk

Anthroposophical Medical Association, Park Attwood Clinic, Trimpley, Bewdley, DY12 1RE, tel: 01299 861444

Aromatherapy Organisations Council, PO Box 19834, London SE25 6WF, tel: 020 8251 7912, website: www.aocuk.net

Aromatherapy Trade Council, PO Box 387, Ipswich, Suffolk, IP2 9AN

The International Federation of Aromatherapists, Stamford House, 2–4 Chiswick High Road, London W4 1TH

British Association of Art Therapists, Mary Ward House, 5 Tavistock Place, London W1H 9SN, tel: 020 7383 3774

British Autogenic Society, Royal London Homoeopathic Hospital, Great Ormond Street, London WC1N 3HR, website: www.auto genic-therapy.org.uk

Dr Edward Bach Centre (Bach Flower Remedies), Mount Vernon, Sotwell, Wallingford, OX10 0PZ, tel: 01491 834678, website: www.bachcentre.com

The Bach Flower Remedy Programme, PO Box 65, Hereford, HR2 0UW

Biofeedback Foundation of Europe, PO Box 75416, 1070 AK Amsterdam, The Netherlands, tel: (0031) 20 44 22 631, website: www.bfe.org

Bowen Association UK (Bowen Technique), PO Box 4358, Dorchester, Dorset, DT1 3BA, tel: 0700 269 8324, website: www.bowen-technique.co.uk

Bowen Therapists European Register, 38 Portway, Frome, Somerset, BA11 1QU, website: www.thebowentechnique.com

Arterial Health Foundation (Chelation Therapy), PO Box 8, Atherton, Manchester, M46 9FY, tel: 01942 878400

General Chiropractic Council, 344–354 Gray's Inn Road, London WC1X 8BP, tel: 020 7713 5155, website: www. gcc-uk.org

British Chiropractic Association, 29 Whitley Street, Reading, Berkshire RG2 0EG, tel: 0118 757557

National Back Pain Association, 16 Elmtree Road, Teddington, TW11 8ST, tel: 020 8977 5474, website: www.backpain.org

Association and Register of Colon Hydrotherapists (Colonic Irrigation), 16 Drummond Ride, Tring, Hertfordshire, HP23 5DE, tel: 01442 827687, website: www.colonic-association.com

International Association of Colour Therapy, 46 Cottenham Road, Histon, Cambridge, CB4 9ES, website: www.international associationofcolour.com

Affiliation of Crystal Healing Organisations, PO Box 100, Exminster, Exeter, EX6 8YT, tel: 01479 841450, website: www.crystal-healing.org

Association for Dance Movement Therapy, c/o Quaker Meeting House, Wedmore Vale, Bristol, BS3 5HX, website: www.dmtuk.demon.co.uk

British Society of Dowsers, Sycamore Barn, Hastingleigh, Ashford, Kent, TN25 5HW, tel: 01233 750253, website: www.britishdowsers.org

British Association of Drama Therapists, 4 Sunnydale Villas, Durlston Road, Swanage

Feldenkreis Guild UK, (Feldenkreis Method), c/o The Bothy, Auchlunies Walled Garden, Aberdeen, AB12 5YS, tel: 07000 785506, website: www.feldenkreis.co.uk

Feng Shui Network International, PO Box 2133, London W1A 1RL

Flotation Tank Association, (Flotation Therapy), 7A Clapham Common Southside, London SW4 7AA, tel: 020 7627 4962, website: www.flotationtankassociation.net

British Flower and Vibrational Essences Association, PO Box 33, Exmouth, Devon, EX8 1YY, tel: 07986 512064, website: www.bfvea.com

Confederation of Healing Organisations, 27 Montefiore Court, Stamford Hill, London N16 5TY, tel: 020 8800 3569

National Federation of Spiritual Healers, Old Manor Farm Studio, Church Street, Sunbury-on-Thames, Surrey, TW16 6RG, tel: 0845 123 2777, website: www.nfsh.org.uk

European Hellerwork Association, Thornfield, Stretton on Fosse, Moreton in Marsh, Gloucestershire, GL56 9RA, tel: 01608 662828, website: www.hellerwork-europe.com

National Institute of Medical Herbalists, 56 Longbrook Street, Exeter, EX4 6AH, tel: 01392 426022, website: www.nimh.org.uk

Association for Holotropic Breathwork International, website: www.breathwork.com

Transpersonal Training and Holotropic Breathwork, website: www.holotropic.com

Faculty of Homeopathy and British Homeopathic Association, 15 Clerkenwell Close, London EC1R 0AA, tel: 020 7566 7800, website: www.trusthomeopathy.org

Society of Homeopaths, 4A Artizan Road, Northampton, NN1 4HU, tel: 01604 621400, website: www.homeopathy-soh.org

British Society of Experimental and Clinical Hypnosis, Department of Clinical Oncology, Derbyshire Royal Infirmary, London Road, Derby, DE1 2QY

British Society of Medical and Dental Hypnosis, 4 Kirkwood Avenue, Cookridge, Leeds, LS16 7JU, tel: 07000 560309, website: www.bsmdh.org

Central Register of Advanced Hynotherapists, PO Box 14526, London N4 2WG, tel: 020 7354 9938, website: www. n-shap-ericksonian.co.uk

National Register of Hypnotherapists and Psychotherapists, Room B, 12 Cross Street, Nelson, Lancashire, BB9 7EN, tel: 01282 716839, website: www.nrhp.co.uk

Guild of Naturopathic Iridologists, 94 Grosvenor Road, London SW1V 3LF, tel: 020 7821 0255, website: www.gniinternational.org

International Association of Clinical Iridologists, 853–5, Finchley Road, London NW1 8LX

Association of Systematic Kinesiology, 39 Browns Road, Surbiton, KT5 8ST, tel: 020 8399 3215, website: www.kinesiology.co.uk

Kinesiology Federation, PO Box 17153, Edinburgh, EH11 3WQ, tel: 08700 113545

Kirlian Research Limited (Kirlian Photography), 25–27 Oxford Street, London W1R 1RR, tel: 020 7287 7980, website: www.kirlian.co.uk

SAD Association (Light Therapy), PO Box 989, Steyning, West Sussex BN44 3HG, website: www.sada.org.uk

British Biomagnetic Association (Magnetic Therapy), 31 St Marychurch Road, Torquay, Devon, TQ1 3JF, tel: 01803 293346

British Massage Therapy Council, 17 Rymers Lane, Oxford, OX4 3JU, tel: 01865 774123, website: www.bmtc.co.uk

Massage Therapy Institute of Great Britain, PO Box 2726, London NW2 4NR, tel: 020 7724 4105

School of Meditation, 158 Holland Park Avenue, London W11 4UH, tel: 020 7603 6116

Transcendental Meditation, Freepost, London SW1P 4YY, tel: 08705 143733, website: www.transcendental-meditation.org.uk

Metamorphic Association (Metamorphic Technique), 67 Ritherdon Road, London SW17 8QE, tel: 020 8672 5951

Association of Professional Music Therapists, 26 Hamlyn Road, Glastonbury, Somerset, BA6 8HT, tel: 01458 834919, website: www.apmt.org.uk

British Society for Music Therapy, 25 Rosslyn Avenue, East Barnet, EN4 8DH, tel: 020 8368 8879, website: www.bsmt.org.uk

General Council and Register of Naturopaths, British Naturopathic Association, Goswell House, 2 Goswell Road, Street, Somerset, BA16 0JG, tel: 01458 840072, website: www.naturopathy.org.uk

British Association of Nutritional Therapists, Monomark House, 27 Old Gloucester Street, London WC1N 3XX, tel: 0870 606 1284

General Osteopathic Council, Osteopathy House, 176 Tower Bridge Road, London SE1 3LU, tel: 020 7357 6655, website: www.osteopathy.org.uk

Federation of Polarity Training (Polarity Therapy), 7 Nunnery Close, Golden Valley, Cheltenham, GL51 0TU

UK Polarity Therapy Association, Monomark House, 27 Old Gloucester Street, London WC1N 3XX, tel: 0700 705 2748, website: www.ukpta.org.uk

Qigong Centre, PO Box 59, Altrincham, Cheshire WA15 8ES, tel: 0161 929 4485, website: www.qimagazine.com

Lamas Qigong Association, 25 Watson Road, Worksop, Nottinghamshire, S80 2BA, tel: 01909 482190, website: www.lamas.org

Radionics Association, Baerlein House, Goose Green, Deddington, Oxford, OX5 0SZ, tel: 01869 338852, website: www.radionic.co.uk

British Rebirth Society, 6 Belsize Park Gardens, London NW3 4LD, tel: 0845 458 1050

Association of Reflexologists, Monomark House, 27 Old Gloucester Street, London WC1N 3XX, tel: 0870 567 3320, website: www.reflexology.org/aor

British Reflexology Association, Monks Orchard, Whitbourne, Worcester, WR6 5RB, tel: 01886 821207, website: www.britreflex.co.uk

Reiki Association, Cornbrook Bridge House, Cornbrook, Clee Hill, Ludlow, Shropshire SY8 3QQ, tel: 01584 891197

Rolf Institute (Rolfing), PO Box 14793, London SW1V 2WB, tel: 0117 946 6374, website: www.rolf.org

Shiatsu Society, Eastlands Court, St Peter's Road, Rugby, Warwickshire, CV21 3QP, tel: 01788 555051, website: www.shiatsu.org

The Listening Centre (Sound Therapy), The Maltings Studio, 16A Station Street, Lewes, East Sussex, BN7 2DB, tel: 01273 474877

T'ai Chi Union, 1 Littlemill Drive, Crookston, Glasgow, GS3 7GE, tel: 0141 810 3482, website: www.taichiunion.com

UK T'ai Chi Association, PO Box 159, Bromley, Kent, BR1 3XX, tel: 020 8289 5166, tel: www.taichieurope.com

Trager UK (Tragerwork), 13 Sycamore Close, Tilbury, Essex, RM18 7TB, tel: 01273 411193, website: www.trager.co.uk

British Wheel of Yoga, 1 Hamilton Place, Boston Road, Sleaford, NG34 7ES, tel: 01529 306851, website: www.bwy.org.uk

Yoga Biomedical Trust/Yoga Therapy Centre, 90–92 Pentonville Road, Islington, London N1 9HS, tel: 020 7419 7911, website: www.yogatherapy.org

Yoga for Health Foundation, Ickwell Bury, Biggleswade, Bedfordshire, SG18 9EF, tel: 01767 627271

Yoga Therapy Centre, Homeopathic Hospital, 60 Great Ormond
Street, London, WC1N 3HR, tel: 020 7419 7195

Index

Bodbh 35
bogeys and monsters 62
Boinn/Etaine (of Ireland) 35
Bonfire Night 90
bread and wine ritual, origins of 81
Bread Sauce 216
breastfeeding 237–8
Breton language 98
Bride/Brigit, veneration of 35, 37, 85–6
British Isles
  Christian missionary period 59–60
  Germanic invasion and settlement
    60–2
  Roman rule 55–9
  Viking raids and settlement 60–2
Bronze Age 28, 30–1
Brythons, arrival from mainland Europe 32

Caesar, on Celtic beliefs and heroic fig-
    ures 33–6
Calanish Stones, Isle of Lewis 126
Calvinists
  ban on Christmas in Scotland 84, 91
  destruction of folk culture 92
Camulos/Cumal 34
Candelmas 85–6, 93
candles, at Christmas 91
carbohydrates 224–7
carols, pagan 118–19
  Christian adaptation of 84
Celtic cross symbol 30–1, 82
Celtic culture *see also* ancient Celts
  acceptance of Christianity 38
  importance of storytelling 68–9
  orientational reckoning for rituals 51
  origins and evolution of paganism
    15–18
  passing on cultural heritage 68–9
  practice of magic 17
  respect for the spoken word 51–3
  timescale 28, 29
  veneration of the natural world 19–20
Celtic Kings, election and inauguration
    40
Celtic languages
  demise of 98–9
  prohibition of 92
Celtic pagan legacy 64–9 *see also*
    paganism
Celtic philosophy
  disregard for death 56
  dualities not seen as conflicting
    opposites 55–6
  enjoyment of life 56
  freedom and responsibility 56
  no concept of absolute truth 56
  view of sin different to Christians 56

Ceridwen (of Wales) 37
Cernunnos 35
children
  cultural icons 345–6
  encouraging aesthetic appreciation
    349–52
  experience of cultural traditions
    349–52
  involving in food preparation 194
  involving in kitchen activities 204–5
  media pressures on 355–61
  parental guidance on popular culture
    371–3
  teaching consumer awareness 361–4
  upbringing of 4–5, 65–6, 345–6,
    354–5
  what they can learn from pets 303–4
Chinese herbal medicine 287
chiropractic 278
cholesterol 223–4
Christ *see* Jesus Christ
Christian blessings, and fertility rites 88
Christian Church
  1969 purge of invented saints 83
  adaptation and reinvention of pagan
    beliefs and practices 81–2
  adoption of pagan symbols and
    designs 73–4, 84
  cult of saints 82–3
  demonisation of pagan
    personifications 82
  evolution of the ecclesiastical calendar
    92–4
  hostility towards science and magic 22–3
  humanism seen as a threat 75
  imposition of its set of beliefs 70–2
  intolerance of folk culture 97
  legislation against witchcraft 78–80
  oppression of women 80
  paganism maligned and discredited
    70–2
  power and control objectives 74–5
  present day influence on government
    and law 101
  prohibition of independent thinking
    74–5
  propaganda against witchcraft 80
  trials for witchcraft 80
  witchhunts 78–80
Christian missionaries in the British Isles
    59–60
  activities of 94–5
  conversion of Anglo-Saxon invaders
    61
  conversion of Viking invaders 61–2
  destruction of pagan artwork and
    artifacts 73